UK Breaks with Bikes

Wales

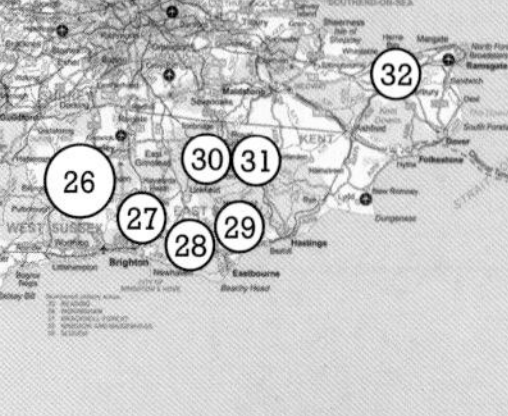

NORTH SEA

First published in 2009 by: Rough Ride Guide Ltd
Walnut Tree Office, The Old Road, Pishill, Oxon, RG9 6HS
ISBN 978-0-954-8829-2-1
Folders printed & by WE Baxters of London
Inside pages printed by: Stephens & George in Wales

The legal stuff...

disclaimer

Mountain biking is a dangerous & addictive sport. The authors and publishers take no responsibility for accident, injury, death, loss of friends, or inconvenience sustained by any user of this guide as a result of information or advice contained within this guide.

This book provides information on routes with a personal insight, but is not necessarily proof of the existence of a right of way, and does not guarantee the safety and well being of any user using the information or advice contained in this guide. Ride safely, within your limits and wear a helmet. RRG accepts no responsibility for any breakage to you or your bike, getting lost! injured, tired, lost! hungry, wet, grumpy, sunburnt, cold or lost!

I would also like to say a really big thank you to everyone that has helped make publishing this book possible, especially the people that have recommended routes & provided pictures.

Breaks with Bikes
in the UK
days, weekends or weeks away
for all abilities
EDITOR Max Darkins

pic by Steve Makin

picture by Steve Makin

picture by Steve Makin in Calderdale

picture by chris Malone

picture by Max Darkins

picture by chris Malone Ladybower Reservoir

picture by Dave Lo

picture by Paul Knott Exmoor

picture by scottishmountainbikeguides.com

Meannach Bothy

foreword by the author...

The idea for this book has come from a love of MTB'ing, an expanding family and a limited budget for holidays. I've never been someone who is very good at relaxing on a hot beach (much to my wife's dismay), so we've always tended to holiday in the UK and it's always been an active type of break, be it MTB'ing, surfing or walking.

From travelling in the UK extensively and riding in some of the most beautiful and awesome places, I've ended up compiling this book of great places to ride that are also fantastic holiday destinations.

If you're planning a trip in the UK then use this book as a resource to get a couple of rides in whilst away. Alternatively, you can use this book as a starting point of where to ride & plan a holiday around that. Also, don't forget to check out our suggested road trips.

I have included 3 types of rides; classic rides using bridleways; trail centres & then suitable places / rides to do with children or riders new to mtb'ing. Holidays should be about escaping the routine, being inspired by new sights (& trails) & bonding with your friends or family through shared adventures. I hope this book helps you to achieve this & discover new friends in a country well worth exploring...

Happy riding

Max Darkins

Feedback: If you know of any info, changes or wish to recommend a route, please contact us and we will endeavour to reward your efforts. e-mail info@roughrideguide.co.uk

INTRODUCTION

Please note that this book does not cover everything a novice needs to know about cycling. We have various expansion packs that can be added to our guidebooks, so you can customise it to your requirements. If you are at all unsure about what equipment you require, how to set-up your bike, how to undertake a safety check on the bike & maintain it, cycling skills, etc have a look on our website (www.roughrideguide.co.uk). You will also find various otherinformation on here for news, reviews, route updates, GPX files and much more.

TOP TIP: SatNav users, use the grid reference provided on the route e.g. SU724898, enter it on www.streetmap.co.uk/streetmap.dll? click 'Landranger Grid', then 'convert', to get the postcode.

TRANSPORT

The nature of this book means that you will probably be travelling to the start of the ride, so its worth looking at the pro's & con's of the different ways;

The 1st choice for most people as it is usually available, quick, reliable, easy & flexible.

The Boot: If there are just one or two of you, putting the bike(s) in the boot is a simple, safe, cheap & aerodynamics way, but it can get the car muddy & both bike & car can get scratched.

Roof racks: Cheap & gets the bikes up out of the way, but also out of mind! Beware of height restrictions. They are also specific to certain cars, not very aerodynamic (slows the car down & increases the running costs) & cumbersome to load/unload.

Rear / boot racks: These allow for easy mounting & dismounting, cause less drag than roof racks, but can obscure your rear view, lights & number plate, are an easier target for thieves & can scratch the car. Tow ball carriers are better but more expensive.

NOTE: It is a fineable offence for the bicycle to protrude more than 30cm's from the side of the car & for the lights & numberplate to be obscured.

TOP TIP: A bike bag keeps everything tidy, hidden, scratch free.

TRAIN

Going by train is better for the environment, can be a pleasant, relaxed, social, economical & exciting way to travel. You can also save all your energy for riding - arrive ready to ride & depart as tired as you want (car journeys are tiring, stressful). However the problem with trains is you are restricted by their timetable (no bikes at peak times), locations & space for bikes – sometimes as few as 2 per train.

We'd advise to book ahead & reserve a space for your bike & be aware that replacement bus services don't usually allow bikes.

For more info on taking bikes on trains see CTC info sheet INF10 or call 08457 484950. Also visit www.nationalrail.co.uk or for Scottish rover tickets & sleeper services see www.firstgroup.com/scotrail or www.walesflexipass.co.uk for Welsh rover tickets.

In England a few local authorities allow bicycles, but in general they don't e.g. the National Express. Wales & Scotland are better though with many councils allowing bicycles on buses e.g. Travelines Cymru in Wales & Stagecoach in Scotland.

See www.traveline-cymru.info for travelling in Wales and www.travelinescotland.com for Scotland.

NOTE: CTC info sheet INF12 has info on taking bicycles on the buses.

FAMILY RIDING

As we have a good collection of rides suitable for young families & new riders I'll just take a minute to help you through the minefield of going riding with your children.

You can introduce a newborn to cycling with an adapted trailer that allows a car seat, or once they can sit up supported (around 6 months usually) you can use a child seat on the back of a bike that reclines & supports their head. Bike seats fit onto hardtail bikes, great for shortish distances & is generally safe as the child is close by & visible.

As the child gets older & heavier a child seat becomes less stable, so a trailer is a good option – it will also allow you to carry luggage and possibly a 2nd child now. Don't worry to much about the weight, it will get a lot heavier once the children & luggage are added. Look for a well made one with bright colours & flag to make road users aware of it.

Once your child gets older they will get bored of just sitting there, so from around the age of 2 you can introduce them to their own bike. I like the balance bike that teaches them how to use two wheels, then around the age of 3-4 they can skip the stabiliser stage when they get their first bike with pedals. Get a bike that fits them now, not one that they will grow into as it will be difficult for them to use and may put them off cycling.

TOP TIPS:

Plan & centre the ride around the children & involve them in planning.

Discuss your cycling adventure a few days ahead & what you might see & do.

On the ride, stop & look at interesting things, feed horses, go to playgrounds, etc.

Get more families & friends involved to share the fun & adventures.

Soft tyres (around5-10psi) makes the ride more comfortable for the child.

Children often go quiet when (too) cold.

Trailer bikes connect to adults bike & bridge the gap between a toddler seat & a child being able to manage roads & longer rides solo.

NOTE: We highly recommend childrens bikes from Isla Bikes, see www.islabikes.co.uk for more info.

NOTE: Our family routes include info on the local attractions & activities for you to incorporate into your cycle ride or holiday, so everyone has something to look forward to, as well as a good experience & fond memories of their cycle holiday.

see 'Family cycling' books by Dan Joyce & Carlton Reid.
and for childrens bicycles see www.islabikes.co.uk.

Other useful websites; www.metcheck.com, www.ukcampsite.co.uk, www.touristinformationcentres.com, www.yha.org.uk, www.find-a-campsite.co.uk & www.roughrideguide.co.uk

USING THE ROUTES

Our aim when producing these guidebooks has been to offer clear, fun and challenging routes, suitable for all abilities. To achieve this we have used the best mapping, sought local riders knowledge, and provided shortcut and extension options. This will ensure that everyone can find and ride the best trails, with minimum effort and hassle.

NOTE: We have made every effort to ensure that these routes only use legal paths, but access rights can change or mistakes be made, so if you are ever unsure, please walk your bike to avoid confrontation.

ROUTE GRADING

Please bear in mind that people's opinions vary, as well as their speed and line choice, which all play a big factor in determining the difficulty level of a route. We have graded our routes from Family to Extreme, bearing in mind the terrain, distance, height gained, and opportunity to bail-out or be rescued (remoteness) should anything go wrong. To keep some consistency and familiarity, we have largely adopted the colour grading system used by the Forestry Commission.

Family (GREEN): Suitable for family riding. Well surfaced, wide, flat trails suitable for young children or bicycle trailers & tag-alongs.

EASY (YELLOW): Suitable for beginners. Generally wide, well surfaced, easy going tracks, but with some technical challenges.

MEDIUM (BLUE): Suitable for intermediate riders. Rougher terrain, some singletrack, requiring some degree of technical ability & endurance.

HARD (RED): Suitable for experienced riders only. Steep gradients & tight singletrack requiring good bike control & quick decision making.

SEVERE (BLACK): Suitable for very experienced and competent riders. Contains some very technical and potentially dangerous terrain.

EXTREME **(ORANGE):** Very technical trails, such as downhill, freeride and jumps for experts only, although some may have escape/chicken runs or easier sections to enable progression.

COUNTRYSIDE CODE

Only ride on open trails
Be in control of your bike at all times
Slow down or stop and let people pass by
Warn people of your presence by calling or ringing a bell, pass slowly and be polite
Don't scare any animals
Don't leave any rubbish
Look ahead and be aware
Be kind & courteous to other trail users
Shut gates behind you

TOP TIP: Fix a bell to your bike to politely warn others of your presence - it has even been known to raise a smile from walkers.

BLOCKED TRAILS

There are a couple of very useful websites provided by the CTC that enable you to report / enter the details of a blocked Right of Way e.g. a locked gate at www.clearthattrail.org.uk or for pot holes in roads (a big cause of cycling accidents) at www.fillthathole.org.uk.

NOTE: You are perfectly within your rights to continue along the path (or where it should be), by passing around or climbing over the obstacle.

NOTE: If an aggressive animal e.g. a dog is stopping you from progressing on a public ROW, inform the police.

ABBREVIATIONS

To reduce the amount of text you have to read on the trail, we have abbreviated frequently used words. It looks a long list, but most are obvious.

L = Left
R = Right
SA = Straight ahead / across
Bear = A bend of less than 90 degrees
T-J = T-Junction (usually at 180 degrees)
Fork = Track splits into two directions
X-rds / tracks = Crossing roads / tracks
DH = Downhill
UH = Uphill
FP = Footpath
BW = Bridleway
ByW = By-Way
(P)ROW = (Public) Right of way
BOAT = By-way open to all traffic
DT = Double track (wide enough for a car)
ST = Single track (narrow trail).

NOTE: Emboldened directions provide the 'must know' information, and the other directions provide greater detail for when you may be unsure.

ROUTE PROFILE

These are at the bottom of the route directions, showing you the cross section / height gained and lost, on the main route. The numbers above the profile correlate to the route text numbering.

DISTANCE & HEIGHT

The (blue) main route is usually around 30 kilometres / 20 miles, which will be suitable for most competent and fit mountain bikers. The (yellow) shortcut and (red) extensions are there for riders who want to adjust the ride to suit their needs. We have provided distances in both kilometres, and miles (in brackets), as although we are starting to become familiar with KM, most of us have grown up using and thinking in miles.

The main route shows the distance and amount of climbing. The extension or shortcut will have a + or - figure, to show the change in distance and climbing from the main route. For example, if the main route is 30 kilometres with 500 metres of climbing, and you ride this and the extension which reads +7 kilometress and +150 meters of climbing, you will ride a total of 37 kilometres with 650 metres of climbing.

TOP TIP: A bike computer is very useful to show you exactly how far you have gone, so you can follow the distances we provide between points. Discrepancies do occur, so use them as a guide, not gospel.

NOTE: The amount of climbing involved on the route is just as important as the distance. Generally, 300+ meters of climbing over 10 miles is strenuous, so any ride of 30 miles with over 900 meters of climbing is going to be very tough. See the route profile below.

ORDNANCE SURVEY (LANDRANGER) MAP KEY

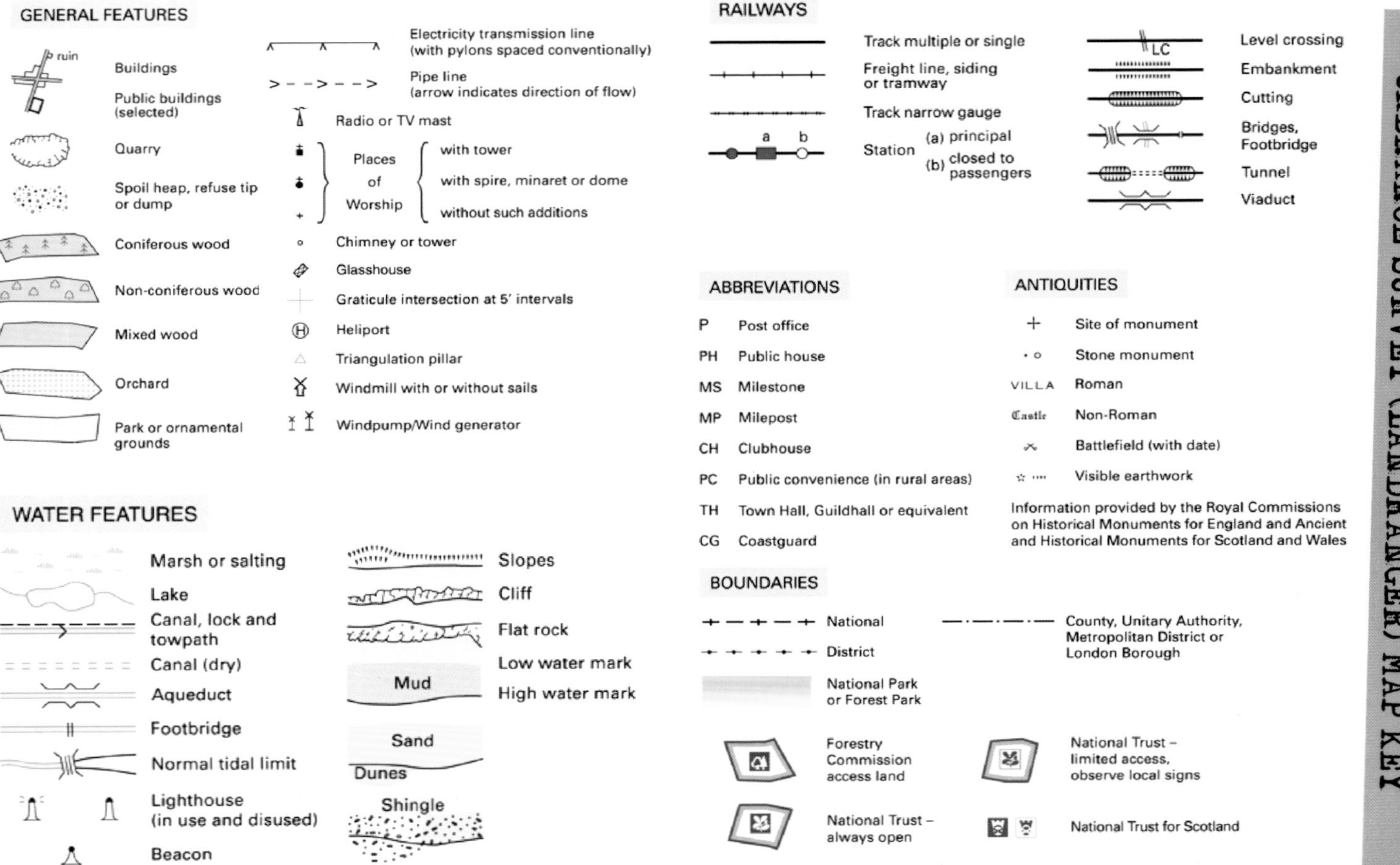

GENERAL FEATURES
ruin
Buildings
Public buildings (selected)
Quarry
Spoil heap, refuse tip or dump
Coniferous wood
Non-coniferous wood
Mixed wood
Orchard
Park or ornamental grounds
Electricity transmission line (with pylons spaced conventionally)
Pipe line (arrow indicates direction of flow)
Radio or TV mast
Places of Worship
with tower
with spire, minaret or dome
without such additions
Chimney or tower
Glasshouse
Graticule intersection at 5′ intervals
Heliport
Triangulation pillar
Windmill with or without sails
Windpump/Wind generator
WATER FEATURES
Marsh or salting
Lake
Canal, lock and towpath
Canal (dry)
Aqueduct
Footbridge
Normal tidal limit
Lighthouse (in use and disused)
Beacon
Slopes
Cliff
Flat rock
Low water mark
Mud
High water mark
Sand
Dunes
Shingle
RAILWAYS
Track multiple or single
Freight line, siding or tramway
Track narrow gauge
a
b
Station
(a) principal
(b) closed to passengers
LC
Level crossing
Embankment
Cutting
Bridges, Footbridge
Tunnel
Viaduct
ABBREVIATIONS
P Post office
PH Public house
MS Milestone
MP Milepost
CH Clubhouse
PC Public convenience (in rural areas)
TH Town Hall, Guildhall or equivalent
CG Coastguard
ANTIQUITIES
Site of monument
Stone monument
VILLA Roman
Castle Non-Roman
Battlefield (with date)
Visible earthwork
Information provided by the Royal Commissions on Historical Monuments for England and Ancient and Historical Monuments for Scotland and Wales
BOUNDARIES
National
District
National Park or Forest Park
County, Unitary Authority, Metropolitan District or London Borough
Forestry Commission access land
National Trust – always open
National Trust – limited access, observe local signs
National Trust for Scotland

ORDNANCE SURVEY (LANDRANGER) MAP KEY

ROADS AND PATHS

Not necessarily rights of way

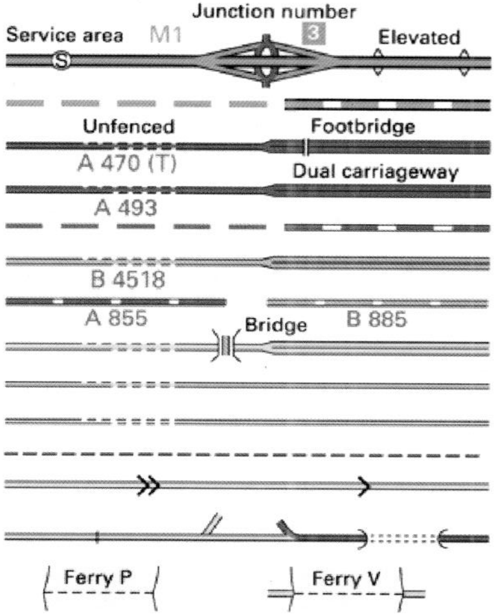

Service area M1 · Junction number 3 · Elevated

Unfenced · Footbridge · A 470 (T) · Dual carriageway · A 493 · B 4518 · A 855 · Bridge · B 885

Ferry P · Ferry V

- Motorway (dual carriageway)
- Motorway under construction
- Trunk road
- Main road
- Main road under construction
- Secondary road
- Narrow road with passing places
- Road generally more than 4 m wide
- Road generally less than 4 m wide
- Other road, drive or track
- Path
- Gradient: steeper than 20% (1 in 5); 14% to 20% (1 in 7 to 1 in 5)
- Gates · Road Tunnel
- Ferry (passenger) · Ferry (vehicle)

TOURIST INFORMATION

- Information centre, all year/seasonal
- Selected places of tourist interest
- Viewpoint
- Parking
- Youth hostel
- Golf course or links
- Bus or coach station
- Picnic site
- Camp site
- Caravan site
- Public telephone
- Motoring organisation telephone
- PC Public convenience (in rural areas)

PUBLIC RIGHTS OF WAY

- Footpath
- Bridleway
- Road used as public path
- Byway open to all traffic

Public rights of way shown on this map have been taken from local authority definitive maps and later amendments. The map includes changes notified to Ordnance Survey by (date). The symbols show the defined route so far as the scale of mapping will allow.
Rights of way are not shown on maps of Scotland.

Rights of way are liable to change and may not be clearly defined on the ground. Please check with the relevant local authority for the latest information.

The representation on this map of any other road, track or path is no evidence of the existence of a right of way.

Danger Area — Firing and Test Ranges in the area. Danger! Observe warning notices

OTHER PUBLIC ACCESS

- Other route with public access

The exact nature of the rights on these routes and the existence of any restrictions may be checked with the local highway authority. Alignments are based on the best information available. These routes are not shown on maps of Scotland.

- National Trail, Long Distance Route, selected Recreational Paths
- National/Regional Cycle Network
- Surfaced cycle route
- 4 National Cycle Network number
- 8 Regional Cycle Network number

ROCK FEATURES

outcrop · cliff · scree · 650 · 600

HEIGHTS

50 — Contours are at 10 metres vertical interval

· 144 — Heights are to the nearest metre above mean sea level

Heights shown close to a triangulation pillar refer to the station height at ground level and not necessarily to the summit.

1 metre = 3.2808 feet

pic by Simon Barnes © 2007 www.bogtrotters.org

Breaks with bikes

pic by Simon Barnes © 2009 www.bogtrotters.org

IN ENGLAND

in the Howgill Fells

England

With so much variety contained within England you really could keep yourself occupied for a serious amount of time. The bleak & humbling terrain of the north york moors are often remote, dramatic & technically challenging. The mountains of the Lake District are epic in their beauty & contain some of the most legendary and classic mountain bike trails around. Add to that the south west which contains some of the most picturesque and charismatic coastal spots and includes riding for families through to more experienced riders and you have an awesome country to ride in just waiting to be explored.

Useful websites; www.enjoyengland.com, www.forestry.gov.uk/england-cycling, www.visitbritain.co.uk & www.roughrideguide.co.uk

picture by Paul Knott

Exmoor

Pic of Peaks by Max

picture by Paul Knott

Exmoor cream tea

picture by Simon Barnes © 2007 www.bogtrotters.org

Entering 'The Beast' in the Dark Peaks

picture by Max Darkins

picture by Max Darkins in Dark Peaks

Skiddaw

picture by Simon Barnes © 2006 www.bogtrotters.o

picture by John Perry © 2005 www.bogtrotters.org on High Cup Nick ride

Maize Beck

picture by John Perry © 2005 www.bogtrotters.org

01 Mineral Tramway
02 St Austell
03 Camel Trail
04 Princetown
05 Bellever
06 Drogo Castle
07 & 08 Hound Tor
09 Babbacombe Bay
10 Woodbury Common
11 Tarka Trail
12 & 13 Saunton
14 & 15 Porlock
16 Dunster
17 Quantocks
18 & 19 Cheddar
20 Moors Valley CP
21 Isle of Purbeck
22 Bournemouth
23 New Forest
24 Freshwater IOW
25 Isle of Wight C2C
26 Downs Link
27 Brighton
28 Friston Forest
29 Cuckoo trail
30 & 31 Bewl Water
32 Crab & Winkle Way
33 Rendlesham
34 Wootton
35 Forest of Dean
36 Malverns
37 Church Stretton
38 Tissingdon Trail

picture by chris Malone

ENGLAND

39 High Peak Trail
40 Bakewell
41 Hope
42 Ladybower
43 Mary Townley
44 Forest of Bowland
45 Horton
46 Pateley Bridge
47 & 48 Swaledale Valley
49 Howgill Hills
50 Whitby to Scarborough
51 Sneaton High Moor
52 High Cup Nick
53 Grizedale Forest
54 Ambleside
55 Keswick
56 Ullswater
57 Skiddaw
58 Isle of Man

Trail centres

59 Haldon Forest
60 Thetford Forest
61 Lee Quarry
62 Dalby Forest
63 Hamsterley
64 Grizedale
65 Kielder Forest

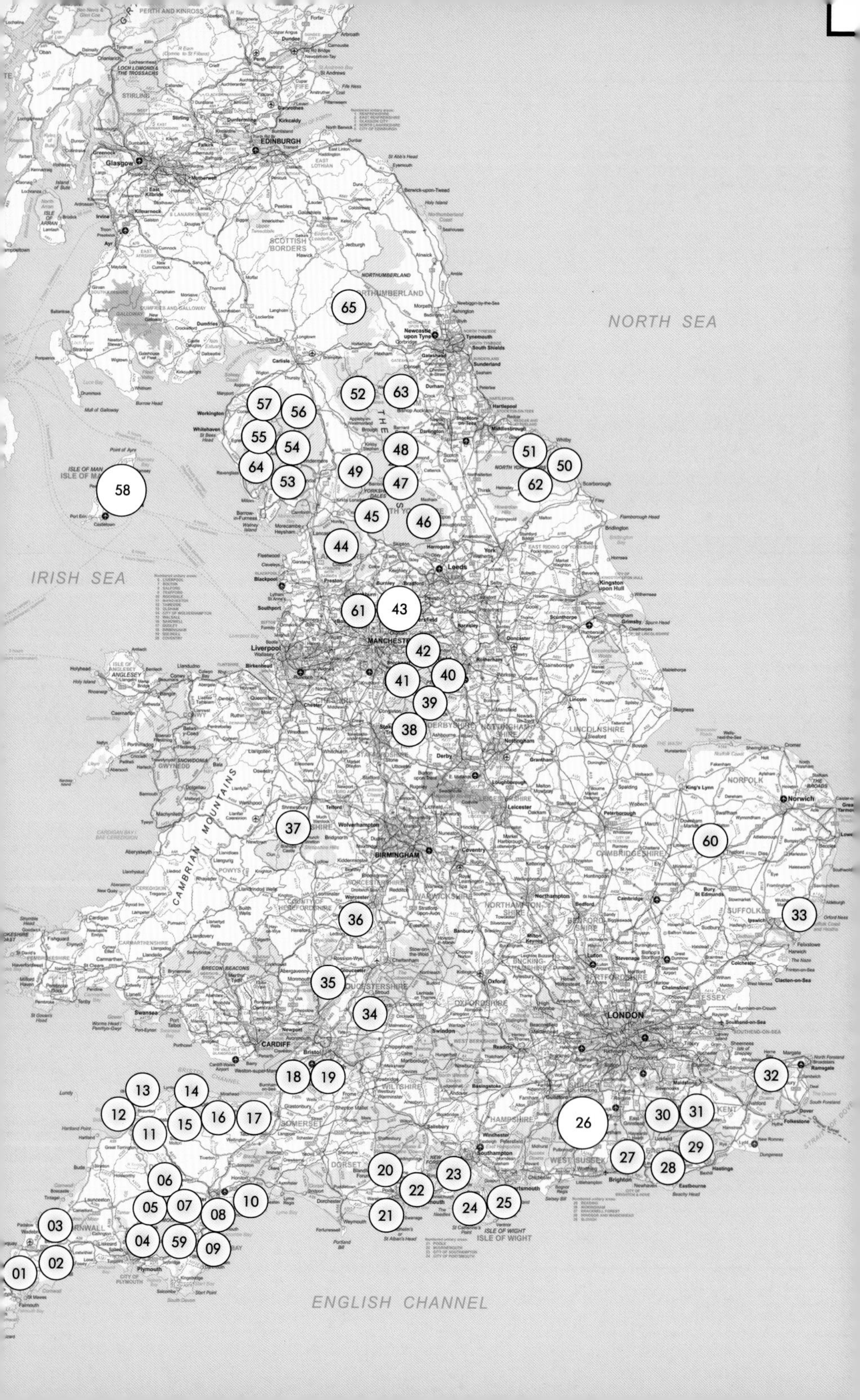

NORTH SEA
IRISH SEA
ENGLISH CHANNEL
CAMBRIAN MOUNTAINS
ISLE OF MAN
ISLE OF WIGHT
EDINBURGH
Glasgow
SCOTTISH BORDERS
NORTHUMBERLAND
DUMFRIES AND GALLOWAY
Newcastle upon Tyne
Leeds
MANCHESTER
Liverpool
BIRMINGHAM
LONDON
CARDIFF
Bristol
Southampton
Plymouth
Norwich
Brighton
LINCOLNSHIRE
NORFOLK
SUFFOLK
KENT
WEST SUSSEX
01
02
03
04
05
06
07
08
09
10
11
12
13
14
15
16
17
18
19
20
21
22
23
24
25
26
27
28
29
30
31
32
33
34
35
36
37
38
39
40
41
42
43
44
45
46
47
48
49
50
51
52
53
54
55
56
57
58
59
60
61
62
63
64
65

ROUTE	GRADE	DISTANCE	+/–
01 Mineral Tramway	Family – Medium	40Km	Various
02 St Austell	Family – Medium	19.2Km & 16.8Km	
03 Camel Trail	Family / Easy	53.6Km	Various
04 Princetown	Family – Hard	23.3Km	+14.2Km
05 Bellever	Easy & Hard	22Km	+3.9 Or −12.
06 Drogo Castle	Easy & Hard	37.8Km	+5.8
07 & 08 Hound Tor	Medium – Hard	23.3Km & 21.6Km	
09 Babbacombe Bay	Medium	17.2Km	+3 & +1.9
10 Woodbury Common	Easy – Medium	19.3Km	Various
11 Tarka Trail	Family – Easy	Various	
12 & 13 Saunton	Easy – Medium	16.9Km & 21.7Km	
14 & 15 Porlock	Medium – Very Hard	Various	
16 Dunster	Easy – Hard	35.8Km	+7.9
17 Quantocks	Medium – Hard	21.6Km	Various
18 & 19 Cheddar	Medium – Hard	25Km & 25Km	3.9Km
20 Moors Valley CP	Family – Medium	Various	
21 Isle Of Purbeck	Family – Hard	29.5Km	+12.5K
22 Bournemouth	Family – Easy	Various	
23 New Forest	Family – Medium	Various	
24 Freshwater IOW	Easy – Hard	37Km	+7.5 Or −18.8K
25 Isle Of Wight C2C	Family – Medium	Various	

ROUTE DESCRIPTION

coast 2 coast cycle track in cornwall, with some old quarries to play in on route.

2 routes; one to the Eden project, the other to quaint seaside town.

A picturesque cycle trail from Bodmin to Padstow – perfect for the family

A classic Dartmoor route, with good, all weather trails over the moors.

Great technical rocky ride in the heart of Dartmoor, with stepping stone crossings

Just off A30 is a lovely dramatic family ride or an epic day out on Dartmoor

choice of two superb technical, rocky singletrack routes. Welcome to Dartmoor!

Some steep stoney trails very close to a popular holiday destination. Get away!

Great mix of trails on the common, from wide stone tracks to twisty singletrack

Lovely family cyclepath along the seafront & estuary. Hire bikes & trailers available

A choice of 2 trails with some nice singletrack just metres from the seafront.

A choice of routes – all rocky, steep & technical, from the lovely Porlock village

Dunster is a tourist hot spot, but these trails are quiet & technical in places

Great all weather trails. Big climbs & long fast singletrack descents. Superb.

2 brilliant technical rides just off the M4 in 'those hills you always drive past'.

A few family cycle trails + some northshore & lots of forests trails to explore

From a family ride to the beach to a coastal, cliff top XC ride on technical trails.

de along the seafront & a ferry ride over to Purbeck if desired.

Lots of wide forest tracks & villages to explore. Perfect for family holidays.

A classic off-road Isle of Wight ride or see about the 2 day round-island-ride

A family friendly coast to coast (Cowes to Sandown) along a good cycletrack

ROUTE	GRADE	DISTANCE	+/−
26 Downs Link	Family / Easy	Various	
27 Brighton	Easy – Medium	18.7Km	+5.5, +1.8 or −11K
28 Friston Forest	Easy – Hard	30.6Km	+11.3 or −14.2
29 Cuckoo trail	Family / Easy	Various	
30 & 31 Bewl Water	Family – Medium	21Km & various	
32 Crab & Winkle Way	Family / Easy	25KM	Various
33 Rendlesham	Family – Medium	36.4Km or 9.7Km	+10Km
34 Wootton	Medium – Hard	31.4Km	−9.5Km
35 Forest of Dean	Easy-medium	Various	
36 Malverns	Medium	14.5Km	Various
37 Church Stretton	Medium to Hard	25.9Km	−16.3 or +8.4K
38 Tissingdon Trail	Family – Easy	Various	
39 High Peak Trail	Easy– Medium	28Km	Various
40 Bakewell	Easy to Hard	34Km	−22.2
41 Hope	Medium – Very Hard	33.8Km	−6.1 or +5.3Km
42 Ladybower	Family – Very Hard	28.2Km	+15Km
43 Mary Townley	Hard – Very Hard	74Km	
44 Forest of Bowland	Easy – Hard	22.7Km	−9.3 or +6.7
45 Horton	Medium	22.3Km	
46 Pateley Bridge	Easy – Hard	3.9Km or 10Km	

ROUTE DESCRIPTION

A well surfaced cyclepath from Guildford to the south coast. Great family ride.

Classic South Downs ride & fun singletrack extensions. Family riding on promenade

A great coastal ride with an added option of some man made trails in Friston forest

A good family cycle trail from the Heathfield to the coast (Eastbourne).

Family ride around Bewl Water or a choice of waymarked trails at Bedgebury Forest

Nice family trail from Canterbury to the coast (Whitestable) & other trails available

Some easy waymarked trails & some nice singletrack trails to search & explore

Some surprisingly technical riding in the Cotswolds. But best avoided when wet

Nice but short man made trail & a big forest to explore – great for whole family

Superb singletrack, but a small area popular with walkers so go off-peak.

Wonderful singletrack trails in the rolling Shropshire hills. A must do ride.

A well surfaced cycle trail for families, through the White Peak countryside.

An old historic railway which is now a great cyclepath suitable for families

A classic White Peak route. Something for everyone & Bakewell tarts post ride!

Typical, technical, rocky, hilly Dark Peaks ride with extreme extension options

Classic, technical Dark Peak moorland ride with or a flat waterside family ride.

An epic ride on the first purpose-built long distance bridleway for horses & mtb'ers

Wonderful riding in the fells, not far from many cities & the north east coast

Great introduction to the Dales trails & countryside (inc Hull Pot) & a great cafe

A gentle ride round the reservoir or classic moorland riding on the edge of the Dales

ROUTE	GRADE	DISTANCE	+/–
47 & 48 Swaledale Valley	Medium – Hard	21Km & 30Km	
49 Howgill Hills	Medium – Very Hard	15.6 & 38Km	
50 Whitby 2 Scarborough	Easy – Medium	Various	
51 Sneaton High Moor	Medium	32.2Km	
52 High Cup Nick	Medium – Hard	52 or 21.7Km	
53 Grizedale Forest	Medium – Hard	27.2Km	various
54 Ambleside	Medium – Hard	9.2Km & 24.3Km	
55 Keswick	Medium – Hard	26.5Km	
56 Ullswater	Medium – Hard	34.4Km	various
57 Skiddaw	Family – Very Hard	52.3Km & 9.7Km	–35.4
58 Isle of Man	Very Hard	67Km	

Trail centres	Green	Blue	Red	Black	Orang
59 Haldon Forest	1	1	1	0	1
60 Thetford Forest	1	1	1	1	0
61 Lee Quarry	0	0	1	1	1
62 Dalby Forest	2	1	1	1	1
63 Hamsterley	1	1	1	1	1
64 Grizedale	2	3	1	0	0
65 Kielder Forest	1	4	5	1	1

ROUTE DESCRIPTION

2 routes providing some classic Dales riding & a great bike centre to base yourself

Just off M6 but often overlooked. Superb 'Big day' ride. Best when dry & no wind

A nice family suitable cyclepath following the coast, passing Robin Hood's Bay

Easy access/escape from the seaside, with some classic moorland riding

An epic or an easier out & back route, but both dramatic. Best on clear, calm day.

Classic Lake District riding on technical, rocky natural trails near the trail centre

A choice of a quick taster loop or a proper classic Lakes ride – drains well.

The infamous Borrowdale Bash from Keswick. A great introduction to the Lakes

Lovely, technical, challenging Lake District ride with a novel shortcut option.

Something for everyone; family cyclepath, epic XC or up & down Skiddaw.

The classic 'End 2 End' ride & LOTS more riding for all, on this great 'cycling' island

Wide choice of trails, including freeride & some natural trails to explore too

No hills, but plenty of flowing singletrack. Easily the best riding for miles around

A technical, rocky & very dramatic setting., but you need a head for heights

England largest trail centre, with a wide range of trails for all abilities. Superb.

Great riding for all abilities on great mix of natural & man made trails.

Nice choice of easy trails & a fun red if you don't fancy the natural stuff.

Nothing too technical, but lots & lots of riding for the intermediate level rider

picture by Simon Barnes © 2007 www.bogtrotte

picture by Paul Knott

picture by Steve Makin

picture by Specialized bikes

picture by Max Darkins

picture by Max Darkins

Drogo castle – Dartmoor

picture by Paul Knott

Exmoor

picture by Max Darkins

Brighton pier

picture by Paul Knott

Ladybower reservoir

picture by Max Darkins

picture by Max

Dartmoor stepping stones

picture by Woodie @ www.bike-dartmoor.co.uk

picture by woodie @ www.bike-dartmoor.co.uk

on Exmoor

picture by Simon Barnes © 2009

www.bogtrotters.org

picture by woodie @ www.bike-dartmoor.co.uk

Bellever rock garden

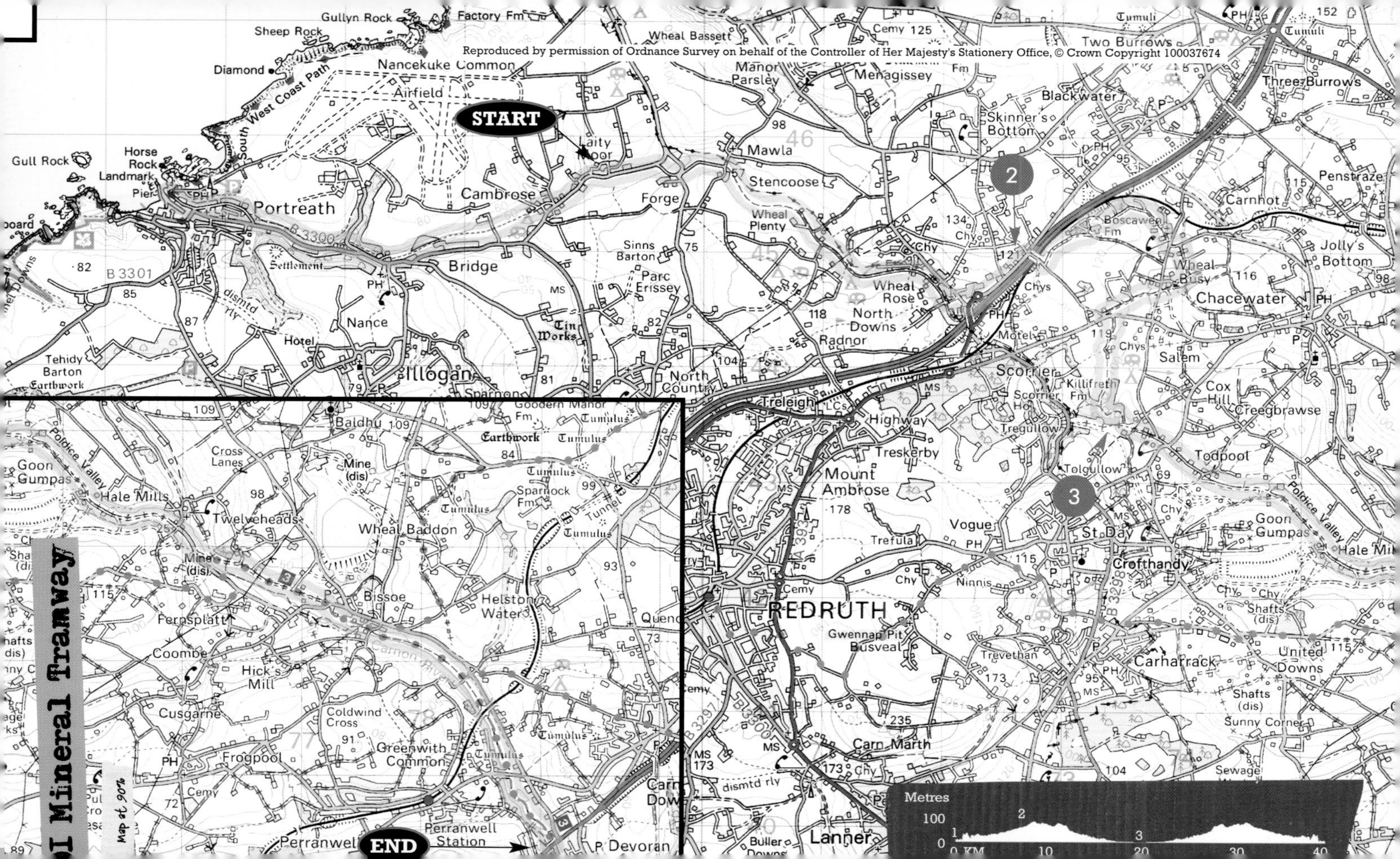

Mineral Tramway
Map at 90%
START
END
Reproduced by permission of Ordnance Survey on behalf of the Controller of Her Majesty's Stationery Office, © Crown Copyright 100037674
Portreath
Illogan
Bridge
Cambrose
Laity Moor
Mawla
Stencoose
Forge
Nancekuke Common
Airfield
South West Coast Path
Gull Rock
Horse Rock
Landmark
Diamond
Sheep Rock
Gullyn Rock
Factory Fm
Wheal Bassett
Manor Parsley
Menagissey
Skinner's Bottom
Blackwater
Two Burrows
Three Burrows
Penstraze
Carnhot
Jolly's Bottom
Chacewater
Wheal Busy
Salem
Cox Hill
Creegbrawse
Todpool
Scorrier
Killifreth Fm
Tregullow
Highway
Treleigh
Radnor
North Downs
Wheal Rose
Wheal Plenty
Sinns Barton
Parc Erissey
North Country
Tin Works
Nance
Hotel
Tehidy Barton
Earthwork
Settlement
REDRUTH
Mount Ambrose
Treskerby
Trefula
Vogue
Ninnis
St Day
Crofthandy
Tolgullow
Goon Gumpas
Poldice Valley
Hale Mills
Carharrack
United Downs
Shafts (dis)
Sunny Corner
Trevethan
Gwennap Pit
Busveal
Carn Marth
Lanner
Buller Downs
Baldhu
Gooden Manor Fm
Cross Lanes
Mine (dis)
Twelveheads
Wheal Baddon
Sparnock Fm
Tunnel
Tumulus
Bissoe
Helston Water
Fernsplatt
Coombe
Hick's Mill
Cusgarne
Coldwind Cross
Greenwith Common
Frogpool
Perranwell
Perranwell Station
Devoran
Metres
100
0
1
2
3
0 KM
10
20
30
40

Mineral Tramway

40KM /25M & 675 METRES OF CLIMBING

START The Mineral Tramway runs right past our recommended start place of The Bike Barn. Simply join the trail, going right to coast at **Portreath or left** to Wheal Rose, then alongside the A30 rd.

2 **Over the A30 rd towards Wheal Busy** and into the old mining area where you follow the named granite way marks. **Turn L at Unity woods,** you follow the trail south-east **through the Poldice valley.**

NOTE: This valley once provided an enormous amount of wealth from the copper found here, but now the old disused quarry provides a wealth of 'freeriding' for mountain bikers.

3 **The trail now follows the Carnon River** through Twelveheads, and Bissoe **to Devoran on the coast, marking the end of this journey's leg.** If you haven't booked a lift for the return journey, turn around and go back the way you came.

Shortcut VARIOUS

Pre-book a lift for the return leg of the Mineral Tramway with www.cornwall-online.co.uk /activeleisure or simply turn back at any point along the Mineral Tramway if/when you feel like it.

For information on the many family activities in the area see www.cornwall-online.co.uk/attractions

Extension VARIOUS

The Poldice Valley is an old quarry which offers lots of superb (freeriding) opportunities (probably the best in Cornwall), so explore these old quarries until your hearts content.....or legs get tired.

Areas to look out for / around include; Tailings dam (751/425), Unity Wood (734/437), and around the United Downs.

Other riding

The Bike Barn will be able to point you in the direction of more cycle rides in the area.

If you are interested in jumping check out www.the-track.co.uk which is just down the road from the Bike Barn (& Treasure Park). Tel. 01209 211073.

picture by Max

Getting there The best place to start is at The Bike Barn with its (free) large car park GR 694/457 / sat nav TR16 5UF. Exit A30 at Redruth & follow signs to/past Treasure Park, then right (Porthtowan), past cambrose sign then look for Bike Barn signs. There is a (smaller) car park at Bissoe Bike hire, off the A39, at the southern end of the route and a railway in Redruth.

Bike shops Elm farm cycle centre, north of Redruth, see www.cornwallcycletrails.com or 01209 891498. with shop, hire, repairs, servicing, tuition & accommodation. Bike chain Bissoe Bike Hire (& cafe) at southern end (nr Devroan) on 01872 870341 or www.cornwallcyclehire.com.

Accommodation: B&B, cottage & campsite at Elm farm (cycle centre), see above for more info. Lots of other places also available, see www.cornwalltouristboard.co.uk

Refreshments

Pubs & shops in Portreath, Chacewater, Porthtowan and a good cafe at the Devoran end, at Bike Chain Bissoe bike hire.

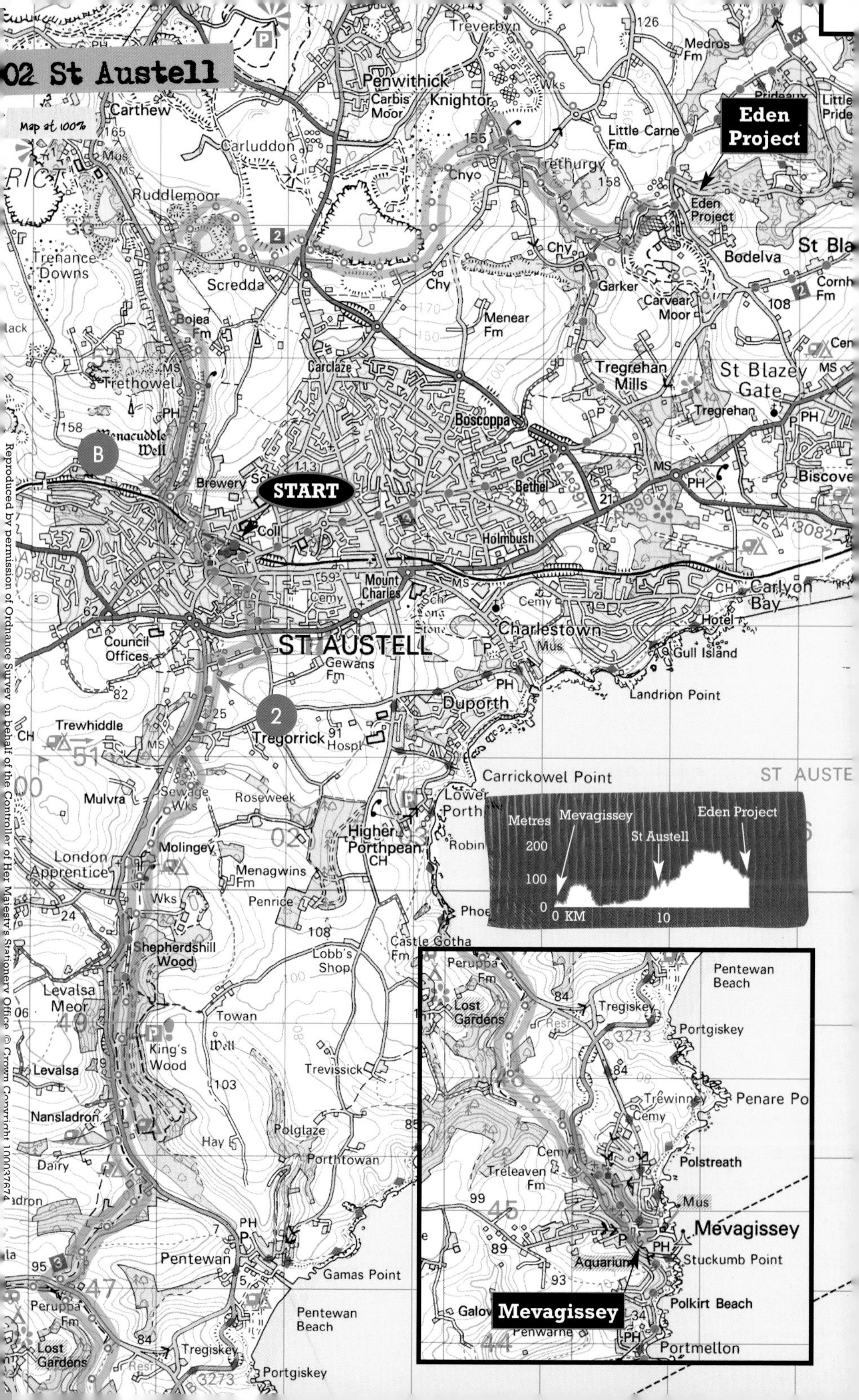

02 St Austell
Map at 100%
START
Eden Project
Mevagissey
Metres
200
100
0
0 KM
10
Mevagissey
St Austell
Eden Project
ST AUSTELL
Carthew
Penwithick
Carbis Moor
Knightor
Treverbyn
Medros Fm
Little Carne Fm
Trethurgy
Carluddon
Ruddlemoor
Trenance Downs
Scredda
Chy
Menear Fm
Garker
Carvear Moor
Bodelva
Cornhill Fm
Bojea Fm
Trethowel
Menacuddle Well
Carclaze
Boscoppa
Tregrehan Mills
St Blazey Gate
Tregrehan
Biscovey
Brewery
Bethel
Holmbush
Mount Charles
Council Offices
Gewans Fm
Charlestown
Carlyon Bay
Hotel
Gull Island
Landrion Point
Duporth
Trewhiddle
Tregorrick
Hospl
Carrickowel Point
Mulvra
Sewage Wks
Roseweek
Lower Porthpean
Higher Porthpean
London Apprentice
Molingey
Menagwins Fm
Penrice
Castle Gotha Fm
Lobb's Shop
Shepherdshill Wood
Levalsa Meor
Towan
Well
King's Wood
Levalsa
Trevissick
Nansladron
Polglaze
Porthtowan
Dairy
Hay
Pentewan
Gamas Point
Pentewan Beach
Peruppa Fm
Lost Gardens
Tregiskey
Portgiskey
Tregiskey
Trewinney
Penare Point
Polstreath
Treleaven Fm
Mus
Aquarium
Stuckumb Point
Polkirt Beach
Penwarne
Portmellon

St Austell

St Austell to Megavissey

19.2KM (11.9M) & 410 METRES CLIMBING

START Follow the Sustrans no3. cycle path from the train station and bear L at church (Trevarithian rd, L on Cross lane, then R then keep L) to cross a rd onto Eastbourne rd and bearing R to the A390 (017/519). Go SA this rd, then just as the houses end, bear R, staying on Sawles Rd to the B3273 (013/516).

2 Turn L alongside this, then L on a wide track (just past a pond on L) towards the sewage works. Bear R at the fork just past the sewage works and follow this good cycle track all the way to the B3273 and go SA on Church Lane, following it around to the R and down into Megavissey (014/449).

St Austell to Eden project

16.8KM (10.4M) & 540 METRES CLIMBING

START Follow the Sustrans cycle route no.2 (north west), bearing R by the church (Market st, and R on Market Hill, to join Menacuddle Hill) over the railway and turn L on Tremena rd, then bearing R, off-road, parallel to the B3274 rd (010/529).

B Bears R, crossing the A391, around the quarry to a rd and go R on this, through Trethurgy, L then R on Chapel lane, then bearing L off this, back off-road, and follow the signs (L) to the Eden Project (049/551).

ROUTE NOTES

Both routes are well surfaced cycle tracks, developed by Sustrans, but be warned, there are some steep hills along the way in places.

The ride to the Eden project is lovely traffic free route along 'The Clay Trails' and has the added bonus that you get a discount on entry to the Eden project. For more information tel: 01726 811911 or see www.edenproject.com.

Heading south leads you through the valley, to the lovely harbour town of Megavissey. Along the way you could detour to the Lost Gardens of Heligan (see www.mevagissey.net /heligan. Megavissey has plenty of refreshments and a nice aquarium (at the far right of the main harbour, under the cliffs, in an old Lifeboat house, tel; 01726 843305). It is free but donations welcomed.

NOTE: Charlestown (nr St Austell) has a fleet of square-rigged sail ships which are open to the public (Easter to October). Tel: 01726 70241 or see www.square-sail.com.

Picture from Eden Project

Getting there: We start the routes from St Austell train station. However if you wanted a shorter ride on the ride to Megavissey there is a car park at King's Wood (006/488).

Accommodation: lots of nice places to choose from. For a full listing see www.visitcornwalluk.co.uk or call St Austell T.I. on 0845 094 0428 for more information.

Refreshments Nothing much along the routes, but there are refreshments at both ends.

Bike shops Pentewan Valley cycle hire, nr Megavissey on www.pentewanvalleycyclehire.co.uk or tel: 01726 844242.

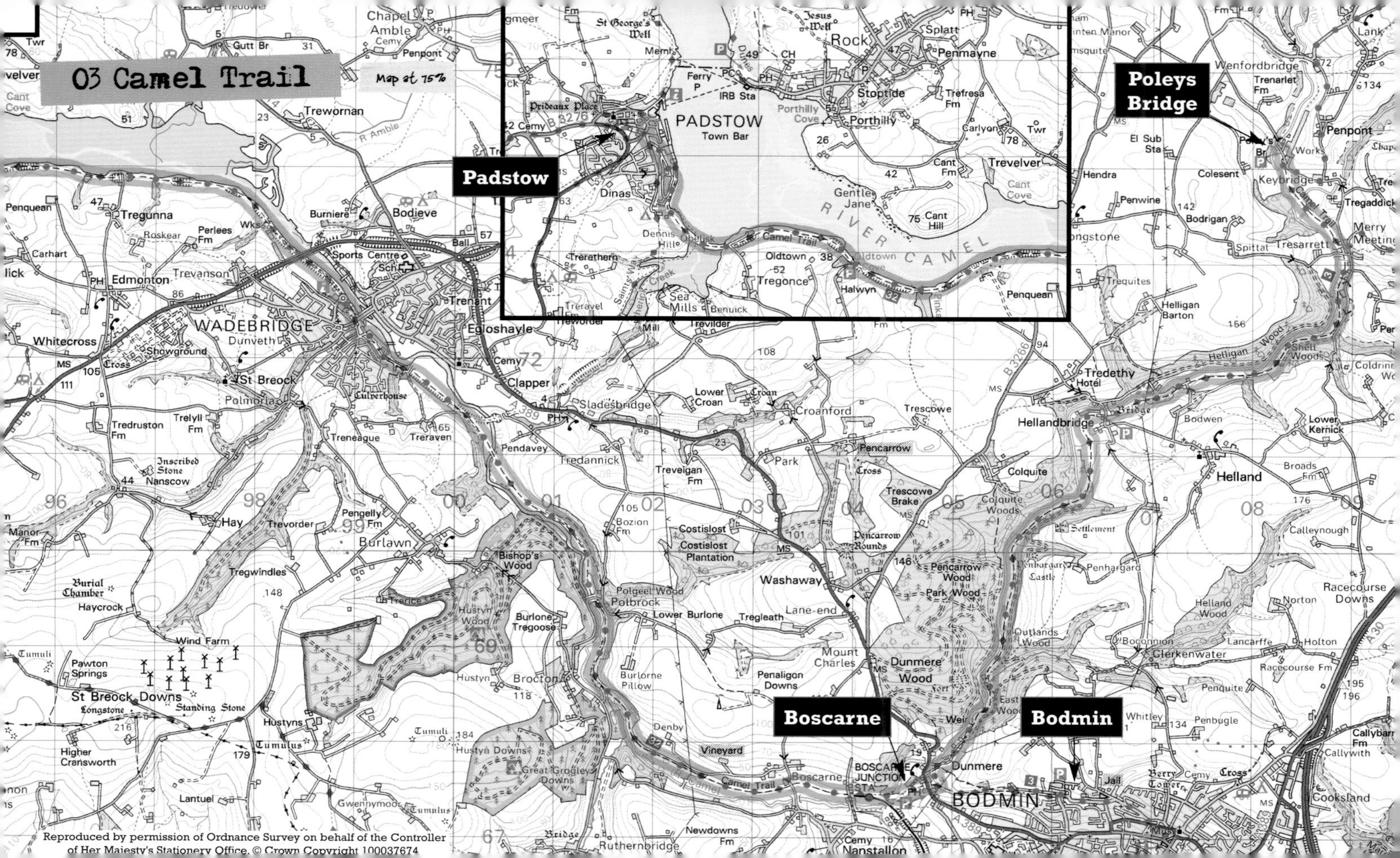

03 Camel Trail
Map at 75%
Padstow
Poleys Bridge
Boscarne
Bodmin
PADSTOW
WADEBRIDGE
BODMIN
RIVER CAMEL
Camel Trail

The Camel Trail

This lovely flat cycle track along an old railway line is very popular, and bikes are easy to hire at Bodmin, Wadebridge and Padstow. There are lots of things to see along the way e.g. Steam railway and museum in Bodmin. It is all traffic free (except in the towns of course), and the surface is mainly gravel, so suitable for mountain and hybrid bikes, making it ideal for families.

NOTE: Cardinham woods on the other side of Bodmin has some nice way-marked (traffic free) cycle routes around it.

pic by Max Darkins

sustrans cycle path sign

Poleys Bridge to Bodmin

9.3KM / 5.8M

There is a car park at the Poley's Bridge (082/741). This trail is quieter than the other 2 sections, and has a slight descent all the way to Bodmin, so bear that in mind if returning back to this point at the end.

Bodmin to Wadebridge

8.5KM / 5.3M

Start either from in Bodmin and use the Sustrans no.3 route to get to Boscarne junction, or from the car park by the Borough Arms pub. There is a tea room and vineyard along this section, which makes a nice stop on the return leg.

Wadebridge to Padstow

9KM / 5.6M

Cycle along the sandy shores of the Camel estuary, to the lovely town of Padstow, which has lots of refreshment stops, including Rick Stein's. The trail is flat & has a good surface, which makes it a very popular, especially for families.

Getting there A good starting point is the (free) car park by the Borough Arms pub, just outside Bodmin, on the trail (047/674). Exit the A30, go through Bodmin on the A389 north west towards Wadebridge. On your way down a steep hill turn left through the Borough Arms pub car park to the Camel Trail car park. By train: At Bodmin use the cycle path to the Camel Trail (involving some hills).

Accommodation Bedknobs B&B in Bodmin on 01208 77553, Holiday cottages at Boscarne 01208 74291, www.trailcottage.co.uk, camping in north east Bodmin (GR081/676) on 01208 73834, YHA on north coast nr Camelford on 0870 7706068 or Golant (nr Fowey) on 0870 7705832, Bodmin T.I. on 01208 76616

Refreshments Lots of places in Padstow, Wadebridge and Bodmin, and a pub at the Bodmin car park. Tea garden at the Boscarne junction, and wine tasting at the Camel Valley Vineyard (west of Bodmin).

Bike shop Babes and Bikes on 01208 815 262 and Bridge Bike hire on 01208 813 050, both in Wadebridge.

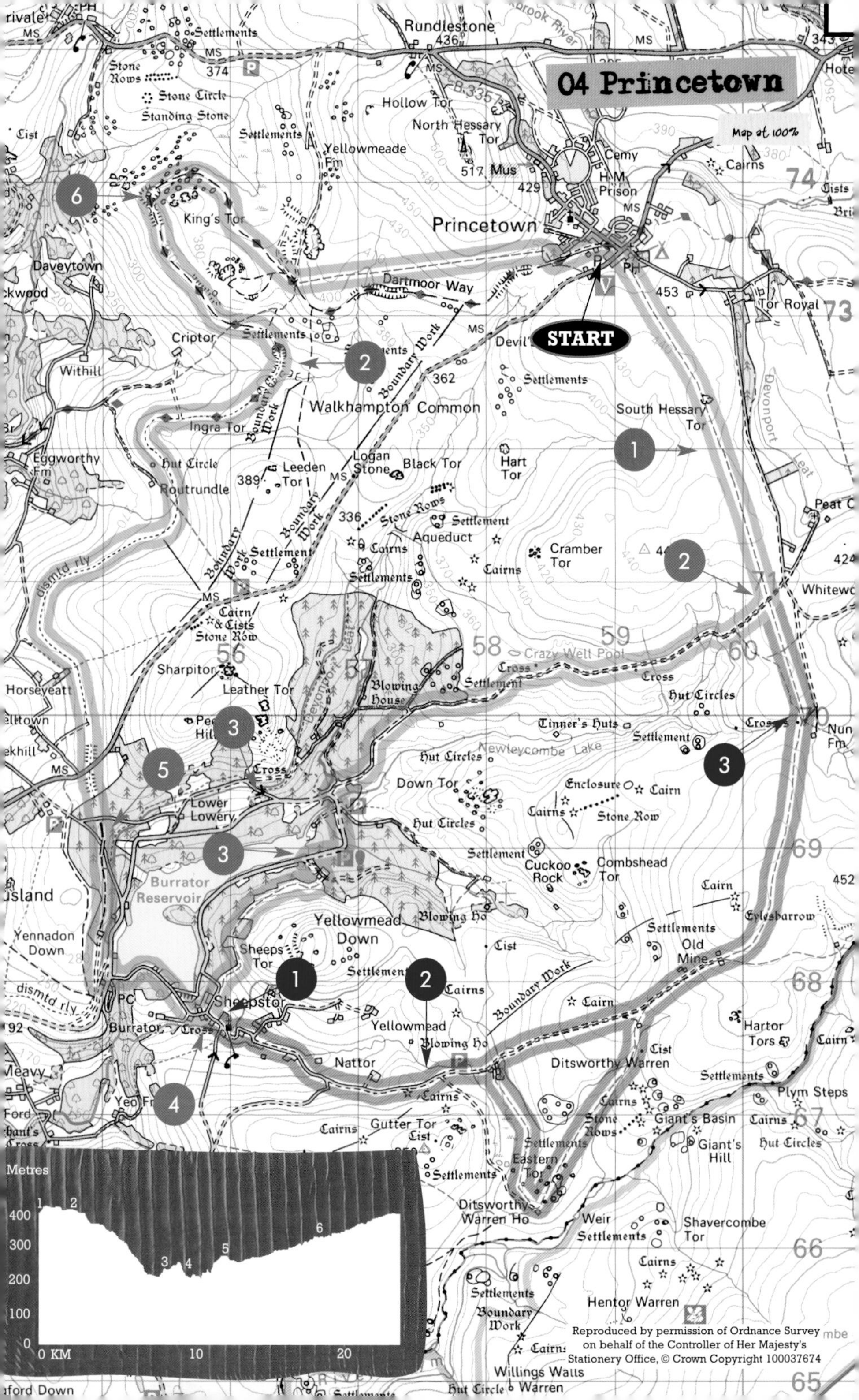
04 Princetown
Map at 100%
START
Princetown
King's Tor
Walkhampton Common
Burrator Reservoir
Sheepstor
Yellowmead Down
Ditsworthy Warren
Dartmoor Way
Metres
0 KM
10
20
Reproduced by permission of Ordnance Survey on behalf of the Controller of Her Majesty's Stationery Office, © Crown Copyright 100037674

Princetown

23.3KM (15.4M) & 415 METRES OF CLIMBING

START **Exit the car park and turn R to a mini roundabout** (591/735) **and go SA between the Plume of Feathers and Railway Inn pubs, on a BW.** Onto the moors, and **keep SA** on this resurfaced track **for 2.9km** (1.8m) **to a X-tracks** (602/709) with a stone marker **and turn R.**

2 Follow this wide, rocky track, **DH, for almost 3km** (2m), to a track on your R, **and keep L,** DH, **for another 1km** (0.6m) **to a rd and car park** (568/964) at the bottom, **by the reservoir. Turn L on the rd, for 0.7km** (0.45m), **then turn L onto a BW** (566/689).

3 **Go through a gate to a T-J** (568/688) **and turn sharp R** onto a narrow path into the woods. **Keep SA at the clearing** onto a track **bearing R and DH to a rd** (559/680). **Turn L on the rd to a T-J** (558/678) **and turn R,** or see the extension.

4 **Follow this rd,** alongside the southern side of the reservoir **for 1km** (0.6m), over a stream **to a T-J** (551/680). **Turn R then shortly L, steep UH to T-J with old railway (permissable) path and turn R on this, keeping SA, over 2 minor rds, DH to the B3212 rd and go SA.**

5 **Follow this main track** across the moors, slightly UH and exposed, but generally easy going, past Kings Torr (pile of rocks) (554/739) **after around 6.4km** (4m) (can see Yellow house in the distance to your L as you bear R, which lets you know you are on the correct track).

6 **Stay on this main track for another 4km** (2.5m) **to a fork** (585/734) **just outside of Princetown, and bear L, past the fire station, back to the car park** (589/735), which is on the R.

Extension

+14.2KM (8.8M) & 335 METRES CLIMBING

1 **Turn L on the rd, to a T-J** in the village **and keep L,** around some tight bends, ignoring the rd on the L after the church. **UH, over a cattle grid, to a fork** (567/673) **and turn L** (Nattor - No through rd).

2 **Go past a car park,** where the rd now disappears, over the river, **to a fork** by a scout hut in the trees (581/674 **and keep L,** (or see **note** below). **Over a ford, UH, keeping L at a fork after 1.2m, and L through Eylesbarrow** (old mine) **for 1.25m, to X-tracks** at Nun's cross farm (604/699).

NOTE: Optional detour to Eastern Tor for a challenging climb west to east. Alternatively keep SA UH to do it East to West for fun descent and do the climb again.

3 **Keep SA to another X-tracks and go SA** again, **to a X-tracks with a concrete post,** you were at earlier (602/709). **Turn L onto the wide stoney DH** (that you rode down earlier) **and rejoin the main route at no.2** (or keep SA back to Princetown).

TOP TIP: Be prepared as the weather can change quickly out on the moors.

Family Rides — VARIOUS

1 The first part of the route, over Hessary Tour, is a good path suitable for children, providing good views on an 'out and back' route.

2 The old railway line from Princetown (downhill) to Burrator reservoir is pretty easy going and suitable for beginners, but is exposed.

3 A simple loop of Burrator reservoir along the roads, with the option of some exploration along the rougher forest tracks if required.

Getting there This ride starts from Princetown (about 8km/5m south of Tavistock) which is in the heart of Dartmoor, where the B3357 and B3212 roads cross. Park in the High Moorland visitor centre car park in Princetown (589/735). There is no railway station nearby.

Accommodation: B&B, hostel and camping at the Plume of Feathers (popular with cyclists) in Princetown on 01822 890240, YHA at Bellever on 0870 7705692. Tavistock TI on 01822 612938 or the High Moorland visitor centre on 01822 890414.

Refreshments: The Plumb of Feathers pub in Princetown is a favourite with cyclists. There is also a shop, cafe, fish & chip shop, etc in Princetown as well, but nothing on the route out on the moors.

Bike shops Tavistock Cycles Ltd (in Tavistock of course) on 01822 617630 or a choice in Plymouth.

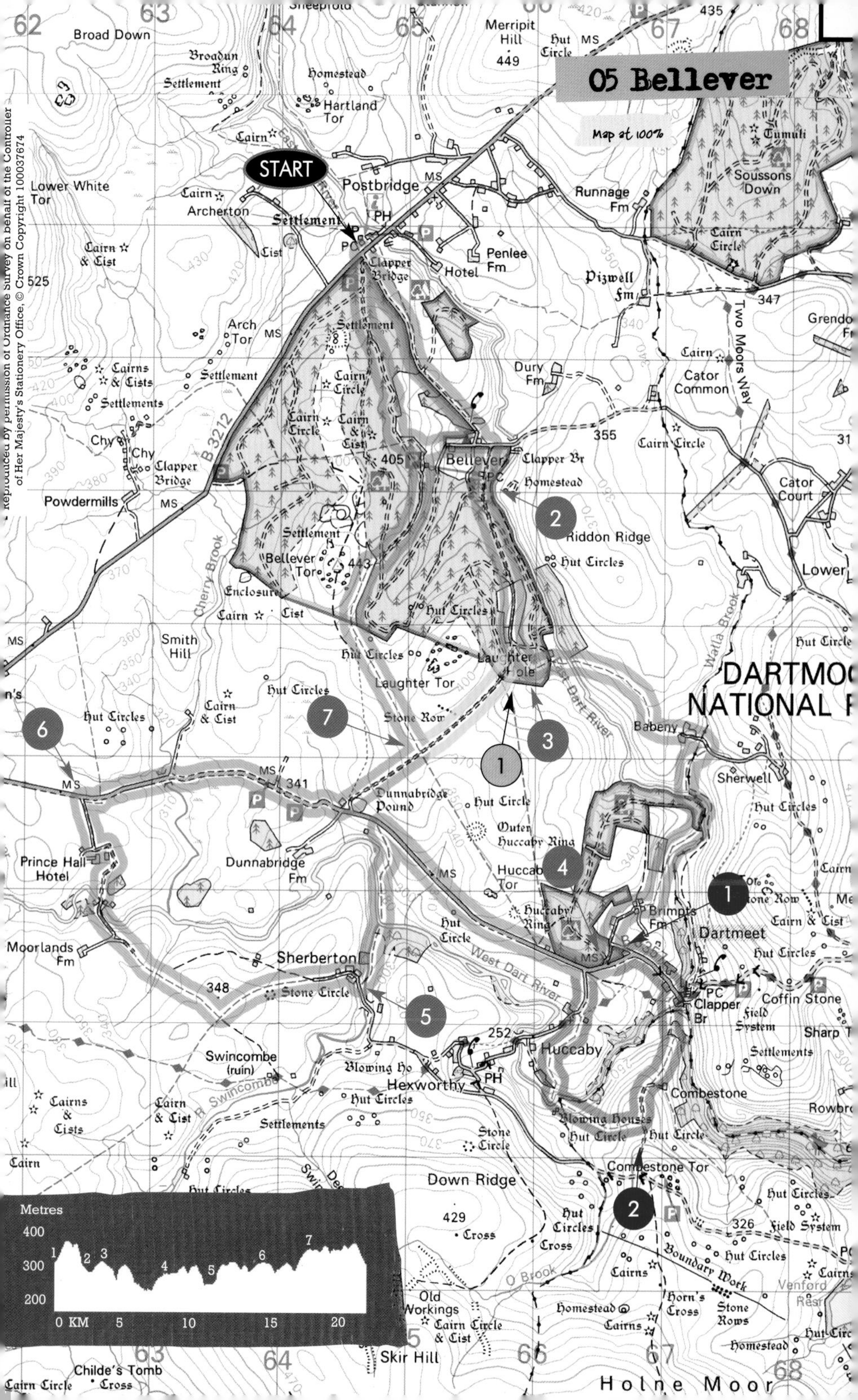
05 Bellever
Map at 100%
START
Broad Down
Broadun Ring
Settlement
Homestead
Hartland Tor
Merripit Hill
449
Hut Circle
Cairn
Postbridge
PH
Lower White Tor
Archerton
Settlement
Cist
Cairn & Cist
525
Clapper Bridge
Hotel
Penlee Fm
Runnage Fm
Soussons Down
Tumuli
Cairn Circle
Pizwell Fm
347
Two Moors Way
Grendon
Arch Tor
Cairns & Cists
Settlements
Cairn Circle
Dury Fm
Cairn
Cator Common
Chy
Clapper Bridge
B 3212
Bellever
405
Clapper Br
Homestead
355
Cairn Circle
Cator Court
Powdermills
MS
Settlement
Bellever Tor
443
Riddon Ridge
Hut Circles
Lower
Cherry Brook
Enclosure
Cairn
Cist
Smith Hill
Hut Circles
Laughter Hole
Laughter Tor
Walla Brook
Hut Circle
DARTMOO
NATIONAL P
Hut Circles
Cairn & Cist
Stone Row
East Dart River
Babeny
Sherwell
Dunnabridge Pound
341
Hut Circle
Outer Huccaby Ring
Prince Hall Hotel
Dunnabridge Fm
Huccaby Tor
Huccaby Ring
Brimpts Fm
Stone Row
Cairn & Cist
Dartmeet
Hut Circles
Moorlands Fm
Sherberton
West Dart River
348
Stone Circle
Coffin Stone
Clapper Br
Field System
Sharp T
252
Huccaby
Swincombe (ruin)
Blowing Ho
Hexworthy
PH
Settlements
Combestone
Rowbro
Cairns & Cists
Cairn & Cist
R Swincombe
Hut Circles
Settlements
Stone Circle
Blowing Houses
Hut Circle
Hut Circle
Combestone Tor
Down Ridge
429
Cross
Hut Circles
Cross
Hut Circles
326
Field System
Boundary Work
Hut Circles
Cairns
O Brook
Venford Res
Old Workings
Cairn Circle & Cist
Homestead
Cairns
Horn's Cross
Stone Rows
Homestead
Skir Hill
Childe's Tomb
Cairn Circle
Cross
Holne Moor
Metres
400
300
200
0 KM
5
10
15
20
1
2
3
4
5
6
7

Bellever

22KM (13.7M) & 580 METRES OF CLIMBING

START **Follow the rd** (or bridleway parallel to it) **towards the YHA. At the T-J** (YHA on right) **go L then R on a forest track** by the Bellever Forest sign on a **BW** (to Laughter Hole fm). Past the toilets, **through a gate and turn L, to a fork and bear L** (Laughtor Hole fm) on a wide track.

2 **Keep SA at the next junction, through a gate** (Path), **through a farm to a X-tracks** (658/759) **and bear L on the Sherwell and Babeny BW,** *or see shortcut.* **Follow the blue** (BW) **marks,** on a technical **DH, to a bridge and stepping stones.**

3 **UH to a walled track at Babeny and follow the markers,** DH, **then R on a BW after the bridge** (673/751), by a passing place. Follow this **over a clapper bridge, stepping stones, alongside riverbank,** UH, **to Brimpts farm and a fork. Bear R, to the rd** (665/734) **and go R on it** or see extension.

4 **After 2.25km** (1.4m) **on the rd turn L on a** narrow, technical **BW track** (647/745), DH **to the river and over the stepping stones. Follow feint grassy track across a field,** by a stream, **then just over another stream turn R, UH through a fm** (646/733)

5 Out onto the open moorland and **keep SA, aiming for a marker post. Bear L to a gate in the wall** (635/731), **and turn R** on a rocky track. Through a ford, **and join a tarmac track and keep R, over a bridge, to the top and keep R to the rd** (625/747).

6 **Turn R on this rd for 2.2km** (1.35m) **then L on a BW track** (645/746) just after a dip in the rd. Go UH on this track, **for 0.8km** (0.5m) **to a X-tracks** (651/750) **and turn L** (to the L of Laughter Tor).

7 Head **across the open moorland,** past a stone, **to a gate at the edge of the forest,** by Bellever Tor, **and turn R** on a narrow track (647/765). Very technical 'Rock Garden' DH. **Go L on a forest track at the bottom and stay on this back to the B3212 rd and the end** (646/788).

Extension

+3.9KM (2.4M) & 160 METRES CLIMBING

A technically challenging extension, and the stepping stones could be under water after heavy rain.

1 **Turn R on the rd for 0.15km** (0.1m) **then L on another rd** (Huccaby & Hexworthy). **After 0.3km** (0.2m) **turn L on a BW** (664/731) (2nd track), **through a gate,** technical DH, **to a river and cross the stepping stones** (662/ 724). **Keep SA over a stream, through a gate and follow the maker posts** UH **to a T-J with a gravel track** (668/723)

2 **Turn L on this for 0.3km** (0.2m) **then bear off L** (669/ 726) before the farm, **on a BW** (Dartmeet). DH, along field edge, with the wall on the RHS, and **join a good track, over some stepping stones.** UH, **past a house and turn R through a gate, to the rd** (671/732) **and L on this, UH, for 0.8km** (0.5m) (past Pixie shop), **rejoin route at** .

Shortcut

-12.9KM (8M) & 350METRES CLIMBING

1 Bear R on the main RH track for 1.1km (0.7m) to a X-tracks at the top (651/750) and turn R and rejoin the route at no.8.

Family

There are some wide forestry tracks in the woodland around Bellever that you can explore on bike or by foot. These range from flat to a gentle gradient, prefect for new riders and trailers.

There is of course the famous Clapper Bridge to look at and a pub at Postbridge.

Getting there start from Postbridge (clapper bridge), which is on the B3212 rd, in the heart of Dartmoor. There is lots of parking, but it does get very busy at peak times. There are no train stations anywhere nearby.

Accommodation B&B at East Dart hotel 01822 880213, Brimpts farm bunkhouse (and tea shop) on 01364 631250, Bellever YHA on 0870 770 5692, camping barn at Runnage fm (GR 667/792) on 0870 7706113. For more info call Moretonhamstead T.I. on 01647 440043.

Bike shops Tavistock cycles, 01822 617 630, Dartmoor cycles in Tavistock on 01822 618178 & Okehampton cycles on 01837 53248

Refreshments
There is a pub at at the start and at Hexworthy, and a tea shop at Brimpts farm.

06 Drogo Castle
Map at 85%
START
Metres
300
200
100
0
0 KM
10
20
30
Cheriton Bishop
Drewsteignton
Castle Drogo
Fingle Br
Prestonbury Castle
Wooston Castle
Clifford Br
Cranbrook Castle
Hore Wood
Butterdon Ball Wood
Whiddon Wood
Hannicombe Wood
Piddledown Common
Sharp Tor
Cod Wood
Bridford Wood
Dunsford
Bridford
Mardon Down
Doccombe
Crockernwell
Sandy Park
Easton
Chagford
Windhill Gate
Steps Br
Hunter's Tor
Rectory Wood
Drewston Wood
Uppacott Down
Butterdon Hill
North Kingwell
Headless Cross
Cairn Circle
Heltor Rock
Moretonhampstead

Drogo Castle

37.8KM (23.5M) & 1,350 METRES CLIMBING

START **At the main rd** with the post office on R, **facing south** in Cheriton Bishop (SX 773/930), **turn L on this rd,** past the Good Knight pub, **and turn R** just past The Old thatch Inn (campsite sign). **After 2km** (1.25m) **turn R** to East & West Down (783/914), **shortly to a fork and keep L.**

2 **Keep SA on the ByW** as track bears L, (can get wet), DH **for 1.65km** (1m) **to a rd** (778/900) **and go L** on this. **0.4km** (0.25m) **to a X-rds** (782/899) **and go SA** (Dunsford) **for 0.65km** (0.4m) **then go R over a footbridge** after the rd bears sharp L (785/893).

3 **Follow the BW signs for 2.9km** (1.8m) **to a rd** (805/884) **and turn R on the rd, over Steps Bridge. After 0.3km** (0.2m) **turn L off the rd, onto a BW** on a concrete track (802/883), towards the YHA, or see the extension.

4 **Keep SA on the BW for 1.3km** (0.8m), **back to the rd** (791/ 880), **and bear on this. After 3km** (1.9m) **to a X-rds** (774/861) at the top and **turn R. UH for 0.8km** (0.5m) **to a fork** (771/869) **and bear L on this rd for 0.5km** (0.3m) **then go L on a BW** (768/868), DH into North Kingwell.

5 **Turn R on the drive for 0.1km then bear L on the BW** just before Yarningale B&B (765/865). Rocky DH, **to a rd** (761/860) **and turn R on this and follow this to a X-rds** in Moretonhampstead (753/861), by the Bell Inn pub.

6 **Turn R on the A382 rd, for 0.55km** (0.35m) (past a hospital) **and turn R,** towards Howton, **then immediately turn L on a rd** past a couple of houses (750/865). **0.8km** (0.5m) **to X-rds** (744/ 871) **and go SA for 1.8km** (1.1m) **to a T-J and turn R, for 0.3km** (0.2m) **then bear L at grassy triangle fork** (742/888) **onto a ByW.**

7 Follow this steep DH, **to a car park** and toilets at the bottom (743/899) **and bear L and L again** just before the Fingle Bridge. **7A Follow the 1st DT** alongside the river, **for 2.6km** (1.6m), out of the woods, **and stay with it bearing L** (ignore the bridge on the R, to some houses).

8 **Follow this grassy DT to a T-J and turn R to a rd** (723/889) **and turn R on this. 0.5km** (0.3m) **to a X-rds** in Easton (719/888) **and turn R on the main rd. 1.1km** (0.7m) **to a X-rds** (712/896) **and turn R** towards Castle Drogo.

9 **UH, for 1.4km** (0.85m) **then turn sharp R** (720/904) towards Coombe farm Gib house (Hunters path / Fingle bridge). **After 0.25m bear L on the Hunters path,** leaving the tarmac track, UH, **following signs for Piddledown common & Sharp Tor.**

10 **Follow this superb trail** along the top of the valley **for 1.3m and keep L,** (keeping your height) **on the** grassy **Hunters path** (737/899). **0.65km** (0.4m) **to a X-tracks and keep SA** on 'Path' **for another 0.65km** (0.4m) **to emerge on a track** (733/906).

11 **Bear R,** DH, **for 0.15km to a T-J and go L for 0.15km to another T-J and follow the signs for Drewsteignton. 0.55km** (0.35m) to the top of the hill (734/908) **and turn R** into the village **and keep SA,** past a telephone box at a grass triangle **to Fingle bridge** (toilets), church on your L.

12 **Bear L just past a white building towards a dead end sign,** past some houses and **keep SA on a DT. 0.15km, past last house and bear L at fork** (740/909) **onto a BW** (use the LHS of the field if it's messy). **To the rd and turn R to a X-rds** (749/915) by some barns **and turn R** (Preston).

13 **After 0.65km** (0.4m) **keep SA/L** as rd bears sharp R, **then immediately L** (753/910) over a cattle grid towards a house. **1km** (0.65m) with house on L and bridge to farm on R, **keep SA on a BW, through an old gate. Cross the stream and bear R,** over a footbridge, and bear L, to a fork **(765/914).**

14 **Turn L here on the old A30,** following the river. Over a bridge, through a couple of gates, over another bridge **to a T-J and turn L,** UH **to a rd** (762/927). **Turn R on the rd, for 1.3km** (0.8m), **back into Cheriton Bishop** (773/930).

Extension

+5.8KM (3.6M) & 250 METRES CLIMBING

1 **0.15km** (0.1m) **over the bridge, and turn L** (803/883), opposite a house (B&B) **then L again on a ByW. UH, for 1km** (0.6m) **to a rd** (811/881) **and turn R on this for 1.6km** (1m) to a junction (819/871) **and turn R then immediately keeping R/SA,** off-road **on a ByW.**

2 **After 0.8km** (0.5m) **keep R/SA joining a rd then shortley keep SA back onto a ByW** (810/869) as the rd bears sharp R. **Join another rd after 0.9km** (0.55m), **then immediately turn R again on a BW** track (Burnicombe).

3 DH, bearing R, then **to L of the buildings on a BW** (Middle path). DH, on this BW (Bridford) **for 1.3km** (0.8m) **back to the start of the loop and go L to the rd** (803/883). **Go L on this, then immediately L again on a** concrete **BW** track, towards the YHA **and rejoin main route at no.4.**

Short Route

1 Do the very western loop of the ride, from Drogo Castle following points 10-11 then 7A-9. A great little loop of 9.5km & 420 metres of climbing, with superb views & pub.

Getting there: Either start in Cheriton Bishop, just off the A30, or at Drogo castle (where the short ride goes from) which is signposted from the A30. Fingle Bridge (nr Drewsteignton) also has a car parks & pub. No train stations nearby.

Accommodation: B&B's at Puddicombe House nr Drewsteignton 01647 281206, Drewsteignton Arms 01647 81224 & White Hart hotel in Moretonhamstead 01647 441340. YHA at Steps Bridge (on ride, nr Dunsford) 0870 7706048, camping nr Whiddon Down 01647 231 695, Newton Abbott TI on 01626 367494.

Refreshments: Pubs in Cheriton Bishop (& shop), Steps Bridge (& cream teas), Moretonhamstead (& shops), Fingle bridge, Sandy Park, Drewsteignton (& shop).

Bike shops: Bigpeaks in Newton Abbot on 01364 654080 & Moor cycles in Okehampton, on 01837 659677

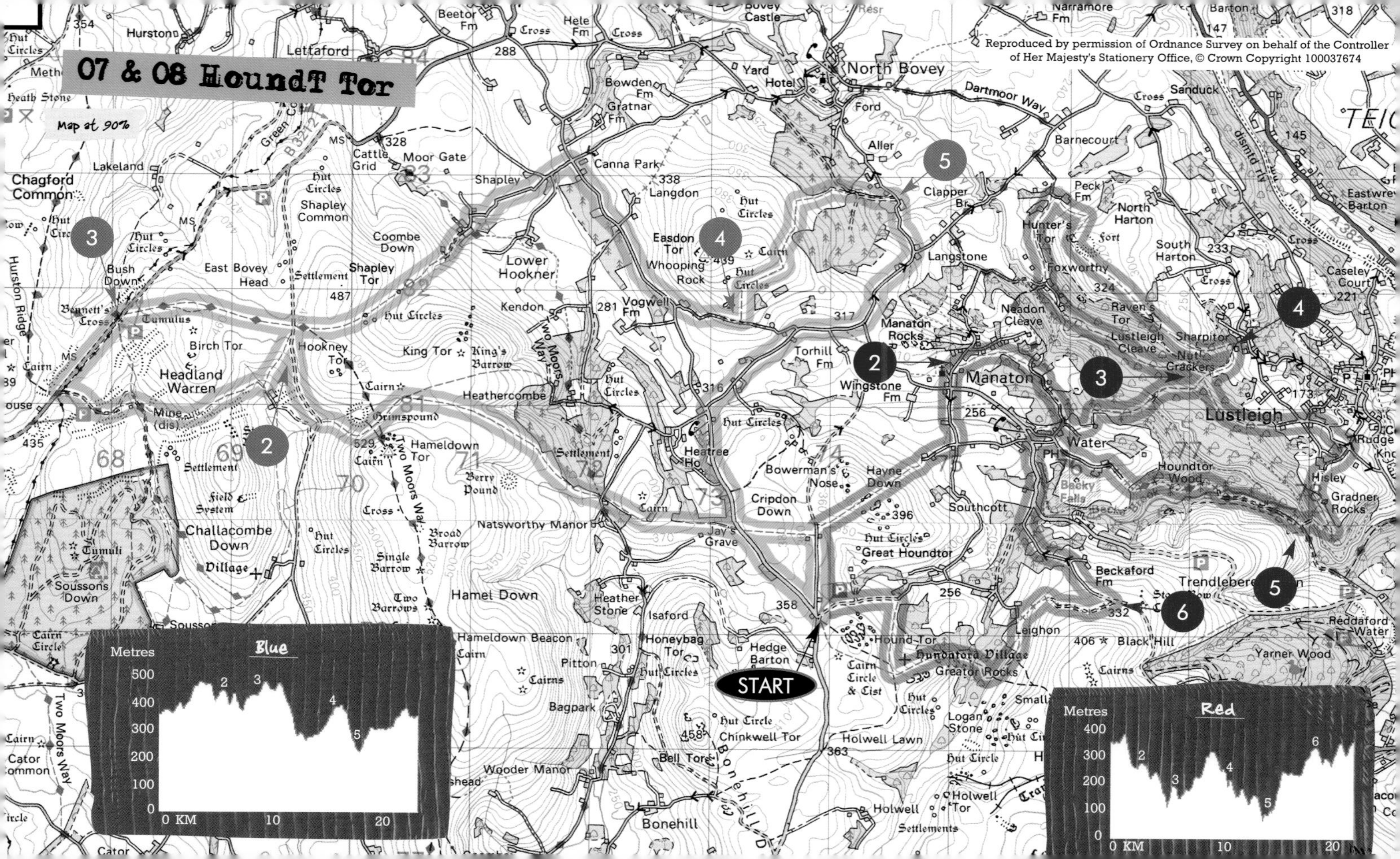

07 & 08 HoundT Tor
Map at 90%
Reproduced by permission of Ordnance Survey on behalf of the Controller of Her Majesty's Stationery Office, © Crown Copyright 100037674
START
Blue
Metres
500
400
300
200
100
0
0 KM
10
20
Red
Metres
400
300
200
100
0
0 KM
10
20
Manaton
Lustleigh
North Bovey
Hameldown Tor
Hamel Down
Headland Warren
Grimspound
Hound Tor
Hundatora Village
Greator Rocks
Becky Falls
Houndtor Wood
Yarner Wood
Easdon Tor
Chagford Common
Challacombe Down
Soussons Down
Dartmoor Way
Two Moors Way

Hound Tor - Blue

23.3 KM (14.5M) & 760 METRES CLIMBING

START Turn R out of the car park to T-J & keep L, UH for 1km then go L on a BW (SX 732/799). UH then DH to a rd & go SA on a BW, long UH, bearing to the LHS of Grimspound. Steep DH to a rd (697/809) & go R on this, UH for 0.9km then turn L on the first BW.

2 UH towards fm & bear R (SP Headland House Inn) UH then DH on great ST, keeping SA past the ruins, keeping SA/L to rd by car park (675/811). Go R on the rd (or L to the pub), UH and go R on a BW shortly after a car park, heading NE (681/817).

3 Follow this (keep R at fork), to rd and go SA on the BW, keep SA/L between the Tors (peaks), UH then good DH, keeping SA as it becomes a rd, to a X-rds (718/ 831). Go R for 1.6km and bear L by Easdon fm, on ByW (SP Barracott), through gate UH to top & turn L on BW (County Rd nr Luckdon (732/817).

4 Bears R alongside a wall, then at corner of wall go R (not SA) on feint track along the hillside & keep SA towards woods. Bear R, DH, 0.2km after big flat boulders on the R, on feint track, keeping SA DH, going R after a wooden barrier, on the BW keeping L through a gate to a rd (745/828) and turn R on this.

5 Keep R at junction in Langstone, UH to to fork and go R, keeping to L, to X-rds (729/809) and go L, UH to BW crossing rd nr Jay's Grave and go L. DH to rd and go R back to X-rds and go 2nd L back to the car park (739/792).

NOTE: The Red route is the more technical route. The two routes together as one, make for a very long & challenging ride.

Hound Tor - Red

21.6 KM (13.4M) & 950 METRES CLIMBING

START Turn R out of the car park to T-J & go R then immediately R again on a rd for 0.8km then go R on a BW (SX 739/799) over Hayne Down. Good DH to X-rds & turn L to another X-rds in Manaton (750/811) & go SA, past church then shortly R on a BW (750/813).

2 Follow the BW to the R, to a track & keep R on this and just before entering the village Water, go L on a BW (759/808). Great (wet!) DH, crossing the bridge at the bottom, UH then L on 1st BW (772/813) for tricky trail along Lustleigh Cleave (to Foxworthy bridge).

NOTE: To avoid this very technical section (inc. 'Nut Crackers') go R on the BW to Lustleigh & rejoin at 4A.

3 Join tarmac by houses & go R by Hunters Barn cottage (758/821) on a BW, through a wooden gate, 0.8km to Peck Farm (758/829). Go R through the fm and a gate, on a BW, steep (walk!) UH on LHS of the fields, then sharp R to a gate and keep L after this on ST along top, then steep technical DH.

4 Turn R before a gate, UH along edge of the wood and bear L at junction you were at earlier (772/813).
4A UH to T-J & go R & keep R to a X-rds (783/806) & go R & keep L on a BW, steeply DH past Gradner rocks, cross bridge over water to T-J & go R (779/800).

5 Follow the ByW, crossing 2nd bridge (772/803) & bear L for steep UH. Keep SA to the top corner of the woods, through a gate on the BW to Water. Join the tarmac and keep L, to X-rds (756/807) & go L for 0.5km then R on another rd, UH for 1.3km then go R on a ByW (763/792) to Leighon.

6 Keep L on the BW, then keep R on this, DH past Greator Rocks, over rocks/bridge then UH, and go R just before the top (745/787), DH to the rd and go L on this, UH, back to the car park (739/792).

Getting there: Hound Tor car park (739/792), west of Bovey Tracey, north off the B3387, towards Manaton. There are car parks nr the Warren House in on the B3212 & in North Bovey for the west route or in & around Lustleigh for the east route if required.

Accommodation: B&B at Ring of Bells in North Bovey on 01647 440375 and Puddicombe House in Drewsteignton 281206, Self catering in Lustleigh 01647 277357, YHA at Steps Bridge on 0870 7706048 or camping barn by Great Houndtor (GR749/795) on 7706113, Bovey Tracy TI on 01626 832047 or Moretonhamstead on 01647 440043.

Refreshments: 'The Hound of the basket meals' vanat the start (car park). The (good) Warren House Inn at the far western end of the West route or the pub in Water on the East route.

Bike shops: Big Peaks in Ashburton on 01364 654080.

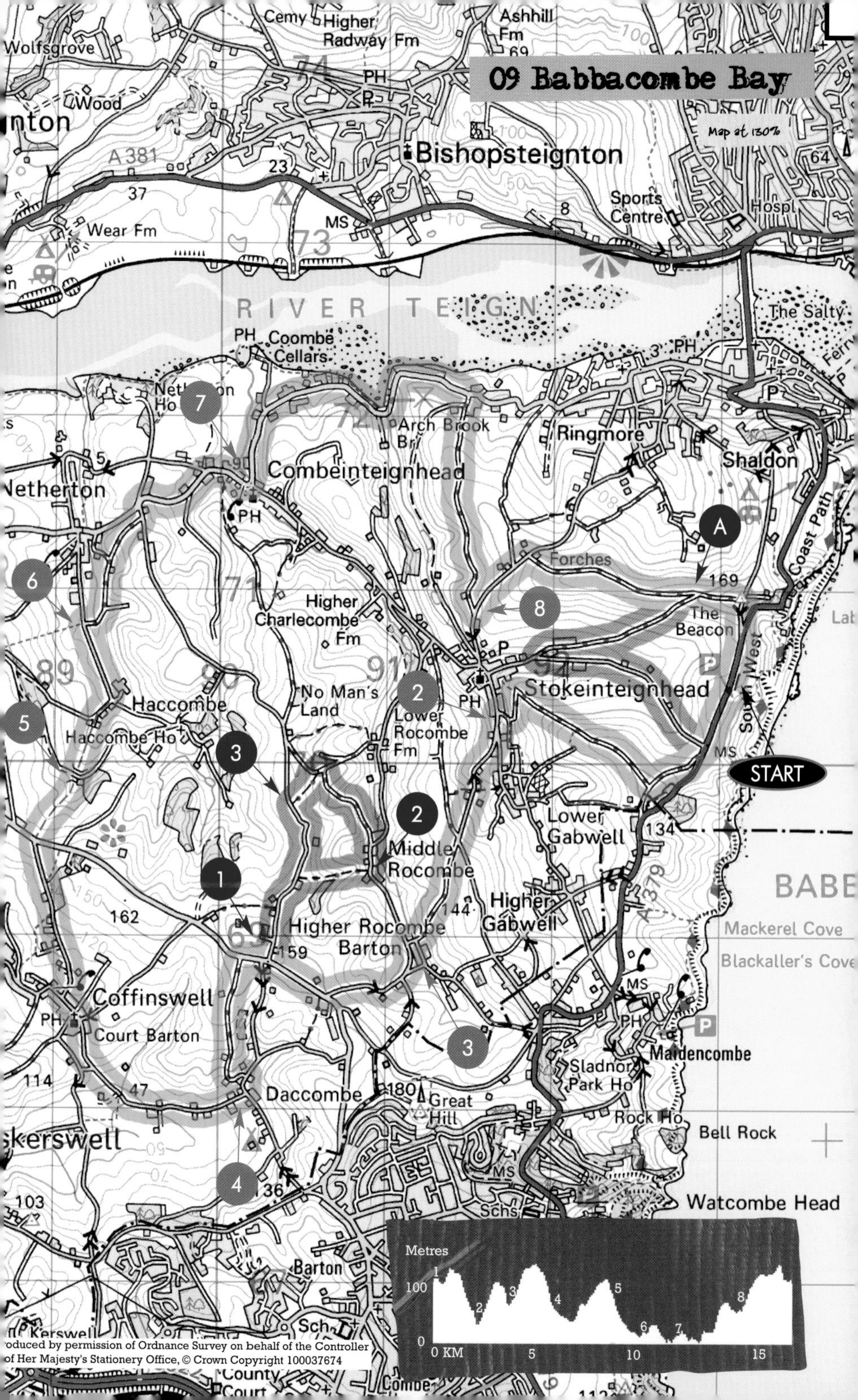

roduced by permission of Ordnance Survey on behalf of the Controller of Her Majesty's Stationery Office, © Crown Copyright 100037674

Babbcombe Bay

17.2KM / 10.7M & 600 METRES OF CLIMBING

START **Exit the car park and turn L** (south) on the A379 rd. **After 0.4km** (0.25m) (just after the rd on the R to Stokeinteignhead) **turn R on a DT off the lay** (SX 929/700). **0.3km** (0.2m) UH **to a fork at the top** (926/699) **and turn R.** DH on a rocky DT which bears sharp L **to a T-J at the bottom and turn R to a rd** (by Chasers Arms pub) (917/703).

2 **Turn L on the rd then shortly R on a rd,** between the two thatched cottages (917/702), UH. **To X-tracks and keep SA to another X-tracks and go SA** (unsuitable for motors) DH, **to rd and keep R to a T-J** (911/690).

3 **Turn L on the rd and keep R,** UH **to the main rd** (907/687) **and turn R on this rd for 0.55km** (0.35m) **then L on a DT** (901/689) by a gate (with view) shortly after a rd on the R or see extension 1. Stoney, DH, **to a rd** (902/682) **and turn R to a T-J** in the village (902/681).

4 Follow this rd **for 1.5km** (0.95m) into Coffinswell and turn R on the rd (Milber) opposite the Fox cottage (891/686). **UH to the main rd at the top** (889/695) **and go SA** on a little used BW. Under the bridge (can get wet here) and **through a gate and go SA** across the field.

5 DH, **to a gate,** out of the field, **onto drive and bear R on this to a T-J** (893/704) with Haccombe House on R, **and turn L** on the rd. **After 0.5km** (0.3m) **turn R on a DT** (892/708) after the conifers, Haws farm (Caravan & Camping Club) FP on L.

6 **Keep SA** (L then R at forks) on this main track **to a rd and turn L to a T-J** with the main rd (895/715). **Turn R on the rd,** DH, into Combeinteignhead **and follow the rd to the L** (Combe Cellers) by the garage, which then follows the coastline.

7 **After 2km** (1.25m) on this coastal rd, **turn R** at the Teignharvey park sign, (915/721) (before the pink thatched Little Harvey farmhouse) steep UH. **Keep SA** between the farm and house, becoming a stoney track, **steep UH, then DH to a rd** (915/709).

8 **Turn L on the rd,** UH, **for 0.5km** (0.3m) **then turn R on a DT** (919/712) and follow this UH. **After 1km** (0.65m) ignore the DT on the R or see extension 2. **Keep SA for 0.25km** (0.15m) **to a rd** (931/ 710) **and turn R,** DH, **joining the A379 rd** heading south (R), **back to the car park on the L** (931/704).

EXTENSION 1

+3KM / 1.9M & +110M CLIMBING

1 **After 0.4km** (0.25m) **turn R on a rd** (903/689) (Combeinteignhead & Netherton), **then after 0.5km** (0.3m) **turn R** on the John Musgrave Heritage Trail (White arrow). Good DH between the trees, **to a rd** at the bottom (909/694) **and go L on the rd.**

2 **After just 0.15km** (0.1m) **bear L on a DT** (909/696) (as the rd bears R) on a rocky track UH. **After 0.55km** (0.35m) **turn L at the T-J** (of DT's), **then shortly L again on a ST** between the trees (906/700) and follow this **to the rd** (904/698).

3 **Turn L on the rd and follow this back to the main rd** (903/689) (where you left the main route) **and turn R then immediately L on the DT** by the gate, **and rejoin the main route near the end of no.3 where you left it.**

EXTENSION 2

+1.9KM / 1.2M & +65M CLIMBING

A **Turn R on the DT,** on a fast stoney DH, past a farm **to a rd** (919/706) **and turn L on this rd** and follow it up **to the A379 rd** (929/701) **and turn L then R back into the car park** (931/704).

Getting there Exit A380 at Newton Abbot & go east on A381 towards Teignmouth. Shortly after the viewpoint parking on the right, get in the right hand lane to turn right at the lights, over the bridge & south on A379 towards Torquay. 1mile past Sheldon the (free) car park is on left (931/704). By train; Newton Abbot or Teignmouth just off the route.

Accommodation LOTS of places but popular holiday destination, so book early. Rocombe country house B&B 01626 873367, coast view holiday park in Shaldon on 01626 872392. NO YHA's close by. Torquay T.I. on 0870 7070010.

Bike shop Bikin Motion in Torquay, on 01803 214145

Refreshments Usually an ice cream van in th car park at the start. There are also pubs and shops in Stokeinteignhead, Coffinswell and Combeinteignhead.

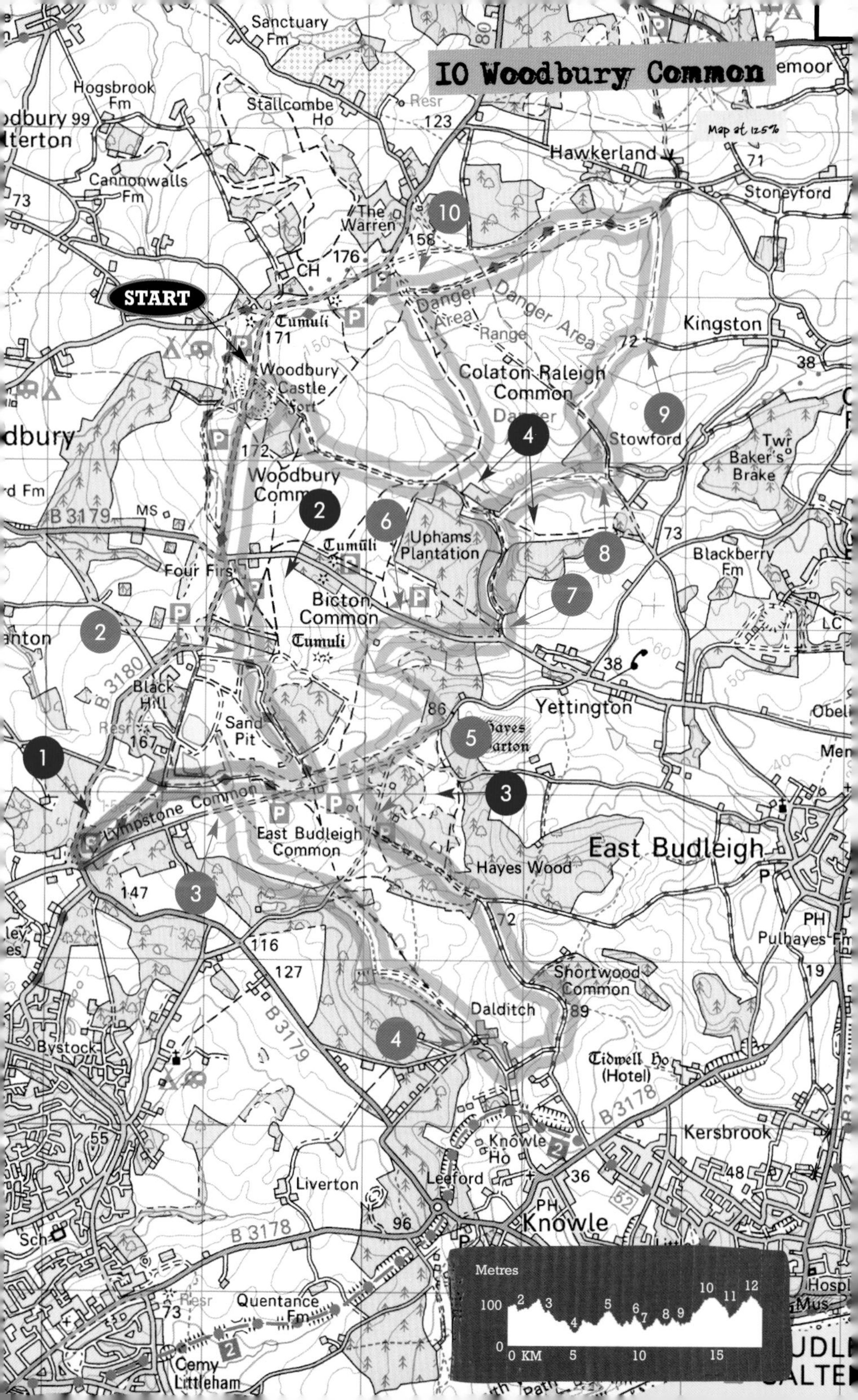

10 Woodbury Common
Map at 125%
START
Sanctuary Fm
Hogsbrook Fm
Stallcombe Ho
Resr
123
Hawkerland
71
Stoneyford
Cannonwalls Fm
73
The Warren
158
176
CH
Tumuli
171
Woodbury Castle Fort
Danger Area
Range
Colaton Raleigh Common
Kingston
72
38
Stowford
Twr
Baker's Brake
172
Woodbury Common
Uphams Plantation
73
Blackberry Fm
B 3179
MS
Four Firs
Bicton Common
LC
Tumuli
B 3180
Black Hill
Resr
167
Sand Pit
38
Yettington
86
Hayes Barton
Obeli
Lympstone Common
East Budleigh Common
East Budleigh
Hayes Wood
147
116
127
72
PH
Pulhayes Fm
19
Shortwood Common
Dalditch
89
Bystock
B 3179
Tidwell Ho (Hotel)
B 3178
Kersbrook
55
Knowle Ho
Leeford
36
48
Liverton
PH
Knowle
96
B 3178
Resr
73
Quentance Fm
Cemy
Littleham
Metres
100
0
0 KM
5
10
15
2
3
4
5
6
7
8
9
10
11
12

Woodbury Common

19.3KM (12M) & 480 METRES OF CLIMBING

START Head south out of the car park (back-right) on the (Pink) East Devon Way, heading for a clump of trees. At the trees (after 0.5km/0.3m) bear L, following the pink arrows on a loose stoney track, DH, over some water, then bearing L, UH.

2 After 1.2km (0.75m) turn R (037/851), still following the pink arrows along a good ST for 0.7km (0.45m) and turn L (031/851) on a BW (easy to miss). Go down to the rd and SA on the FP SA, but immediately bear R off this on some ST (032/849).

3 Follow this ST (and tell-tale tyre tracks) DH and bearing L to emerge at a rd (038/844) and go SA and follow this track (south-east) alongside some water, to a DT (041/839). Bear L on this and follow it to a T-J and bear R to some houses (047/835).

4 Keep SA/L on a drive for 0.25km (0.15m) then turn L on a ROW (049/833). UH, to a T-J (052/835) and turn L and follow this, bearing L and keep L to a T-J at the bottom (048/844) by Hayes Wood. Turn L and follow this track for 0.8km (0.5m) to a rd (041/848).

5 Go SA but immediately bear R, off the FP, heading north, to a rd (039/851). Go over the rd and turn R alongside it, then bearing L (west) after a while, then R (north) past the water tunnels and UH, over a concrete slab, (deep puddle in dip), to a split in the path, by the rd (042/860).

6 Turn R, DH, alongside the rd, then bear L to join the rd and head east on it. Shortly as the rd bears R, turn L (north) (049/860) on a gravel DT (BW) at the edge of the woods and follow the BW signs.

NOTE: There are some good singletrack trails in the woods to the R and L (Uphams Plantation_.

7 After 0.8km (0.5m), UH, to a DT at the top and turn R then immediately turn L on an unmarked BW (048/867). Follow the BW sign, bearing L through the woods and past a wooden barrier to a DT.

8 Turn L through the water and back UH. 0.5km (0.3m), past another wooden barrier, turn R (before exiting the woods) on easy to miss BW (053/873). Great twisty ST through the woods on the BW, keeping L at the clearing, over a plank bridge.

9 Keep on the RHS in the trees for 1.6km (1m), out the other side, and keep SA, past a green barrier and turn L at the junction (058/885). Turn L and follow this (East Devon Way) track west for 1.6km (1m) to a main X-tracks (042/880) with car park on the R.

10 Turn L and follow the middle track, DH, for 1km (0.6m), to the end and bear R, down a gully, through a stream and back UH, to a DT on the corner of Uphams planation (044/869).

11 Turn R on a BW / DT and follow this wide track to the trees / castle in the distance (037/871). Keep L/south of the woods/castle, to a car park (033/872).

12 Take the ST in the back-right corner of the car park, alongside the rd, between some gauze bushes. Follow this trail south, DH, for 0.8km (0.5m) to a rd and go SA, back to the Four Firs car park (032/864).

D.I.Y. route — VARIOUS

Woodbury Common is a great place explore. The main route isn't too long route as it is aimed to introduce you to the area, and point you in the right direction of some good places to explore. With this information you can easily make your ride as long or short as you require. Places of particular interest are:

1 Bomb holes, home-made Northshore, and dirt jumps to the west and north of the car park in Lympstone common.

2 Various single track trails in Bicton - go past the Tumuli and down to water tunnels.

3 There are various single track trails in East Budleigh Common worth exploring.

4 There are various single track trails in and around Uphams plantation.

Getting there Exit the M5 at junction 30 (by Exeter) & go south on A376 (Exmouth). After 2 miles go left on the B3179 through Woodbury to a X-roads (with the B3180). The Four Firs car park is straight ahead, then immediately right (032/864). Other car parks are available. Train: In Exmouth - follow the cyclepath no.2 (north-east) towards Budleigh Santerton, to get to Woodbury common.

Accommodation: Holbrook Farmhouse B&B in Clyst Honiton on 01392 516441, Ladram Bay holiday centre on 01395 568398 off the A3052, St John's Caravan & Camping in Exmouth on 01395 263170, YHA in Exeter on 0870 7705826. Exmouth TI on 01395 222299

Bike shops Knobblies in Exmouth on 01395 270182 & The Bike Shed in Exeter on 01392 426191.

Refreshments Nothing on the ride, but places close by.

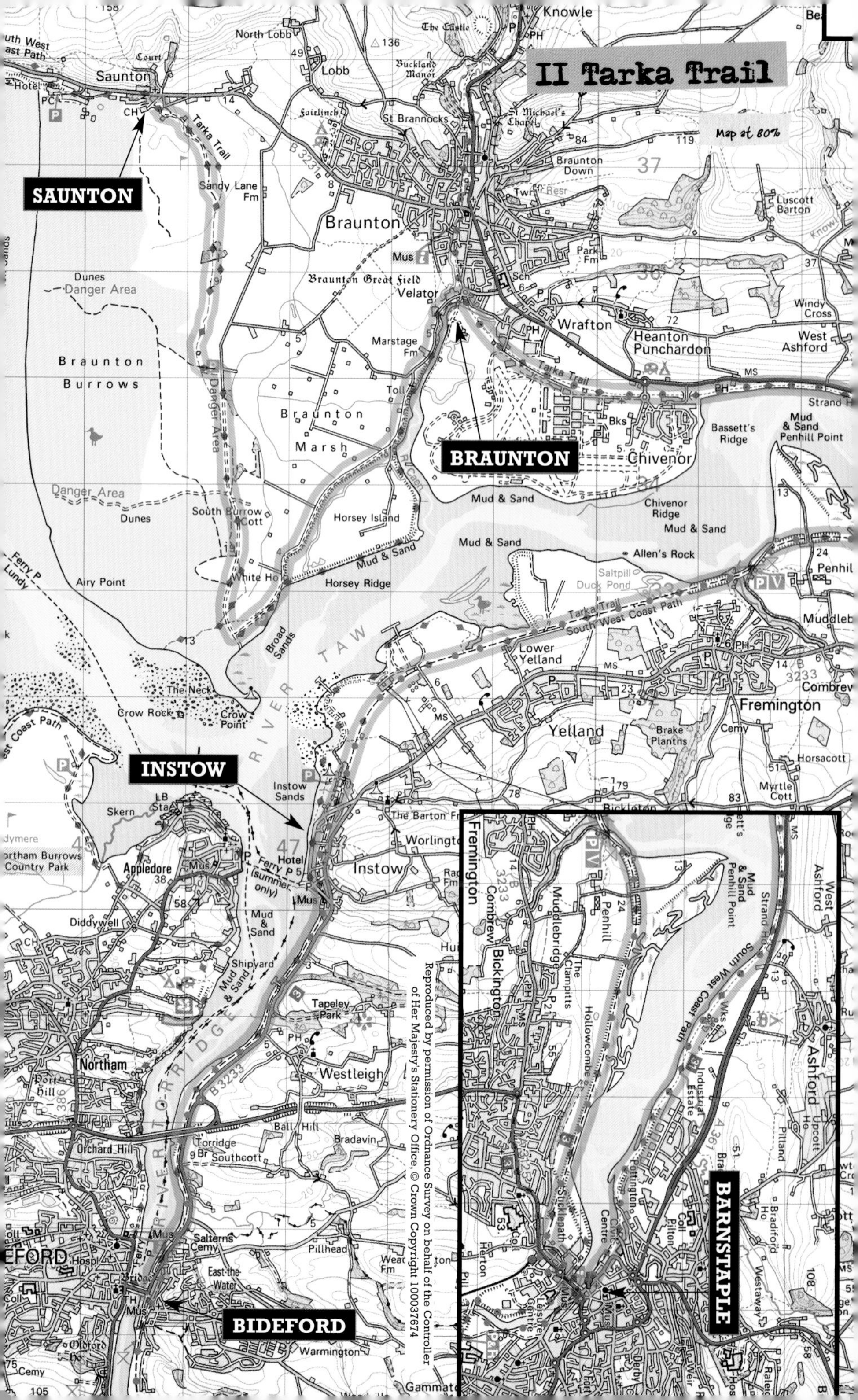
II Tarka Trail
Map at 80%
SAUNTON
BRAUNTON
INSTOW
BIDEFORD
BARNSTAPLE
Saunton
Braunton
Braunton Burrows
Braunton Great Field
Braunton Marsh
Velator
Wrafton
Heanton Punchardon
Chivenor
Horsey Island
Horsey Ridge
Airy Point
Crow Point
The Neck
Crow Rock
Broad Sands
River Taw
Lower Yelland
Yelland
Fremington
Instow
Instow Sands
Appledore
Northam
Westleigh
Tapeley Park
Bradavin
East-the-Water
Warmington
River Torridge
Tarka Trail
South West Coast Path
Penhill Point
Bickington
Muddlebridge
Ashford
Reproduced by permission of Ordnance Survey on behalf of the Controller of Her Majesty's Stationery Office, © Crown Copyright 100037674

Tarka Trail

VARIOUS

The Tarka Trail is a lovely family friendly and mostly traffic free, flat cycle path that hugs the waterside of this beautiful & popular holiday destination.

NOTE: The first section from Saunton has some single track and bumpy doubletrack which won't be suitable for everyone. However, from the southern car park at Braunton Marsh, it becomes smooth and easy going all of the way to Bideford.

Saunton to Braunton

9.7KM (6M)

1 Car park to west of Saunton, by beech (or in the layby past the hotel) & use BW on R before B3231 rd (bend in drive). At rd, go R & shortly R into golf club carpark and bear L through a gate on the Somerset & North Devon coast path (456/375).

2 Follow this BW, south, through the golf course, for 1.75km (1.1m) (by a sign) and turn L through a gate into a carpark (462/351). Go through this to a (rough) DT and turn R (south) on this for 2.6km (1.6m) to a car park at the end (465/326).

3 Turn L and go through the (sprawling) car park to join a road and follow this through Braunton marsh. Bear R at the T-J past the Toll (482/351) for 1km (0.6m) to a roundabout (487/358) and either turn R on teh Sustrans route 27 to Barnstaple or L, on the same cyclepath, to Braunton.

Braunton to Barnstaple

8KM (5M)

Follow the Sustrans cycle route no.27 along the River Taw/estuary, for 8km (5m) to 'The Square' in Barnstaple (558/330).

Barnstaple to Instow

10KM (6.2M)

Cross Long Bridge (A3125 rd) (or to avoid this road, use the Sustrans cycle route which goes south along the river for 1km, before doubling back to the other side of the bridge) (557/328). Follow the Sustrans no.3 route signs to join the southern side of the river Taw/estuary, and follow this for 9.6km (6m) to an old signal box (474/301) and either go SA on Tarka Trail, or turn R into Instow village.

Instow to Bideford

4.5KM (2.8M)

Follow the obvious Tarka Trail for 4.3km (2.7m) , to the cafe in the old train carriages (456/263). To go into Bideford, head R, over the bridge to a round-about (454/264) and go R.

Family activities

SURFING

When you are in this part of the country you need to get in the sea. For some surfing lessons (at Saunton or Croyde) tel 01271 890400 or see www.surfsouthwest.com. Otherwise there are lots of surf shops to hire boards from in Braunton

THE BIG SHEEP

Fun activities for the whole family, including; sheep races, pony rides, mountain boarding, lamb feed-ing, indoor playground, laser gun game, a garden centre, and even a brewery. There is also an ice rink in winter time. Just 2 miles west of Bideford, tel 07866 398599 or see www.thebigsheep.co.uk.

Getting there This will depend on which section(s) you want to ride. There are car parks at various locations, but be warned, it gets busy.

Accommodation: There are soooo many places. Call Barnstaple T.I. on 01271 375000. Instow is a nice peaceful village and Croyde is a surfers favourite.

Bike shops: South Fork in Braunton are excellent see www.southforkracing.co.uk or tel; 01271 817247 & The Bike Shed in Barnstaple on 01271 328628.

Refreshments cafe at Saunton car park and lots of places in the villages/towns along the route.

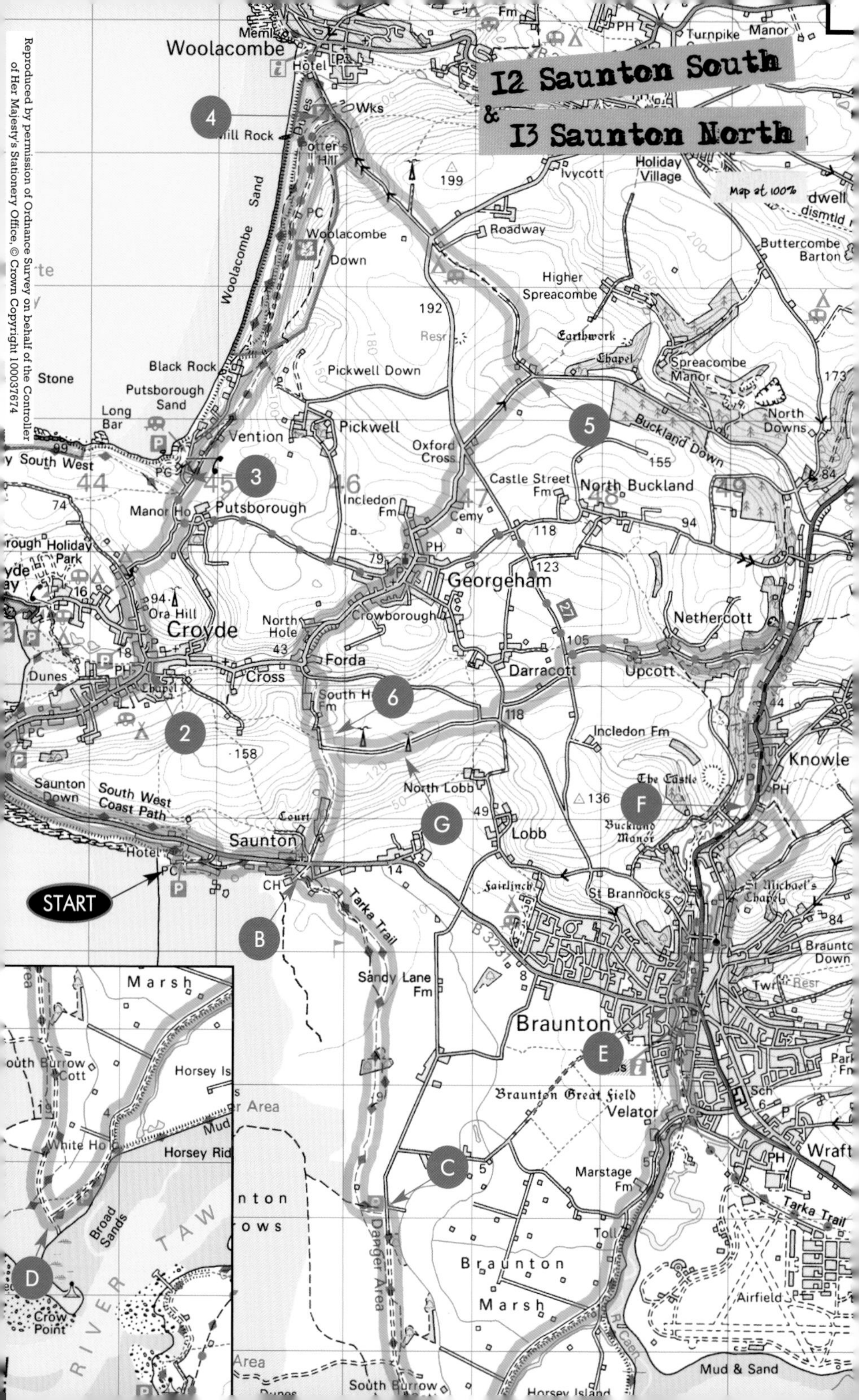
12 Saunton South
&
13 Saunton North
Map at 100%
START
Woolacombe
Hotel
Wks
Mill Rock
Potter's Hill
Woolacombe Sand
PC
Woolacombe Down
199
Ivycott
Holiday Village
Roadway
Turnpike
Manor
Buttercombe Barton
Higher Spreacombe
192
Resr
Earthwork
Chapel
Spreacombe Manor
North Downs
Black Rock
Stone
Putsborough Sand
Long Bar
Pickwell Down
Pickwell
Vention
Oxford Cross
Buckland Down
155
South West
Castle Street Fm
North Buckland
Manor Ho
Putsborough
Incledon Fm
Cemy
118
94
Holiday Park
Georgeham
123
Ora Hill
Croyde
North Hole
Crowborough
Nethercott
Forda
Cross
Darracott
105
Upcott
Dunes
Chapel
South Hole Fm
Incledon Fm
Knowle
158
The Castle
PH
Saunton Down
South West Coast Path
North Lobb
136
Buckland Manor
Court
Lobb
Saunton
Hotel
CH
Fairlinch
St Brannocks
St Michael's Chapel
Tarka Trail
Braunton Down
Sandy Lane Fm
Braunton
Marsh
South Burrow Cott
Horsey Is
White Ho
Horsey Rid
Mud
Braunton Great Field
Velator
Sch
Wrafton
Marstage Fm
Broad Sands
RIVER TAW
Danger Area
Toll
Tarka Trail
Braunton Marsh
Airfield
Crow Point
South Burrow
Horsey Island
Mud & Sand
R Caen
1
2
3
4
5
6
B
C
D
E
F
G

Saunton North

16.9KM (10.5M) & 490 METRES OF CLIMBING

START Go back up the steep car park entrance, to the rd (SS 450/377) and turn L on this. Follow this around the coast (433/383), DH, into Croyde. Rd bears L (surf shop opposite), past more surf shops, and a good pasty shop on the L.

2 As the main rd bears R, keep L/SA on another rd (444/392), (Putsborough beach), past the toilets, and (Seat) garage. After 0.65km (0.4m) turn R (Cherry Tree Farm SA) following the brown sandcastle signs. Steep twisty UH, for 0.65km (0.4m) to a T-J and turn L to Putsborough beach.

3 Keep SA past Clifton Court, on a DT, coastal BW. Follow this along the hillside, with great views to Woolacombe. Joins a big long car park, to the rd (459/433) and turn R on this.

4 1.2km (0.75m) steep UH to a X-rds (467/424) and keep SA 'Little Roadway Farm' campsite. Keep SA on the grassy DT as the drive bears L to the farm. Track improves past the gate, and bears L through a gate on a DT, DH to a rd (475/413).

5 Turn R on the rd, UH, to (Oxford Cross) X-rds and keep SA, DH, for 2.25km (1.4m), through Georgeham, to Forda and turn L on another rd. Just past South Hole Farm B&B turn R on the BW (457/390). Steep UH, through a gate, and keep L, to the top.

6 Keep SA on the BW, between trees, good ST, DH, join a drive, to the rd (458/377) and turn R on this, for 0.8km (0.5m), then L back to the car park (447/377).

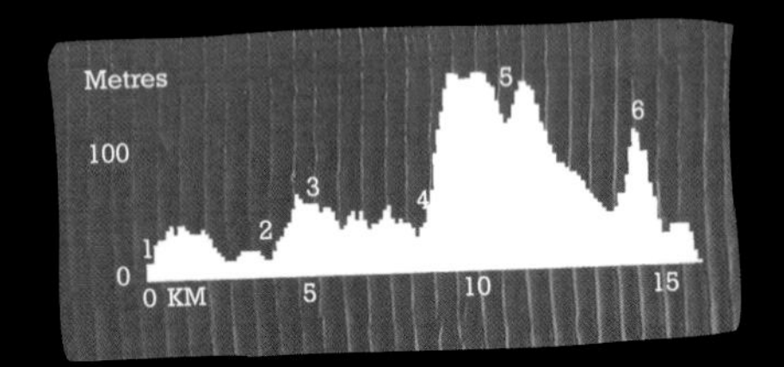

Saunton south

21.7KM (13.5M) & 350 METRES OF CLIMBING

START Go R on BW before the bend (449/376) up to B3231 rd, and go R on this, then shortly R on the gold club driveway. Look for (and join) the Somerset & North Devon BW coast path on the L just along here.

B Go through a golf course, and bear R (south), following the BW signs (south) along some nice ST between the trees. After 1.8km (1.1m) (by a sign) turn L through a gate into a car park (462/351).

C Go through the car park to the DT and turn R (south) on this. Follow this rough DT for 2.6km (1.6m) to a car park at the far end (465/326).

D Bear L, through the long, sandy car park to join the tarmac road and follow this for 3.2km (2m), past a Toll booth to a rd junction (482/350) and bear R. To a roundabout (486/358) and bear L on the Tarka Trail cycle path, into Braunton.

E 0.5km (0.3m) after crossing the B3231 rd go R on a rd, to the main A361 rd (487/371) and go SA on Church St. Over the river and go L on Silver St, for 0.3km (0.2m) then go R, UH, on this track for 0.65km (0.4m) then L on another track, steeply DH, to the A361 rd (492/381) and turn R on this.

F After 1.3km (0.8m) (through Knowle) turn L on Nethercott road (route no.27). At the junction turn L (leaving route no.27), then very shortly R, to a T-J and turn L to a X-rds (472/387). Turn R here and very soon keep SA on a track as the rd bears R, UH towards the radar masts.

G Go past the masts, DH to T-J and go L on a BW (458/385). ST, DH, between trees, joining a drive, to the rd (458/377). Turn R on the rd, for 0.8km (0.5m), then L down into the car park (447/377).

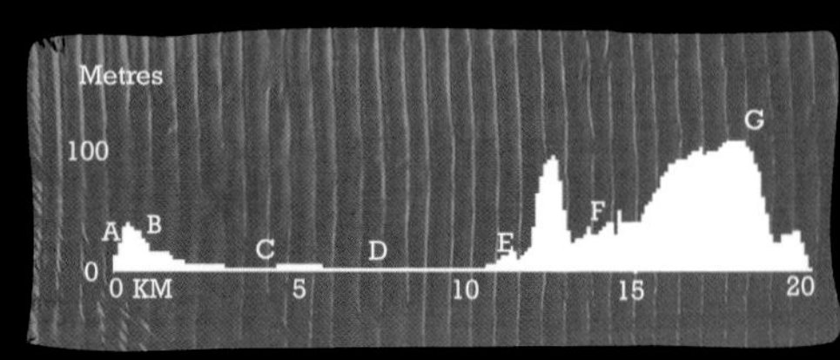

Getting there Go through Barstaple, to lights in Braunton and go left on B3231 (Saunton & Croyde). After 2.5 miles turn left (just before a hotel), down to a car park by the sea (447/377). There is (limited) free parking past the Hotel in a layby overlooking the sea. Train: Go to Barnstaple & join the Tarka Trail to Braunton.

Accommodation: B&B at South Hole farm on self catering cottages (sleeps 4–8) in Croyde on 01271 890 083, camping at Midland Holiday Park, near Ashford on 01271 343691, YHA camping barn in Illfracombe on 0870770 5878. Barnstaple TI on 01271 375000 for more info.

Refreshments Cafe at start in carpark. North route: shops etc in Croyde, cafe at Putsborough beach carpark, shops etc in Woolacombe & pub in Georgeham. South route: Choice in Braunton, and a pub in Knowle.

Bike shops
Southfork in Braunton on 01271 817247 or The Bike Shed in Barnstaple, on 328 628

I4 & I5 Porlock

Map at 85%

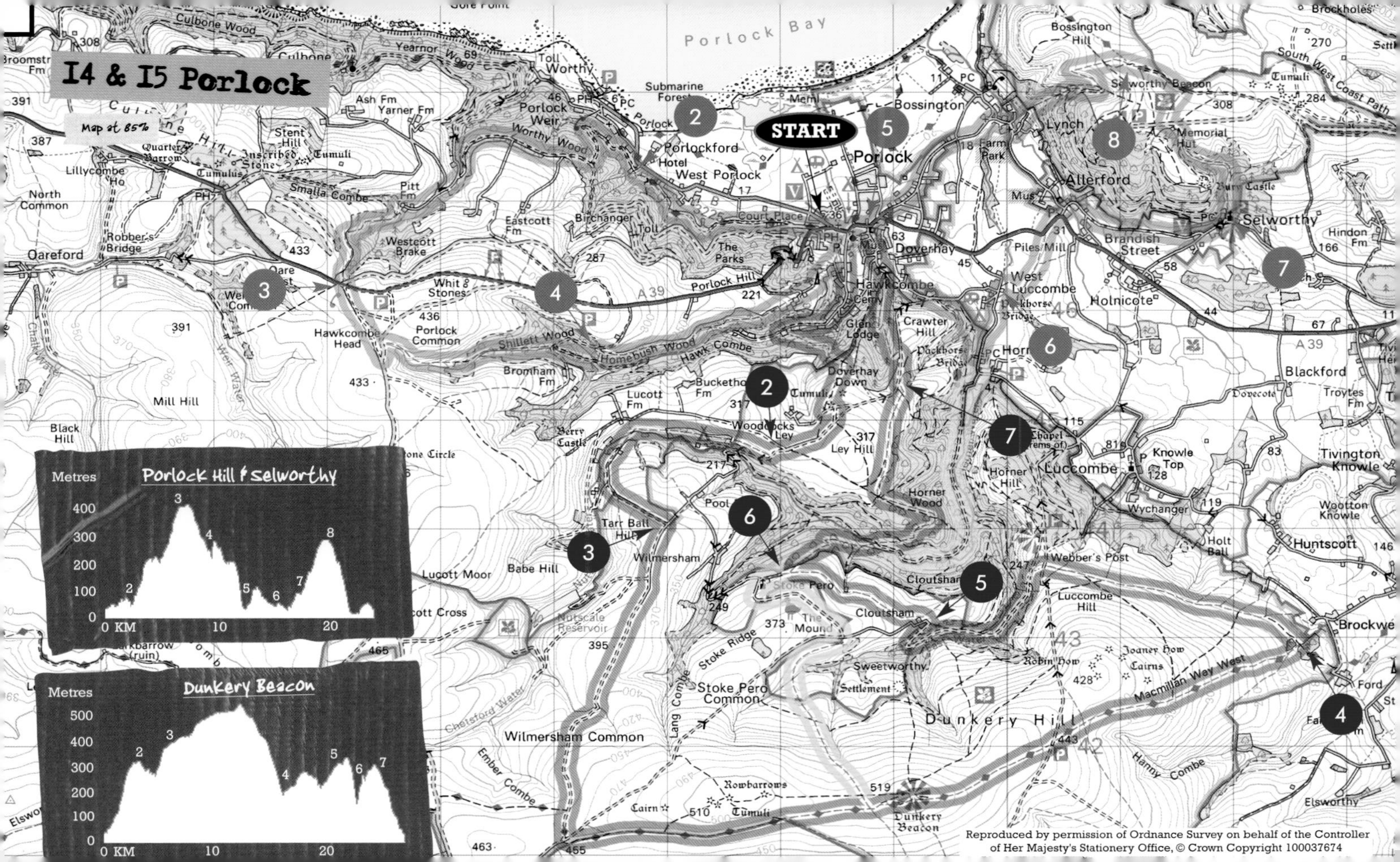

Dunkery Hill

27KM (16.8M) & 1,010 METRES OF CLIMBING

START Go back to the High st/A39 & go R on Parson's St, past village green, SA/R at fork on dead end lane and just past the last house turn L, over footbridge, on a BW SP Ley Hill (880/457). Keep SA, UH, keeping R at fork in dip, steep UH to a tarmac track (Woodcocks Ley fm on R). Go L on tarmac then shortly R on a DT, to a rd & go R on it for 0.65km then R on BW (879/446) as rd bears L, DH.

2 Follow this & cross the water at the bottom and bear R (866/448) on a BW, steep UH. Becomes a better track past house, UH and follow this to the rd (869/440). **NOTE**: A BW does bear off to the R over the moors, but there isn't much of a trail on the ground.

3 Turn R on the rd, UH for 3.2km to a T-J (861/411) and go L then R on the BW, UH to Dunkery Beacon (891/414). Keep SA (or see note below), DH, on the Macmillan Way West, over a rd, keeping SA, DH for another 2.4km (1.5m) to a X-tracks by some trees (925/429).

NOTE: The (yellow) bail-out / shortcut option (north) down from Dunkery Beacon & along Horner Water (valley bottom) to Horner helps avoids some big hills if your legs & lungs have had enough.

4 Turn L and follow the rocky BW climbing along the bottom of Luccombe Hill, keeping L/SA for 2.4km (1.5m) to a rd (903/437). Go SA on the BW opposite and shortly to a rd and go L on this, (big) DH then UH to (Cloutsham) farm and bear R here, up to a gate & BW.

5 Go L at T-J through another gate and across a field and follow this for 1km to a gate (881/436) with BW SA, but go R through BW gate (before fm at Stoke Pero). DH, into the trees, on a fast fun windy ST to a stream at the bottom and cross the footbridge.

NOTE: For the 'Escape' route (avoiding big hill SA) go R on the track alongside Horner Water, to Horner (897/454)

TOP TIP: Horner Wood has lots of excellent trails worth exploring, but note, not all are legal to ride.

6 Bear L then R (effectively SA), UH, on Granny's Ride (888/439) for tough UH, keeping SA at X-tracks, UH (walk!) on a ST. Follow the Horner Gate & BW signs, to a T-J with a good track (888/443) at edge of the woods and turn R on this, DH to a rd (890/453) and go R on this.

7 After 0.3km (0.2m) turn L on a BW (890/456) going R and very steeply DH for 1km (0.6m) to a rd at the bottom (889/463). Turn L on the rd, steep DH, keeping SA (north) back into Porlock (887/467).

Porlock Hill & Selworthy

12.6KM (7.8M) & 600M CLIMBING / +11.4KM (7.1M) & 445M CLIMBING

START Go back to & R on the A39, & immediately R on 'New rd' (Toll rd) for 0.15km then go R on permissive path (when dry) or use B3225. Keep R at fork, then SA/R at the BW fork, to a stoney DT (867/472) with hut on L. Follow this DT SA/L, UH, turning R on steep DT UH at (863/473).

2 Bear sharp R for 0.25km (0.15m) to a fork (FP just before on L) and keep R. 1.3km to a rd & go L, UH on this, keeping SA/L when it bears R after 0.25km. At Pitt fm (846/469) bear L at the BW fork, steep UH on a stoney BW for 1.1km (0.7m) to and L on the A39 (841/462).

NOTE: The BW in Worthy Wood at (856/475) going steeply DH to the rd is a good fun. At the rd go L and L again on the BW, parallel to the rd, UH to Pitt farm.

3 Almost immediately go R off it again, onto hard-pack BW (south-west) across the moor for 0.8km (0.5m) to a rd (845/455) and turn L on this. After just 0.15km turn R on a BW (845/457), DH, into the valley, and follow this fast fun rocky ST down through the valley for 2km, bearing L to (BW) T-J and go L (863/455), bearing R on DT, steep UH.

4 Turn R on a ST BW, nr the cattle grid at top, fun ST to a junction & go SA through the gate across the field (nice views). DH through field & exit it and go SA/R on a BW by a house (881/461). Follow the BW for steep fun DH, over narrow footbridge and continue down the lane back into Porlock (886/466) & **optional early end**.

5 At eastern end of the High St in Porlock, go R (south) on Doverhay rd (887/467) for 0.5km (0.3m) to a fork and bear L. After 0.6km ignore rd on R, and join a BW on the R just past it (894/460). Bear L at a fork, over a bridge, to a rd (898/456) and go L on this for 0.7km then go R (just after rd on L) through the water on a BW (899/462).

6 Bears L, then keep L at a fork, to the A39 rd (903/467) and go R on this for 0.25km then SA/L back off it, as it bears R, going SA, over a bridge (905/469). Bears R, then keep SA, as rd bears R and DH, on a rough DT (SP Selworthy). Keep SA at the farm, to a rd and turn L, UH on the rd for 0.25km then turn L through a gate on a BW, (920/468), as the rd bears R, by a church.

7 After 0.4km of steep UH bear L at the fork, over a stream, keeping L, to a rd and turn L on this then shortly R, UH on a grassy BW (914/477) UH to a X-tracks (916/480). R to the top, or L (on South West Coast path) for 0.55km DH to a fork (910/482) & bear L (Porlock) on BW.

8 **NOTE**: R is FP only. Lovely steep zig-zag DH, then bearing R, SP 'Lynch Combe' DH to a rd (900/476). Turn R on this, then shortly keeping L to follow the Sustrans cycle signs, keeping SA (R) back into Porlock (887/467).

Getting there: car park by Porlock Visitors centre (884/468), off the B3225 or there are various other possible starting points all over the place e.g. Dunkery Hill (904/419).

Accommodation: campsites at Burrowhayes fm, 01643 862463 in west Luccombe, Sparkhays in Porlock, 01643 862470, Pool Bridge (west of Horner wood) 01643 862521 & Minehead nr Moor Wood, 01643 704138. YHA in Alcombe, south of Minehead, 0870 7705968. Porlock T.I. on 01643 863150.

Refreshments Porlock has plenty & tearooms in Selworthy, Horner & Allerford.

Bike shop Porlock cycle hire on 01643 862535 for basics & Pompy's in Minehead for wider choice, tel: 01643 704077

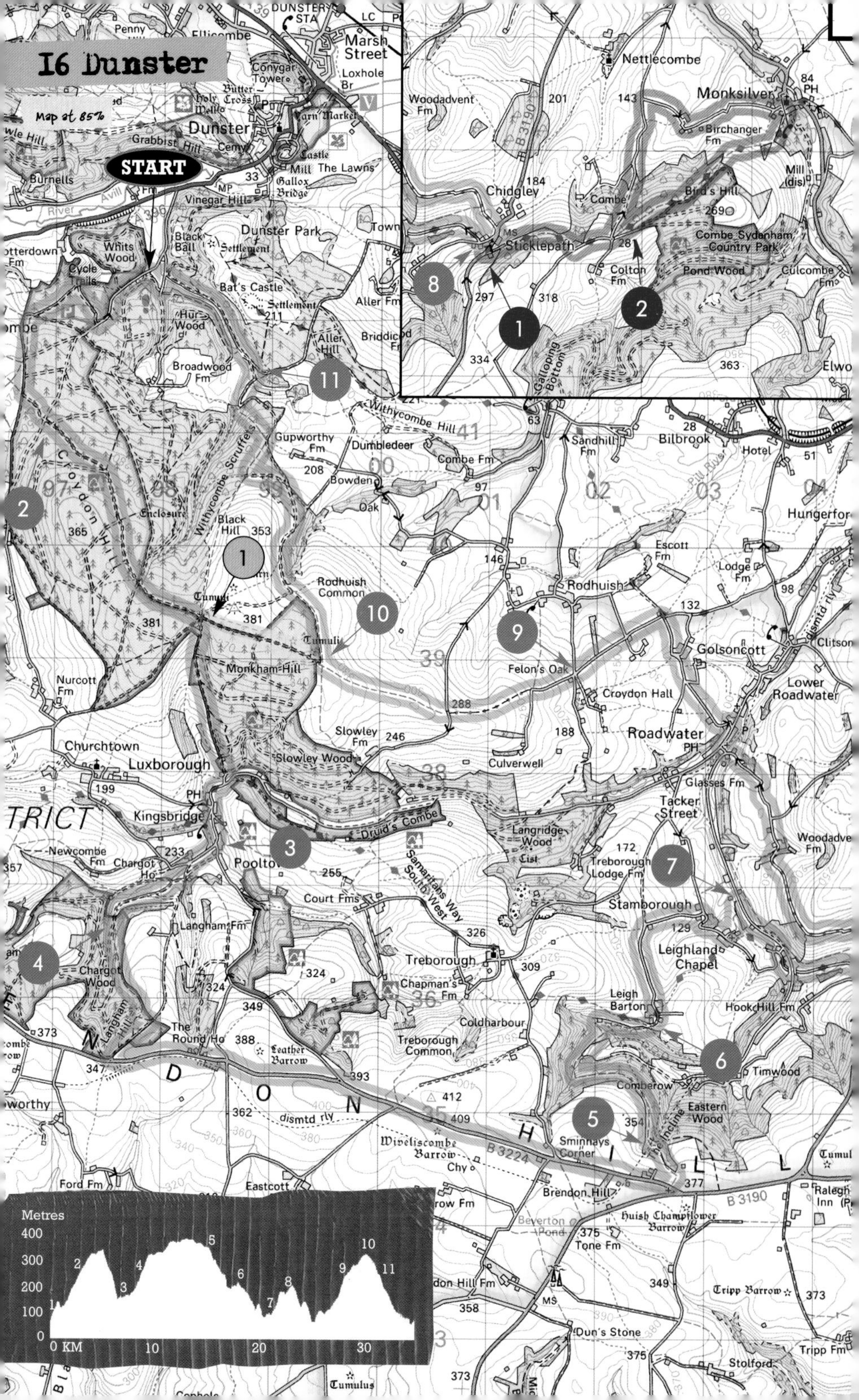
16 Dunster
Map at 85%
START
Dunster
Marsh Street
Conygar Tower
Loxhole Br
Butter Cross
Holy Wells
Yarn Market
Grabbist Hill
Castle
Mill
The Lawns
Gallox Bridge
Vinegar Hill
Burnells
River Avill
Whits Wood
Cycle Trails
Black Ball
Dunster Park
Settlement
Bat's Castle
Hur Wood
Broadwood Fm
Aller Hill
Aller Fm
Croydon Hill
Enclosure
Withycombe Scruffets
Withycombe Hill
Gupworthy Fm
Dumbledeer
Bowden
Combe Fm
Black Hill
Tumuli
Rodhuish Common
Monkham Hill
Nurcott Fm
Churchtown
Luxborough
Kingsbridge
Slowley Fm
Slowley Wood
Druid's Combe
Samaritans Way South West
Langridge Wood
Cist
Newcombe Fm
Chargot Ho
Pooltown
Court Fms
Langham Fm
Chargot Wood
Langham Hill
The Round Ho
Leather Barrow
Treborough
Chapman's Fm
Coldharbour
Treborough Common
dismtd rly
Wiveliscombe Barrow
B 3224
Brendon Hill
Sminhays Corner
Incline
Comberow
Eastern Wood
Timwood
Leigh Barton
Leighland Chapel
Hookhill Fm
Stamborough
Treborough Lodge Fm
Tacker Street
Glasses Fm
Roadwater
Croydon Hall
Felon's Oak
Culverwell
Rodhuish
Golsoncott
Lower Roadwater
Clitsom
Lodge Fm
Escott Fm
Hungerford
Sandhill Fm
Bilbrook
Hotel
Pill River
Nettlecombe
Monksilver
Woodadvent Fm
Birchanger Fm
Chidgley
Combe
Bird's Hill
Mill (dis)
Sticklepath
Colton Fm
Combe Sydenham Country Park
Pond Wood
Culcombe Fm
Galloping Bottom
B 3190
Huish Champflower Barrow
Beverton Pond
Tone Fm
Tripp Barrow
Tripp Fm
Dun's Stone
Stolford
Ralegh's Inn
Eastcott
Ford Fm
Metres
400
300
200
100
0
0 KM
10
20
30

Dunster

35.8KM (22.2M) & 1,300 METRES CLIMBING

START Exit the car park to the rd and turn L, following the Orange trail, steep UH, for 0.65km then R on a DT (SS 974/420). Follow the DT past a clear (parking) area on the L, past a barrier, DH, for 0.15km to a fork at the bottom (972/423). Bear L, UH, to a T-J and go R on this DT, which bears L along the edge of the woods. After 0.7km (gate on the R), bear L on the DT (967/ 413), into the woods, for 0.3km to a rd and go SA on the DT (orange signs) opposite, to a fork (970/411).

2 Keep SA on this main track for 1.8km to a X-tracks (978/ 397), just after a FP on the L, and keep SA (no signs). After 0.65km at a 5-way junction (984/394) take the 2nd R (the only rough DT, into the trees) on the BW to Luxborough or keep SA for a Shortcut (-24km/15m & -875 metres of climbing). Rocky DH for 1.6km to a rd and turn R on this, down to another rd (986/379), and turn R on this. After 0.65km (through Kingsbridge), turn R just past cream tea garden, on a rd to Dunster (985/374).

3 After 0.3km turn L on a BW (Wheddon Cross & Langam Hill), down to the houses (982/371) and bear R (or keep SA through a gate by the house, for an easier climb). Keep L, over a cattle grid (Langam Hill), into well kept grounds and keep SA/R after 0.15km as a track bears off sharp L and UH. To a fork as you enter another field (977/369) (can see a house down below on the R) and bear L, UH. Go through a gate into the woods and immediately bear L at the fork, steep UH, on a DT (976/367).

4 Follow this to the corner of DT and turn L on this, UH, to a T-J (979/358) with a good track. Turn R on this, to the rd (975/354) and turn L on this. After 5.4km (just before meeting the B3190 rd) and turn L through a gate on a BW (ST 027/344). Keep to the LHS of the field, kinks around the corner and turn L through a gate (028/345). Past some stagnant water on a bumpy, grass track, through a gate, into the woods. Short, steep, DH, through a small stream (no public access sign L & R) and turn R, short steep UH (blue dot on tree), to a T-J (FP R).

5 Turn L, UH, shorlty to the top then R (blue dots), and follow this main track, keeping R at all of the forks, DH, on the main track (blue dots) for 1.95km, to an old hut (020/358). Turn R on the BW to Leigh Barton (can get overgrown), UH. Through a gate after 0.55km (farm buildings SA) and turn R on the track, bearing L around the farm buildings, to a X-rds (026/359).

6 Turn L on the better surface, past a farm house, becoming a rd (good views), DH on ST rd for 1.45km (bearing R), down to a grass triangle T-J (030/368), and turn R, DH, then UH on this twisty rd for 0.4km to the top (032/366). Turn L on the Roadwater BW just by the houses. Down to the Wessex Water building and turn L on a high sided ST BW. Keep R, around the back of the houses, over a small wooden bridge to the rd (033/369).

7 Turn R on this rd for 0.55km then R (FP to Leighland) before you enter the woods SA. Past a hand made paper mill, and bear L on the grassy DT, past some workshops/sheds, to a rd (037/364) and go L on it, under a bridge. UH on this minor rd. 0.8km to a T-J by farm & go L to the main rd (046/362) and turn L or see the extension. **7A** Immediately go L off the rd on a grassy DT (before a wooden gate with 'Chidgley hill farm' SP).

8 Through a metal gate and keep SA on the dirt ST in the grassy DT, (not the BW L). UH, to a metal gate and go SA/R on a rough track. DH, keeping SA at a X-tracks (037/373) (FP on the L). Bears round to the RHS of a house, and joins a rd going UH. Keep L on this ST rd, DH for 1.1km to a fork and bear R, over the water, into Roadwater. To a T-J and turn R for 0.15km then L on a rd (032/384), steep UH. 0.8km to a fork and bear L, 0.4km to a X-rds (026/394) and turn L on the rd for 1km to a X-rds and keep SA (no through rd).

9 After 0.4km keep SA on a ROW (014/387) as the track bears L and a BW on the R. 0.8km, UH, to a rd (006/385) and go SA on the BW (muddy in places), through a gate out into open. Tough grassy UH, into bumpy field (but great views), use the worn track on the LHS by the trees, going SA, through a gate at forest edge, and turn R (SS 995/389).

10 Along forest edge on the Dunster BW, 0.8km to a DT X-tracks (992/396). Go SA/R on DT for 0.65km to a fork and keep L, 0.4km to another DT fork by trees (991/ 406) and bear L for 0.4km, then R on a BW (988/406) into trees. Technical DH to a DT (989/409) and go L, L immediately, on a BW, DH to multiple-junction (987/412) and go R on a DT, DH.

11 0.3km to a fork and bear L, to a T-J (988/416) and go L on the RUPP, alongside the stream, to a clearing and rd, and go L on the rd over a bridge then turn R (980 /423) as rd deteriorates, through a wooden gate (white arrows 1, 2 & 3), on track back to the start (978/424).

Extension

+7.9KM (4.9M) & 340 METRES CLIMBING

1 Turn R on the rd, steep UH then shortly L on a stoney track, on the Monksilver BW (ST 046/361). UH to a T-J and turn L Monksilver via colton B, UH, to T-J with a DT and go SA through a gate across a field, to a rd (054/ 361). Turn L on this for 0.3km to a T-J (057/362) and go SA into the woods (Wildlife Conservation area).

2 DH on the BW, for 2.1km to a rd in Monksilver (073/374), and turn L on it, UH for 1m to a T-J (060/ 375). Go L, UH for 1.4km to a T-J (057/362) and retrace your earlier steps, back to the main route, and rejoin the main route at 7A (047/363).

Getting there: From the A39 (following the north coast) turn south on the A396, through Dunster, then after 1/2 mile turn left on a minor road, signposted 'Luxborough' for another 1/2 mile (keep right at fork just before) then left into the car park (978/424), just before a steep hill. There is a train station in Dunster.

Bike shop
Pompy's in Minehead on 01643 704077

Accommodation: Independant Base Lodge in Minehead on 01643 703520 private rooms or dorms & bike friendly. Alcombe coombe YHA (west of Dunster) on 0870 7705968, camping barn at Woodadvent farm nr Roadwater (GR 037/374) 0870 7706113 & nice Minehead caravan & campsite nr Moor Wood up on the hills, west of Minehead, on 01643 704138. Minehead T.I. on 01643 702624.

Refreshments: Pub & cream tea graden (open 2-6 Tuesday-Sunday) in Kingsbridge, pub & general stores in Roadwater and pubs & shops in Dunster.

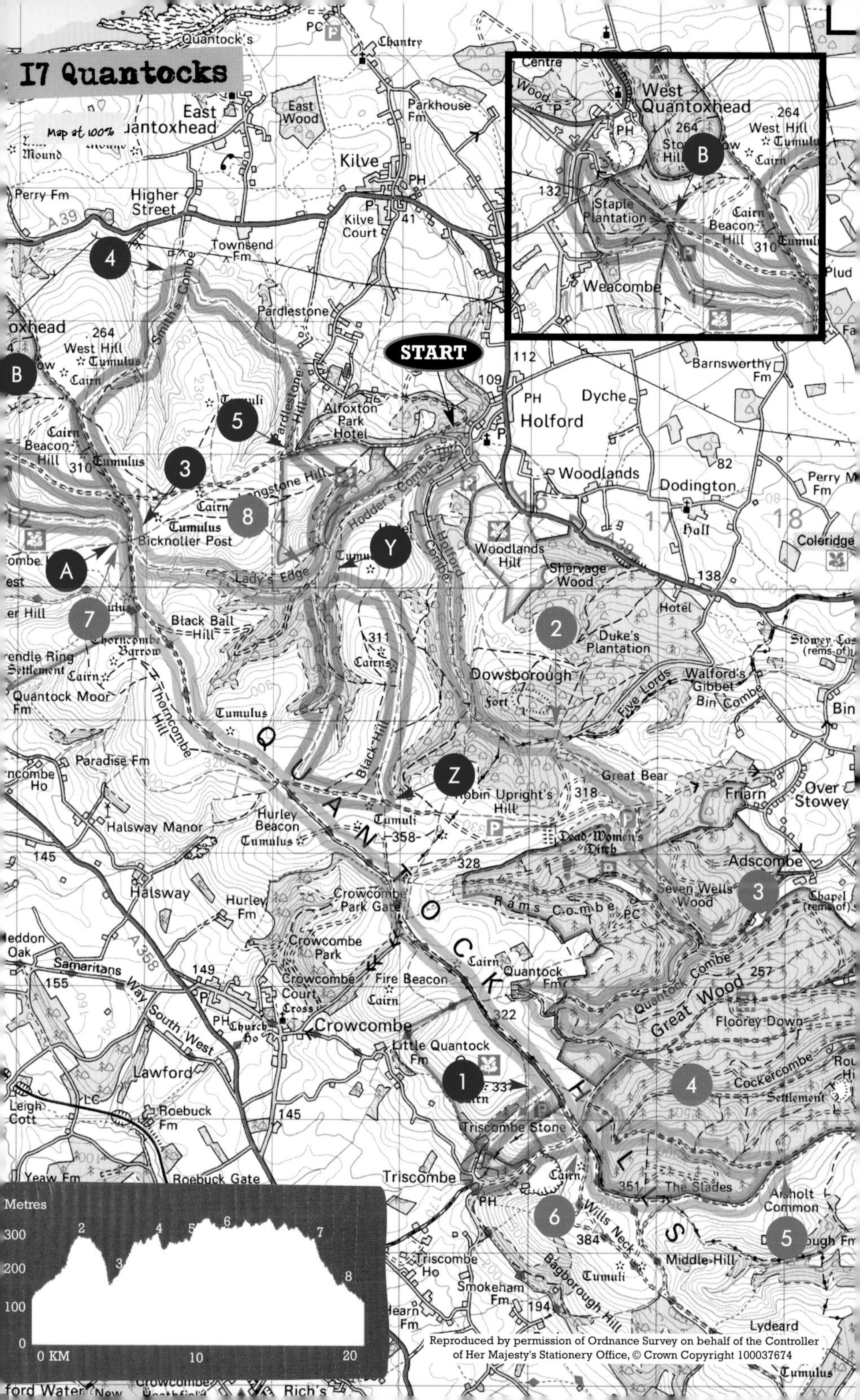
17 Quantocks
Map at 100%
START
A
B
Y
Z
1
2
3
4
5
6
7
8
East Quantoxhead
Kilve
Kilve Court
Chantry
Parkhouse Fm
East Wood
Higher Street
Perry Fm
Townsend Fm
Pardlestone
Alfoxton Park Hotel
West Quantoxhead
Staple Plantation
Weacombe
Beacon Hill
West Hill
Holford
Dyche
Barnsworthy Fm
Woodlands
Dodington
Hall
Coleridge
Woodlands Hill
Shervage Wood
Duke's Plantation
Dowsborough
Fort
Five Lords
Walford's Gibbet
Bin Combe
Smith's Combe
Longstone Hill
Hodder's Combe
Holford Combe
Lady's Edge
Bicknoller Post
Black Ball Hill
Thorncombe Barrow
Thorncombe Hill
Quantock Moor Fm
Paradise Fm
Halsway Manor
Halsway
Hurley Beacon
Hurley Fm
Black Hill
Robin Upright's Hill
Great Bear
Friarn
Over Stowey
Dead Women's Ditch
Rams Combe
Seven Wells Wood
Adscombe
Quantock Combe
Great Wood
Floorey Down
Cockercombe
Settlement
Crowcombe Park Gate
Crowcombe Park
Crowcombe Court
Crowcombe
Fire Beacon
Quantock Fm
Little Quantock Fm
Triscombe Stone
Triscombe
Triscombe Ho
Smokeham Fm
Wills Neck
Bagborough Hill
Middle Hill
The Slades
Aisholt Common
Lydeard
Samaritans Way South West
Lawford
Roebuck Fm
Roebuck Gate
Leigh Cott
QUANTOCK HILLS
Metres
300
200
100
0
0 KM
10
20
Reproduced by permission of Ordnance Survey on behalf of the Controller of Her Majesty's Stationery Office, © Crown Copyright 100037674

Quantocks

21.6KM (13.4M) & 680 METRES OF CLIMBING

START Go back to the rd and turn R on it then R after a LH bend (ST 155/410) (Holford Combe). Follow this, past a hotel, becoming off-rd, to a fork after about 2.4km to a clearing (156/390). Bear L, for 0.7km to a T-J and go R to a rd (162/388) and go SA on a BW.

2 0.8km to a rd and go R on this, then L on a track just past the car park (168/384). To a gate and go through this for 0.25km to a fork (169/380) and bear R (off BW) DH for 1km to car park (174/373).

3 Turn R then L onto a track, past a 'No Vehicles' sign, on the LHS of a stream, for 1.3km, then steeply UH, out of the woods. 0.25km to a track at the top (160/370) and turn sharp L on this to the rd (168/365).

NOTE: The BW down to Quantock Combe is a good DH and there is a (man-made) DH from Floorey Down, south, continuing over the rd, down into the Cockercombe valley.

4 Turn R on the rd for 0.5km then turn L on a fire road (BW) (165/361) going DH. Keep R at a fork on a sharp left-hand bend (167/359), going UH, for 0.5km to a fork and bear L (on the BW), for 1km to the edge of the woods (180/357).

5 Bear R out of the woods to a DT and turn R on this, alongside the (outside) edge of the woods, UH. 2.1km, dropping down to a rd and car park on the R (164/360) and keep SA on a good wide, tree-lined DT.

6 Follow this for 2.1km to a rd (150/375) or see extension 1. At the rd, go SA, UH, to a car park and bear L, following this main track for another 3.5km to a multiple-junction and wooden sign, at Bicknoller Post (129/404) and Beacon Hill SA.

7 Turn sharp R (south-east), or see extensions 2 or 3.
7A There are a few trails here, but aim to go down into the valley and you should pick up the right one. A good 1.6km DH, to a fork just over a stream (143/400) and bear L or see extension 4.

8 Follow this lovely trail, alongside the stream, down Hodder's Combe, for 1.4km back to the car park (154/411).

Extension 1

+2.3KM (1.4M) & 140 METRES CLIMBING

1 After 0.3km turn L off main track on a BW (162/362), steep DH into a valley. At rd (156/356) go L and keep L, UH, alongside a stream. Keep SA, rd deteriorates past a quarry, to a T-J at the top (164/359). Turn L and go SA on the tree-lined DT, and rejoin at no.6.

Extension 2

+5.5KM (3.4M) & 240 METRES CLIMBING

A Bear L down into Weacombe Valley, for 2km to nr Weacombe (112/408) turn R along the bottom of the woods to a rd. Turn R on this rd for 0.4km then R on another rd (110/416). UH, to a car park and keep SA, to the right-hand side of Beacon Hill.

B 1.2km to a X-tracks at the top (128/407) and go R (south) (or see extension 3). 0.4km back to Bicknoller Post (129/404) and follow the BW on the L of the main track going SA (south) and rejoin at no.7A.

Extension 3

+3.5KM (2.2M) & 240 METRES CLIMBING

3 Keep SA on main track for another 1km (0.65km if joining from extension 2) to a wooden post (125/413) and go R on a grassy track. Becomes ST, steep DH for 1.45km to a X-tracks (132/423) and turn R.

4 UH, then around the edge of the hill for 1.1km (just after DH over stream then UH) turn R (141/ 418) steep UH. To a DT and go SA over this, 0.15km to another DT (142/410) and go SA on a wide grassy trail.

5 Follow this around the hillside, then go DH into the woods on some great ST, to a stream (144/403) and turn L, (or turn R for 0.3km to a fork and turn L for extension 4) and rejoin the main route at no.8.

Extension 4

+5KM (3.1M) & 200 METRES CLIMBING

Y Turn R at the fork (ignore this if joining from ext 3), then shortly L over the stream to a T-J and bear L, steeply UH on a BW. 0.65km to a X-tracks (148/400) and turn R, for 1.6km, UH, along the hill top to a X-tracks (149/384) with a main track.

Z Turn R on this for 0.8km then R on a narrow ST (142/385), DH, into the trees, through streams. Keep L, then after 1.8km at a fork (143/400) (been here before), keep R and rejoin main route at no.8.

Getting there Start in Holford, just off the A39. Exit the M5 at Bridgewater (junction 23 or 24) and head west on the A39 for 10 miles to Holford. Turn left by the pub and follow this small road right to the (free) car park on the left (154/411). Train: Bridgewater – 13km/8m east of Quantocks.

Accommodation: B&B in Nether Stowey at the Old Cider House on 01278 732228, YHA near Holford on 0870 770 6006 Camping at St Audrie's Bay (nr West Quantoxhead) on 01984 632515, Bridgewater TI on 01278 427652.

Bike shops Bicycle Chain 01278 423 640 Thorne Cycle Ltd 01278 423632 & John's Street Cycles 01278 441500 – all in Bridgewater.

Refreshments Pubs in Holford, Triscombe & West Quantoxhead.

ROUGH RIDE GUIDE

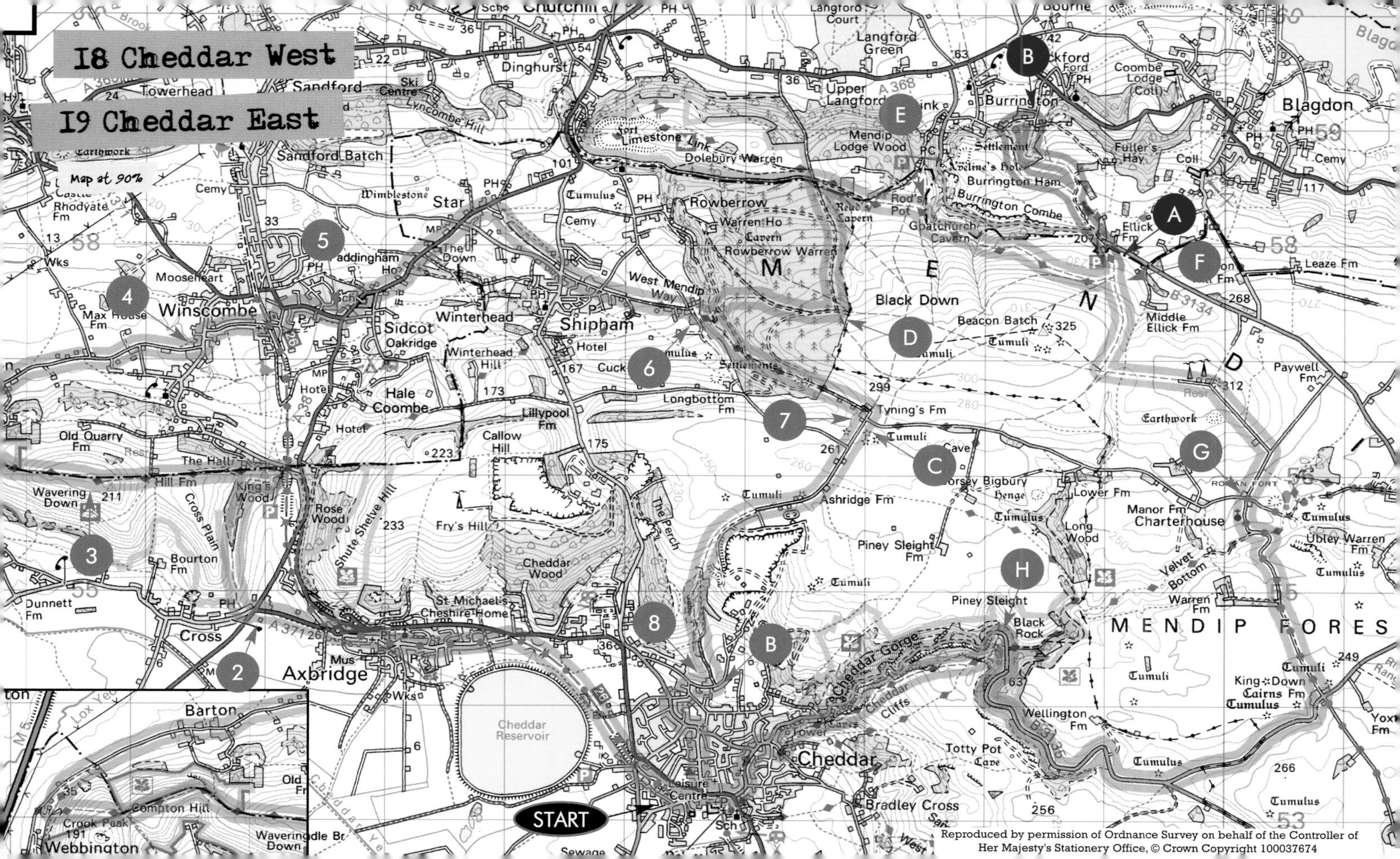
18 Cheddar West
19 Cheddar East
Map at 90%
START
MENDIP FOREST
Cheddar
Axbridge
Winscombe
Shipham
Blagdon
Burrington
Cheddar Gorge
Cheddar Reservoir
Black Down
Charterhouse

Cheddar west route

25KM / 15.5M & 650 METRES CLIMBING

START Head north-west on the Strawberry Line cycle path (no.26), around the reservoir, to a rd (ST 441/546). Turn L on this rd through Axbridge, join the A371 and bear L to the A38 (419/548).

2 Cross the rd and turn R (north) on the BW (by the pub), UH, on the edge of the wood, bearing L then R to a car park (422/560). Turn L, joining the Mendip Way, UH, through the woods, out into the open, and continue west, UH, to Wavering Down.

3 Follow the BW along ridgetop to Crook Peak then steep DH, to a wood (383/560) and bear R, to a rd (385/563). Turn R on this rd for 3.2km (2m) to a T-J (415/571).

4 Turn L (Winscombe) for 0.15km then R on The Lynch rd and follow this round to the L and A371 (421/574). Turn R on the A371 for 0.55km (0.35m) to the A38 (426/574) and turn L (north) on this.

5 After 1.6km (1m) (in Star) turn R on a narrow lane (439/583), which becomes a BW, going UH, to a rd in Shipham. Turn L on the rd, and go SA over the X-rds, and keep SA on this rd, UH, to a T-J at the top (455/575).

6 Go SA on the West Mendip Way (WMW), steep DH, and keep R on the WMW, UH. Keep R of the stream, and follow the blue BW arrows, UH, keeping SA, exit the woods, and keep SA to Tynings farm (470/565).

7 Go SA/R (south-west) on this (unsuitable for motors) rd, past a race track, becoming a stoney ST, DH. Bear L at the bottom and R onto a wide track, DH to the rd (458/542).

8 Turn R on the rd, bearing L on Hannay Way, to a X-rds with the B3125 (454/541) and turn L. Take the 3rd R (The Hayes) south to the A371 and cross this, onto Station rd, and right back into the Industrial Estate (453/533).

Getting there: Cheddar is easily accessed from the M5. In Cheddar, turn right on Station rd just before the High St, by the memorial, then shortly right again into the Valley Line industrial estate and park (may be busy at weekends) down the far end by the bike shop, on the left (ST 453/533).

Accommodation: Market Cross hotel, Cheddar 0870 2407060, B&B in Priddy 01749 676465 & Churchill 01934 854800, camping at Broadway House 01934 742 610, YHA in Cheddar 0870 7705760 & T.I. 01934 744071.

Bike shop: Cheddar Cycle Store on 01934 741300

Refreshments: West route: pubs in Axbridge, Cross, Winscombe, Star, & Shipham. East route: drinks at Tynings farm, cafe in Burrington.

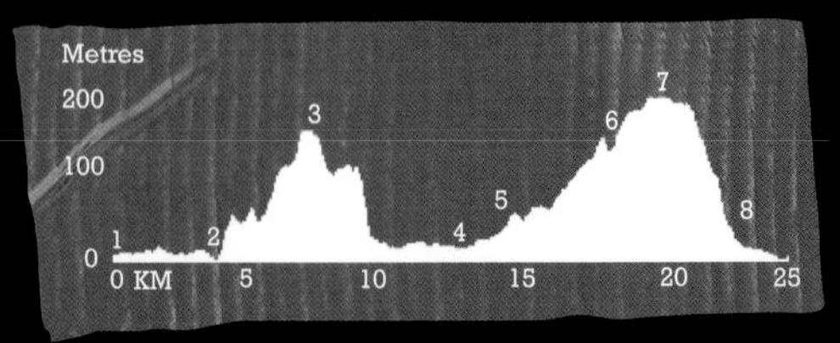

Cheddar east route

25KM / 15.5M & 790 METRES CLIMBING

START Go to the A371 rd and turn L then R on 'The Hayes', to a T-J with B3135 (456/538). Go L on this for 0.4km (0.25m) then R on Hannay Way, bearing L then R on Warrens Hill, for 0.25km then L on a BW (457/542).

B Steep UH, for 1.65km (1m), past a motor racing track, becoming tarmac at top and keep SA on this. Keep SA to Tyning's farm (470/565), where the rd turns R, but you bear L (west) through the farmyard, onto a good track.

C Go into some woods and keep SA at the X-tracks, then (easy to miss) L at a fork. DH, by a stream, to a fork and bear R, UH, over 2 X-tracks to 5-way X-rds and go SA on gravel track, then L just before exit the woods (468/574).

D DH, keep SA/R for 1.2km (0.75m) to a X-tracks (466/586) and turn R. Keep SA on this BW (Limestone Link) to a T-J (475/583) and turn R on the 2nd BW (Limestone Link).

E Follow this good track through the bracken for 1.95km (1.2m), through stream crossings, to a major junction with a signpost (491/577) and keep SA/R or see the extension.

F Go UH for 0.9km (0.55m) to a X-tracks (490/569) and turn L (east) to the radar masts, where you join a rd (499/568) at the top here. Go DH on the rd to a T-J and turn R to a X-rds (502/558) and go SA.

G Follow this rd (cyclepath no.3) for 2.1km (1.3m) to a X-rds with the B3371 (508/541) and turn R on this B rd. 1.6km (1m) to a T-J (496/534) and go R on B3135 rd. After 2.8km (1.75m) go L on a BW (just past access to Black Rock on R), as the rd begins to go DH (481/546).

H UH, through the woods, then steep DH, past the tower to a rd and turn R, then L on the B3135/Cliff St to the A371 (459/532). Turn R on the High St, then L on Station Rd, and R back into the Industrial Estate (453/533).

Extension

+3.9KM (2.4M) 175 METRES CLIMBING

A Turn L, DH, to a rd and turn L on this, then R up a stoney ramp behind the car park / lay-by. Follow the track across the open ground to a fork and keep L, DH, on ST into the woods, to a T-J (482/590). Turn R then shortly, where the rd bears sharp L, R and keep SA on the BW.

B UH into the woods, as the track bears L. Follow this BW back UH, to rejoin the track you came along earlier, back over the rd, and UH to the junction (491/577) and keep SA (south) and rejoin the main route at F.

TOP TIP: Explore Rowberrow Warren & Black Down. For family friendly ride, follow the Strawberry line from the bike shop (13.5km to Congresbury). Non-cyclists, see Cheddar caves www.cheddarcaves.co.uk or tel: 01934 742343.

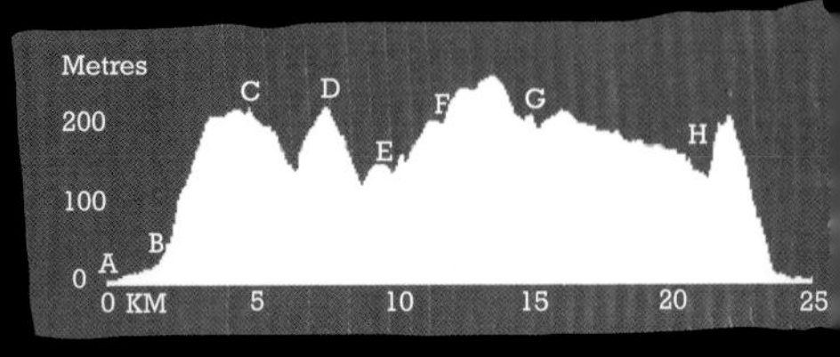

20 Moors Valley
Country Park
Map at 110%
START
Cross
Drove End
Warren Park Fm
Cranborne Common
Alderholt Common
Telegraph Plantation
Bleak Hill
Pistle Down
North Plumley Fm
Gravel Pit
Harbridge Green
Tumuli
Mount Ararat
Kent Hill
Turmer
Boveridge Heath
Tumulus
Stephen's Castle
Plumley Wood
Plumley Fm
Wild Church Bottom
Lower Turmer
Harefield Plantation
Noon Hill
Home Fm
Gravel Pit
Ellingham
Ringwood
Forest
Somerley Park
Somerley
Cemy
Ebblake
Sand Pit
Gravel Pit
Blashford Fm
Blashford
Weir
Ashley Fm
Gouldings Fm
Lower Common
Moors Valley Country Park
Baker's Hanging
CH
Legged Cross
Watchmoor Wood
B 3081
River Avon
Woolsbridge
PH
Ashley Heath
Ashley
Wools Br
A 338
Lions Hill
St Ives
David's Hill
Avon Heath Country Park
West Moors Plantation
Hotel
St Leonards
East Moors Fm
Avon Castle
dismtd rly
Whitefield Bottom
Weir
PC

Moors valley CP

VARIOUS

1 From the Ashley Twinning car park off the A31, exit the car park by the rd entrance, zig-zag over Hurn Lane, onto cycleway/pavement under the A31. Bear L past a phonebox, then carefully cross the A31 slip road, then bear L on to the Castleman Trail (towards Ashley Heath).

2 Cross the lane at Holly Grove fm to another rd crossing at Ashley Heath. Cross Horton rd & rejoin the Castleman Trail then 0.6km past the old platform at Ashley Heath, go R on narrow exit into Forest Edge Drive. Follow the rd to a T-J with Horton rd and zig-zag L & R into the Moors Valley Country Park. Follow the tarmac entrance rd for 0.8km to the visitor centre.

Corsican Circuit — 3.2KM

The central route which can be extended with the other trails. Head east from the visitor centre & ride it anti-clockwise. Uses wide, flat gravel forest tracks and is well suited for families.

TOP TIP: The trail waymarkers are round posts with coloured banks around near the top.

Watchmoor Loop — +2.3KM

The Watchmoor Loop adds 2.3km to the Corsican Circuit, following some sand, dirt & gravel tracks into some quieter parts of the forest. Some gentle hills along the way and passing close to some northshore trails in Watchmoor wood.

Somerley Loop — 1.6KM

Adding a further 1.6km, this trail weaves along gravel & dirt tracks through a dense part of the forest, along undulating trails, with a steep downhill section near the end.

Crane Loop — 3.2KM

Either use this as another extension to the Corsican Circuit or as a family ride by itself. Passing through the gold course, past Crane lake and alongside the river, before returning alongside the mini railway. Using mainly tarmac tracks, with some dirt & gravel sections You'll mainly follow tarred trails, though there are some gravel and dirt sections, with one short hill & some narrow sections.

Other Riding

There are some technical northshore trails in Watchmoor Wood (see no.1 black arrow) & lots of trails to explore in Ringwood Forest. Also, the Castleman Trail continues all the way to Poole & most of it open to cyclists. For more information & maps on this trail see www.dorsetforyou.com.

Family Activities

There are lots of activities here for everyone, including: Go Ape (high ropes course), mini steam railway, golf, fishing, childrens play area & Play trail. For more info. see www.moors-valley.co.uk.

picture by East Dorset District council

Getting there: Moors Valley country Park car park (SU107/055) off the B3081, between Ringwood & Verwood, just off the A31. Alternatively there is a free (Ashley Twinnings) car park off the A31 where you join the B3081 (take the Hurn Lane exit from the junction roundabout) at GR SU139/048.

Accommodation: self catering cottage in Horton; very comfy, log fire, sleeps 6, bike storage, clothes drying, etc, see www.classic.co.uk cottage no.1934 or call 01258 840969. For more options see www.pooletourism.com or Ringwood T.I. 01425 470896.

Bike shop cycle hire at Moors Valley vc on 01425 470721 or see www.moors-valley.co.uk or Bicycle World shop in Ringwood 01425 470835

Refreshments: cafe / restaurant in the Moors Valley country Park visitors centre.

21 Isle of Purbeck

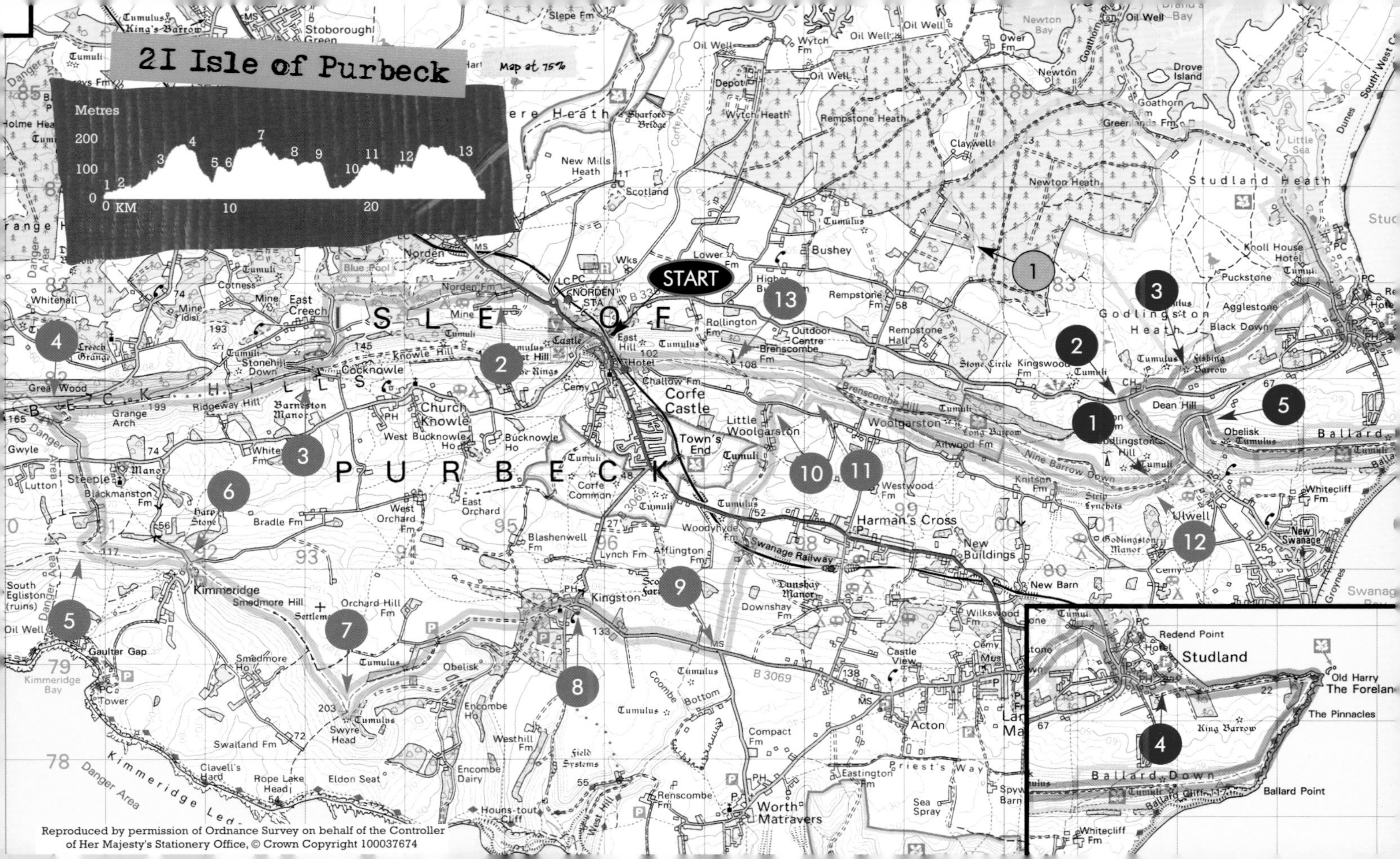

isle of Purbeck

29.5KM / 18.3M & 820 METRES CLIMBING

START **Turn R** (north-west) **on the A351, SA at the roundabout** (Wareham) **for 0.3km** (0.2m) **then L to Norden Farm** (SY 952/829). **Go past the campsite reception, SA to the caravan site and to the far R corner of the field to a BW,** into the woods (947/829).

2 **Follow this BW** (and occasional signs to East Creech) **for 1.6km** (1m) **to a rd** (933/829). **Turn L on this rd, and keep SA** (south) as it turns R, past a chalky embankment, **then hairpins UH. At the top** (after 1.45km/0.9m) **turn R on the Ridgeway** Hill & Tyneham BW (931/821).

3 **Go through the wooden gate onto the gravel BW,** keeping the fence to your L. **0.8km** (0.5m) **to a X-tracks** (922/ 819) (farm track R and grassy DH L) **and go through the gate to your L.** Continue on the grassy BW (still headed generally W), now with the fence to your R, **SA for 1.8km** (1.1m) **to a car park** (at a viewpoint) (905/817).

4 **Turn L** (Steeple), DH on a steep gravel track **for 0.2m to a rd. Turn L** on this, DH, **for 0.5km** (0.3m) **to a X-rds** (907 /812) (where the rd turns L) **and go SA on the gravel track** (Steeple Leaze Farm). **Past a farmhouse and campsite,** into the trees, UH, on a rough track, **bearing R, and ending at a rusty metal gate** (908/803).

5 **Go through this into and around the LHS of the field,** east then south **to the far corner and a silver metal gate after 0.3km** (0.2m). **Go through the gate, and head east on a grassy track** with a fence to the R, **for 1.1km** (0.7m) to a rd (918/801).

6 **Turn R to a T-J, and turn L then R** (effectively SA) **on a gravel BW and follow this for 2.4km** (1.5m) (steep drop and view of the sea R), **to a large tumulus at Swyre Head** (934/785) (just ahead is a bench with great views). **Turn L almost back on yourself, following the sign for Kingston.**

7 **1.45km** (0.9m) **to a car park** (943/793), **and turn R on the narrow tarmac rd, into Kingston. Keep SA to a T-J** (957/796) with the B3069 rd (Scott Arms Hotel L).

8 **Go R** on the 'B' rd (Swanage) **for 1.6km** (1m) **then L through a metal gate on a BW** (Wooyhynde & Little Woolgarston), opposite a rd to Worth Matravers, (972/791).

9 **1.6km** (1m), DH, under railway, past Woody Hyde farm **to the A351 rd** (973/805). **Cross the rd to go SA through 2 silver metal gates on the** (Woolgarston) **BW.** Follow the grassy track, becoming tarmac, **past farm buildings, to a T-J with a narrow rd** (after 1.3km/0.8m) (976/817).

10 **Turn R, UH on the rd for 0.3km** (0.2m) **to the top and turn L on** (Brenscombe Hill) **BW** (980/817). Grassy UH, **for 0.15km** (0.1m) **to a gate** (980/819) **and go through this and turn R** (or L for a shortcut back).

11 **Turn R and follow this** (SP to Ulwell), **along the hillside and keep SA over a couple of X-tracks** (after 0.5km/0.3m, and 2.75km/1.7m) heading east along the hillside, **for 3.7km** (2.3m) **to a wider track going steeply DH** (SZ 013/ 808) **and turn sharp L on this, UH,** or see the extension.

12 **To the top** (008/811) **and bear L** along the field edge, **and keep SA on the obvious track,** along the hill top. Follow this along the hilltop **for 3.8km** (2.35m) **to a mast** (SY 973/822) **and bear L at the fork on the ST DH** (west).

13 **0.9km** (0.55m) **to a rd and go R on this,** under the railway **to a T-J** (961/822) **with the A351 rd. Go R on this for 0.4km** (0.25m) **then R back to the car park** (959/825).

Extension

+12KM (7.5M) & 415 METRES CLIMBING

1 **Keep SA/R on this broader track, DH, keeping L at a round hill, SA, to a rd** (after 0.5km/0.3m) (018/812). **Turn L on the rd then immediately keep L at the fork,** UH, for 0.8km (0.5m) **to a T-J** (012/818) with the B3351 rd.

2 **Turn R on the B rd** (past the golf club) **for 0.5km** (0.3m) **then L on a BW** through a small gate at a little parking area (017/819). **Keep SA for 0.25km** (0.15m) **past open part of the golf course to a fork** (018/821) **and bear R.**

3 **Follow the BW DH for 1.6km** (1m) **to a track** (030/829) **and turn R to the B3351. Go R on this for 0.4km** (0.25m) into Studland **and turn L on School Lane** (034/825) by Studland Stores. **At the end of this rd,** by the toilets, **and continue on the BW** (Handfast Point) around the coast.

4 Along top of the cliff edge, **to a fork** (048/815) (after 2.6km/1.6m) **and bear R, UH, on Ballard Down BW. Follow this** (west) along the ridge **to an obelisk** (022/813). **Go through the gate, bearing R, DH, to the rd** (020/816).

5 **Turn L on this rd, 0.65km** (for 0.4m) **then turn R on the BW you came down earlier** (018/812) (just after a rd on the R). **UH, for 0.5km** (0.3m) **to a fork** (014/809) **and bear R, UH,** on a track you haven't been on **and rejoin the main route at no.11.**

Family ride

1 From Burnbake campsite, use the quiet forest tracks (a mix of tarmac and stone based tracks) to reach Studland (Bay). Good range of beaches and refreshments, including a nice pub overlooking the sea in Studland.

Getting there: start at Corfe Castle car park (south of Poole/Bournemouth) on the Isle of Purbeck (which isn't actually an island, but a penisula). Go through Wareham (west of Poole) then south-east on the A351 (Corfe) for 5 miles to the visitor centre car park (959/825). By train: Get a train to Bournemouth then a ferry (regular & cheap) from North Haven Point (037/871) to South Haven Point (and join the ride in Studland).

Accommodation: B&B in Corfe on 01929 480 374. B&B in Church Knowle on 480712. Campsites at Burnbake on 01929 480570 in Rempstone, Ulwell on 422823, Norden farm on 480098 & Bucknowle farm on 480280. YHA in Swanage on 0870 7706058. Swanage T.I. on 01929 422885.

Bike shops: Bikelab on 01202 330011, and Action Bikes on 680123 both in Poole. Xtreme in Bournemouth on 01202 741744 and Bikeabout in Swanage on 01929 425050.

Refreshments: A National Trust cafe in the castle entrance, and a choice of pubs & shops in Corfe, and the Scott Arms Hotel in Kingston.

22 Bournemouth

Bournemouth VARIOUS

This is a lovely cycle ride along the Promenade, but please be aware that it is closed to cyclists in the peak of summer i.e. July & August, between 10am & 7pm. During this time there is an alternative road route, running parallel to it.

This flat seafront trail is perfect for families and a great way to get further along the beach to search out the quieter spots. It is all off road apart from a short section at the Hengistbury Head end.

WARNING: In July & August, promenade cycling is restricted to before 10am & after 6pm and carries a £1,000 fine if broken.

The route stretches from Hengistbury Head (SZ 180/908) nr Christchurch and runs west, for 14km, along the seafront, past Bournemouth, to Poole Head. You can extend the ride from here (using the ferry, to Studland) see the extension for details.

NOTE: You can get the ferry (which takes bicycles) to & from Christchurch to Hengisybury Head. See www.mudefordferry.co.uk or call 07968 334441.

TOP TIP: The wind usually blows from the west, so starting from the east and heading west, should mean you are wind assisted for the return journey.

NOTE: There is a BMX track in Bournemouth with hard packed gravel, two berms made of concrete, some easy doubles for novices and 2 big doubles for more advanced riders. Sat Nav BH6 5NF / GR SZ 145/195 or see www.bournemouthbmx.com.

Extension VARIOUS

Keep following the cycle path, past Poole Head, alongside the B3369 to Sandbanks, and join the road to catch the ferry over to Studland (South Haven Banks). Here you can enjoy the (nudist) beach or see our 'Isle of Purbeck' ride.

Alternatively, for some superb Freeriding, at Okford Hill, nr Blandford Forum see www.ukbikepark.com.

Family activities

As you will probably guess there are LOTS of holiday & family activities in and around Bournemouth, here are just some of them:

SURFING

Although not renown for surfing you may be lucky and get some waves when there. Hire boards from Sorted Surf Shop, www.sortedsurfshop.co.uk or tel: 01202 309638 or for lessons call 0800 0437873 or see www.bournemouthsurfschool.co.uk.

AQUARIUM

The Oceanarium in the centre of Bournemouth, right next to the route and has an excellent selection of fish. Tel; 01202 311 993 or see www.oceanarium.co.uk for more details.

GUS GORILLAS JUNGLE PLAYGROUND

Slides, ball pool, etc in Poole, tel; 01202 717197 or www.gusgorillas.co.uk.

Getting there There are car aprks at the start and end points of the route, as well as a few inbetween, just choose whatever suits you best.

Accommodation: LOTS of places on offer, see www.bournemouth.co.uk. A favourite camping spot of ours is Burnbake, just a ferry ride over to the Isle of Purbeck, tel: 01929 480570 or www.btinternet.com/~burnbakecampsite.

Bike shops Primera Sport on 01202 775588 or www.primera-bournemouth.co.uk, Pedals cycle centre on 01202 301683 and On Yer Bike, tel; 01202 315855 or www.onyerbike.co.uk does bike hire.

Refreshments There are lots of places all along the route.

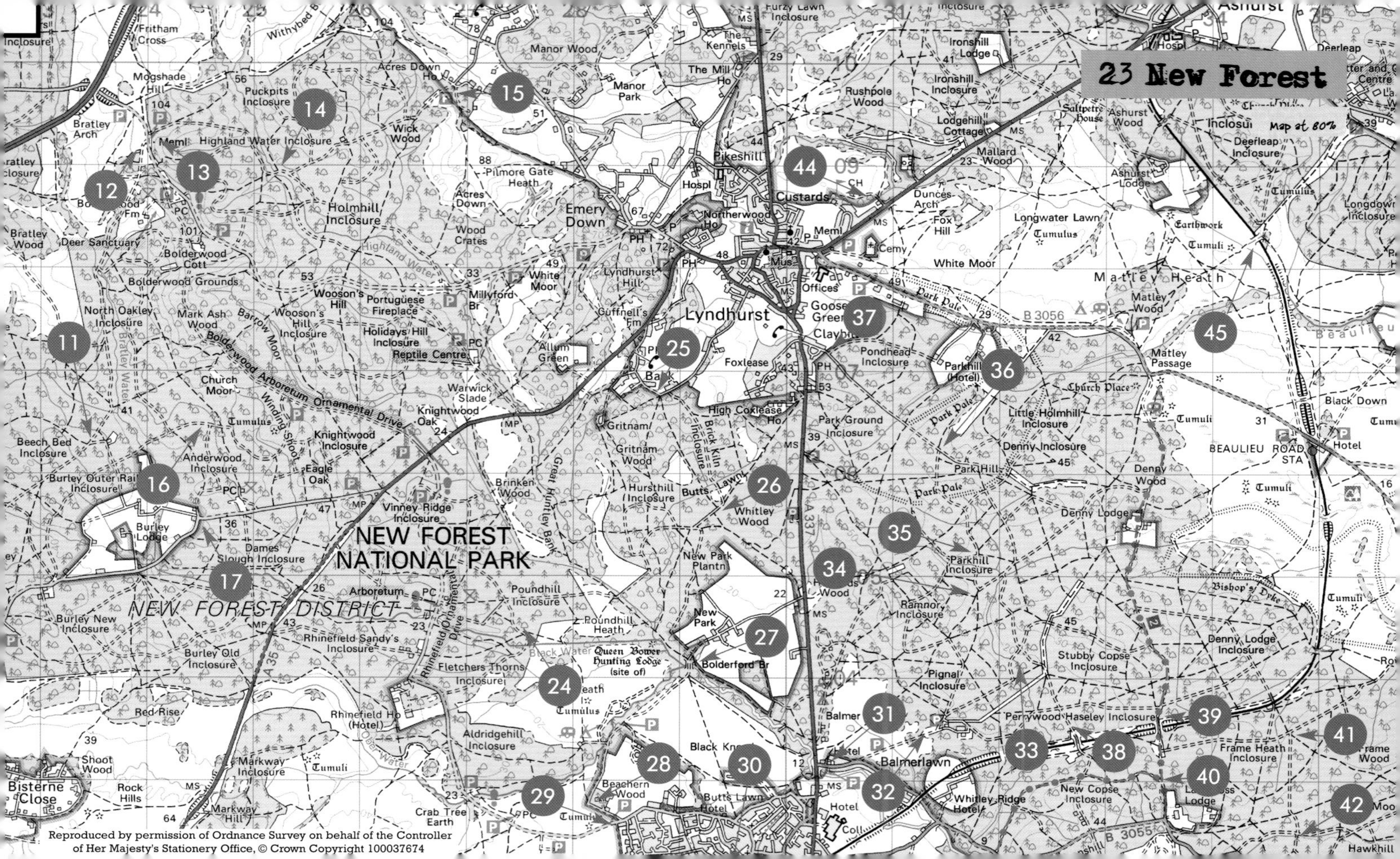
23 New Forest
Map at 80%
NEW FOREST NATIONAL PARK
NEW FOREST DISTRICT
Lyndhurst
Emery Down
Custards
Pikeshill
Balmerlawn
Matley Heath
BEAULIEU ROAD STA
Bisterne Close
Burley Lodge
Bolderwood Arboretum Ornamental Drive
Rhinefield Ornamental Drive
Highland Water Inclosure
Holmhill Inclosure
Denny Inclosure
Denny Lodge Inclosure
Parkhill Inclosure
Knightwood Inclosure
Puckpits Inclosure
White Moor
Longwater Lawn
Queen Bower Hunting Lodge (site of)
Reproduced by permission of Ordnance Survey on behalf of the Controller
of Her Majesty's Stationery Office, © Crown Copyright 100037674

New Forest

D.I.Y. route

The broad tracks around the forest are all very similar, so rather than trying to follow a set route, just ride as much or as little as you like (see right for ideas of places to visit), and use the numbered markers to orientate yourself.

RULES OF THE FOREST

1 Keep to waymarked gravel tracks when cycling.
2 Be aware of animals, cyclists, pedestrians & drivers.
3 Always ride in a single file when roads are narrow and never ride more than two abreast.
4 Keep your speed down, give way to walkers.
5 Make sure you are visible by wearing bright clothing.
6 Always use your lights in the dark or in poor visibility.
7 Keep well away from any work going on in the forest.
8 Don't pass vehicles loading timber until told to do so.
9 Plan your route to be out of the forest by dusk.
10 No campfires. Barbecue sites provided by the Forestry Commission (023 8028 3141).

See www.forestry.gov.uk/newforest for more info.

This ancient woodland is mainly made up of old oak and beech trees, and has a wonderful peacefulness about it, as well as a timeless character. There is a 40 mph speed limit for cars on unfenced roads to protect the wildlife (and cyclists). There are also lots of car parks, so please use one of them and take any valuables with you. Obviously there is no driving allowed on the forest tracks.

Please don't feed the animals as it encourages to stray on to roads. Also, they have plenty of natural food in the forest and they can become quite aggressive.

FOREST HISTORY

William the Conqueror made this area a royal hunting ground in 1079 when he discovered it's beauty (and the many deer that lived there). He couldn't have been a very good hunter though, as there are lots of deer still living here, as well as over 5,000 ponies and cattle which roam wild on 45,000 acres of open forest. This has been a right for many of the locals, and as many 400 (commoners) exercise the right to graze their stock.

The towns & villages

BEAULIEU

(in south-east) is a lovely village with National Motor Museum, Palace House, 13th Century Abbey and a pub.

BROCKENHURST

(in the south) is a lovely village where the ponies often graze on the village green. There is a 1,000 year old yew tree in the churchyard and at the west end of the main shopping street (Brookley Road) is a wide ford, known as 'The Water Splash'. Good selection of shops, pubs, etc.

BURLEY

(south west) is a picturesque village with cattle often wandering around it. There are a few tea shops, art galleries and a pick your own farm. It is also famous for its smuggling history and witches.

LYNDHURST

(central) is the 'Capital' of the forest, and home to the New Forest Museum and Visitor information centre. Big car park and a various shops, tea rooms and cafes, etc.

FRITHAM

(north) a small village, home to the famous Royal Oak Inn where smugglers were believed to gather years ago.

NOTE: An open-top bus calls at Lyndhurst, Beaulieu, Brockenhurst & Lymington (on the Isle of Wight) and it has room for your bicycle. There is also a network of on & off-road cycle routes that has been created to link the main villages and railway station at Brockenhurst. You may walk on any footpath or track, unless it says otherwise, but cyclists must keep to the main gravel surfaced forest roads.

Family activities

Purpose built MTB trails (aimed at kids & beginners) - see www.avontyrrell.org.uk for more details.
Burley Deer Park & tractor / trailer rides 01425 402559
Longdown activity farm, see www.longdownfarm.co.uk.
Marwell Zoological Park, see www.marwell.org.uk.
Otter and Wildlife park, see www.ottersandowls.co.uk.
Paultons Leisure Park, see www.paultonspark.co.uk.

Getting there south-west of Southampton. From the M27 (junction 1), go south on the A337 (Lyndhurst). There are lots of free car parks all over the forest and in the centre of Lyndhurst. Train station in Brockenhurst.

Accommodation Lots of places, but they fill up quickly. Call the New Forest T.I. on 01703 282269 or Forestry Commission campsites on 0131 314 6505. YHA in Burley on 0870 7705734.

Bike shops Cyclexperience in Brockenhurst on 01590 624204 and in Christchurch on 01202 486278, and Forest Leisure Cycling in Burley on 01425 403584 & Beaulieu on 01590 611029 (all do bike hire).

Refreshments Lots of pubs around the forest, but if you don't bump into any by chance, head to a village which will most likely have a pub, shop and usually a tea room or two.

ROUGH RIDE GUIDE

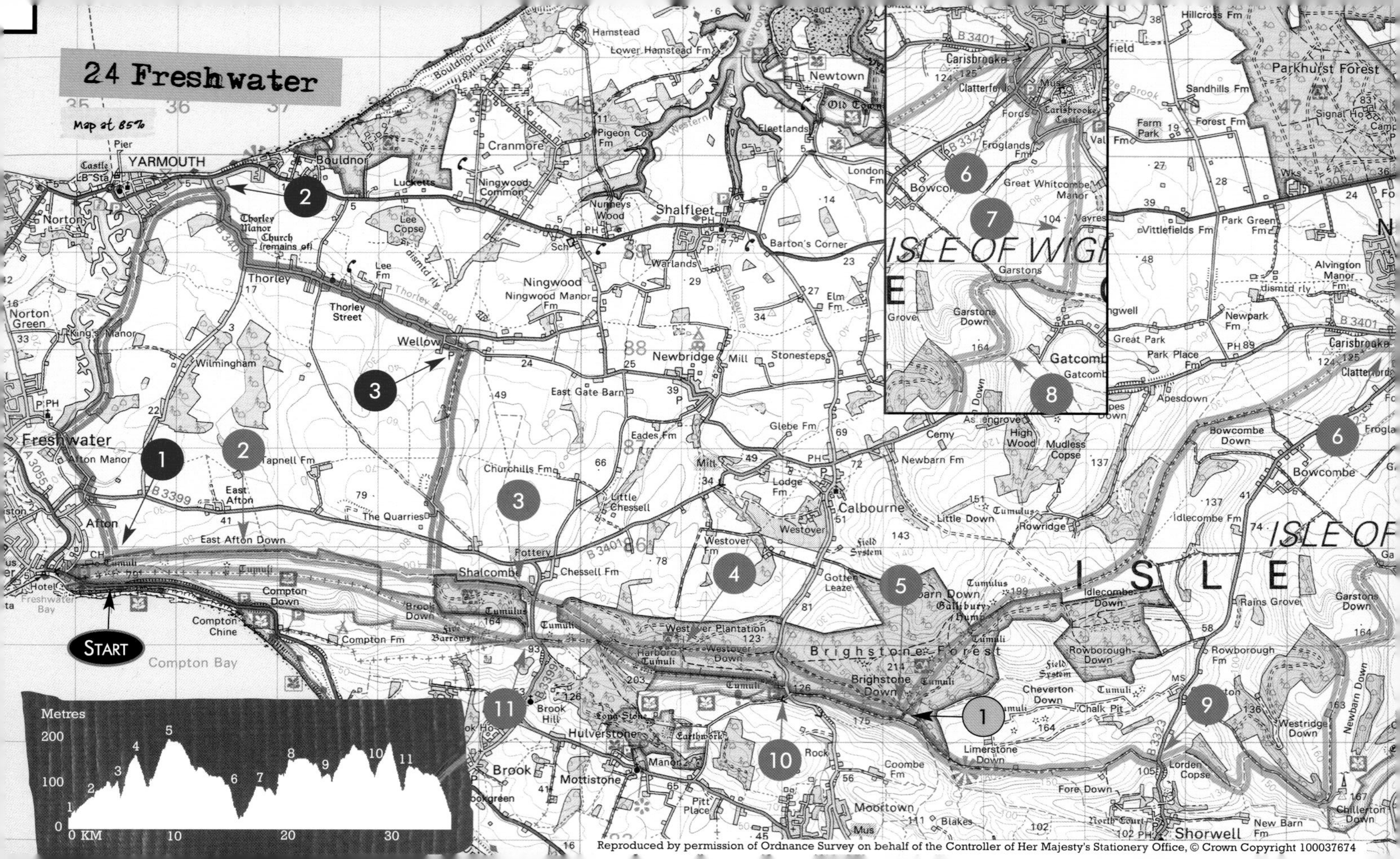
24 Freshwater
Map at 85%
START
Metres
200
100
0
0 KM
10
20
30
YARMOUTH
Freshwater
Freshwater Bay
Compton Bay
Afton
East Afton
East Afton Down
Thorley
Thorley Street
Wellow
Ningwood
Shalfleet
Newbridge
Newtown
Calbourne
Shalcombe
Brook
Mottistone
Hulverstone
Brighstone Forest
Brighstone Down
Carisbrooke
Bowcombe
Shorwell
Parkhurst Forest
ISLE OF WIGHT

Freshwater

37KM (23M) & 870 METRES CLIMBING

START Go towards Freshwater on the A3055 rd, after 0.15km turn R on Southdown rd (SZ 349/857), and shortly R again on the Old Highway, Carisbrooke BW towards the Golf club. 0.7km (0.45m) to a fork and bear L, DH on the (F32 Freshwater way) BW, then shortly R on the Pilgrims way, along the edge of the golf course or see extension.

2 After 1.3km (0.8m), at the end of the golf course, go through some gates onto a grassy track, along the bottom, (east). After 2.2km (1.35m), go through a gate, and bear R into the woods (386/857).

3 Follow this BW to a T-J and turn R on the farm track, DH, to the rd (395/855). Cross the rd onto the (Bridgestone forest) BW SA, for 0.5km (0.3m) through a gate, and R at the fork, UH, for 0.65km (0.4m) to a DT (403/851), and turn L on this, for 0.7km (0.45m) to multiple X-tracks.

4 Keep SA on the main track, DH, for 1km (0.6m) to a rd (419/849) and keep SA on the BW. Keep SA at X-tracks on the (BS9 Carisbrooke) BW, keeping R, on the lower track, for 1.45km (0.9m), to Bridgestone down five lane ends (432/ 843) and turn L on the Tennyson trail (N139) or see the shortcut.

5 Keep SA on this ByW (SA at some X-tracks, through a gate on the N136a, bearing R on the main track Old Highway N128 Carisbrooke, and SA at the X-tracks on the N123) for 4.2m, DH to a tarmac T-J (481/881).

6 Turn sharp R to the rd and go SA (R then L) at the off-set X-rds onto Clatterford Shute (481/877). After 0.65km (0.4m), through 2 fords, bear L at Froglands triangle (483/872). After 0.4km (0.25m) (castle on L), turn R on the (Gatcombe N108) BW (486/874), before Whitcombe rd.

7 1km (0.65m) to a fork and bear L on (Gatcombe G6) BW (486/863), 0.65km (0.4m) to a X-tracks (486/ 857). Turn R, for 0.8km (0.5m) then turn L on the (Downs, Shorwell) BW, just past a house on the R (478/858). Around a chalk pit, steep UH, through a gate, and keep SA around the side of the hill for 0.8km (0.5m) to a tree (478/850).

8 Turn R at the tree, through a gate to a T-J in the woods (474/849) and turn L, to a barn. After 1.6km (1m) bear R by the radar mast and keep R at the X-tracks onto a concrete rd (474/834). After 1km (0.6m) turn L on BW (blue arrow) (466/ 838), to gate and keep R through more gates and R along edge of woods, DH to a rd (457/838).

9 Go SA on the (SW51 Freshwater) BW, and keep SA for 2km (1.25m) (surface changes) to the viewpoint at top of Limerstone down (438/837). Keep SA on the main (BS10 Tennyson trail, Lynch lane) track, through some gates, keeping the wood on the RHS, for 1.95km (1.2m) to a rd.

10 Turn R on the rd, for 0.1km then L through a car park (420/845), on a ByW (Mottistone Down, Freshwater). After 2.1km (1.3m) keep SA at some X-tracks with a dirt road, through a gate into a field (402/850) and bear L on the DT, through fields, for 0.65km (0.4m) to a rd (395/850).

11 Go SA on the track opposite, turning L at the bottom of the chalk pit, to some gates and bear R at the fork, UH on a chalk track. Follow this ByW for 4.5km (2.8m) along the ridge top (Brook Down), through a golf course, to a fork (359/ 857). Go L/SA on the (Tennyson Trail, old highway) ByW, to the A3055 rd and L back to the start (351/856).

Extension

+7.5KM (4.5M) & 45 METRES CLIMBING

1 Stay on the (Freshwater) F32 BW, for 0.65km (0.4m), DH to a rd and bear R on this to the main B3399 rd (350/865). Go SA/L on the (Causeway) rd, for 0.7km (0.45m), then turn R on a (cycle path) BW (348/871). Follow this for 3.2km (2m) along the riverside, bearing to the R of Yarmouth, to the B3401 rd (364/896).

2 Turn R on this rd, staying L on this after 0.9km (0.55m) (366/888), through Thorley village. After another 2.2km (1.35m), turn R, in Wellow village, on the round island cycle route (386/881), for 0.25km (0.15m) then turn R on the (S19 Hamstead Trail) BW, (388/880), by the brook.

3 UH for 1.6km (1m) to a rd (by a thatched cottage) and turn L then immediately R on a driveway (The Quarries) (385/863). Keep SA on the BW, to the B3399 rd and go SA on the BW opposite, UH for 0.4km (0.25m), to a X-tracks (386/857) and turn L, and rejoin route at No.3.

Shortcut

-18.8KM (11.7M) & 375METRES CLIMBING

1 Turn R at the X-tracks, to another X-tracks (FP only SA) and turn R on a DT ByW , and follow this for 1.2km (0.75m) to a rd (421/845), and rejoin main route at 10.

TOP TIP: For a 80+km ride (best done over 2 days) see the link for a map & directions: www.extremists.co.uk/randonnee.PDF

Getting there: Ferry to the Isle of Wight (WightLink ferries on: 0870 582 0202, www.wightlink.co.uk or Hovertrave onl: 01983 811 000 or www.hovertravel.co.uk) and aim for Freshwater. Park in the cliff side car park (351/856), off the A3055. Day trippers could go as a foot passanger (to save money) from Lymingt-on to Yarmouth and join the ride on the extension.

Accommodation: Lots but gets busy. Yarmouth T.I. on: 01983 813818. Palmerston Hotel on: 01983 865547, campsites at Grange farm, Brighstone on: 01983 740296, Stoats farm, Totland bay on: 01983 755258 & Compton farm on: 01983 740215. YHA in Totland Bay (West coast) 0870 7706070.

Bike shops: Wight mountain, 01983 520530 in Newport, Isle cycle hire on 01983 760219, in Yarmouth.

Refreshments: None on route but Freshwater, Yarmouth, Carisbrooke & Shorwell are just off the route.

25 Isle of Wight C2C
Map at 75%
START
END
Cowes Roads
COWES
Old Castle Point
Breakwater
Norris Castle
Marina
Ferry
Springhill
East Cowes
Osborne Bay
Osborne Ho
Swiss Cott
Barton Wood
Barton Manor
King's Quay
Mud & Sand
Woodside
Wootton Creek
Somerton Fm
Nodes Fm
Power Sta
Whippingham
RIVER MEDINA
Ludham Cottage
Woodhouse Fm
Dallimores
Holiday Village
Quarr Abbey
Wootton
Fishbourne
Quarr Abbey (rems of)
Quarr Hill
Mus
Show Ground
Werrar Fm
Heathfield Fm
Alverstone Fm
Palmer's Brook
Westwood
Kite Hill
Marina
Binfield Fm
North Fairlee Fm
Crem
Wootton Bridge
Mill Pond
Puck Ho
Parkhurst
Dodnor Ho
Wootton Common
Packsfield
Firestone Copse
Newnham Fm
Horse Centre
Meml
Lower St Cross Fm
Hospl
Albany Prison
Butterfly World
Littletown
Woodhouse Fm
Blackbridge Brook
Havenstreet
The Grange
El Sub Sta
Briddlesford Lodge
Great Briddlesford Fm
Fairlee
Cemy
Hunny Hill
Kitbridge
New Fairlee Fm
Sch
Barton
Staplers
Staplehurst Grange
Great Pan Fm
ROMAN VILLA (rems of)
Durton Fm
Burnt Ho
Shide
Priory
New Close Ho
Valleys
Bembridge Trail
Garretts Fm
Little East Standen Fm
Standen Ho
Marvel Fm
Birchfield Ho
Gravel Pit
St George's Down
Great East Standen Manor
Craft Village
Arreton Manor
Arreton
Blackwater
Whitecroft
Stone Fm
Longdown
Langbridge
Haseley Manor
O F W I G H T
Gatcombe Mill
Birchmore Fm
Champion
Pidford
Merston Manor
Merstone
Perreton Fm
Stickworth Hall
Redway
Horringford
Newchurch
Hill Fm
Wackland
Hale Manor Fm
Zoo
Hale Common
Queen's Bower
Winford
Sheat Manor
Sibdown Fm
Chillerton
Rookley
Pagham Fm
Country Park
Bohemia Corner
Little Budbridge Fm
Loverstone Fm
Harts Fm
Rookley Green
Bathingbourne
Bigbury Fm
Cheverton
VILLA (rems of)
Manor
Morton
Alverstone
Adgestone
Yaverland
Wks
Zoo
Borthwood Fm
Scotchells Brook
Schs
Mus
SANDOWN
Isle of Wight Airport
Black Pan
Pier
IRB Sta (summer only)
Lake
Mersley Fms
Knighton Fm

Isle of Wight

22.3KM (13.9M) & 195 METRES OF CLIMBING

This route runs from Cowes, through Newport, to Sandown and is all off-road apart from the use of quiet, traffic controlled roads through the towns. It is also very flat, making it perfect for all the family.

Cowes to Newport 7KM (4.3M)

From the High st/Ferry port, head south on Birmingham rd, joining the A3020/Medina rd (L), then R on Bridge rd (B3320), and 2nd L off this, on Pelham rd. Before the (dead) end of this, turn R on South rd, then L on Arctic rd. Keep SA, leaving this rd as it bears R, off-road, past all the moored yachts along the river, to Newport.

1 Follow Sustrans route 23 (yellow highlighted route on map) from Newport to Wootton **to catch the steam train.**

Newport to Sandown 15.2KM (9.4M)

Join the Riverway, under the A3054 and L at the roundabout, then R at the next roundabout on Holyrood st, jinking over the High st, joining Church litton rd, then go L, then R on Medina Ave. To the B3401 (Shide rd) and go L then R just before the A3020 back off road through lovely countryside, to Sandown.

At Sandown, go R on Perowne Way, to the end (T-J) and go L, under the railway. Either finish here or continue on Station Ave (becoming the B3329), to Albert rd, and go L (against one-way), cross the High St, to the Esplanade (coast).

Family activities

Sandown Pier has various activities such as adventure golf, dodgems, amusements, cafes, etc.

Amazon World in Newchurch (nr Sandown) is a great all weather destination. See www.amazonworld.co.uk 01983 867122

Isle of Wight Zoo in Sandown has a great collection of tigers as well as other animals. See www.isleofwightzoo.com or call 01983 403883.

Carisbrooke Castle Museum on the west edge of Newport. Tel 01983 523112 or see www.carisbrookecastlemuseum.org.uk.

Space Island is an indoor soft play area for kids aged 4+, in Lake, Sandown. See www.space-island.co.uk or tel: 01983 405070.

Robin Hill country adventure park, east of Newport and north of Arreton has a whole host of rides, slides, play areas, walks, maze, etc. See www.robin-hill.com for more info.

Dinosaur Isle is a museum housed in a spectacular building in Sandown. See, smell, tough and learn about their life and world. Call 01983 404344 or see www.dinosaurisle.com.

Shanklin Chine is a gorge with dramatic waterfalls and a nature trail. See www.shanklinchine.co.uk

Isle of Wight Steam railway that runs (5 miles) from Wootton to Smallbrook (nr Ryde). See note left and www.iwsteamrailway.co.uk for more info.

Getting there Get Red Funnel (0844 844 9988 / www.redfunnel.co.uk) from Southampton to (east) Cowes, then the chain link ferry to west Cowes/start of the ride..

Accommodation: This is a ver popular holiday destination, so there are lots of options available, but you need to book up well in advance. See www.isleofwight.com for a comprehensive listing of places.

Bike shops Wight off road in Sandown 01983 408587, Wight Mountain in Newport on 533445, and cycle (& car) hire in Cowes 299056 & Sandown on 400055.

Refreshments There are lots of choices in the 3 towns, Cowes, Newport and Sandown, but only a pub in Newchurch off the southern part of the route(4km out of Sandown).

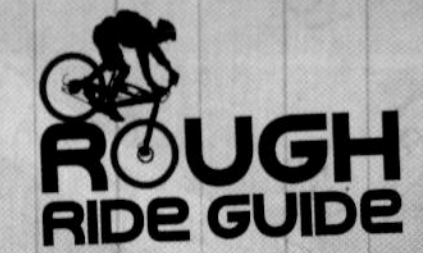

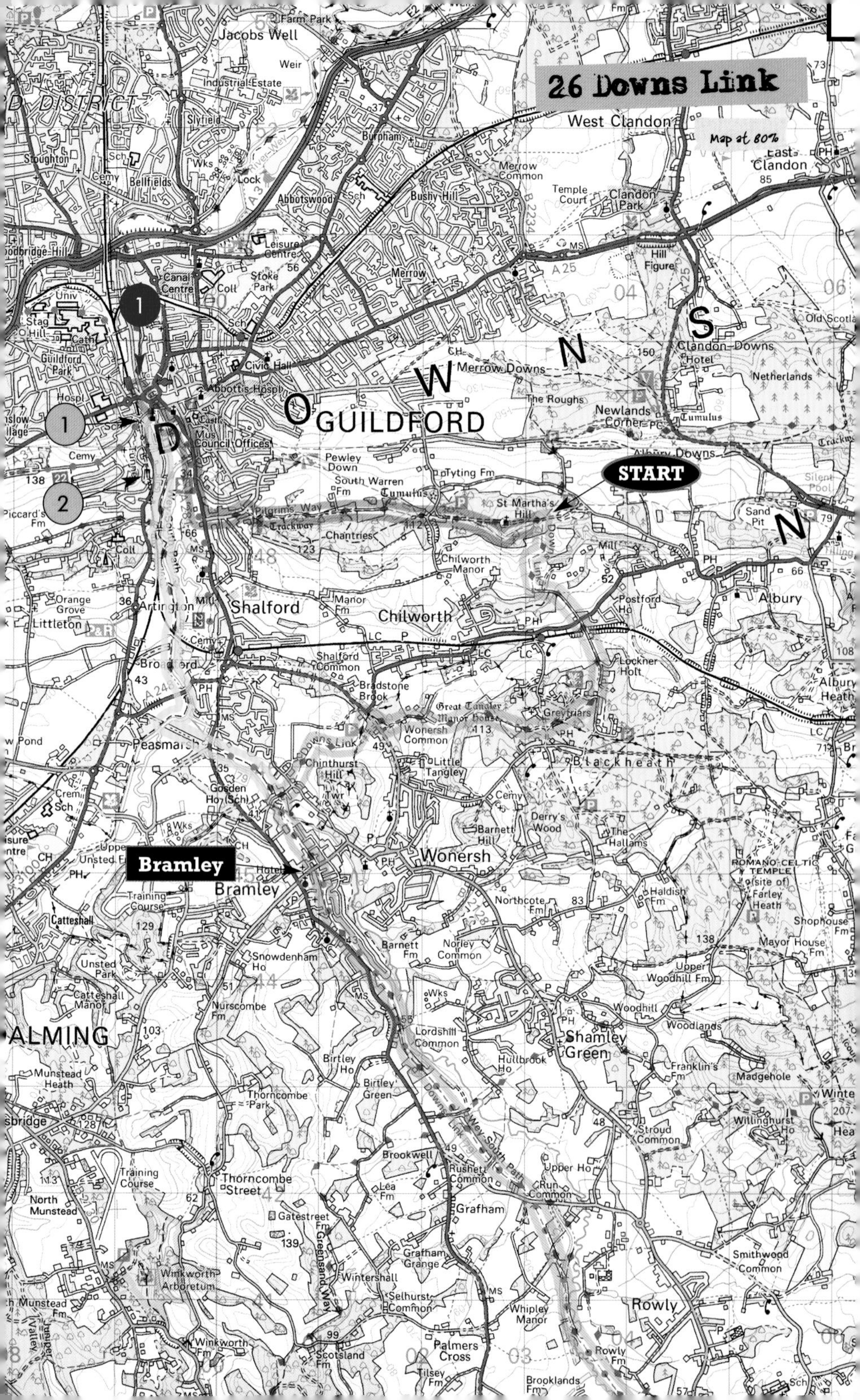

26 Downs Link
Map at 80%
START
Bramley
GUILDFORD
Jacobs Well
West Clandon
East Clandon
Merrow
Shalford
Chilworth
Albury
Wonersh
Bramley
Shamley Green
Grafham
Rowly
Peasmarsh
Blackheath
St Martha's Hill
Newlands Corner
Artington
Littleton
Thorncombe Street
Winkworth Arboretum
Greensand Way
Downs Link
Wey South Path

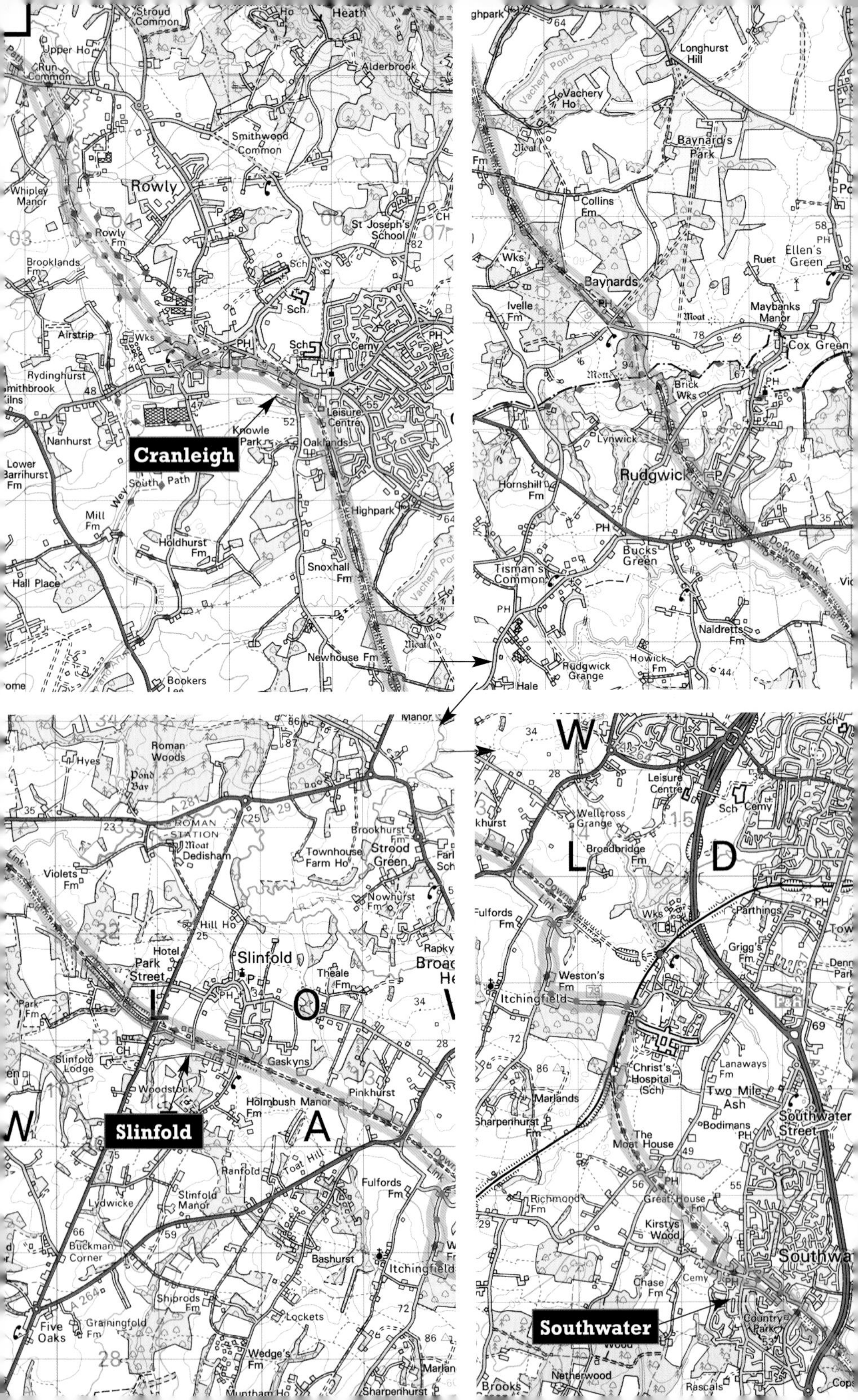

Cranleigh
Rudgwick
Slinfold
Southwater
Stroud Common
Heath
Upper Ho
Run Common
Alderbrook
Smithwood Common
Rowly
Whipley Manor
Rowly Fm
St Joseph's School
Brooklands Fm
Airstrip
Rydinghurst
Smithbrook Kilns
Nanhurst
Lower Barrihurst Fm
Knowle Park
Leisure Centre
Oaklands
Highpark
Wey South Path
Mill Fm
Holdhurst Fm
Hall Place
Snoxhall Fm
Newhouse Fm
Bookers Lee
Longhurst Hill
Vachery Pond
Vachery Ho
Baynard's Park
Collins Fm
Ellen's Green
Ruet
Baynards
Ivelle Fm
Maybanks Manor
Cox Green
Brick Wks
Lynwick
Hornshill Fm
Bucks Green
Tisman's Common
Naldretts Fm
Howick Fm
Rudgwick Grange
Hale
Downs Link
Roman Woods
Hyes
Pond Bay
Roman Station
Dedisham
Violets Fm
Townhouse Farm Ho
Brookhurst Fm
Strood Green
Nowhurst Fm
Hill Ho
Hotel
Park Street
Theale Fm
Broadbridge Heath
Park Fm
Slinfold Lodge
Gaskyns
Pinkhurst
Woodstock
Holmbush Manor Fm
Ranfold
Toat Hill
Fulfords Fm
Lydwicke
Slinfold Manor
Buckman Corner
Bashurst
Itchingfield
Shiprods Fm
Lockets
Five Oaks
Graingingfold Fm
Wedge's Fm
Muntham Ho
Sharpenhurst
Marlands
Wellcross Grange
Broadbridge Fm
Leisure Centre
Fulfords Fm
Weston's Fm
Parthings
Grigg's Fm
Christ's Hospital (Sch)
Lanaways Fm
Two Mile Ash
Sharpenhurst Fm
Bodimans
Southwater Street
The Moat House
Great House Fm
Richmond Fm
Kirstys Wood
Chase Fm
Country Park
Netherwood
Brooks
Rascals
W
L
D
O
A

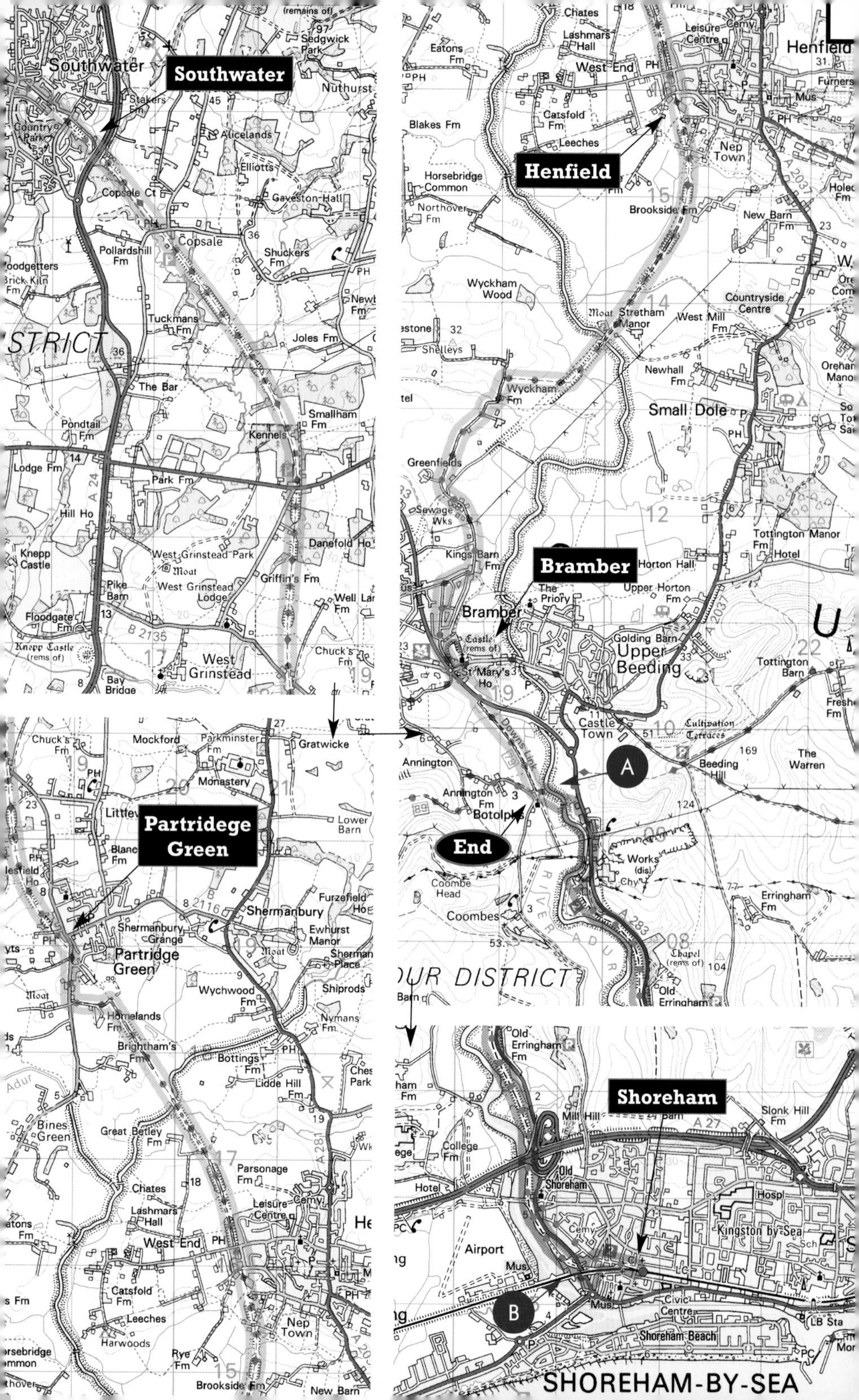
Southwater
Henfield
Bramber
Partridege Green
End
A
B
Shoreham
Upper Beeding
Small Dole
Copsale
West Grinstead
Shermanbury
Partridge Green
Botolphs
Annington
Kingston by Sea
Shoreham Beach
SHOREHAM-BY-SEA
Airport

The Downs Link

Guildford to Downs Link

The Downs Link (DL) starts just out of Guildford. You could leave your car here, although we recommend catching the train to Guildford (& back from Shoreham) and cycling to the DL start by either:

1 Follow the cyclepath from the centre of Guildford, to Shalford, then join the Pilgrim's Way, to St Martha's Hill (031/483), and the start of the Downs Link. This uses hilly, tough off-road trails, so will not suitable for family riding.

1 For an easier ride out to the Downs Link from Guildford, join the Wey South Path along the river. You can pick this up from the High St/bridge, by heading south on Millmead lane (by St Nicholas church). Bear L over the (black & white) footbridge then R by Millmead lock, through the park and keep R, to the river and turn R alongside this.

2 Follow the river, cross the A248, through field to a gate by a black footbridge. Cross the bridge/river (L) and follow the gravel track to the (busy) A281 and cross this (carefully) to join the Downs Link.

The Downs Link

This is a great family trail, as is mostly along wide, stone based, traffic free trails and follows an old railway line, so is also pretty flat for the most of it. It also makes a great winter ride as it drains well, easy to navigate and keeps you off the roads.

The whole of the Downs Link (from St Martha's Hill, to just past Bramber) is 54km (33.5m), plus another 11km (6.8m) to get to and from the start and end (train stations). If this sounds too ambitious have a look at our suggested shorter sections, which all make great, easy going family rides.

BRAMLEY TO CRANLEIGH 9KM

Park in Bramley Business Centre (009/450) (Old Bramley & Wonersh Old station), on Station rd (B2128). Cross the rd, heading south to Cranleigh. Cranleigh's main car park is right next to the DL (056/391). Exit out the back of the car park and bear L, to minor rd and go L then immediately R (SP Downs Link), and pass the playing fields. Slinfold has a few parking places just by the DL trail (117/308) by the caravan park.

CRANLEIGH TO SLINFOLD 10.2KM

Shortly after Baynards (old pub), go under a bridge then bear L to rd (FP only SA), and go L, over bridge and left on a BW SP Downs Link, and follow this, to rejoin the DL route.

SOUTHWATER TO PARTRIDGE GREEN 8KM

Park at Southwater Country park. Cross the rd onto Sakers lane (SP Copsale), pass under the A24 and bear R as tarmac bears L, off-road.

HENFIELD TO BRAMBER 7KM

Park by the Old Railway Tavern (pub), on the route. Head down Station rd and turn R (as rd bears L) at the bottom, then shortly L on the DL (206/159). Parking available in Bramber.

Bramber to Shoreham-by-Sea

A At a T-J (193/094) turn L (SP South Downs Way) over the river and turn R on the 'Coastal Link'. Follow this along the river Adur for 5km (3m) to the A283 rd in Old Shoreham (212/053) by railway.

B Turn R, under the railway bridge, then L on Victoria rd, back under the railway, to a X-rds and go R, on Hebe rd. Keep SA, following the cyclepath signs, to the end of Queens place and Shoreham-by-Sea train station (218/053) is just to the right.

Getting there: Get the train to Guildford and back from Shoreham-by-Sea. Otherwise see our suggested shorter rides.

Bike shops: Cycleworks in Guildford, GR 015/519 on 01483 302210 & Pedal Pushers GR 998/500 on 502327. (Near) Cranleigh: Beyond MTB's GR 026/390 on 01483 267676 on the A281, along the B2130.

Refreshments: Lots in the towns, cafe at Southwater country park, pubs nr Southwater (GR 148/272), Copsale (GR 171/249) over the A24, Partridge Green, pub (& Oriental food) in Henfield, various in Bramber & Upper Beeding & water tap at Cranleigh leisure centre.

Accommodation: Guildford TI 01483 444333, Horsham TI 01403 211661, Shoreham-by-Sea T.I. 01273 292589

27 Brighton

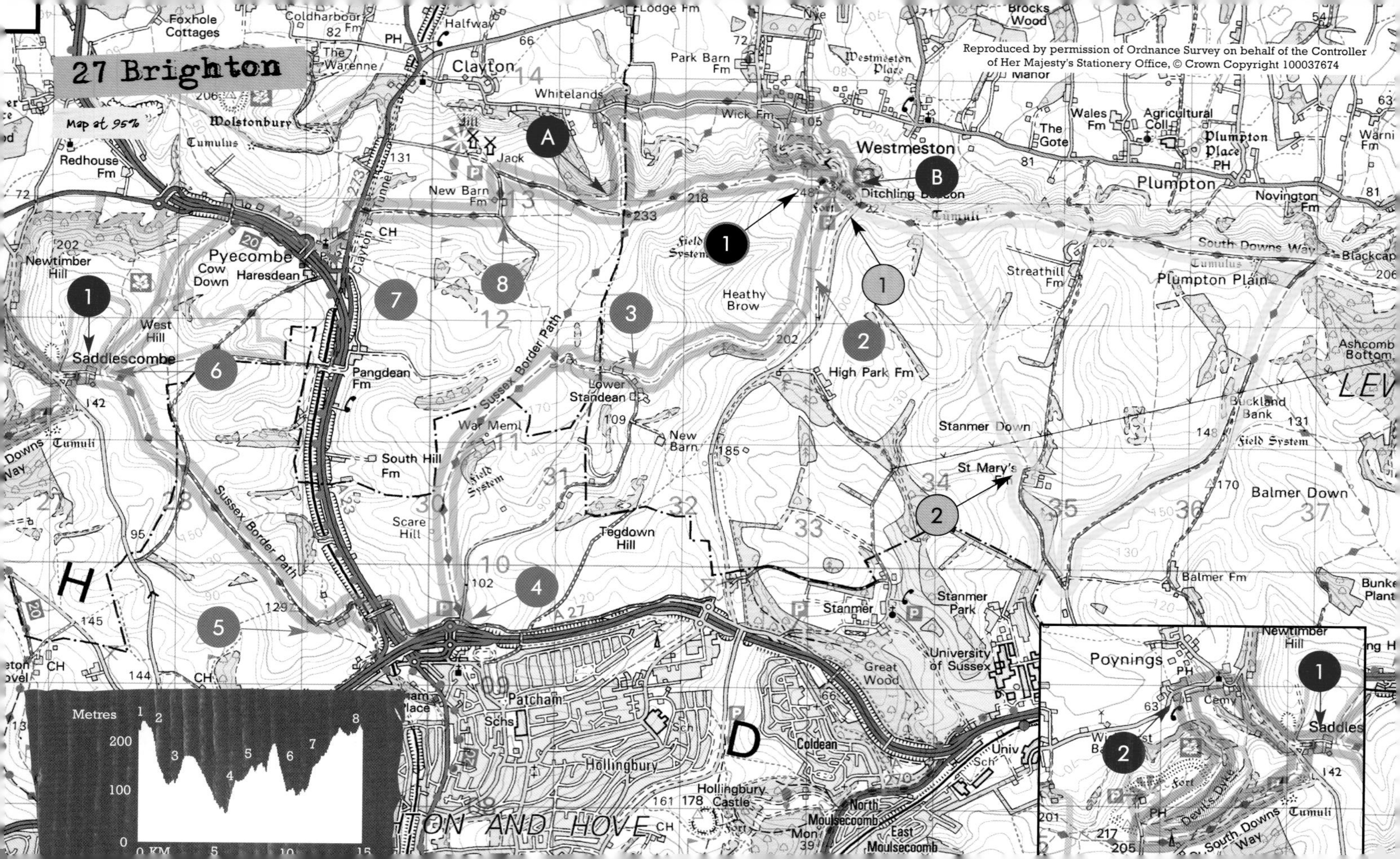
Map at 95%
Clayton
Whitelands
Westmeston
Ditchling Beacon
Plumpton
Plumpton Plain
South Downs Way
Pyecombe
Saddlescombe
Sussex Border Path
Heathy Brow
High Park Fm
Lower Standean
Stanmer Down
St Mary's
Balmer Down
Tegdown Hill
Scare Hill
South Hill Fm
Pangdean Fm
Stanmer Park
University of Sussex
Great Wood
Patcham
Hollingbury
Coldean
Moulsecoomb
Poynings
Devil's Dyke
Metres
200
100
0
0 KM
5
10
15

Brighton

18.7KM (11.6M) & 495 METRES CLIMBING

START **Head west** away from the rd, through a gate, on BW no.13 (main SDW track) **for 0.3km** (0.2m), just around a LHB **then turn L** (TQ 330/131) off the main/SDW track, through a gate, **on BW no.16** (Heathy brow). Go DH, **for 1.1km** (0.7m) **to a fork**, just past a gate **and bear R on Lower Standean BW** (328/128).

2 DH, into the valley, **through a gate** by the trees, on BW no.37, through a field **and bear R to a** single wooden **gate. Immediately through this turn L** on BW no.38, **for 0.15km to a fork and bear R,** on BW no.39. **Keep L to a DT** (315/115) **and turn R** on BW no.21.

3 **Keep SA** at BW no.20, **to a gate and turn L on BW no.19,** UH, **to some X-tracks** (309/117). **Turn L,** through a gate onto the West Sussex border path, **and keep SA on this** as the ST gets very feint, **for 2.6km** (1.6m) on the RHS of the field, **through a gate to a rd** (302/095).

4 **Turn R, to a T-J** (A27 just ahead), **and turn R, keeping SA at the roundabout for 0.55km** (0.35m), bears R, **then turn L on the** (Waterhall) **BW** (297/096). **Over the** A23 and railway, **and turn R, bearing L,** UH, **on a DT, to a T-J** (291/095) by a barn **and turn R,** UH.

5 **1.6km** (1m) **to a X-tracks** (280/107) where the main track bears R, **and go SA** through a silver gate, ST. **After 1km** (0.6m) **go through a gate and bear L,** DH, through a tunnel of trees **for 0.15km then R through a gate** before the houses and a drive, **and immediately sharp R again,** UH, **on a DT** (273/115) **or see** extension 1.

6 **Keep SA, to a gate** by some trees (New Timber hill), **and go SA,** DH, **on the grass,** to the A23 rd. **Go over the bridge** (over the A23) **and to a rd** (284/129) **and turn R on this. Joining the slip rd** off the A23, **and keep SA** (Pyecombe/A273) **for 0.4km** (0.25m) **then turn L on Church lane** (291/124) into Pyecombe.

7 **Bear R by the church,** on School lane, **to the A273 rd and turn L on this for 0.25km** (0.15m), **then turn R over** this rd (294/129).**On the SDW,** through the golf club **for 1.1km** (0.7m), through a gate, **to a X-tracks** (305/128).

8 **Turn L** on the SDW, towards the (Jack & Jill) windmills **for 0.4km** (0.25m) **to a T-J** (305/132) **and turn R** on the SDW. **Keep SA on the main track** (SDW) **for 3.2km** (2m), **back to the car park** (333/130) **or see** extension 2.

Extension 1

+5.5KM (3.4M) & 185 METRES CLIMBING

1 **Turn L on the SDW, to a rd** (271/114), **then turn R on the rd, then shortly L on a BW** parallel to the rd, **to a rd in Poynings village** (265/120). **Turn L on the rd, then L again by the church, through the village, for 0.3km** (0.2m) **and turn L on a BW** (261/119).

2 **Follow this BW,** UH, **for 1.6km** (1m), keeping SA **to a rd and turn L on this (or R to the pub) for 0.15km** (0.1m), **then turn L on the SDW** (258/107). **Keep bearing R at the forks in the BW, DH, to a rd at Saddlescombe (270/114). Go over the rd** on the SDW, UH, **back to the start of the extension and rejoin the route at no.6.**

Extension 2

+1.8KM (1.1M) & 135 METRES CLIMBING

A **Turn L at the Keymer post** (315/129) (before the Sussex Border Path which is good but can be busy with walkers), DH, (bombholes to the R of main track) **keeping L at a fork after 0.65km** (0.4m), **to a rd** (313/137). **Turn R on the rd, for 1.3km** (0.8m) **to a X-rds** (325/137) **and turn R on the rd,** UH on the infamous Ditchling Beacon (333/130).

B **Through a gate after 0.8km** (0.5), **to a X-tracks** (369/125), **and keep SA on the SDW. Keep SA on this for 3.9km** (2.4m), past Dews pond, **to a rd and go SA back to the** car park at the **end / start** (333/130).

Short Ride

11KM (6.8M) & 260 METRES CLIMBING

1 **Head East,** across the rd from the car park, **on the** (SDW) **BW for 0.35m then turn R** (post but no BW sign), (338/128). Through some trees, **to a single gate and bear R on BW no.11,** on a feint track through the field, **for 1.4m** to the farm **rd** (347/108).

2 **Bear R/SA on this for 1km** (0.65m) **to a rd** (350/098) and turn L and follow this DT, SA, UH for 3.6km to a X-rds with the SDW at the top (369/125). **Turn L, on the SDW, and follow this for 3.75km, all the way back to the start at Ditchling Beacon car park (333/130).**

TOP TIP: For a nice family ride, follow sustrans no.2 cycle path along Brighton seafront.

Getting there Start from the car park at Ditchling Beacon (333/130) south of Ditchling village, at the top of the hill, off Ditchling road. By train: stations at Sussex uni, Keymer & Lewes.

Accommodation Blackberry Wood campsite in Streat (nr Ditchling) is lovely, tel: 01273 890035 or see www.blackberrywood.com. B&B at Poynings Manor farm on: 01273 857371, B&B in Kingston near Lewes on: 01273 472295. YHA in Brighton on: 0870 7705724 Brighton backpackers on: 01273 777717. Brighton T.I. (premium rate) on: 0906 7112255 & Worthing T.I. on: 01903 210022.

Bike shop Bicycleworks in Lewes on: 01273 483399

Refreshments Often an ice-cream van at the start, a pub & tea shop in Pyecombe, a pub (& maybe ice cream van) on extension 1 /Devils Dyke.

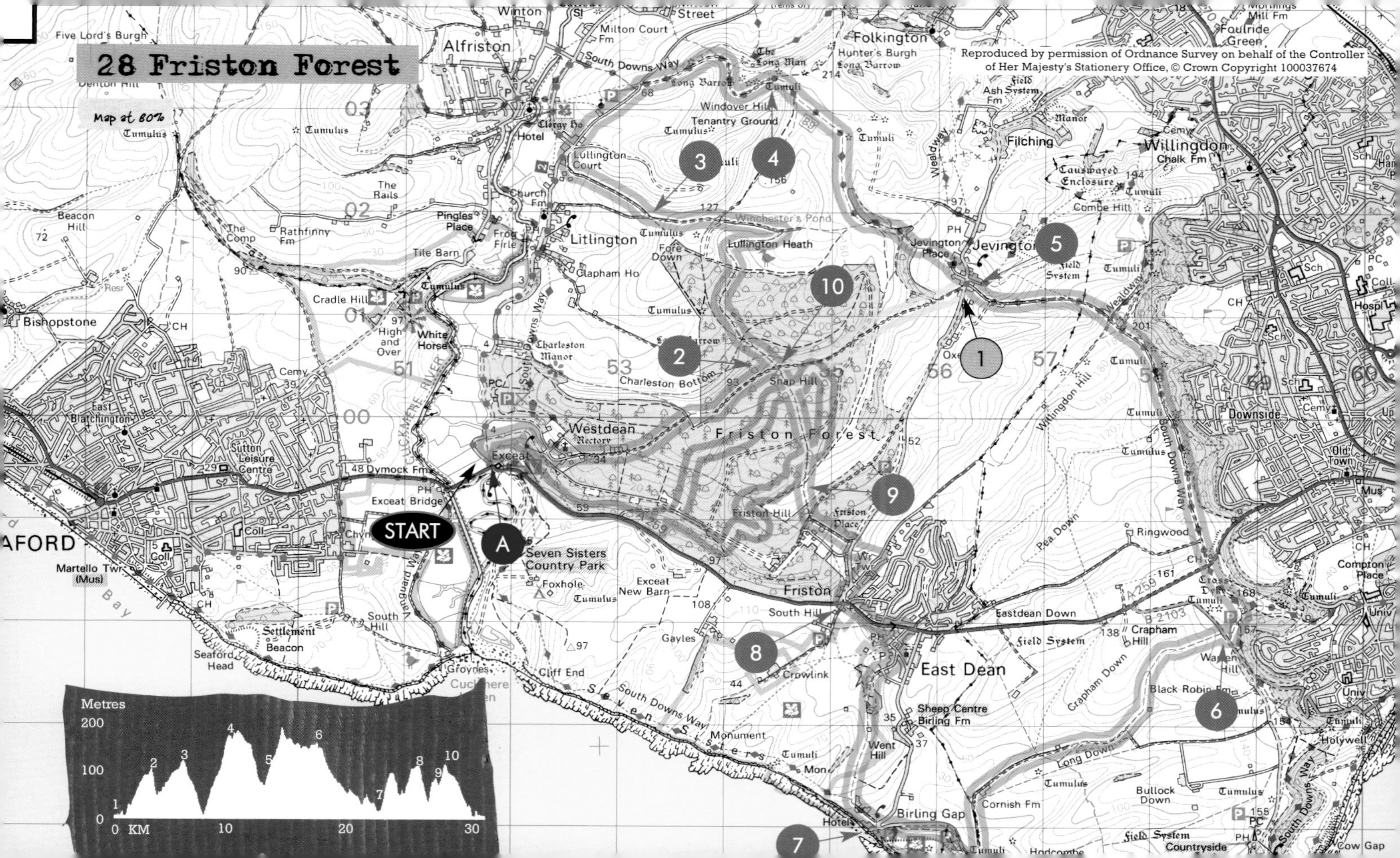

28 Friston Forest
Map at 80%
Reproduced by permission of Ordnance Survey on behalf of the Controller of Her Majesty's Stationery Office, © Crown Copyright 100037674
START
Seven Sisters Country Park
Friston Forest
Alfriston
Litlington
Westdean
Exceat
Exceat Bridge
Jevington
Friston
East Dean
Birling Gap
Willingdon
Folkington
Seaford Head
South Downs Way
Vanguard Way
Wealdway
Cuckmere River
Metres
200
100
0
KM
10
20
30

Friston Forest

30.6KM (19M) & 845 METRES CLIMBING

START **Go through a gate at the north end of the car park, onto a BW and follow this,** around the bottom of the wooded hill. **After 1km** (0.6m)**, at the houses, turn L then immediately R on a narrow lane,** UH. **Follow this main track for 2.25km** (1.4m)**,** becomes a gravel surface, through a field, back into the woods, **to a X-tracks** (544/005), by Snap hill.

2 **Turn L** (Lullington heath), DH, **keeping R at a fork after 0.15km** (0.1m) **for 0.3km** (0.2m) **to a multiple** (7) **junction** (541/007). **Bear R** (Lullington heath), UH, going through a gate into the nature reserve, **and follow the BW to a gate and T-J** (545/018). **Turn L on a** (DT) **BW,** (Litlington) UH **for 0.65km** (0.4m) **to a X-rds,** at Winchester's pond.

3 **Keep SA for 0.65km** (0.4m) **to a fork** (532/019) **& bear R** or see extension 1. **1km** (0.65m) DH **to a rd** (525/025) **and turn R on this, and keep SA,** UH, **for 1km** (0.6m)**then turn R on the SDW** (532/032). Up Wendover hill, **for 0.9km** (0.55m) **to a fork** (540/035) **and bear R** (L is a FP), along the top of a valley, **to the summit** (544/033).

4 **Keep following the blue SDW signs,** along, then down the hill, alongside, then **into some woods after 1.95km** (1.2m) (553/018). **Keep R then SA,** DH, steep, technical track, **to a** (St Andrews) **church and keep SA on the rd. To a T-J** in Jevington, **and turn R then immediately L on Eastbourne Lane** (BW), (562/013) or see the shortcut.

5 UH, rejoining the SDW, **for 1.5km** (0.95m) **to a X-tracks** (576/009), **and keep SA on the SDW. 2.65km** (1.65m) **to the** A259 **rd** (585/985). **Go SA on the SDW, to a trig point and keep R, to the** B2013 **rd. Cross the rd, into a car park and turn R for 0.1km, to a gate, and follow the BW** (586/979), DH, into the valley.

6 **Keep SA for 3km** (1.9m) **and bear L,** on a drive, **just past the farm** (563/963), **for 0.65km** (0.4m) **to a rd** (564/956). **Turn L on the rd, then shortly R, through a gate,** on a BW, **parallel to the rd** (heading west). **Later, rejoin the rd, and turn L on this for 0.25km** (0.15), **then keep SA on the SDW,** as the rd bears sharp R.

7 UH, **for 0.3km** (0.2m) **then bear R** (552/962), on the BW, up Went hill, **joining a good track. After 0.3km bear R,** DH, **to a rd** (West way), **then bearing L on Lower street, then R on Upper street** (nr Tiger Inn), **to a T-J** (557/ 979) in East dean. **Turn L** on the A259, UH, **for 0.7km** (0.45m), **then R on Old Wilmington rd** (Jevington) (550/982).

8 **After 0.25km** (0.15m) **bear R at a fork, for 0.4km** (0.25m) **then turn L** (554/986), through a gate, **on a BW,** steep DH, **to a rd. Turn R on this for 0.1km then turn L** (552/988) **on a BW** (dirt track on the RHS of the drive). **After 0.5km** (0.3m)**, keep SA on a BW,** into the trees, as the drive bears L, UH, across a field, **into Friston forest.**

9 **Follow this forest track** (or the purple cycle trail, for a longer, more technical finish to the ride) **for 1.3km** (0.8m), through a clearing, SA over a path, up, then down some of Snap hill, **to a X-tracks** (544/005) **and turn L.**

10 **Follow this track** (you came along at the start) **for 2.25km** (1.4m) (keeping R after 0.25km/0.15m), **back to the houses** in Westdean, **and turn L on the BW, back to the car park** (518/995).

Extension

+11.3KM (7M)

1 Waymarked (purple markers) 11.3km (7m), challenging ride around Friston Forest.

Shortcut

-14.2KM (8.8M) & 395 METRES CLIMBING

1 **Stay SA on the rd for another 0.1km and turn R on a BW** (562/012), UH, **for 0.9km** (0.55m)**, into Friston forest. Keep SA on this BW** forest track, DH, **for 1km** (0.65m) **to a X-tracks** (544/005) **and go SA and rejoin route at no.10.**

Family activities

There are plenty of trails in Friston Forest suitable for families, including a (green) waymarked family cycle route of 7.25km (4.5m). For more information and a route map, call in at Cuckmere Cycles which is at the start of the ride.

Lots of great coastal walks, see www.beachyhead.org.uk

Drusillas Park (Zoo) nr Alfriston, has a wide range of animals as well as a play areas for the kids, and Thomas the Tank Engine trains. www.drusillas.co.uk or 01323 874100.

Sheep Centre, nr East Dean, with other farm animals to cuddle & feed, inc rabbits, pigs, chicks. Tel; 01323 423302 or see www.sheepcentre.co.uk.

Getting there: start in Friston Forest at the National Trust (pay & display) car park (gets locked at dusk) (518/995). This is between Seaford and Eastbourne, on the A259 by a narrow bridge over Cuckmere river. Train: stations in Seaford and Eastbourne (follow the A259 west).

Accommodation: B&B's at Exceat farmhouse on: 01323 870218, the George Inn on: 870319, Dean's barn on: 870319, The Giants Rest pub in Wilmington on: 870207, YHA in Alfriston on: 0870 8705666, camping in Alfriston on: 01323 870560, or Sussex Ox (nr Alfriston) on: 870840, Eastbourne TI on: 01323 411400.

Refreshments: cafe at the start, a pub over the bridge in Jevington, a cafe at Birling gap, and shops, pubs etc in East Dean.

Bike Shops: Cuckmere cycles at the start on 01323870310 or Evolution cycles in Eastbourne on 01323 737320.

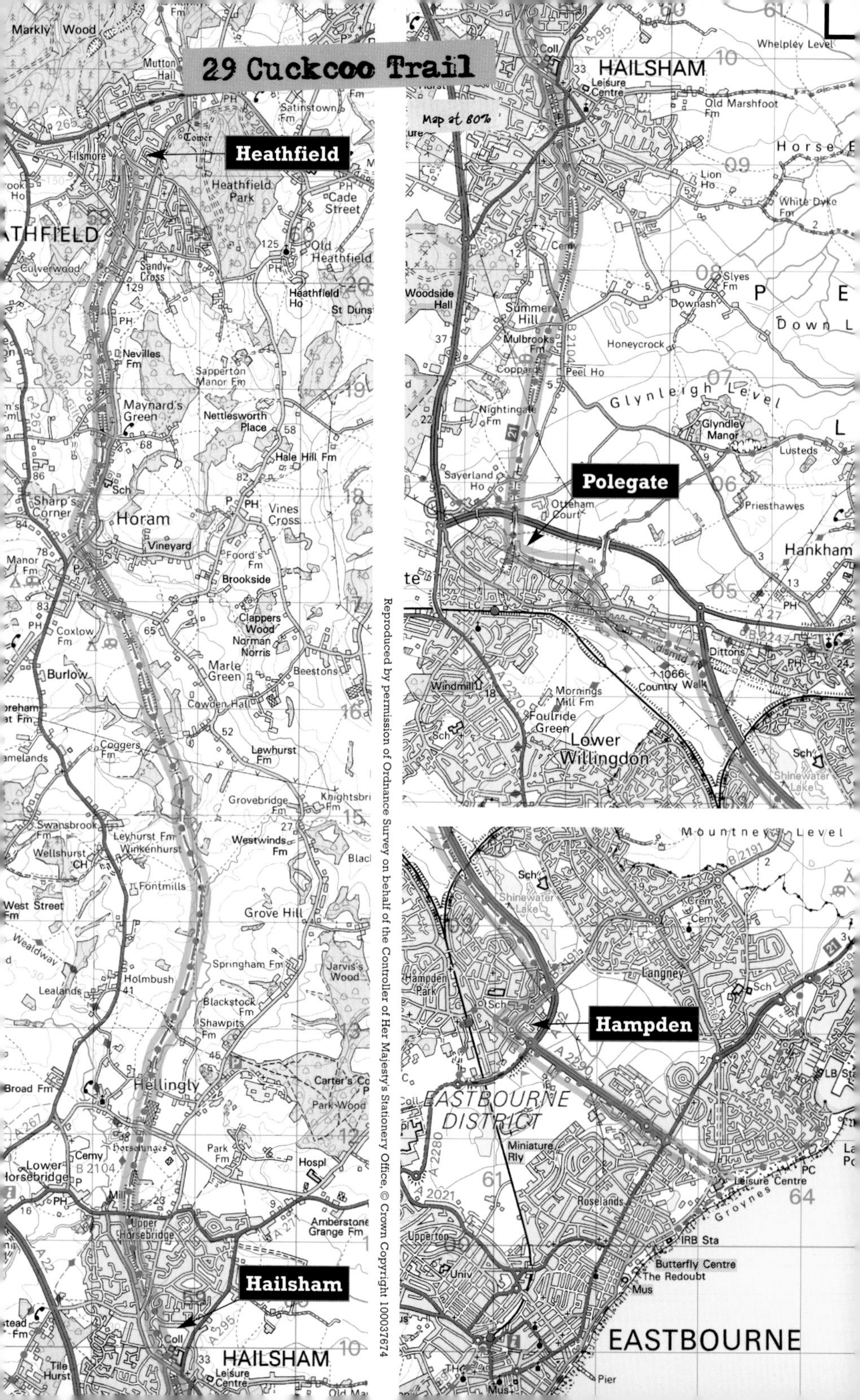

29 Cuckcoo Trail
Map at 80%
Heathfield
Polegate
Hampden
Hailsham

Cuckoo Trail

This lovely cycle track was given its name from the tradition that the first cuckoo of spring was released at Heathfield Fair. It is (mostly) traffic free cycling trail, with good surface and only a gentle gradient (around 120 metres over the 17.7km /11m) which makes it an ideal family cycle route.

NOTE: There are some road sections from the railway stations and when passing through Hailsham.

Hampden

Exit the station and go R (Station Approach) to Mountfeild rd, and go R on this, SA at a roundabout, then R on Dallington rd. Take 2nd L (Ashington rd), and R at the end of this, then L on the Cuckoo trail, before going under the A22. **NOTE**: Hampden to Eastbourne is 2.7km & Hampden to Polegate is 5.5km.

Polegate

Exit the station and go R (north) on the High street, to station rd, cross this (using crossing) and turn R, then L on School lane, and keep SA on the corner, to the R of Polegate Primary school, and join the Cuckoo trail just up here, crossing the A27. **NOTE**: Polegate to Hailsham is 4.3km

Heathfield

The trail starts/ends at a car park in Heathfield, off Newnham Way, which is off Station rd (582/212), between the B2203 and A265. Please note that the Cuckoo trail ends here, but the Sustrans route no.21 continues north. **NOTE**: Heathfield to Horam is 4km & Horam to Hailsham is 8.4km.

Family activities

There are things along the trail to look out for i.e. metal scultures and carved wooden benches, as well as some alterntive forms of entertainment.

KNOCKHATCH ADVENTURE PARK

nr Hailsham has a whole range of things to entertain the kids, including mini quad bikes, laser adventure game, karting, rowing boats, crazy golf, trampolines, and children's farm. Prices vary between the activites. For more info call 01323 442051 or see www.knockhatch.com.

MINATURE RAILWAY

Nr Hampden station. Follow the A22 to Lottbridge Drove, then follow brown 'Mini Railway' signs. Tel: 01323 520 229 or see www.emsr.co.uk.

EASTBOURNE

There are various activities & attractions in Eastbourne, such as visiting the butterfly centre, Museum, Aquarium, walk along the Pier, etc.

To get to Eastbourne, follow the Sustrans no.21 signs from the end of the Cuckoo Trail, to the coast and turn right (south-west).

For more information on the Cuckoo Trail and other cycle routes visit www.eastsussex.gov.uk and do a search on 'Cuckoo Trail'.

Getting there: There are a number of possible start/end points, including Heathfield, Horam, Hellingly, Hailsham, the 2 stations (Polegate & Hampden Park) and even Eastbourne.

Accommodation: see www.enjoysusses.info. The Hidden Spring Vineyard nr Horam, has caravan & camping, tel: 01435 812640 and comes recommended. Sussex country info centre are happy to help book accommodation for you, free of charge, call 01323 442667.

Refreshments: Lots of choice in Hampden Park, Polgate, Hailsham and Heathfield. Cafe in Horam and tea shop on the trail, Old Loom Mill craft centre (just before south of B2104, 5km (3 miles) north of Polgate.

Bike shops: M's cycle hire on www.m-cyclehire.co.uk or 07852 986 165 or 163, can deliver & collect. Cycle Revival in Heathfield 01435 866118, M & S Accessories, Hailsham 01323 845409, & Kontour cycles, Polegate 01323 482368.

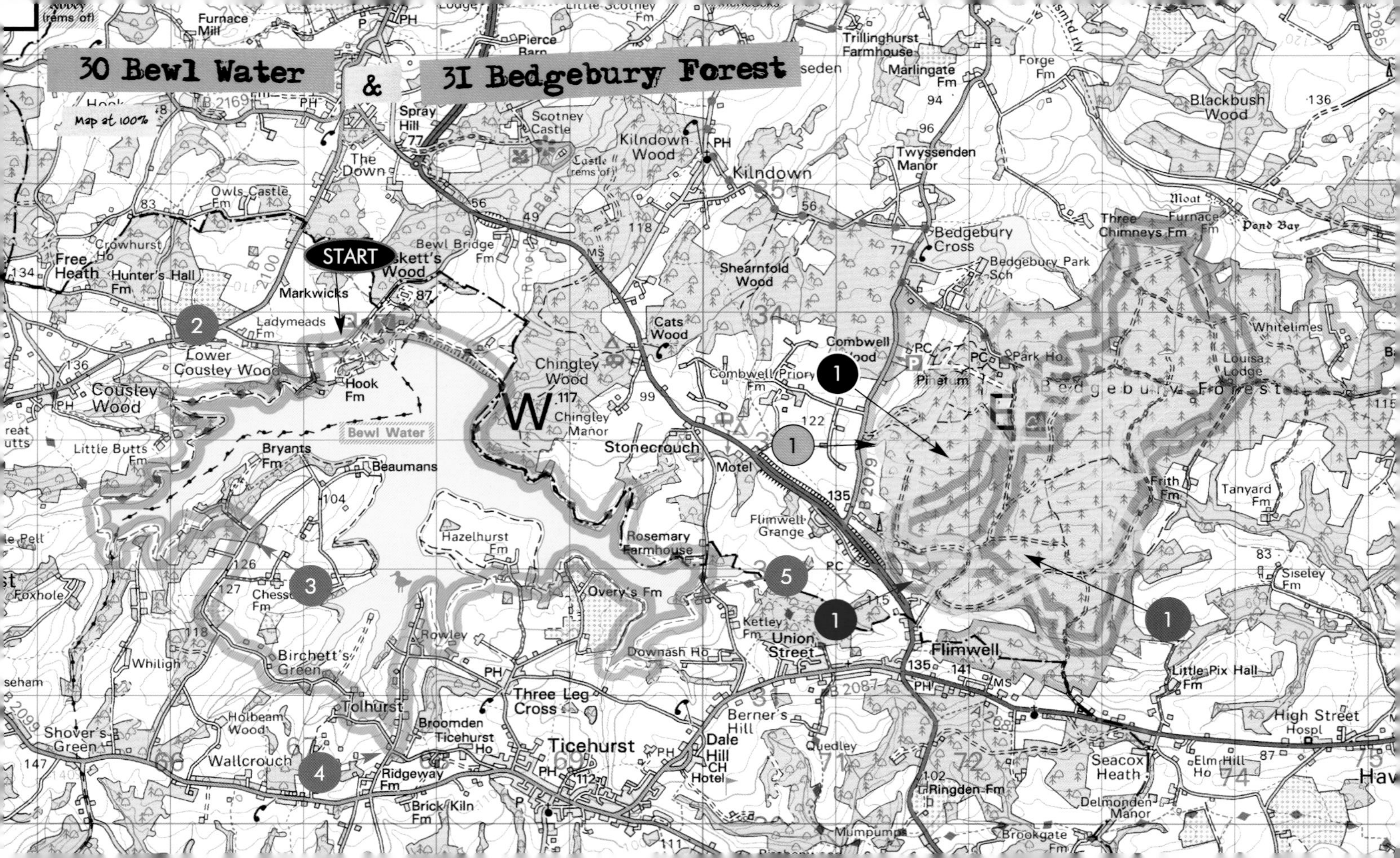
30 Bewl Water
&
31 Bedgebury Forest
Map at 100%
START
Bewl Water
Bedgebury Forest
Free Heath
Hunter's Hall Fm
Crowhurst Ho
Owls Castle Fm
Markwicks
Ladymeads Fm
Lower Cousley Wood
Cousley Wood
Hook Fm
Little Butts Fm
Bryants Fm
Beaumans
Hazelhurst Fm
Chess Fm
Birchett's Green
Whiligh
Holbeam Wood
Wallcrouch
Shover's Green
Tolhurst
Broomden
Ticehurst Ho
Ridgeway Fm
Brick Kiln Fm
Ticehurst
Three Leg Cross
Rowley
Overy's Fm
Downash Ho
Rosemary Farmhouse
Stonecrouch
Chingley Wood
Chingley Manor
Bewl Bridge Fm
The Down
Spray Hill
Scotney Castle
Kilndown Wood
Kilndown
Shearnfold Wood
Cats Wood
Combwell Priory Fm
Combwell Wood
Motel
Flimwell Grange
Ketley Fm
Union Street
Berner's Hill
Dale Hill
CH Hotel
Quedley
Flimwell
Ringden Fm
Mumpumps
Seacox Heath
Delmonden Manor
Brookgate Fm
Elm Hill Ho
High Street Hospl
Little Pix Hall Fm
Sisseley Fm
Tanyard Fm
Frith Fm
Louisa Lodge
Whitelimes
Park Ho
Pinetum
Bedgebury Park Sch
Bedgebury Cross
Twyssenden Manor
Three Chimneys Fm
Furnace Fm
Moat
Pond Bay
Blackbush Wood
Forge Fm
Marlingate Fm
Trillinghurst Farmhouse
Pierce Barn
Furnace Mill
Foxhole
B 2079
B 2087
B 2100
B 2169
B 2099

Bedgebury Forest

Easy/Family Route 9KM (5.6M)

1 An easy, well surfaced ride on wide tracks making it perfect for children/families.

Single track route 13KM (8M)

1 A singletrack trail, that's great for newer rider, but it gets more challenging (and fun) the faster you go, so should appeal to more experienced riders also.

Freeride Area

1 North-shore (wooden constructions) riding for experienced riders only. Includes elevated ladder trails going up to about 2 metres, skinny balance logs (as thin as 4 inches wide), various drops, see-saws, wooden kickers, a set of linked see-saws, wooden bermed corners, and others. Next to the freeride area is a dirt jump area.

Cycle skills area

① With planks to balance along, logs to hop & a course to weave along

NOTE: There is a good adventure playground for non-cyclists here too.

Bewl Water

21KM (13M) & 290 METRES CLIMBING

START **Follow the 'Bewl water route' signs,** heading **west, for 1.2km** (0.75m) **to the lake and turn R** (TQ 669/333).

2 **Follow the lake** (on your LHS) **for 5.1km** (3.15m), **then turn R through some gates** (661/324) by a hut, **following the BW sign.** Short UH, **to a DT and turn R on this,** following the BW signs **to a rd** (665/322).

3 **Turn R on this rd, for 1km** (0.6m) **to a fork** (663/314) **and bear L,** following the brown signs. 1.9km (1.2m) **to a T-J** (676/306) **and turn L,** on Burnt lodge lane.

4 **After 0.7km** (0.45m), **keep SA** on Lower Hazlehurst, **for 0.5km** (0.3m) **then through a** 'Bewl water' **gate** (678/318). **Follow the Bewl water signs for 5.3km** (3.3m) alongside the water, **to a T-J with a rd** (700/318).

5 **Turn L,** over the bridge, (or use the B2087 to Flimwell and include the Bedgebury loops) **for 0.25km** (0.15m) **then turn L back onto the Bewl water track** (700/320) and **follow the signposts around Bewl water, for 5.2km** (3.2m) **back to the visitors centre** (677/338).

TOP TIP: Bedgebury Cycle Club do social rides & trail maintenance. Members get an annual car parking pass, free showers, bikewash and discounts on parts and accessories in the Bedgebury bike shop. For more info see www.boarsonbikes.co.uk.

Getting there: Bedgebury Forest route starts at the (expensive) visitors centre car park (715/337), off the B2079, but there is a cafe, bike hire, bike wash, showers and a bike shop. Bewl Water Visitors centre (not so expensive) car park (675/337) is the start for the other and is just off the A21 – follow the brown signs. Train station at Stonegate – head north, through Stonegate village, and over the B2099 rd to Bewl Water, by Ticehurst.

Accommodation: B&B at the Cherry Tree Inn in Ticehurst on: 01580201229, B&B in Wadhurst on: 01892 783896, B&B in the 'Best Beach Inn' in Wadhurst, on: 01892 782046, camping (on the north of Bewl water) off the A21, on: 01892 890566. Tunbridge Wells TI on: 01892 515675 or www.heartofkent.org.uk

Bike shops: Evernden cycles at the Visitors centre in Bedgebury Forest, on 01580 879694 or see www.everndencycles.co.uk. Bewl Water bike hire (summer only) on: 07801 610999.

Refreshments: Pinetum centre in Bedgebury Forest and Eugene's ice cream van. Bewl Water visitor centre has a cafe.

32 Crab & Winkle Way
Map at 85%
START
Swalecliffe
Studd Hill
Chestfield
Greenhill
West End
South Street
Radfall
Thornden Wood
West Blean Wood
Clowes Wood
Blean
Tyler Hill
Broad Oak
Sturry
Rough Common
Harbledown
CANTERBURY
Tankerton
Tankerton Bay
Whitstable Street
Saxon Shore Way
Long Rock
Frogs Island Fm
Bleangate
Bullockstone
Bodkin Fm
Red House Fm
Shrub Hill
Bogshole Fm
Burgess Fm
Tumulus
Clapham Hill
Duncan Down
Court Lees
Pean Hill
Clowes Fm
Red Lion Ho
Denstroude
Honey Hill
Parsonage Fm
Wildlife Park
Amery Court
Butler's Ct
Well Court
Frog Hall
Honey Wood
Hothe Court Fm
Church Wood
Homestall Wood
Upper Harbledown
Hall Place
Wildwood Wealden Forest Park
West Blean Ho
Blaxland Fm
Calcott
Brambles Fm
Vale Fm
Mayton Fm
Langton Lodge
Alcroft Grange
Shelford Fm
Den Grove Wood
Little Hall Fm
Hales Place
Sewage Wks
Stour Valley Walk
Leisure Centre
Council Office
DVROVERNVM
Museum
Castle
North Downs Way
Bigbury
Denstead Fm
Howfield Wood
Petty France
Tonford Manor Moat
Chartham Hatch
Poldhurst Fm
Little Barton Fm
Motel
CANTERBURY DISTRICT
Aquarium
Harbour
IRB Sta
Sports Centre
Strode Fm
Northwood Ho

Crab & Winkle way

12.5KM (7.8M) & 110 METRES CLIMBING

ONE-WAY

START At the Westgate / northern end of the High St (146/580), where the junction of Pound Lane & St Peter's St, cross the rd and follow the Sustrans 'Route 1 Whitstable' signposts down Westgate Grove and Whitehall rd.

NOTE: You simply follow the Sustrans no.1 cycle route signs, all the way to Whitstable harbour.

2 After running parallel with the A2050 it heads R (north), off-rd, UH, providing good views of Canterbury. Past a water tower, use the crossing, over the A290, onto a cycle/foot path, and go R opposite Kent College, past car park (131/595).

3 Nice section of off-road, past fruit farms, going R at a X-rds in Clowes wood, then L at the T-J (126/626). After 1km bear L off the forest DT, crossing the A299, to a rd in South St (123/650).

4 Turn L on this for just 0.3km, joining the (SP Station & Centre) cycle path after Millstrood rd, to its end. Turn L then R, following the signposts, DH, to the centre of Whitstable, and on to the harbour.

RETURN JOURNEY

You can catch the train from Whitstable, back to Canterbury (east station), via Faversham.

5 If you are cycling back, you could use the alternative Sustrans no.1 cycle path as you re-enter Canterbury, passing the University, back to the same start/end point (146/580).

other riding — VARIOUS

1 **Thorden / West Blean wood** - There is a good surfaced double track going through the centre of the woods, leading to the wildlife park, and lots of superb twisty single track all through these woods.

2 **Clowes wood** - This open access Forestry Commission wood has a few nice single tracks in places, but they are harder to find. There is also a wide forest road that goes around the wood.

3 **Rough common** & Church wood - A few well surfaced double tracks, and lots of single track - although some of it is (signposted) out of bounds to cyclists.

Family

The route is ideal for family riding, as it is mostly stone based paths which provide a good all weather surface, and is mostly off-road, apart from quiet lanes & cycle paths used in the towns.

Half way along the ride is the Druidstone (wildlife) park, www.druidstone.net or tel 01227 765168.

Wildwood discovery park in West Blean wood offers close encounters with native wildlife; from owls to otters, badgers to beavers, and wild boar to wolves. Great for children www.wildwoodtrust.org.

INTERESTING FACTS

The Crab & Winkle way name comes from the old railway line that ran from 1830 to 1952.

Whitstable is famous for Oysters and has a festival in July.

Getting there: Park in the small car park near Kent college (131/595) on the route. There is also a (free) Rough common nature reserve car park just down the road (121/594). By train: there are train stations in Canterbury & Whitstable.

Accommodation: B&B at Cathedral gate hotel in Canterbury on tel: 01227 464381, B&B in Whitstable on: 01227 263506, YHA in Canterbury on: 0870 7705744, camping in Canterbury, just off the A257 on tel: 01227 463216, Canterbury TI on 01227 378100.

Bike shops: Tibbs in Canterbury on: 01227 787 880. Herberts in Whitstable on 01227 272072, and Downland cycles (bike hire) at Canterbury West station, tel: 01227 479 643.

Refreshments: There are lots of places in Canterbury & Whitstable.

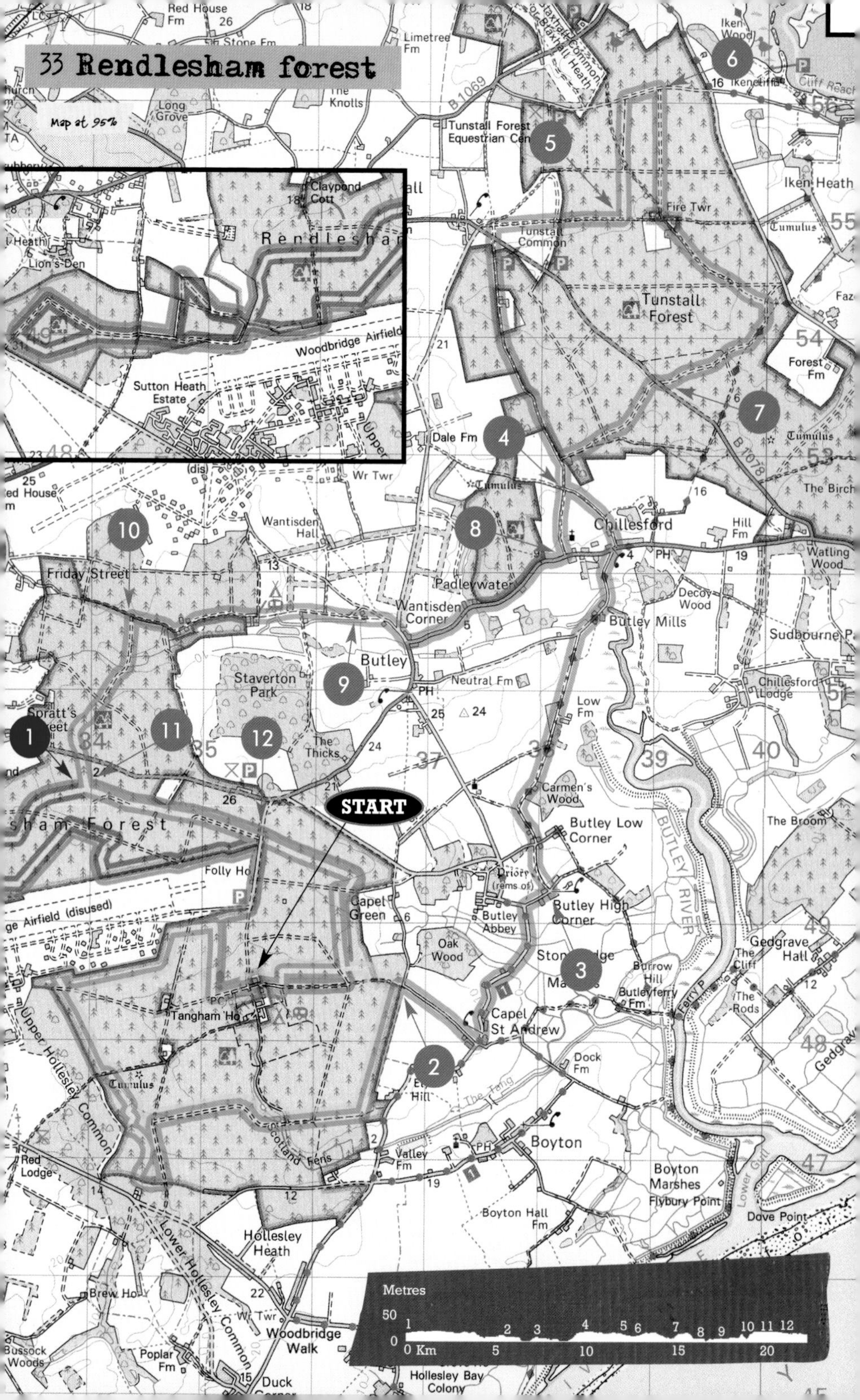
33 Rendlesham forest
Map at 95%
START
Red House Fm
Stone Fm
Limetree Fm
The Knolls
Long Grove
Tunstall Forest Equestrian Cen
Iken Wood
Ikencliff
Cliff Reach
Iken Heath
Fire Twr
Tunstall Common
Tunstall Forest
Forest Fm
Tumulus
The Birch
Claypond Cott
Rendlesham
Lion's Den
Woodbridge Airfield
Sutton Heath Estate
Upper
Wr Twr
Dale Fm
Wantisden Hall
Chillesford
Hill Fm
Watling Wood
Friday Street
Padleywater
Wantisden Corner
Decoy Wood
Butley Mills
Sudbourne P
Butley
Neutral Fm
Staverton Park
The Thicks
Spratt's Street
Low Fm
Chillesford Lodge
Carmen's Wood
Butley Low Corner
Rendlesham Forest
Folly Ho
Airfield (disused)
Capel Green
Priory (rems of)
Butley Abbey
Butley High Corner
Butley River
Oak Wood
Burrow Hill
Butleyferry Fm
Ferry P
Gedgrave Hall
The Cliff
The Rods
The Broom
Tangham Ho
Capel St Andrew
Dock Fm
Upper Hollesley Common
Tumulus
The Tang
Boyton
Scotland Fens
Valley Fm
Red Lodge
Boyton Marshes
Flybury Point
Dove Point
Lower Gull
Boyton Hall Fm
Hollesley Heath
Lower Hollesley Common
Brew Ho
Wr Twr
Woodbridge Walk
Bussock Woods
Poplar Fm
Duck Corner
Hollesley Bay Colony
Metres
50
0
0 Km
5
10
15
20

Rendlesham forest

36.4KM (22.6M) & 150 METRES OF CLIMBING

START **Head west from the car park, following the yellow cycle track signs.** Stay on this waymarked track, which bears north, before going around the southern part of the forest, **for 8.9km** (at the end of a 1.1km stretch of singletrack, along the edge of the forest) **where the cycle trail bears L, by a gate, near the corner of a rd** (367/484).

2 **Turn R to the rd, and go SA/R on this for 0.8km to a X-rds** (374/479) at Capel St Andrew, **and turn L** (Butley). **After 1.4km** on this rd, **turn R** (Butley high corner) (378/491) on the dead end rd, **for 0.25km, then turn L on a ROW** (380/492), 0.4km to a rd and go SA on this.

3 **After 0.3km to a fork** (378/499), by the power lines, **and turn R. Keep SA on this main track for 1.6km to a rd and turn R on this, for 0.8km to a T-J** in Chillsford village. **Turn R then immediately L on a BW** (386/522) by a post box, **for 0.6km to a X-tracks** (381/527).

4 **Turn R and keep SA on this DT for 2.3km to a rd and go SA on a ST** (bird sign) **for 0.15km to a** sandy **DT** (375/549) **and go R on this** (leaving the bird trail). **Enter the forest after 0.5km and keep SA on the DT for a 0.6km then go L** (387/550) following a signpost with a bicycle on it.

5 **0.4km to a X-tracks and go SA for 0.1km to another X-tracks and go SA** (L then R), **on a ST** (not the bird trail on L). **Keep SA on this track for 0.6km to a rd** (387/560) **and turn R on this rd for 0.3km then go R** past a green barrier (by a 2/4 sign) **on a wide forest track** (390/561).

6 **Follow this main track, for 1.2km,** which bears L **to a X-tracks** (390/550) **and go SA,** past a house on the LHS. **Keep SA over 2 X-tracks, for 1.2km to a T-J** (399/543) **and turn R. Keep SA on this forest track for 1.3km** (under some power cables), **to a rd** (390/536).

7 **Go SA,** past a barrier, **on a wide forest track,** by no.32 sign **and keep SA** (at X-tracks after 0.7km) **for a total of 1.1km** past a barrier, **to a T-J** at the edge of the woods (381/529) (been here before). **Turn L for 0.25km to a X-tracks & go SA** (not been here before), **to a rd** (382/521).

8 **Turn R on the rd for 1m** into Butley village, **then turn R** (Tunstall, Camping) as the rd bears L (368/514). **Bear L immediately at the fork, for 0.25km & bear L on a** (grassy DT) **BW** just past a house on the L. Follow the telegraph poles, through a farm, **to a DT track, and go SA/L on this.**

9 **Keep SA after 0.4km on a grassy DT** (BW), as the good track bears L. **Keep SA,** becoming a ST, **to a good DT** (354/516) **and keep SA on this** into the trees (the campsite on L sells food). **Keep SA on this DT for 1.2km** (alongside the telegraph poles) **to a wide forest track on the L** in an open area (343/516).

10 **Turn L** (following the bird sign) past a green barrier, **and keep SA,** DH, (over X-tracks with red top posts) **bearing R. To a fork & bear L, to a X-tracks and keep SA,** following the bird sign **to a rd. Go SA for 0.3km to a** (DT) **T-J** (340/501) **and turn L** (bird sign) or see the extension.

11 **0.5km to a T-J and go L** (old shipping containers on the L), **and join a good, wide forest track. Keep SA on this,** following the (green) bike signs **to a rd** (355/497).

12 **Go SA, and follow the** (green) **cycle trail for 2km, to a** (small) **X-tracks** in the trees (362/486). **Turn R on the yellow cycle trail** (signs on other side of the wooden post), **leaving the green cycle track, and follow the yellow signs, to a tarmac rd** (under power cables) **and keep SA on this, back to the car park** at the start/end (353/484).

Extension

+10KM (6.2M) & 120 METRES CLIMBING

1 **Turn R and follow the** (green) **cycle trail signs** (going to the western edge of the forest, then back east, using some of the same tracks), **for 7.2 miles, to a rd** (355/497), **and rejoin the main route at no.12.**

NOTE: This is the 'Green' waymarked cycle trail (of 17km/11m).

Short route

9.7KM (6M) & 30 METRES CLIMBING

1 Follow the 'yellow' cycle trail markers from 'START'.

Family rides

The Yellow and Green cycle trails start at the car park ('START') and can be cycled in either direction. Alternatively you can just ride the forest tracks as you please. All of these options are suitable for families.

NOTE: New tracks do appear over time and signposting is not always obvious. There are some fun unmarked single track trails in the forest to explore.

Getting there This ride starts from the Tangham car park in Rendlesham forest, which costs £1 for the day. Exit the A12 on the A1152, by Woodbridge, through Melton, and follow the Rendlesham forest signs. Bear right on the B1084, for just over 3 miles, then turn right into Rendlesham forest, for 1 mile to the car park (353/484). There is a railway station in Melton.

Accommodation: B&B in the Ship Inn, Blaxhall (nr Tunstall forest) on: 01728 688316, YHA in Blaxhall on: 0870 7705702, campsite in Rendlesham forest (by the car park), on 01394 450707 & Woodbridge TI on : 01394 382240

Refreshments cafe & campsite shop at start, pubs at Butley & Chillesford, tea shop in Butley, campsite shop in Rendlesham forest & a tea shop and two pubs in Snape

Bike shops Thomas's Cycle Revolution on tel: 01473 716 604, and Ranelagh Cycle Warehouse on: 01473 250610 in Ipswich.

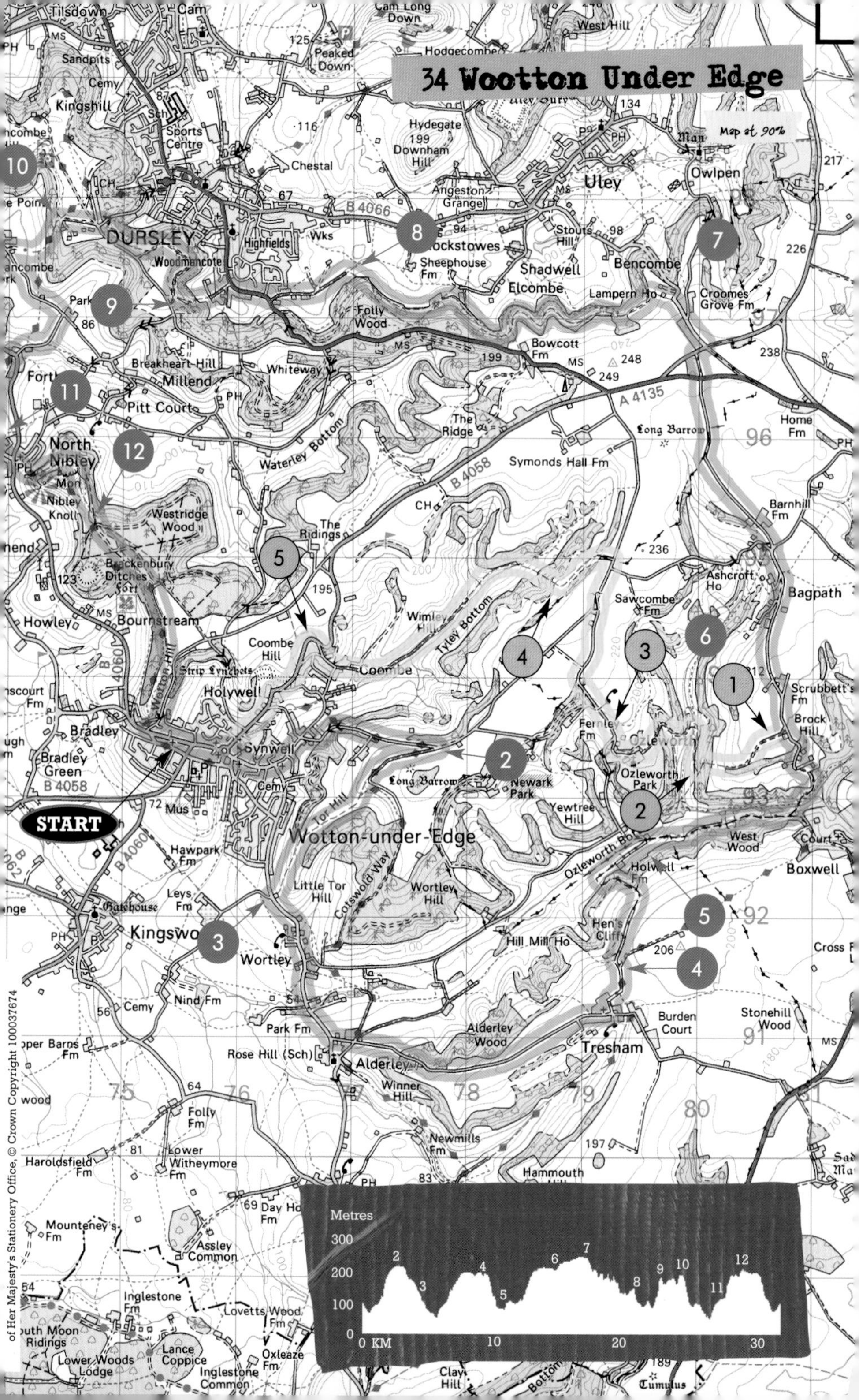

34 Wootton Under Edge
Map at 90%
START
Tilsdown
Cam
Cam Long Down
West Hill
Peaked Down
Hodgecombe
Sandpits
Cemy
Kingshill
Sports Centre
Hydegate
Downham Hill
Chestal
Angeston Grange
Uley
Owlpen
DURSLEY
Woodmancote
Highfields
B 4066
Wks
Stouts Hill
Sheephouse Fm
Shadwell
Bencombe
Elcombe
Lampern Ho
Croomes Grove Fm
Folly Wood
Bowcott Fm
Breakheart Hill
Millend
Whiteway
Pitt Court
A 4135
North Nibley
The Ridge
Waterley Bottom
Long Barrow
Symonds Hall Fm
Home Fm
Nibley Knoll
Westridge Wood
B 4058
Barnhill Fm
The Ridings
Brackenbury Ditches
Howley
Bournstream
Ashcroft Ho
Bagpath
Sawcombe Fm
Wimley Hill
Tyley Bottom
Coombe Hill
Coombe
Strip Lynchets
Holywell
Scrubbett's Fm
Brock Hill
Fernley Fm
Ozleworth
Bradley
Bradley Green
Synwell
Newark Park
Ozleworth Park
Yewtree Hill
Wotton-under-Edge
Tor Hill
Cotswold Way
West Wood
Boxwell
Hawpark Fm
Little Tor Hill
Wortley Hill
Holwell Fm
Kingswo
Leys Fm
Gatehouse
Hen's Cliff
Hill Mill Ho
Wortley
Nind Fm
Cross
Park Fm
Alderley Wood
Burden Court
Stonehill Wood
Rose Hill (Sch)
Alderley
Tresham
Winner Hill
Folly Fm
Newmills Fm
Haroldsfield Fm
Lower Witheymore Fm
Hammouth Hill
Day Ho Fm
Mounteney's Fm
Assley Common
Inglestone Fm
Lovetts Wood Fm
South Moon Ridings
Lower Woods Lodge
Lance Coppice
Inglestone Common
Oxleaze Fm
Clay Hill
Tumulus
Metres
300
200
100
0
0 KM
10
20
30
of Her Majesty's Stationery Office, © Crown Copyright 100037674

Wootton-Under-Edge

31.4KM (19.5M) & 1,060 METRES CLIMBING

START Exit the car park and turn R on Glouster Street, DH, to a roundabout and go SA, 0.45m to an off-set X-rds (766/935) and turn R. UH on this narrow rd for 0.8m then sharp R on a BW (777/934).

2 After 0.4m keep SA through a gate, where the track turns L. Feint track, DH, to/through a gate, through another field and another gate. Into the woods and continue, DH, to a rd (763/922).

3 Turn L on the rd, through Wortley, and keep L as you enter Alderley (768/910) onto a narrow rd and follow this (east) UH. 1.6m to Tresham and turn L on a farm track (793/ 912), which bears R, 0.25m to a fork and keep L.

4 After 0.4m, just before a gate, turn L along the field edge (795/922), DH, into the woods. Track improves and exits the wood, past Holwell fm, and shortly as the rd turns L, keep SA on a dirt track.

5 After 0.8m, in the woods, bear L at the fork (808/929), DH, then steep UH, and join a rd. Head north on this rd for 1.25m to a X-rds or see shortcut.

6 Keep SA for another 1m, to the A4315 rd and go SA to T-J and turn R to a X-rds (801/968). Turn L on this rd for 0.3m, DH, to a sharp RHB and turn L onto a BW (798/972).

7 DH, to a gate and go L on the BW track (795/972) and follow it westwards, through the wood. After around 2m on this (ignoring the 2 BW's on the L), and exit the woods, on a good track) to a T-J (769/974).

8 Turn L & keep SA to the A4135 rd & turn R on this, for 0.25m then L back off it (759/973). Immediately bear R at the fork, UH, and turn R on a BW, just before the rd (755/971), and go through the woods.

9 To a T-J and turn L, then R on another DT just before the rd, and follow this to another rd (748/978). Turn L on this rd, to another rd and go SA, across the edge of a common, DH, into the woods.

10 Turn L, staying on the main track, DH, to a rd (740/976) and turn L on this for 0.5m then turn R on another rd (745/970). DH, to the A4060 & go SA on a BW opposite, UH for 0.45m, to a rd (738/960).

11 Turn L to the main rd in in North Nibley and turn R on this, then immediately L on a BW (741/958), past the pub. Steep UH, to open ground and keep SA into the woods, keeping R at major fork, then L near the edge of the woods.

12 Follow this track bearing R and DH to a rd (757/943) and turn L then immediately R on Adey's Lane. Steep DH, to a T-J and turn R to a roundabout (been here before), and go R, along the main street, back to the car park (756/934).

Shortcut

-9.5KM (-5.9M) & -330 METRES CLIMBING

1 After 0.25m on this rd turn L on a BW track just past a large house (808/936) and go across a field. Keep R at the gates, and go across the next field and into the woods.

2 DH, to a BW fork (800/932) and turn R (north), dropping DH, and go L (west) over the water (800/936). Go UH to the gates into Ozleworth Park Manor House and turn R just before them & follow this track past the ponds and church, to a rd (793/935).

3 Turn R on the rd, and follow this UH, keeping R to a T-J by a radar mast and turn R on this rd for 0.2m then turn L on a BW (792/950). Pass through a gate and keep SA, track fades away, go SA through a field, to a gate, going into the woods.

4 Steep DH, across a field and join a track alongside a stream, on the southern side for about 0.5m then turn R through a gate, over the stream. Join a wide track and follow this to a rd at the end, and keep R, to the B4058 rd (767/943).

5 Turn L on this rd and follow it DH, for 0.8m to a roundabout (759/934) (been here before). Turn R, along the main street and back to the car park on the L just up here (756/934).

Getting there Exit the M5 at junction 14 and go east on the B4509, then left on the B4058, through Charfield, into Wotton-under-Edge. Turn left on Glouster Street to a free car park (signposted), behind the civic centre (756/934). Train station in Dursley.

Accommodation: Royal Oak B&B on 01453 842316, the coffee shop on 01453 843158 & Holly House on 01454 294296 – all in Wotton. YHA in Slimbridge (over the M5) on 0870 7706036. Camping at Canons Court in Bradley Green/Wotton on 01453 843128. Stroud TI on 01453 760960

Refreshments Nothing until North Nibley nr the end. Lots of choice in Wootton though.

Bike shops Severn Cycles in the centre of Dursley on 01453 544866 and Cytek on the outskirts of Stroud on 01453 753330

35 Forest of Dean
Map at 95%
START
Woodside
Nailbridge
The Pludds
Upper Lydbrook
Brierley
Serridge Green
Quarry (dis)
Worrall Hill
Birch Wood
Industrial Estate
Boey's Pike
Sports Centre
Edge Hills
Wysis Way
Bilson Green
Serridge Inclosure
Crabtree Hill
Gloucestershire Way
Sallowvallets Inclosure
FOREST OF DEAN DISTRICT
Stockwell Green
Edge End
New Beechenhurst Inclosure
Hospl
Wimberry Slade
Sculpture Trail
Llama Trekking
Speech House Hotel
Cemy
Arboretum
Speech House Walk
Cannop
Mine Museum
Mine
Ruspidge
Spruce Ride
FOREST OF DEAN
Barnhill Plantation
Saintlow Inclosure
Russell's Inclosure
Cannop Ponds
Air Shaft
Staple-edge Wood
Upper Soudley
New Fancy View
Mallards Pike
The Barracks
Brandrick's Green
Nagshead Plantation
Blakeney Walk
Moseley Green
Blackpool Br
Bradley Hill
Factory
Church Hill
Parkend
Danby Lodge
Blakeneyhill Woods
Ellwood
Air Shaft
Parkend Walk
Little Drybrook
Cockshoot Wood
Parkhill Inclosure
Oakenhill Wood
Yorkley Slade
Yorkley
Mill Hill
Whitecroft
Viney Hill
Pillowell
The Eaves
Yorkley Court
Oldcroft
Hayes
Soilwell
Kidnalls
Bream
The Lyd
Sutton Bottom

The Forest of Dean

VARIOUS

There are a variety of trails to ride in this 27,000 acre forest, from well surfaced wide forest roads, to tight twisty single track. The way marked trails offer a good starting point, but the technical cross country trail isn't very long so you'll probably want to explore the forest further by yourself, or see below.

TOP TIP: The best way to get a guaranteed great ride is to book a guide, who will cater to your requirements, and will cost around £50 for half a day (not a lot if there is a group of you). See www.wyevalleymountainbiking.co.uk or ask at Pedalabikeaway.

FoDCA XC trail

4.5KM (2.8M)

This is a short but sweet flowing single track trail just behind the centre/pedalabikeaway. Its worth riding this course a couple of times, then exploring the unmarked trails further.

NOTE: Head up the hill, past the start of the FoDCA trail, to find some downhill trails. There are also some other good sections of singletrack leading off from around the top here.

Family trails

VARIOUS

Follow the Sustrans cycle route no.42 as far as you wish, or follow any of the following routes that all start at Pedalabikeaway, who have maps etc..

17.7km (11m) Family trail (yellow waymarkers) on good trails, such as disused railways.

8km (5m) Iron Road route (not waymarked), gentle, flat family trail - ask about it in the bike shop.

22.5km (14m) Rally around the forest (blue waymarkers), offering more climbs & descents.

Family activities

STEAM RAILWAY

Dean Forest Railway, runs between Parkend to Lydney (south of the forest), tel: 01594 845840 or see www.deanforestrailway.co.uk.

MINATURE RAILWAY

Perrygrove miniature railway, in Coleford, tel: 01594 834991 or see www.perrygrove.co.uk.

ELTON FARM

Themed mazes, a mountainboard centre and fishing lake at Elton farm (to east of forest), tel: 01452 760795 or see www.eltonfarm-leisure.co.uk.

CLEARWELL CAVES

9 caves going down to 100ft below the ground, www.clearwellcaves.com or tel: 01594 832535.

DICK WHITTINGTON FARM

Countryside centre with play barn, pedal karts, lots of different animals, picnic area, etc. Nr Longhope (north east of forest), see www.dickwhittington.org or tel: 01452 831000.

PUZZLE WOOD

Eerie woodland with in & outdoor play area, cafe, picnic area and ponies. Nr Coleford, tel: 01594 833187 or see www.puzzlewood.net.

GO APE

High rope course, with rope bridges, zip slides, etc. See www.goape.co.uk or tel: 0870 4445562.

SCULPTURE TRAIL

Pick up a leaflet from Beechenhurst Lodge, and follow the blue ringed posts and directional arrows for an impressive 5.6km (3.5m) Sculpture trail walk.

Getting there: M4 over the river Severn on the older bridge (M48) & exit at junction 2. Follow A48, through Chepstow, to Lydney, then head for Dean Forest Railway and stay on the B4234. 1/2 mile past a X-roads with the B4266, turn left to the Pedalabikeaway shop. Railway at Lydney.

Accommodation: Lots of choice; visit www.visit-forestofdean.co.uk and search for something that fits your requirements.

Bike shop: Pedalabikeaway have a bicycle service centre and bike hire, tel: 01594 860065 or see www.pedalabikeaway.co.uk. They also have shower, toilets, bike wash & refreshments.

Refreshments: The Pedalabikeaway café serves hot drinks and snacks during the week and hot food at weekends.

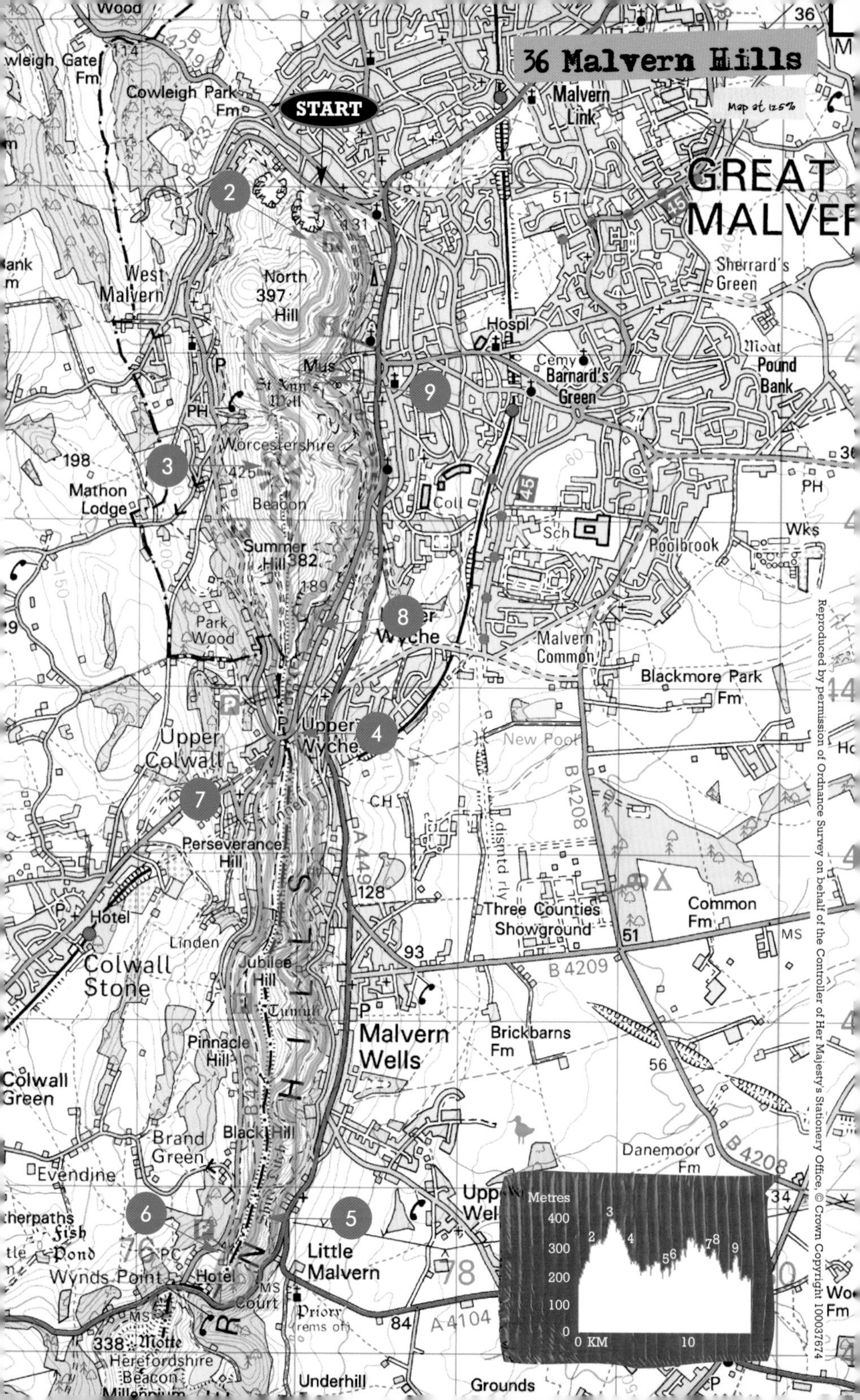
36 Malvern Hills
Map at 125%
START
Malvern Link
GREAT MALVERN
Cowleigh Park Fm
West Malvern
North Hill
397
Sherrard's Green
Hospl
Moat
Pound Bank
Cemy
Barnard's Green
Mus
St Ann's Well
Worcestershire Beacon
425
Mathon Lodge
198
Coll
Sch
Poolbrook
Wks
Summer Hill
382
Park Wood
Malvern Common
Blackmore Park Fm
Upper Wyche
Upper Colwall
New Pool
B 4208
Perseverance Hill
A 449
dismtd rly
Hotel
Colwall Stone
Linden
Jubilee Hill
Three Counties Showground
Common Fm
B 4209
Tumuli
Malvern Wells
Brickbarns Fm
Pinnacle Hill
Colwall Green
Black Hill
Brand Green
Evendine
Danemoor Fm
Fish Pond
Wynds Point
Little Malvern
Court
Priory (rems of)
A 4104
338
Motte
Herefordshire Beacon
Underhill
Grounds
Metres
400
300
200
100
0
0 KM
10

Malvern Hills

14.5KM (9M) & METRES OF CLIMBING

START From the North Quarry car park, head straight up main track at south end of car park. When the track flattens, switchback R onto small path before Ivy Scare Rock, climb up round three switchbacks to join main path.

2 Go L, follow past stone circle and bear L, still on main track, ignore small path on L by bench, continue until next main path on L. Follow to the top of Worcestershire Beacon and turn R on a tarmac rd, then L through gap in rock and follow round L to ridge, then go R.

3 Straight down over tarmac road and to small path on L of ridge, to bottom, straight on take middle path of three, past stone circle. Follow path past car parks to Wyche Cutting, turn L through Cutting then R past house onto main path.

4 Follow until path splits into 3 & take R path, UH, at top go L, DH, and bear L at the bottom. Follow path down, then climb up round side of hill ignore path up on the R by a bench, through a small quarry, straight over at a X-tracks.

5 Follow around the side of hills, when in trees round sharp right hand bend, bear R, up path and switchback R and follow path to top & turn R as trees end.

6 Over ridges and over main path aim for large track on left of ridge path, stay on main path towards ridge, then bear L and head up large track on L of ridge path.

7 Stick to paths on L of ridge to the Wyche Cutting (mind steps), cross road and turn R back up Beacon Road to stone circle and take small path to R signed Quarry Walk and St Annes Well via Earnslaw Quarry.

8 Go down & stay right on small path following concrete wall, when path breaks into clearing & bear R, DH, onto a wider path and follow this. Stay on this main path to St Annes Well, bear L up behind Well and straight over past large path on L.

9 To start of tarmac road on R, go L and then immediately R and follow this path all the way back to North Quarries car park (772/468).

NOTE: This route has kindly been supplied by Back on Track MTB shop, which is very close to the start of the route & full of advice for more riding.

TOP TIP: There are lots of great trails all criss-crossing one another over the hills, making navigation very difficult. If you don't mind not knowing exactly where you are all of the time, we'd recommend just riding around & exploring any (legal) trails you like the look of.

Family Activities

Out to Grass mountain boarding centre (to the west, in Cradley) makes a great day out - see www.outtograss.co.uk or call 01886 880099.

Eastnor Castle (with various different events on through the year) to the south of the hills, on 01531 633160 or www.eastnorcastle.com.

Getting there Just off the M5, south-west of Worcester, we start in the North Quarry (P&D) car park (SO 772/468) at the northern tip of the hills, in Malvern, on the B4232 rd, nr Back on Tracks bike shop.

Bike shops Back on Track on 01684 565777 / www.backontrack-bikes.com is a great bike shop right by the start off the B4232. Unit 2, no.6 North Malvern Rd, WR14 4LT.

Accommodation: YHA on 0870 7705948, campsite at Out To Grass (Mtn board centre) on 01886 880099 / www.outtograss.com & Eastnor castle, on 01531 633160 / www.eastnorcastle.com. For B&B's, etc, see www.malvernhills.gov.uk or call Malvern T.I. on 01684 892289.

Refreshments Lots on choice in the town.

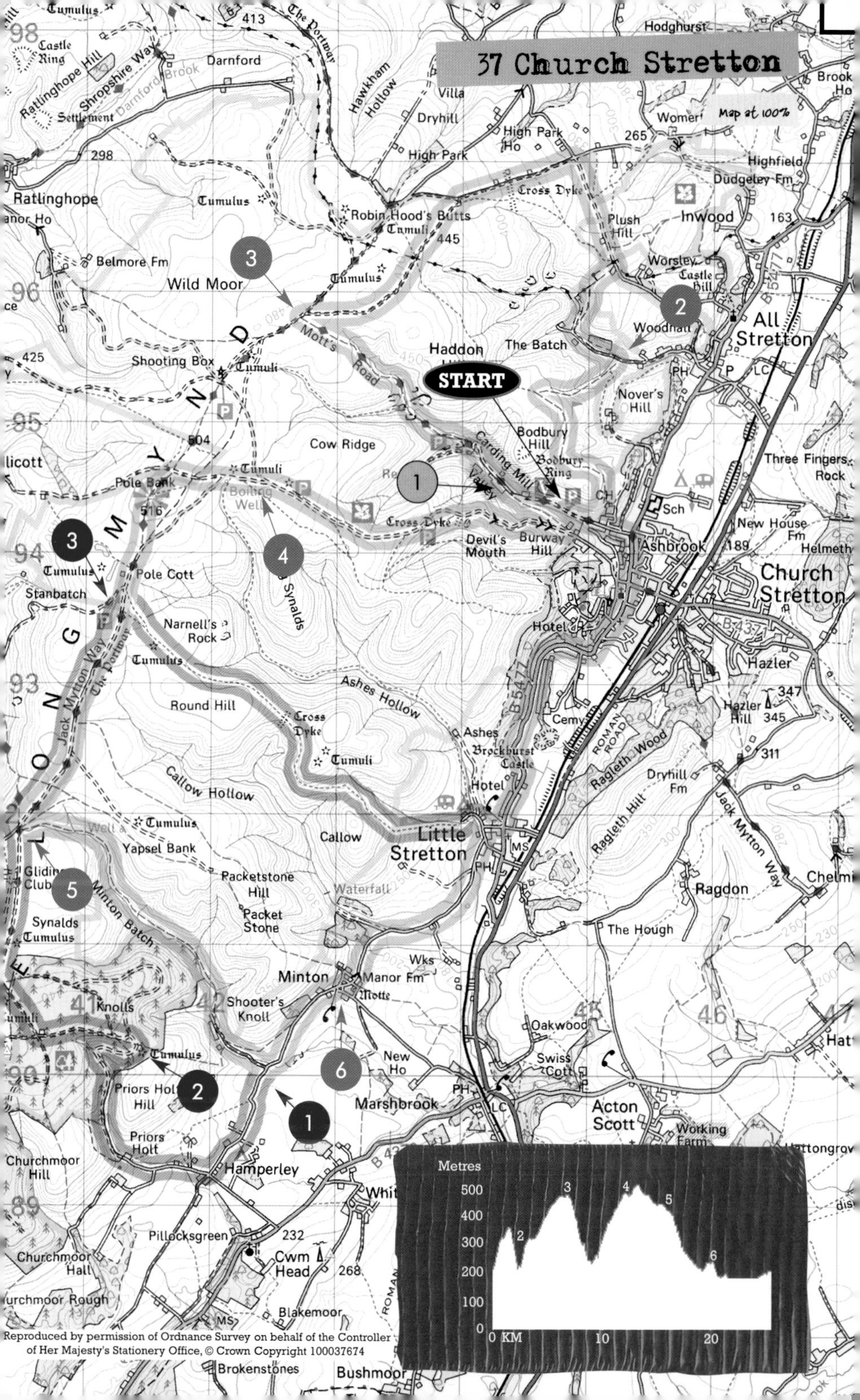
37 Church Stretton
Map at 100%
START
Church Stretton
All Stretton
Little Stretton
Carding Mill Valley
Long Mynd
Pole Bank
Shooting Box
Mott's Road
Wild Moor
Boiling Well
The Synalds
Ashes Hollow
Callow Hollow
Minton Batch
Minton
Marshbrook
Hamperley
Priors Holt Hill
Acton Scott
Ragleth Hill
Hazler Hill
Jack Mytton Way
The Portway
Shropshire Way
Ratlinghope
Robin Hood's Butts
Gliding Club
Metres
500
400
300
200
100
0
KM
10
20

Church Stretton

25.9KM (16.1M) & 990 METRES CLIMBING

START Go left on rd then shortly R off-rd on a ST, UH, keep L, following fence on R & through a gate. To a T-J (SO 451/946) & go L, UH on DT through golf course & R (yellow posts) DH to DT (452/954).

2 Go L on this, then bear R over stream, UH to a rd (452/962) and turn L on this, gradual climb to a X-rds and go L on BW. UH, keep L at fork, bearing slight R, to X-tracks just before a better DT (427/958) and go L on Mott's Rd (BW).

3 Fun descent to Carding Mill Valley and just past the buildings & car park on L, bear R on a BW or see the shortcut. Follow this BW UH to a rd (448/941) and go R on this rd, UH, using the sections of BW along the way if you wish, to a fork in the rd at the top (424/945).

4 Go L at fork, shortly keeping SA off-rd as rd bears L, UH, then L on a track (Jack Mytton Way) to summit of Pole Bank (415/944). Drop down the other side, rejoining the rd and keep SA/R on this to the entrance to the Gliding Club (404/918) and turn sharp L on grassy track.

NOTE: Stanbatch offers a fun, fast DH - use the ROW to Asterton, then UH on rd to Gliding Club.

5 Can be very difficult to find, but you aim for the valley through the heather and bear R. This is a superb ST (BW) descent through Minton Batch valley which you follow all the way to the rd at the bottom (424/900) and turn L or see the extension.

6 Bear L at fork, into Minton and keep SA at the X-rds on the rd to Little Stretton and bear L at T-J (441/917) then R at wide rd junction. 6A At X-rds with B4370 and go L on this, all the way back to Church Stretton and go L back up Carding Mill Valley (453/941) to where you left the car.

Shortcut

-16.3KM (10.1M) & -500 METRES CLIMBING

1 Keep L along the main track, back to where you parked the car (for 9.6km & 490m climb ride).

Extension

+8.4KM (5.2M) & +300 METRES CLIMBING

1 Go R on rd to X-rds in Hamperley by a farm (420/892) & go R on rd, keeping SA UH into the woods, becoming forest track and follow this (not the BW's), wiggling around and keep L at 2 forks in track close to one another (413/902).

2 UH to X-tracks (406/902) and go R, keeping SA through gate and follow SP's over hill to wide track and bear R on this, past Glider Club, through a gate to the rd (top Minton Batch) (404/918). Go R on the rd, to the start of an enclosure on the L & turn R (413/936) on a permissive BW (opposite the Stanbatch track on the R).

3 Go L on wider track & follow the permissive route off to the left, DH to a rd in Little Stretton (441/919) just past campsite. Go L to X-rds with the B5477 & rejoin the main route at 6A.

Getting there: Where the A49 & B4371 cross one another in Church Stretton, go west on the B4371 (Sandford Ave), over railway. At X-rds with B4370/High St, go R on this for 0.5km then left on Carding Mill Valley & park just past last house on left in little layby or further up on right. Also parking (etc) at Blazin Bikes (Marshbrook). Railway in Church Stretton.

Accommodation: See www.blazingbikes.co.uk for camping & pods. If full, lots of choice in Church Stretton. Call tourist information on 01694 723133. YHA Bunkhouse in All Stretton on 01694 722593 & Long Mynd Bridges Youth Hostel on 01588 650656. Small Batch camping in Little Stretton on 01694 723358 www.smallbatch-camping.webeden.co.uk

Refreshments

Blazin Bikes in Marshbrook and lots in Church Stretton.

Bike shops See www.blazingbikes.co.uk a mtb & outdoor centre in Marshbrook (nr Little Stretton), with bike hire, cafe, accommodation, parking, guiding, skills courses & showers.

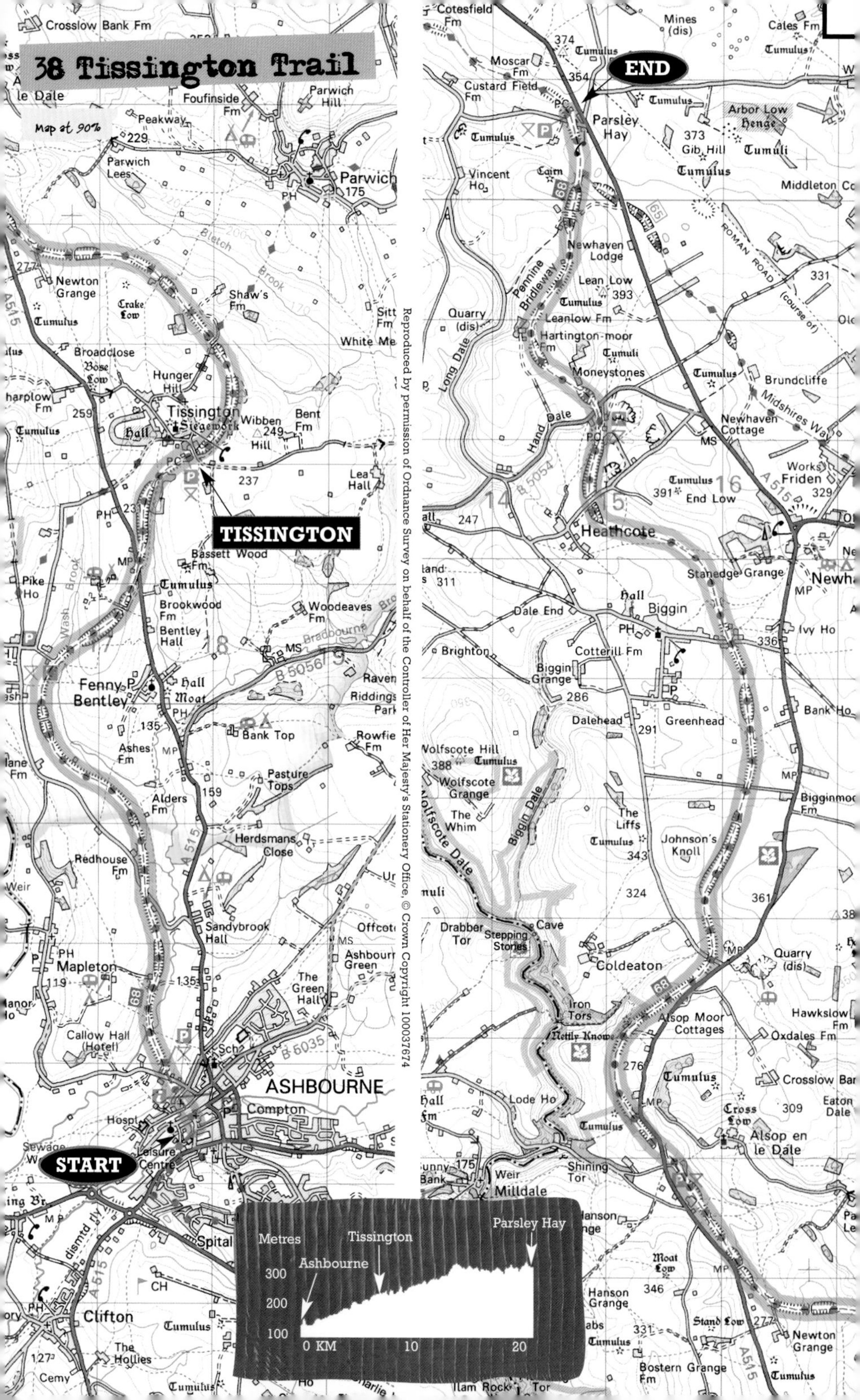
38 Tissington Trail
Map at 90%
START
TISSINGTON
END
ASHBOURNE
Tissington
Parsley Hay
Parwich
Fenny Bentley
Mapleton
Clifton
Biggin
Heathcote
Friden
Alsop en le Dale
Milldale
Coldeaton
Metres
300
200
100
0 KM
10
20
Ashbourne
Tissington
Parsley Hay

Tissington Trail

42KM (26M) & 800 METRES OF CLIMBING

The Tissington Trail was a former railway, between Ashbourne and Buxton, completed in 1899 and closed in 1967. In 1971 it was re-opened as a recreational trail and has been one of the most popular trails of its kind in the UK ever since.

If riding the whole route in both directions, start in Ashbourne, in the car park on station rd (178/465) and head north, through the long (lit) tunnel. This way you climb gradually to Parsley Hay, which means a lovely long descent all the way back.

This is a VERY easy trail to follow and once you are past the incline at the (southern) start, the well surfaced trail is relatively flat and perfect for families. It winds it's way northwards, climbing very gradually, all the way to Parsley Hay, where it meets the High Peak Trail.

TOP TIPS

Starting from Ashbourne means you have gravity on your side for the return jouney.

The village of Tissington is very nice, and offers a great place to get refreshments.

You can link the Tissington Trail with the High Peak Trail at Parsley Hay. This leads to High Peak Junction, just south of Matlock. Please see the High Peak Trail route.

Shorter / family rides

If you don't want to cycle the whole route, here are some suggested sections:

ASHBOURNE TO THORPE

Start from Asbourne (178/465) and cycle 4.5km (2.8m) to the car park at Thorpe (166/503). there is a pub in Thorpe where you can refresh, then head back down the hill to Ashbourne or continue to Tissington.

THORPE TO TISSINGTON

Continue northwards for 2.3km (1.4m) to Tissington (178/521). This is a lovely village where you can find more refreshments before heading back down, southwards, or continuing northwards to Biggin.

TISSINGTON TO BIGGIN

Head north on the Tissington trail for 9.5km (5.9m) to the steps down to the road (west) into Biggin and a pub (152/594). Alternatively continue along the Tissington trail for another 2.5km (1.6m) to a parking & picnic spot, by the B5054, (151/611).

HARTINGTON TO PARSELY HAY

Head north from Hartington, for 3km (1.9m) to Parsley Hay (146/637) where there are refreshments available at the cycle hire.

Getting there: Ashbourne has a number of good roads leading to it. The A517 from Belper, A52 from Derby & Stoke-on-Trent, and the A515 running north to Buxton and south to the A50 and Birmingham. See above for other starting points.

Accommodation: There are a lot of places to stay around this area, so call Ashbourne TI 01335 343666 or Buxton TI 01298 25106. Bassett Wood farm just south of Tissington on 01335 350254 with B&B, camping and caravan site is very nice

Refreshments: Lotsof choice in Ashbourne, pubs in Thorpe, Biggin, Heathcote and refreshments at Parsley Hay cycle centre at the end.

Bike shops: Cycle Hire in Ashbourne 01335 343 156, and in Parsley Hay on 01298 884 493.

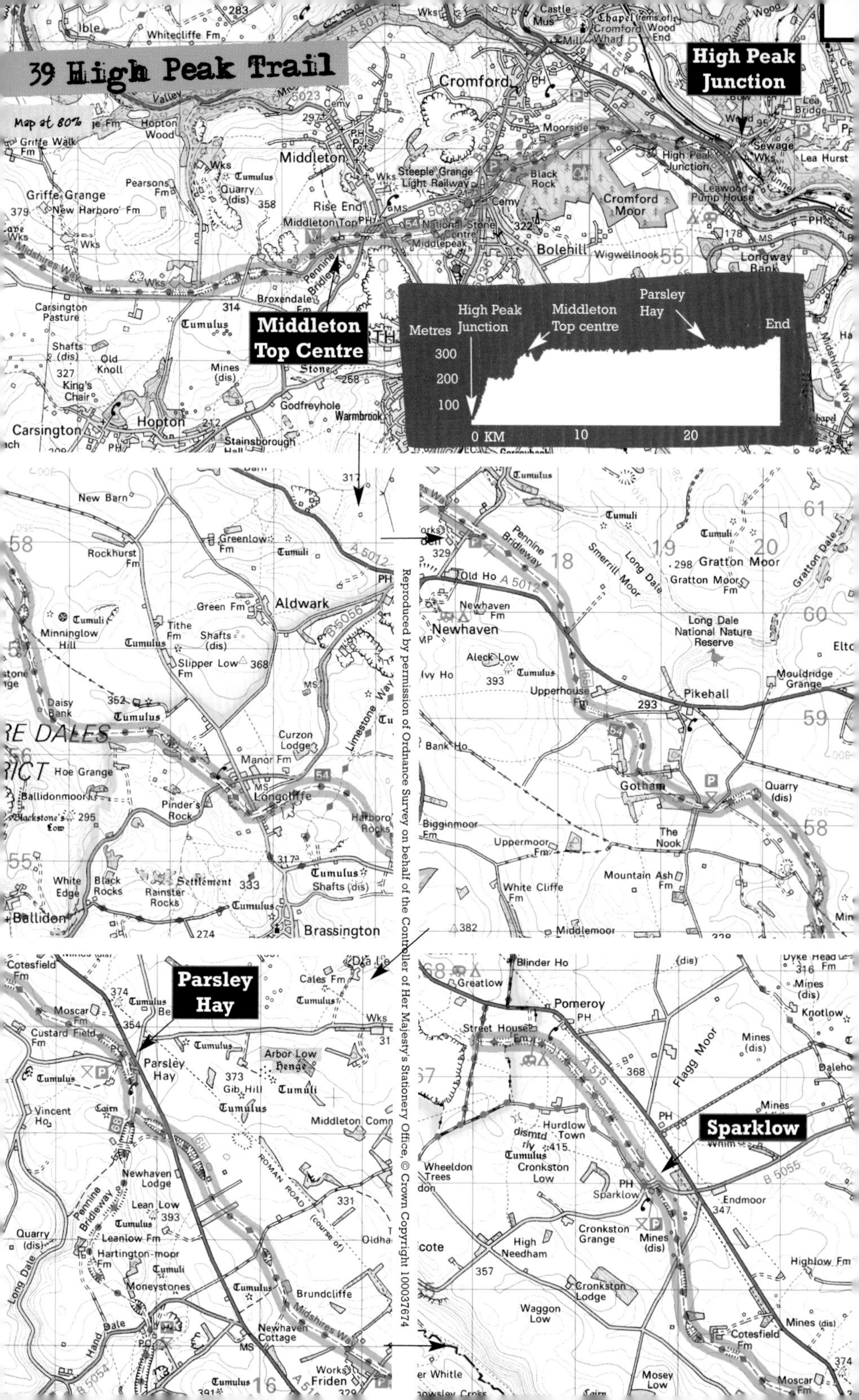
39 High Peak Trail
Map at 80%
High Peak Junction
Middleton Top Centre
Parsley Hay
Sparklow
Metres
300
200
100
0 KM
10
20
High Peak Junction
Middleton Top centre
Parsley Hay
End
Cromford
Middleton
Bolehill
Cromford Moor
Black Rock
Steeple Grange Light Railway
National Stone Centre
Carsington
Hopton
Aldwark
Longcliffe
Brassington
Newhaven
Pikehall
Gotham
Gratton Moor
Long Dale National Nature Reserve
Arbor Low Henge
Gib Hill
Pomeroy
Hurdlow Town
Cronkston Low
Friden
Pennine Bridleway
Midshires Way

High Peak Trail

28KM (17.4M) & 660 METRES OF CLIMBING

The High Peak Trail follows the old Cromford and High Peak railway, which was one of the first to be completed in the country, in 1830. Now converted into a trail for walkers, riders, It runs from the High Peak Junction (315/561) to Dowlow, nr Pomeroy (110/673), 6km (3.7) past Parsley Hay.

Unlike conventional railway routes, this one twists and turns and goes up & down hills along the way. When travelling from the southeast, to the north-west i.e. from High Peak Junction to Parsley Hay the route is mostly going uphill. The section between the High Peak Junction to Middleton involves a big climb on rough terrain, so it is best avoided for family rides.

Middleton Top visitor centre (276/552) is a popular place to start the ride, as it has good facilities and avoids the steep hill from High Peak Junction. You will probably prefer to end/turn around at Parsley Hay or Sparklow where you can get some refreshments, rather than ride to the very end where there is effectively nothing.

NOTE: At the end of the High Peak Trail, you can join Sustrans route no.68 to continue to Buxton.

Carsington Water

Just to the south of the High Peak Trail is Carsington Water, which has a (13km) family friendly cycle path around the perimeter. Start from Carsington Water visitor centre (GR 241/517) www.carsingtonwater.com & bike hire on 01629 540478 and lots of other activities such as sailing, & has a childrens play area.

HIGH PEAK JUNCTION 4.4KM to MIDDLETON TOP VISITOR CENTRE

High Peak Junction (315/561) has toilets, a picnic site and a car park (off the Cromford to Holloway road). There is also railway workshops & memorabilia, a visitor centre and shop selling books, maps, gifts and refreshments. Just 4.4km (2.7m) but 255 metres of climbing, with some rough surfaces make this a tough start to the ride. See below for the facilities available at Middleton Top visitor centre.

MIDDLETON TOP TO PARSELY HAY 18.3KM

The visitor centre (276/552) provides a car park, toilets, cycle hire, picnic site, information, maps, walk leaflets, books, gifts, refreshments and the story of the High Peak Railway, There is also a steam winding engine, built in 1892, to pull wagons up and down the hill, which can be seen running on the first weekend of the month in the summer & bank holidays (sadly not to pull you up though). After some initial climbing, and passing through a short dark tunnel, this is the flattest section of the trail, providing wonderful changing views as you wind your way to Parsley Hay, some 18.3km (11.4m) and 310 metres climbing, away.

PARSELY HAY TO SPARKLOW 3.3KM

This short 3.3km (2m) flat section of the trail provides a nice gentle family ride between the cycle hire centre (with refreshments) at Parsely Hay (146/636) to the pub in Sparklow (126/660).

NOTE: Another 2.5km (1.6m) past Sparklow will get you to the end of the trail (110/673).

Getting there: There is parking available at High Peak Junction, Middleton Top visitor centre and (pay& display) at Parsely Hay, as well as some other car parks along the trail.

Accommodation: Lots of places to choose from, so call Matlock T.I. on 01629 55082 or Buxton T.I. on 01298 25106. There is a campsite at the end of the trail in Pomeroy, tel: 01298 83259 and a good pub just down the road.

Refreshments: cafe at Middleton Top visitor centre and a pub in middleton, refreshments at Parsley Hay, and a pub in Sparklow.

Bike shops: cycle Hire is available at Middleton Top cycle Hire centre, tel: 01629 823 204 and at Parsley Hay, tel: 01298 84493.

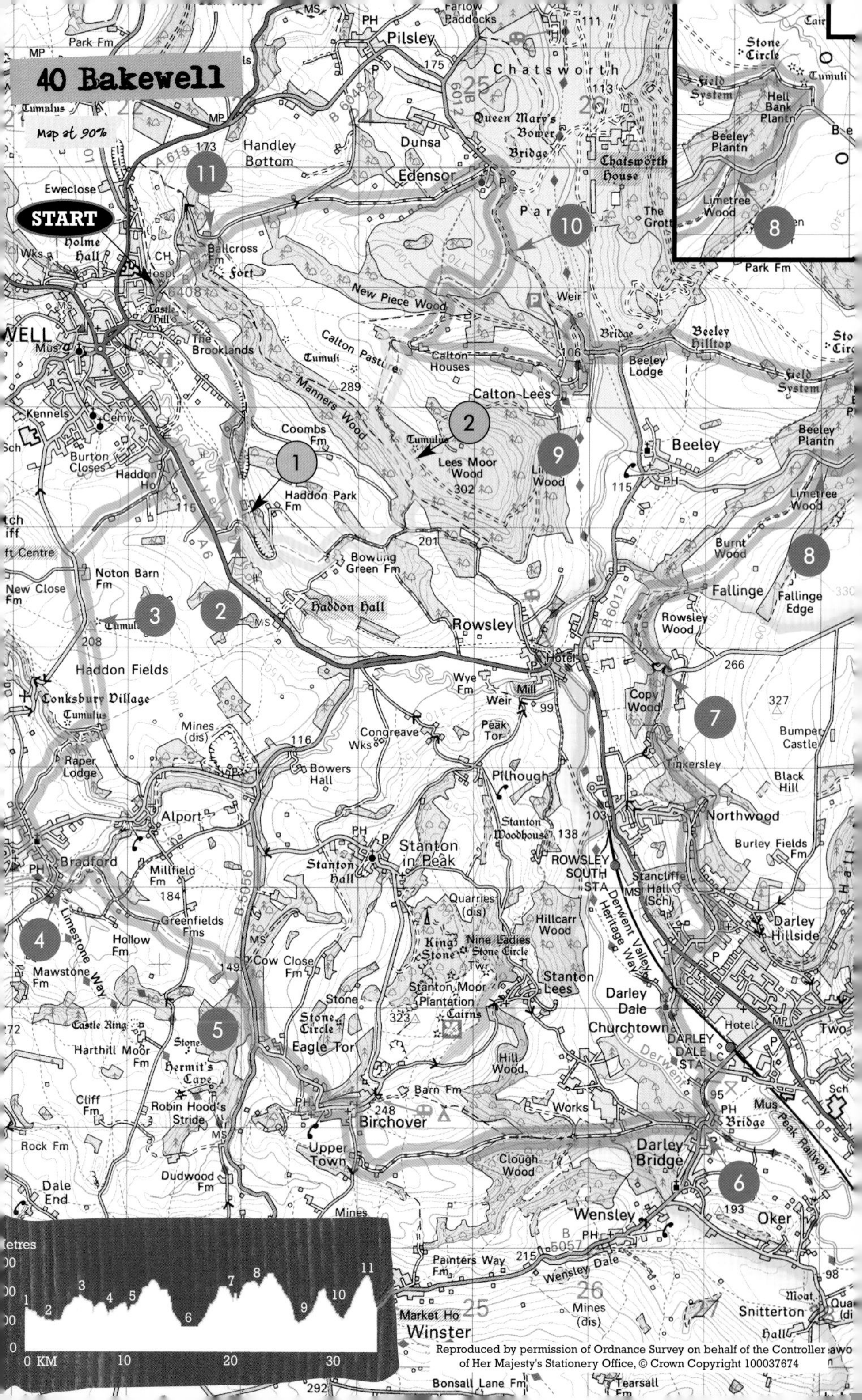
40 Bakewell
Map at 90%
START
Pilsley
Chatsworth
Queen Mary's Bower
Bridge
Chatsworth House
Dunsa
Edensor
Handley Bottom
Eweclose
Holme Hall
Ballcross Fm
Fort
Castle Hill
The Brooklands
New Piece Wood
Calton Pastures
Calton Houses
Tumuli
Manners Wood
Calton Lees
Coombs Fm
Lees Moor Wood
Haddon Park Fm
Kennels
Burton Closes
Haddon Ho
Noton Barn Fm
New Close Fm
Bowling Green Fm
Haddon Hall
Rowsley
Beeley
Beeley Lodge
Beeley Hilltop
Field System
Beeley Plantn
Limetree Wood
Burnt Wood
Fallinge
Fallinge Edge
Rowsley Wood
Copy Wood
Bumper Castle
Haddon Fields
Conksbury Village
Raper Lodge
Mines (dis)
Wye Fm
Weir
Mill
Congreave
Peak Tor
Bowers Hall
Pilhough
Tinkersley
Northwood
Black Hill
Alport
Bradford
Millfield Fm
Greenfields Fms
Stanton in Peak
Stanton Hall
Stanton Woodhouse
Rowsley South Sta
Derwent Valley Heritage Way
Stancliffe Hall (Sch)
Darley Hillside
Burley Fields Fm
Limestone Way
Hollow Fm
Mawstone Fm
Cow Close Fm
Quarries (dis)
King Stone
Nine Ladies Stone Circle
Hillcarr Wood
Stanton Moor Plantation
Cairns
Stanton Lees
Darley Dale
Churchtown
Darley Dale Sta
Castle Ring
Harthill Moor Fm
Hermit's Cave
Robin Hood's Stride
Stone Circle
Eagle Tor
Hill Wood
Barn Fm
Works
Cliff Fm
Birchover
Upper Town
Clough Wood
Darley Bridge
Rock Fm
Dudwood Fm
Dale End
Wensley
Oker
Peak Railway
Painters Way Fm
Wensley Dale
Market Ho
Winster
Snitterton
Hall
Stone Circle
Hell Bank Plantn
Tumuli
Beeley Plantn
Limetree Wood
Park Fm
Metres
0 KM
10
20
30
Reproduced by permission of Ordnance Survey on behalf of the Controller of Her Majesty's Stationery Office, © Crown Copyright 100037674

Bakewell

34KM (21.1M) & 1,040 METRES OF CLIMBING

START Exit the car park at the far corner by the old station building, to the Monsal trail and go R (south east) on this, passing under a bridge. Follow this for 1.3km, to the end of the trail, dropping down to the field towards the river and follow the BW along the bottom of the valley to a track/rd (229/670).

2 Go R or see the shortcut. To the A6, and go R on this for 0.8km then L on Intake lane (just before entering Bakewell). Follow this, keeping SA, through a field to a rd and go L on this for 0.5km then keep SA through a gate on a BW, as the rd bears R (216/661).

3 SA on RHS (muddy DT), just before old trees by the farm buildings, turn R through a gate, along the edge of the field and follow the BW into the trees, DH, to cross the bridge at the bottom (214/651). Go UH to rd and go L to a X-rds in Youlgreave (by church), and go SA, DH, looking out for BW SA/L as rd bears R.

4 Cross the bridge and go L by the river then shortly bearing R (away from river), UH, SA at X-tracks, then as track bears L, go SA/R by Greenfeilds fm. Cross the fields, through gates, keep SA at a minor rd, DH, over the bridge/river and up to the B5056 rd (230/632).

5 Go R on this rd then 1st L on rd (SP Birchover), UH, into the village and go R (after the shop) on Upper Town lane. after 0.4km turn L on Clough lane and follow this, to X-tracks and go SA (R then L) DH on rough track. Keep SA/R as rd joins from L, DH to T-J with B5057 rd in Darley Bridge (269/620).

6 Turn L, over the river, 0.4km to a X-rds and go L (Church rd), and follow this, over railway, to the A6. Go R then first L (Whitworth rd) and follow this rd, bearing (and keeping) L, for 1.3km then fork R on Lumb lane (just after Bent lane). UH to BW on L, through the woods, and keep SA, to a rd (266/658).

7 Turn L on the rd, DH around bends and turn R on the on the BW track (just after a house). 7A UH for 0.2km and follow the BW to the L. Go DH into the woods, then UH, over a bridge and turn sharp R, UH, through gate into a field, and follow the track past the buildings, UH to a rd (279/675).

8 Turn R on the rd for 1km, then as rd bears R, go L on a DT (at end of woods) and follow this around edge of woods, DH, becoming tarmac past Beeley Hilltop, to the B6012 rd (262/684). Turn R on this rd, over the bridge and go into the car park here, out the south end of it.

9 Bears R to off set X-rds, keep SA (SA/R at grass triangle and L at fork), UH on this (BW) track for 1.2km Zig-zag past some buildings, to small woods and bear R (north) on a BW. **9A** Across a field, into the wood, keeping SA where the tracks merge, down through the park, towards a small clump of trees. Follow the SP, turning R just before the trees, to the rd (252/692

10 Turn L on the rd, then shortly after the rd bears R go L on a BW (basically cutting the corner), back to rd and very shortly L (SP Edensor tea room) (251/699). Keep SA UH on this rd, all the way to the rd at the top, and go SA/L on this, UH.

11 Just after rd starts to descend and before it bears R, go SA/L on BW (just after a farm track), (227/693) for fun, steep DH through the trees. Emerge from trees, across the gold course and back down to the Monsal trail, and turn R on this, back under the bridge and L, to the car park (222/690).

Shortcut

-22.2KM (13.8M) & 620 METRES CLIMBING

1 Bear L up the rd, over the tunnel entrance, and shortly R through a gate into a field on a BW (232/668). To a good track and go R for 1km (0.6m), ignore a track on R, to a X-rds (244/670). Go SA up the dirt ST into the wood (hard climb), to the top.

2 Shortly bear R, UH again, levelling off again for twisty ST, to a gate. Go through the double gates, DH, to a wood and a gate and go R (not SA), then bear L at the BW fork.) & rejoin main route at 9A.

Family

The family friendly Monsal Trail cycle track is perfect for families, as it offers a good flat surface away from the traffic. The trail starts from (just east of) Bakewell, and passes the start of the ride, heading north, then west, for about 4km to Great Longstone. After a refreshment stop return along the same track, back to Bakewell (and the obligatory Bakewell tart at a cafe).

Getting there Take A619 over the stone bridge / river Wye, as rd bears L & after bridge got right on B6408 (Industrial estate). The Monsal trail car park is on the left after 0.4km (SK 222/690). Train: to Matlock & cycle 3.5km from Darley Dale along the A6 or back roads via Upper Hackney).

Accommodation There are a few places, check out www.visitderbyshire.co.uk (accommodation tab). YHA in Bakewell on 0870 042 9290 and Greenhills holiday park in Ashford in the Water, just outside Bakewell, on 01629 813467.

Refreshments Lots in Bakewell, pubs & local village shops in the first half, and Edensor tea room shortly before the final climb.

Bike shop Bespoked in Bakewell on 01629 815076

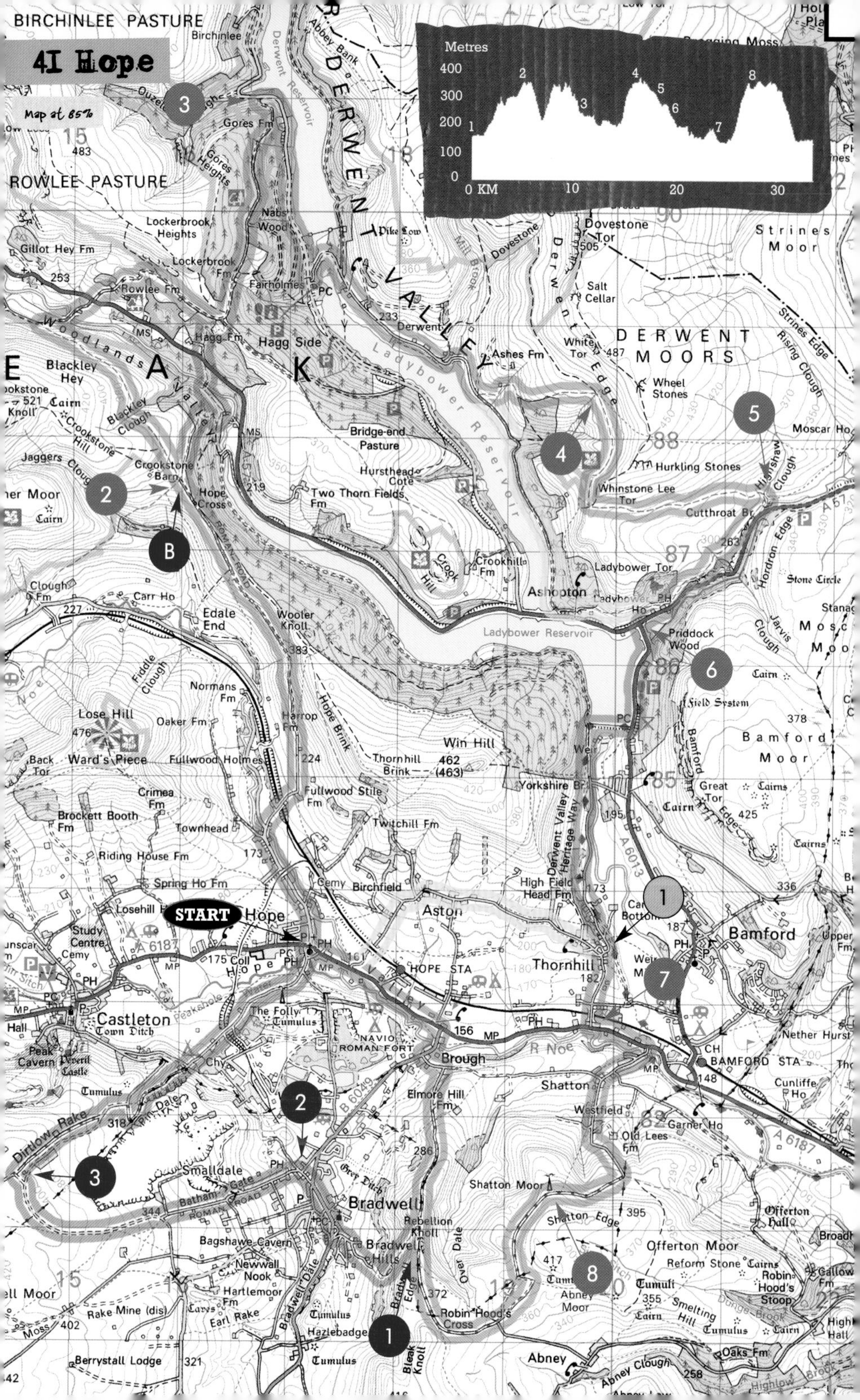
41 Hope
Map at 85%
Metres
400
300
200
100
0
0 KM
10
20
30
BIRCHINLEE PASTURE
ROWLEE PASTURE
DERWENT VALLEY
DERWENT MOORS
Derwent Reservoir
Ladybower Reservoir
Birchinlee
Abbey Bank
Gores Fm
Gores Heights
Lockerbrook Heights
Lockerbrook Fm
Nabs Wood
Gillot Hey Fm
Rowlee Fm
Fairholmes
Hagg Fm
Hagg Side
Pike Low
Derwent
Ashes Fm
Dovestone Tor
Salt Cellar
White Tor
Wheel Stones
Hurkling Stones
Whinstone Lee Tor
Cutthroat Br
Strines Moor
Strines Edge
Moscar Ho
Highshaw Clough
Woodlands Valley
Blackley Hey
Crookstone Knoll
Crookstone Hill
Crookstone Barn
Jaggers Clough
Hope Cross
Bridge-end Pasture
Hursthead Cote
Two Thorn Fields Fm
Crook Hill
Crookhill Fm
Ladybower Tor
Ashopton
Ladybower PH
Priddock Wood
Field System
Bamford Moor
Bamford Edge
Great Tor
Stone Circle
Hordron Edge
Jarvis Clough
Clough Fm
Carr Ho
Edale End
Wooler Knoll
Fiddle Clough
Normans Fm
Lose Hill
Oaker Fm
Harrop Fm
Hope Brink
Win Hill
Thornhill Brink
Back Tor
Ward's Piece
Fullwood Holmes
Fullwood Stile Fm
Twitchill Fm
Yorkshire Br
Derwent Valley Heritage Way
Crimea Fm
Brockett Booth Fm
Townhead
Riding House Fm
Spring Ho Fm
Birchfield
High Field Head Fm
Losehill Hall
Study Centre
START
Hope
Aston
Thornhill
Bamford
HOPE STA
BAMFORD STA
Castleton
Town Ditch
Peak Cavern
Peveril Castle
The Folly
Tumulus
NAVIO ROMAN FORT
Brough
R Noe
Shatton
Westfield
Garner Ho
Old Lees Fm
Nether Hurst
Cunliffe Ho
Dirtlow Rake
Pin Dale
Smalldale
Batham Gate
ROMAN ROAD
Elmore Hill Fm
Grey Ditch
Bradwell
Rebellion Knoll
Bradwell Hills
Bagshawe Cavern
Newwall Nook
Hartlemoor Fm
Rake Mine (dis)
Earl Rake
Bradwell Dale
Bradwell Edge
Hazlebadge
Bleak Knoll
Berrystall Lodge
Over Dale
Shatton Moor
Shatton Edge
Offerton Moor
Offerton Hall
Reform Stone
Abney Moor
Robin Hood's Cross
Robin Hood's Stoop
Smelting Hill
Abney
Abney Clough
Oaks Fm
Highlow Brook
START

Hope

33.8 KM (21M) & 1,220 METRES CLIMBING

START Head north on Edale rd (by the pub) (SK172/835), cross a bridge / river & keep SA as rd bears L, on Fullwood Stile Lane, UH. Keep L & through gate onto a rocky track, UH, to top. Keep SA through gates, to BW X-tracks (159/876) and go SA on Blackley Hey or see 'The Beast' below.

B The Beast - Go R, through gates, into the woods on a VERY rocky DH. Follow it to bottom, bear R over bridge then UH to the A57. Go SA (walk) UH past Hagg fm or L on A57 to rejoin the main route.

2 Rocky DH, to a lane and turn R to the A57 and go SA, UH on a lane, past Rowlee fm. Through couple of gates, to X-tracks at the top (163/890), and go SA/L (& SA for extension riders coming past Hagg farm) for rocky DH, past Lockerbrook fm, to rd by the reservoir (166/910).

3 Turn R on the rd, for 1.85km, then go L at mini-roundabout by/before Fairholmes car park, past the Dam and follow rd to the R. After 1.85km turn L on a BW, SP Derwent Edge (187/883). UH on flagstone track, bearing R at hut by the gates.

4 Keep wall on R, steep rocky UH, to another gate and keep SA on track (open ground) to a gate and bear R along track on side of the hill. At the pass, nr Winstone Tor, keep SA (bearing L) on ST, opening out & getting rocky, DH (197/ 874). Watch out for the boggy section at bottom (213/875).

5 Join alongside a fence, trail bears L then R, to a (ST) fork and keep R (nr rd). Through gate & keep L at the fork, down to the pub & rd. Go R on the rd, then shortly L at lights, on the A6013 (202/863).

6 After 1km turn R (walk) over dam wall (201/ 854), then at end of this turn L and look for a permitted BW after 0.25km on the R. Keep SA on this to a rd & go R on this. Keep L in thornhill (by phonebox) (198/834) or R on rd for the shortcut.

7 Turn L on the A6187 for 0.55km then cross on Stratton lane, through Shatton, then long UH, becoming hardpack surface. Past the mast, where trail levels out.

8 Keep L at T-J on BW, bearing to R, past rd on L, and keep SA for fast rocky DT, becoming tarmac near the bottom. Keep L into Brough and go R to the A6187 and go L on this, into Hope (172/835).

Shortcut

-6.1KM (3.8M) & 260 METRES CLIMBING

1 Follow rd to Aston & keep SA, DH, under railway bridge to A6187 and R to Hope (172/835).

Extension

+5.3KM (3.3M) & 250 METRES CLIMBING

1 As good track starts to descend, look for (easy to miss) gate/BW on L and go through this. Head R on a small track across the field to/through a gate and keep R along the wall. Bear L, steep DH, through gate, joining tarmac to Bradwell. Keep R and turn R on the B6049, through village, after the lights fork L on Town lane, UH.

2 Keep SA then go L on a track as rd starts to descend, and go L at X-rds, on the main track to a gate by X-rds. Go through the small gate on R, along wall, to gateway and bear R on feint track over a feild, through a gate and keep SA (nice track on RHS of track) to a gate.

3 Technical rocky section, then fast open section, before more rocks, though a gate to a rd. Turn R (Pindale rd), keepng R at fork, UH, and look for the (Pin Dale) track on the L. Rough rocky DH to rd and keep SA, back to Hope (172/835).

Getting there: In the heart of the Dark Peak, Hope is on the A6187, just south of Ladybower reservoir, which is on the A57 between Glossop & Sheffield. Train station in Hope.

Accommodation: The woodbine B&B (and cafe) in Hope is excellent and very bike friendly, tel: 01433 621407 & a YHA in Castleton on 01433 621767. There are lots more places; call Castleton TI on 01433 620679.

Refreshments: The woodbine cafe (& others) in Hope, fairholmes visitor centre by the reservoirs, pub nr Ashopton, and in Bampton.

Bike shop: 18 Bikes in Hope, tel: 01433 621111 & basic spares at the Fairholmes bike hire.

42 Ladybower – Cut Gate

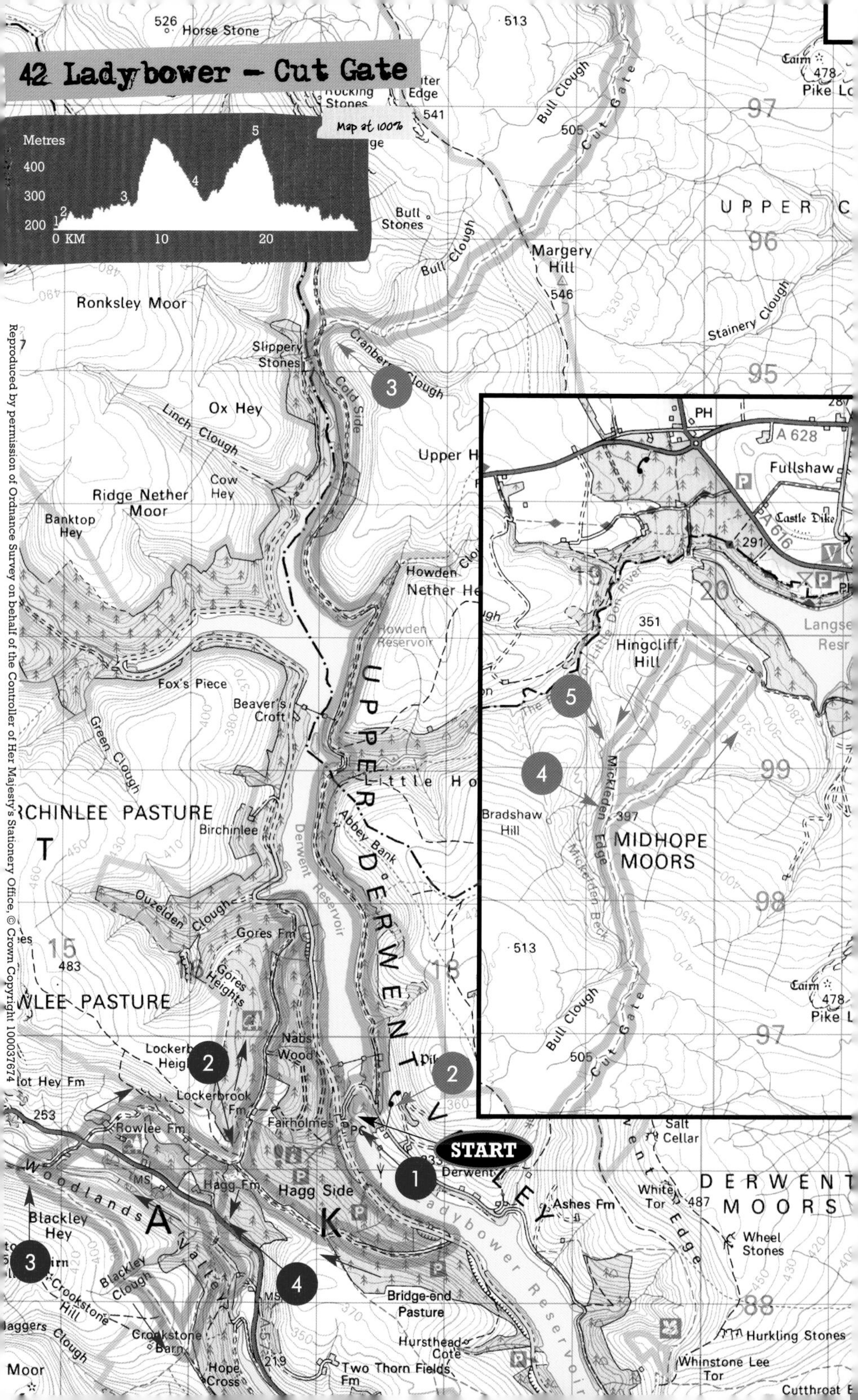

Ladybower

28.2KM (17.5M) & 1,015 METRES CLIMBING

START Exit Fairholmes car park and go R then R again at mini roundabout (172/893) (2nd exit, through gate), past the Derwent dam wall. UH, bearing R, to a T-J (174/894) and turn L on a BW (SP Slippery Stones) through a gate, off-rd, along the edge of the reservoir.

2 Towards the end of reservoir the track bears R into moors, then DH near Slippery Stones (169/951). Keep SA (SP Langsett), across the stream and shorlty R at fork, on LHS of stream.

3 Over another stream, keep R (FP only L), up the steep zig-zags UH, becoming more rideable later. Followed by some nice ST, then flagstones and UH to Howden Edge. Some nice changable terrain, with stony ST, for total of 3km, then bear R (SP Langsett & Penistone) (192/986).

4 ST, DH, joining alongside a wall (on L), SA, to T-J at the bottom, by a gate (to ruins). Turn L through the gate and past the ruins of North America farm, and up to a T-J and go L (R goes DH), ST followed by short DH then UH, becoming a better stone track (Cut Gate).

5 Retrace your wheels tracks back across the moor and enjoy the descent from Howden Edge, taking care on the DH through Cranberry Clough, and follow the BW back to Slippery Stones (169/951). Now follow the (same) reservoir side track, back to the visitor centre (172/893).

NOTE: This is a pretty remote ride, which leaves you exposed, so go prepaired. The Cut Gate path over the moors also suffers in wet weather so avoid it anytime soon after it has been raining. Not only will it make the ride more enjoyable (and doable) but it will stop the trail getting damaged.

TOP TIP: The extension on its own, makes a great technical ride, with some of the Peaks best technical trails. It may be short, but it packs a punch.

Extension

+15KM (9.3M) & 650 METRES CLIMBING

1 From Fairholmes, head south on the rd for 1.4km, then turn R on a BW, just past parking area, (180/884) before cattle grid. UH on loose gravel-becoming better, to top and go R across the top, through a gate to a X-tracks (163/890).

2 Turn L through a gate, superb steep stoney DH, through 2 gates, to the (busy) A57 (161/887). Turn R on this rd for 1.15km then turn L on a track (151/892) over 2 bridges and turn L on a BW track just along here (147/889).

3 Follow this track across Blackley Hey, past Blackley Clough, to a X-tracks (159/876) and turn L. Go through a gate at edge of woods, for start of 'The Beast', a very rocky DH, keeping L (north) at the bottom, on BW to the A57 again.

4 Go L on the rd for 1.15km again and turn R on track to/past past Rowlee fm (or go SA to walk back up past Hagg fm). Back at X-rds (164/890), head north, past Lockerbrook fm for fast DH, to rd by the reservoir. Turn R on this rd and follow it back to Fairholmes / end (172/893).

Family ride

16KM (10M) & 200 METRES OF CLIMBING

You can do a loop of the reservoir by continuing along the road at the northern tip of the reservoir, by the Slipery Stones. This is a nice quiet road, that leads you all the way back to the start.

OTHER ACTIVITIES

There are some nice walks around the area for non-cyclists, as well as the impressive dam to admire, and the cafe at the visitors centre to eat cake in. The visitor centre also has exhibitions for all ages and cycle hire (see below for more details).

Getting there: Ladybower reservoir visitor centre is just off the A57, which runs between Glossop/Manchester & Sheffield. Follow the signs to Fairholmes visitor centre, where the rd crosses the reservoir, by Ashopton.

Accommodation: The Woodbine Café & B&B in Hope is very good, tel: 07778 113 882 or see www.woodbine-hope.co.uk, YHA's in Castleton on 0870 7705758 and another in on Edale 0870 7705808. For more choices call Fairholmes T.I. on 01433 650953.

Bike shops: cycle hire at Fairholmes visitor centre has basic spares, tel 01433 651261 or 18 bikes, in Hope is very good, tel; 01433 621111.

Refreshments: only at the visitor centre at the start/end, but it is good.

43 Mary Townley Loop

Map at 70%

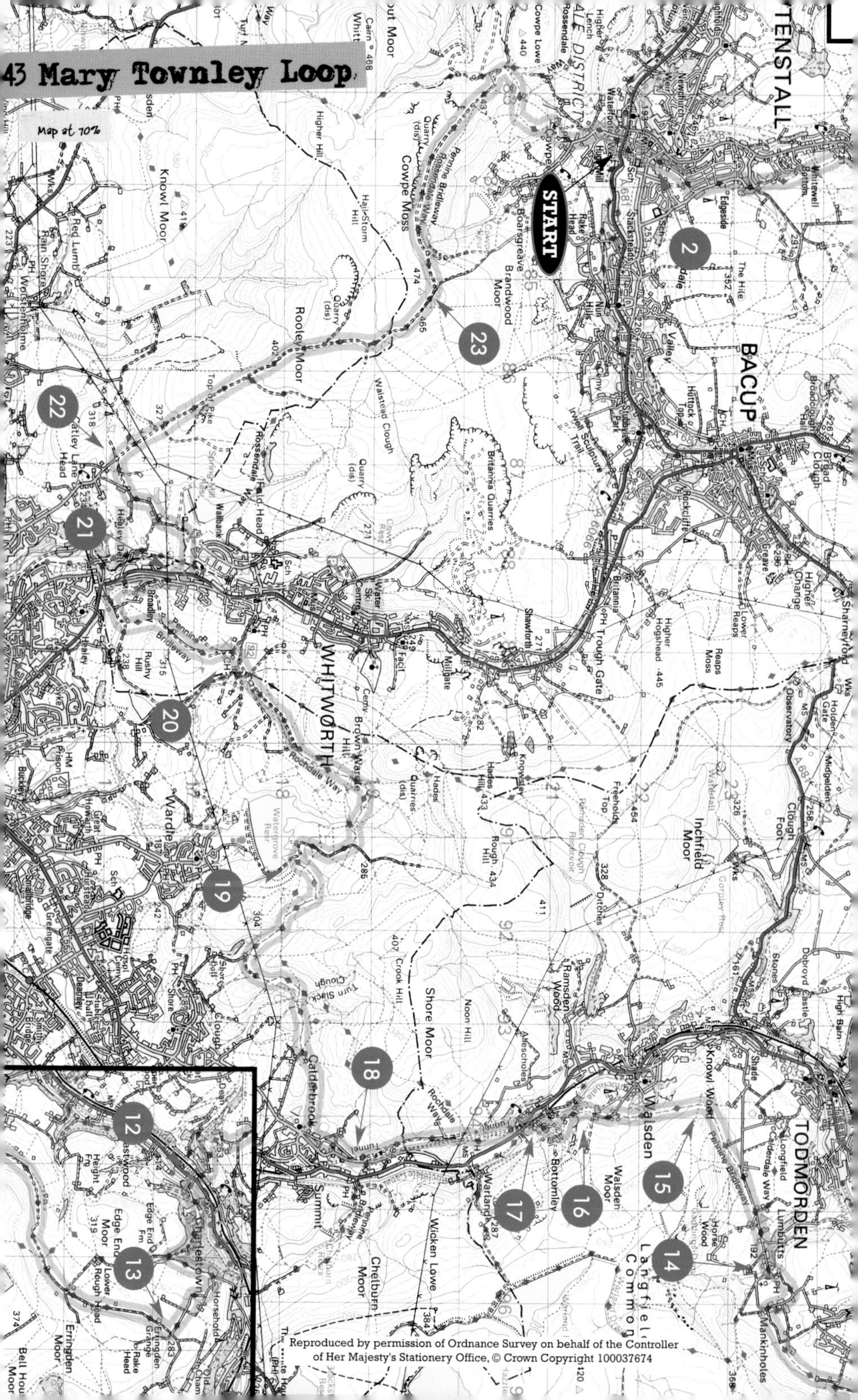

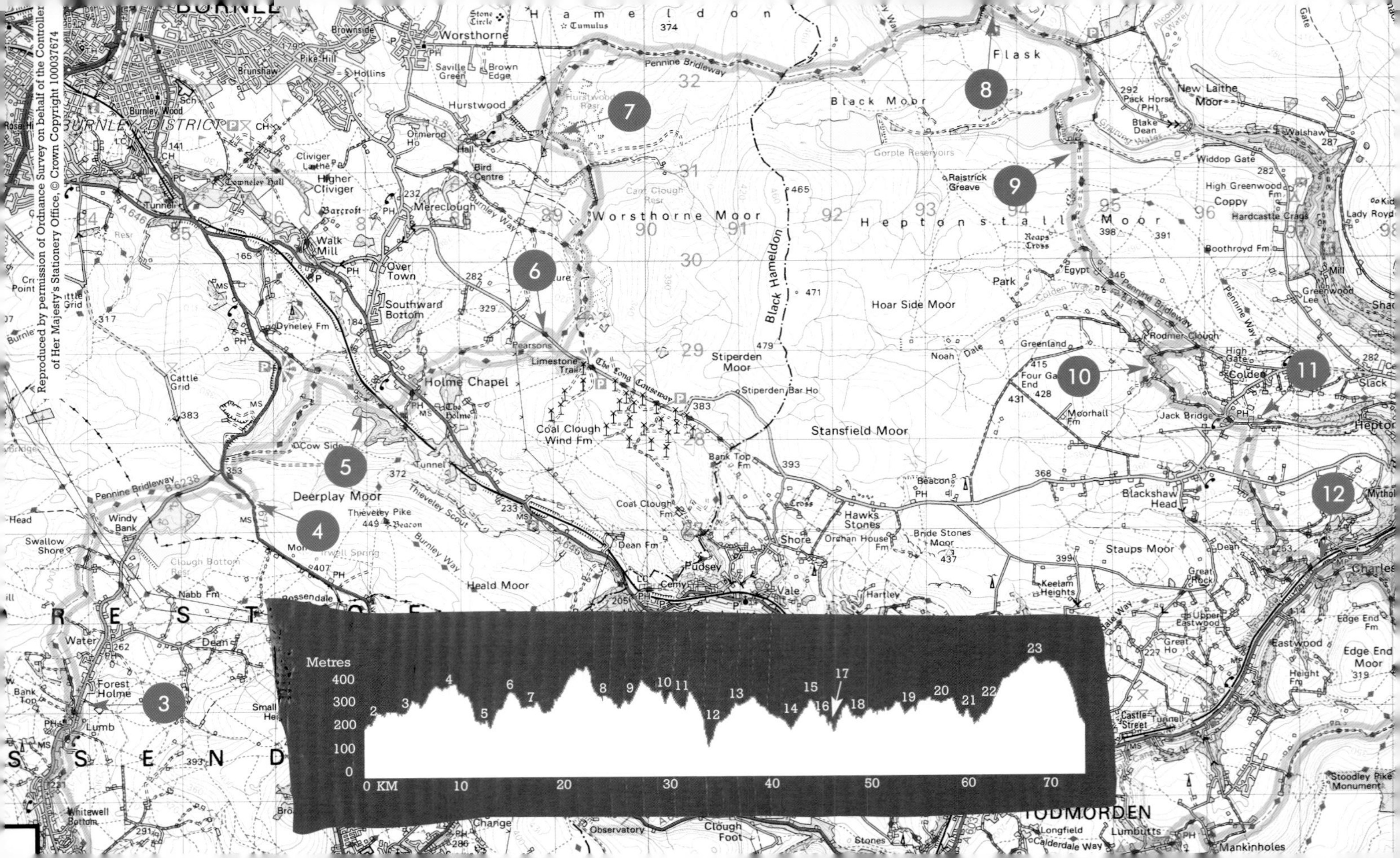

Metres
400
300
200
100
0
0 KM
10
20
30
40
50
60
70
Deerplay Moor
Thieveley Pike
Holme Chapel
Coal Clough Wind Fm
Worsthorne Moor
Black Hameldon
Stiperden Moor
Stansfield Moor
Hoar Side Moor
Heptonstall Moor
Black Moor
Hurstwood
Worsthorne
Walk Mill
Higher Cliviger
Todmorden
Heald Moor
Staups Moor
Blackshaw Head
Colden
Pennine Bridleway
Pennine Way
Burnley Way
Calderdale Way
Gorple Reservoirs
Widdop Gate
New Laithe Moor
Lumbutts
Mankinholes
Stoodley Pike Monument
Edge End Moor
Jack Bridge
Hawks Stones
Bride Stones Moor
Keelam Heights
Clough Foot
Pudsey
Shore
Flask

Mary Townley Loop

74KM (46M) & 2,270 METRES CLIMBING

START Waterfoot is 3km east of Rawtenstall along the A681, go L/north by the Pegasus (rd crossing designed with horses in mind) on Townsend St. Keep SA on this, past a school, to a T-J & go L then R on Todd Carr rd (838/224).

2 At end & bear R alongside the park (Prospect st), then Wales rd, bearing L to Edgeside lane () & go L on this, coming to a X-rds & go SA on Lumb lane. Becomes BW & on to B6238 & go R on this then L, UH on Peers Clough rd (838/250).

3 Go through a gate past last fm, on a BW to 5 gates, take last on R, DH through field, through couple gates, then another over fm track, through field. DH over stream, L cross farm rds, to gate by tree & continue UH over farm track then R at the end to B6238. Cross rd & follow the BW L, parallel to rd, bearing R then L to A671 (857/273).

4 Cross rd & go L parallel to it, through gate SA, to the end of the track and go R on 2nd track (SP Holme Chapel) (864/287). Follow trail as it bears to L of the fm, past fm & keep SA through gate into field as fm track bears L. DH to bottom & bear R between old buildings, past Scout fm, then keep SA alongside the railway line (not under it).

5 Go under the next bridge, to the A646 in Holme Chapel (874/285). Pub here to R. Go SA on lane opposite, UH & bear R at fork on Holme Chapel rd, bearing off to the L after 0.3km through gate in wall. Pass through more gates, bear to R before fm, (880/289) DH, through gate on L, UH & R through (yet) another gate to Long Causeway rd (888/292).

6 Go R, alongside 'The Long Causeway' then L (before the windfarm) onto the moor & DH towards Cant Clough reservoir. Go L at T-J, over stream & on track between old spoil mounds either side, to another stream and go L to another stream crossing. Go over the packhorse bridge& go R, UH to Cant Clough reservoir (894/306).

7 Go over the dam, through gate at other end & UH on concrete track, towards Hurstwood reservoir (889/314). Bear R on the track alongside the reservoir & keep SA, UH to DT (Gorple rd) & go R on this good track for 3km (crossing border from Lancashire to Yorkshire) & dropping down to Widdop reservoir, over the dam & bridge to a rd (936/328) & go R on this.

8 Keep to R after 1km, for 0.1km then go R through a gate opposite car park (947/323). Over bridge & follow the DT to Lower Gorple reservoir (944/317) and bear L, over the bridge & dam. Follow track L at far end, shortly past the waterboard house turn R on DT (946/312).

9 Over bridge & climb UH to top, through gate onto farm track, keep L, DH, becoming tarmac, for 1.6km then turn R (959/390) on steep DH (School Land Lane) to the woods. Just a bit further along is May's Aladdin's Cave' which really lives up to its name - superb place to get some refreshments.

10 Over the bridge & UH past Land Farm (gardens open to public in summer) through a few gates to farm rd (called New rd). Go L on this, DH to Jack Bridge (962/282) and go R on the rd then very shortly bear L (opposite a car park) on Husdon Mill rd then next R on Bow lane (964/281).

11 Easy to miss. Keep SA on this UH, to houses & rd & bear L then very shortly R on (farm rd) Marsh Lane (964/274). Keep SA on the main track, DH, ignoring other tracks, to gate at bottom (Dove Scout fm) & go L on the packhorse trail, steeply DH, zig-zags, under railway to the A646 & turn R then L over a crossing (971/264).

NOTE: If you have come out on Jumble Hole Wood rd, turn L alongside the A646, then R over it.

12 Over the canal onto the Pennine Way lane, UH through woods & go L on ST shortly after track on R (979/261), just before the top & track bears slight R. DH, over packhorse bridge, to L, along edge of the wood, through 2 gates to corner of a rd (982/266). Go R into Horsehold then R again, UH, follow the rd to 2nd X-tracks (988/262).

13 Go R through a gate (Kilnshaw lane) & keep SA on this (becoming London rd), to RHS/under Stoodley Pike monument & keep SA to a rd at Mankinholes (960/234). Go R, past the YHA, then L on a BW (lumbutts lane), DH to pub & go SA on track steep DH to rd in Lumbutts (956/234).

14 Go R on the rd, UH for 1.1km then bear L through gate on a BW just before a pub on R. Keep SA on the packhorse track, UH, walled section, then narrower trail in open moors, bearing to the L & X-tracks, where you keep SA (938/226).

15 Heading south, DH, emerge on drive (house to L) keep SA to junction (big house to L) & go SA/L on Hollingworth lane (939/217) between 2 houses. Follow this rd, then just past gate/house on the L, go SA (through gate) on BW as the DT bears L (939/214), staying alongside the wall.

16 DH, bear to LHS of a house, through gate, over bridge, UH into Bottomley (942/210). Go R & R again through gate, steep DH, over water to tarmac rd & follow this L, to the A6033 (940/207) & use the crossing to L, to the other side of this rd.

17 Follow trail off Top O Th Close rd, through field & gates on grassy track, through more gates, over track, UH, to a DT (942/199). Go L on this, between 2 pylons, DH, joining a better track, to a rd & go R then shortly next R on next rd 'Higher Caldbrook rd' (944/188) by a ventilation shaft.

18 Keep SA, ignore fm track on R, past houses, bears L then R & bear R on the BW as the rd starts to go DH (942/183) before Calderbrook house. UH (fisheries to L), to a fm & bear L and stay on this track, under the power lines & bearing R back under them again, then bearing L, DH to Watergrove reservoir (912/181).

19 Go R on the track by reservoir, then R by building, UH for 0.7km then L at fork (910/188). DH, over stream then R, bearing L, UH, to (BW) track halfway up the hill (905/189) & go L on this. Keep L at fork & SA at X-rds, towards the golf club & past the LHS of it & L at fork just past it (890/173).

20 Shortly after going under power cables keep SA/L, off main track, DH, over track to building on L, to another DT (wall SA) & go R (887/161). Through gate, keep SA/L then R, past old quarries, to High Gate lane & go L on this, DH to T-J with Tonacliffe rd & go R then L on Oakenshaw Ave, to the A671 (882/168) & cross this.

21 Go SA, DH, alongside the river (on L), over bridge & go back L (river on L still), then R & keep SA on this UH, path joins from L, Uh, stream on L. To DT & go L, keep R at fork by houses, on Knacks Lane, follow it bearing R, to fork by more houses and keep R again & keep SA to X-rds (869/161).

22 Turn R, UH, under power cables, (Rooley Moor rd) & keep SA for long climb onto Rooley Moor. After 3km bear R at fork (857/184), (quarry to L) for 1.5km to another fork & keep L on main track, Cowpe reservoir DH on RHS (851/196).

23 After 2.75km, drop to foot of Cowpe Lowe (827/204) & drop down the hill to the R, to lane & go SA/R on this, DH to T-J. Go R then L on Cowpe rd & follow it all the way to the A681 back in Waterfoot & the end (834/217).

NOTE: If you started the route elsewhere, turn R alongside the river, then L over the crossing/main rd & go up Townsend st (835/217) & see no.1.

picture by Ian Donohoe

Getting there There are various places to start. We start the ride in Waterfoot (835/217), just east of Rawtenstal, where there is parking, shops & train station not far away + Hebden Bridge & YHA is well places 1/2 way around.

Accommodation: Various options depending on where you start/end. Call Rawtenstall T.I. on 0161 253 5111 or Hebden Bridge on 01422 843831. If stopping halfway Mankinholes YHA in Todmorden makes a good stop, tel 0845 371 9751

Refreshments: Good choice at start/end, pub in Holme Chapel, the wonderful Alladins cave at Rodmen Clough, Hebden Bridge just off the route, pub in Mankinholes & some shops etc just off some southern parts of the route.

Bike shops: Ride On in Rawtenstall on 01706 831 101 / www.ride-on.co.uk is very good as is Blazing Saddles in Hebden Bridge on 01422 844435 / www.blazingsaddles.co.uk

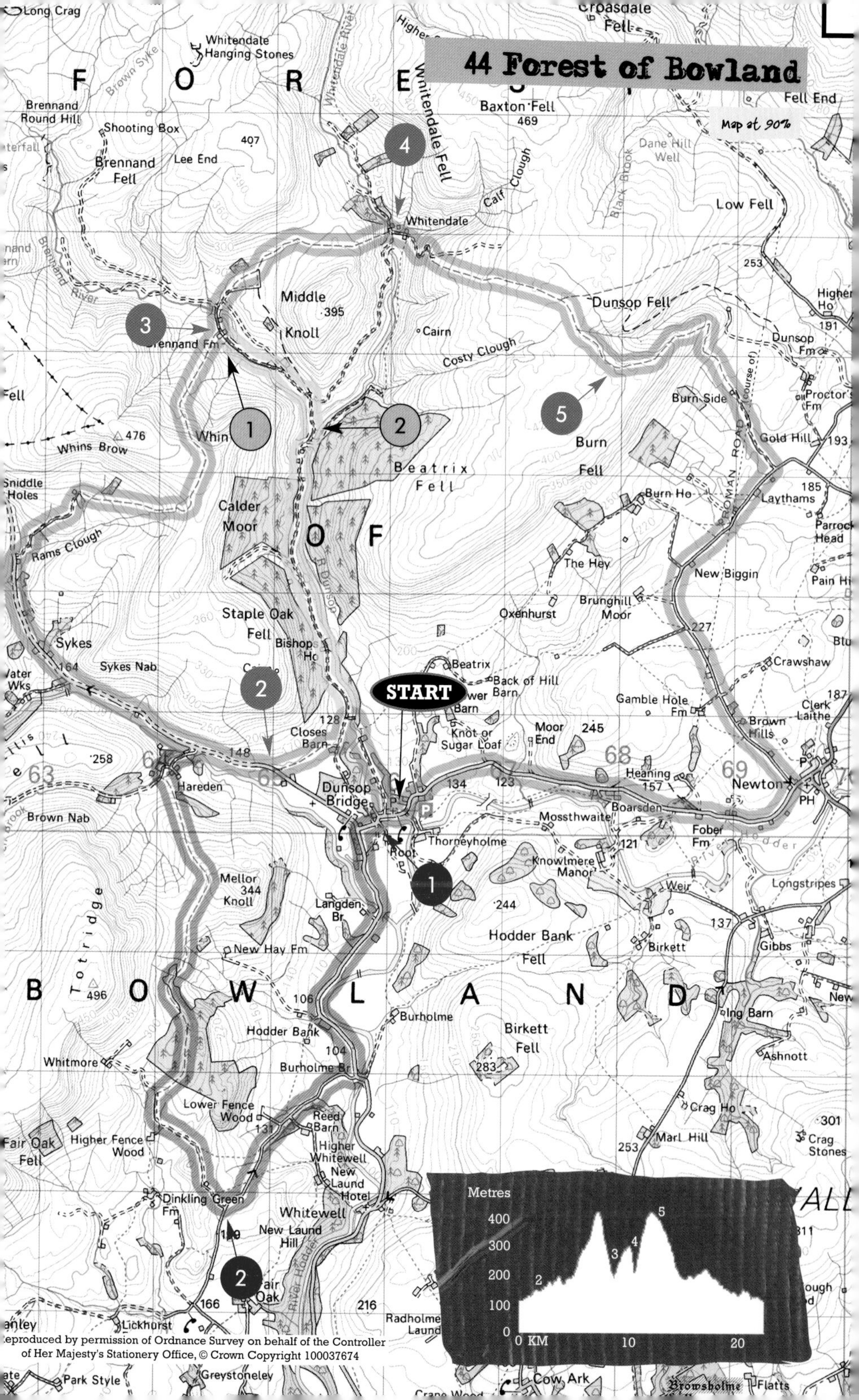
44 Forest of Bowland
Map at 90%
START
Metres
400
300
200
100
0
0 KM
10
20

22.7KM (14.1M) & 865 METRES CLIMBING

START Turn R on the rd for 0.1km then R on (BW) track before the bridge (SD 659/501) and follow this, joining alongside river by house, then L over a bridge (656/509). Go L/south, then R before a fm & follow the BW to a rd (650/505).

2 Go R on the rd, UH for 3.2km, then go R on a BW just after a barn (627/522), UH on good track, which gives way to (soggy) grassy track climbing to top. Go through a gate, DH on nice technical track & keep SA through gate & field to a fm (645/541). See shortcut here.

3 Pass the house (on R) & turn L, on good track, over a bridge & bear R, UH (ignore tracks on R), to end of the track, at a gate (648/546). Slight DH around grassy knoll & up the valley (wall on RHS), to the top then steep DH to Whitendale (659/550).

4 Keep SA, over the bridge & past fm, bearing R to go steeply UH on zig-zagging track, keeping R at fork, on the BW (663/547). Climb to top, through gate in wall & bear R on feint track to RHS of the valley, bearing L for grassy ST on RHS of the valley.

5 To farm & bear L then R to join the drive, to a rd (693/530) and turn R on this. Follow this for 3.4km to T-J in Newton (695/504) and go R on this, mostly on slight DH, for 3.8km, back to Dunsop Bridge (661/502).

-9.3KM (5.8M) & -330 METRES CLIMBING

1 Turn R on the good track and follow this back through the valley bottom, keeping R, alongside the river, over a bridge (652/532) & continue alongside the river on the opposite side.

2 Follow this all the way back to the bridge you came over earlier & retrace your earlier steps back to Dunsop Bridge (661/502).

Extension

+6.7KM (4.2M) & +270 METRES CLIMBING

1 Go over the bridge in Dunsop Bridge, to a T-J and go L, after 2.5km turn R on a rd just before crossing the (Burholme) bridge (657/479). Steep UH for 1.7km then go R on a BW track (646/469)

2 UH, keeping R at fork (L goes to fm), UH for 0.25km then as DT bears L, go R on a BW, (640/478). UH into the woods and follow the BW, climbing to LHS of Mellor Knoll then steep DH, bearing R at the bottom, to the rd (643/506) & rejoin main route at no.2 (but 2.5km, not 3.2km).

NOTE: Gisburn Forest (north-east on the B6478) has 3 nice, easy going (9, 12 & 16km waymarked XC trails) which are perfect for beginners. There are plans for some singletrack trails too, see keep an eye on www.forestry.gov.uk for developments.

Getting there: From the west, use the minor roads from junction 33 of the M6, through Dolphinholme & Abbeystead and from anywhere else it's best to use the B6478 that runs between Clitheroe & Long Preston. There is a car park at GR SD 661/502. No train stations very close (Clitheroe is 10km away on B6478).

Accommodation: Wood End farm B&B in Dunsop Bridge on 01200 448223, Slaidburn YHA (in Slaidburn) on 0870 770 6034, or for more options call Clitheroe T.I. on 01200 425566.

Refreshments: Only pub in Newton nr the end or the village store in Dunsop.

Bike shops: A.E. Hargreaves in Clitheroe on 01200 442683, Leisure Lakes in Preston on 0870 8004487 & The Edge cycleworks in Lancaster on 01524 840800.

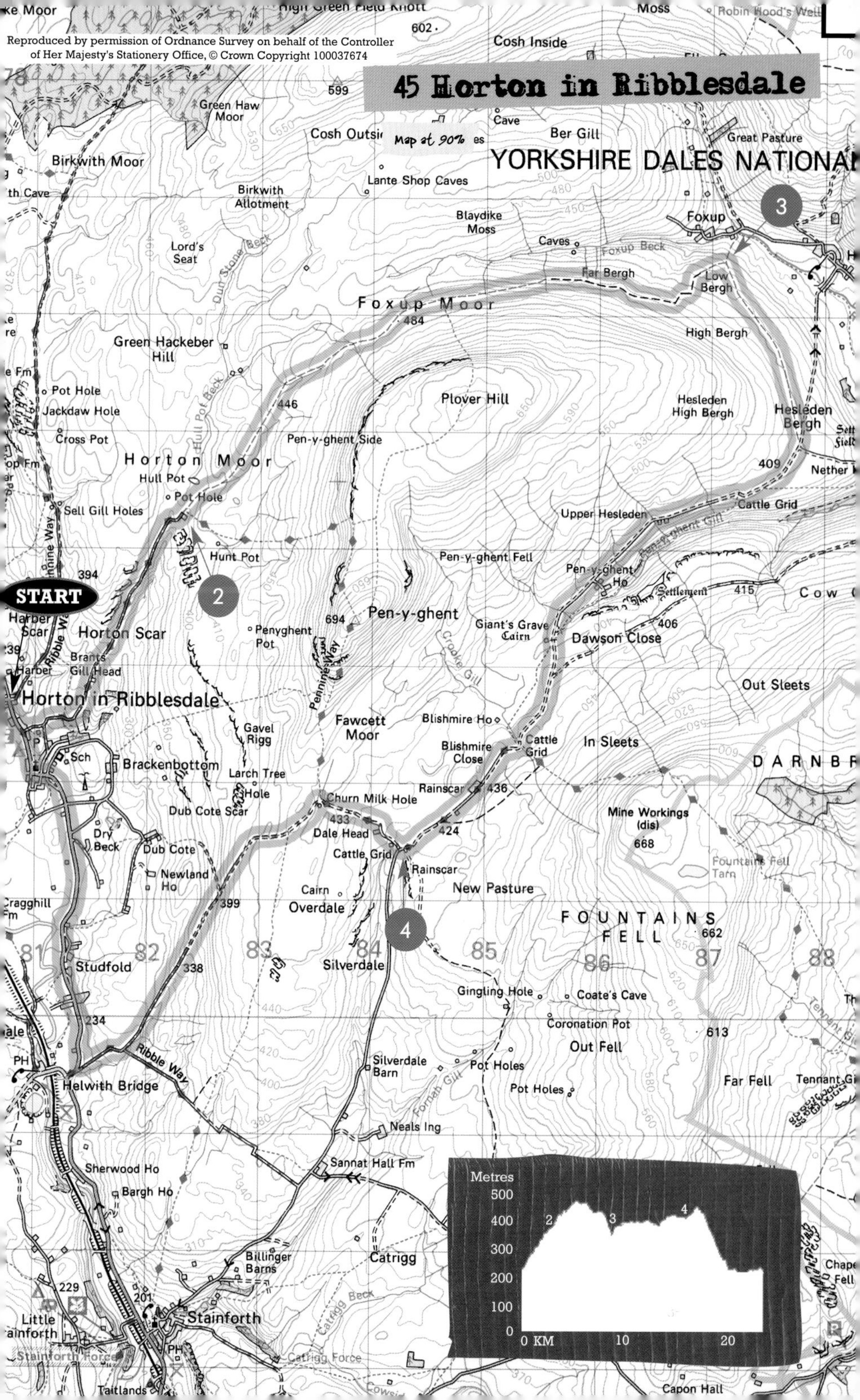
Reproduced by permission of Ordnance Survey on behalf of the Controller of Her Majesty's Stationery Office, © Crown Copyright 100037674
45 Horton in Ribblesdale
Map at 90%
YORKSHIRE DALES NATIONAL
START
2
3
4
Horton in Ribblesdale
Harber Scar
Horton Scar
Brants Gill Head
Horton Moor
Hull Pot
Pot Hole
Hunt Pot
Sell Gill Holes
Birkwith Moor
Green Haw Moor
Birkwith Allotment
Lord's Seat
Green Hackeber Hill
Pot Hole
Jackdaw Hole
Cross Pot
Cosh Inside
Cosh Outside
Cave
Ber Gill
Great Pasture
Lante Shop Caves
Blaydike Moss
Caves
Foxup
Foxup Beck
Far Bergh
Low Bergh
Foxup Moor
High Bergh
Plover Hill
Hesleden High Bergh
Hesleden Bergh
Pen-y-ghent Side
Upper Hesleden
Cattle Grid
Pen-y-ghent Fell
Pen-y-ghent Ho
Pen-y-ghent Gill
Settlement
Pen-y-ghent
Penyghent Pot
Giant's Grave Cairn
Dawson Close
Out Sleets
Pennine Way
Fawcett Moor
Blishmire Ho
Blishmire Close
Cattle Grid
In Sleets
Gavel Rigg
Brackenbottom
Larch Tree Hole
Dub Cote Scar
Rainscar
Churn Milk Hole
Dale Head
Cattle Grid
Mine Workings (dis)
Fountains Fell Tarn
Dry Beck
Dub Cote
Newland Ho
Rainscar
New Pasture
Cairn
Overdale
FOUNTAINS FELL
Cragghill Fm
Studfold
Silverdale
Gingling Hole
Coate's Cave
Coronation Pot
Out Fell
Helwith Bridge
Ribble Way
Silverdale Barn
Pot Holes
Pot Holes
Far Fell
Tennant Gill
Neals Ing
Sherwood Ho
Bargh Ho
Sannat Hall Fm
Billinger Barns
Catrigg
Catrigg Beck
Stainforth
Little Stainforth
Stainforth Force
Catrigg Force
Taitlands
Capon Hall
Metres
500
400
300
200
100
0
0 KM
10
20

22.3KM (13.9M) & 530 METRES CLIMBING

START From the train station keep SA (east) on the B6479/Station rd, following rd bearing sharp R, past the car park on R (go out of car park) for 0.2km then turn L on BW past Pen-y-Ghent cafe, by post office (809/724) and follow this track (Pennine Way), UH, for 2km to open moorland.

2 Ignore Pennine Way (FP) on R & bear L on feint track, UH, by Hull Pot to gate on R, following track to corner of wall and bear R (wall on L). Keep SA, through a number of gates, then as track bears L, DH, wall on R, go through a gate & bear L, DH, then R at gate before the bottom (871/764).

3 Follow the grassy track along the hillside to a rd and go R on this and follow it (through the impressive scenery) for 5.5km, then go through a gate on the Pennine Way after the cattle grid (842/714).

4 Pass some houses then bearing L at Pot hole (835/718), short UH then a good 2km long descent to a junction and bear R , DH to the rd (814/695). Go R on the rd and follow it for 3.5km, back to the car park (807/725).

pic © Simon Barnes 2008 www.bogtrotters.co.uk

A great introduction to the area, with classic moorland riding and impressive views, such as Hull Pot above. A friendly cafe & locals add to the experience too.

Getting there Exit the A65 to go thorough settle, on the B6479 to Horton-in-Ribblesdale, just through the town, there is a car park (807/725) on the left, before the rd turn sharp left, by the pub. Train station in the village.

Accommodation: Golden Lion in Horton with B&B or bunk room on 01729 860206, YHA in Stainforth (just north of Settle) on 01729 823 577, camping barn in Halton Gill (east side of route) on 01756 770241 or plenty of places in settle, see www.settle.org.uk

Refreshments

The Pen-Y-Ghent in Horton. Or a pub in Helwith Bridge if you really can't make it any further.

Bike shops

The Bike Shop, in Settle on tel: 01729 824232

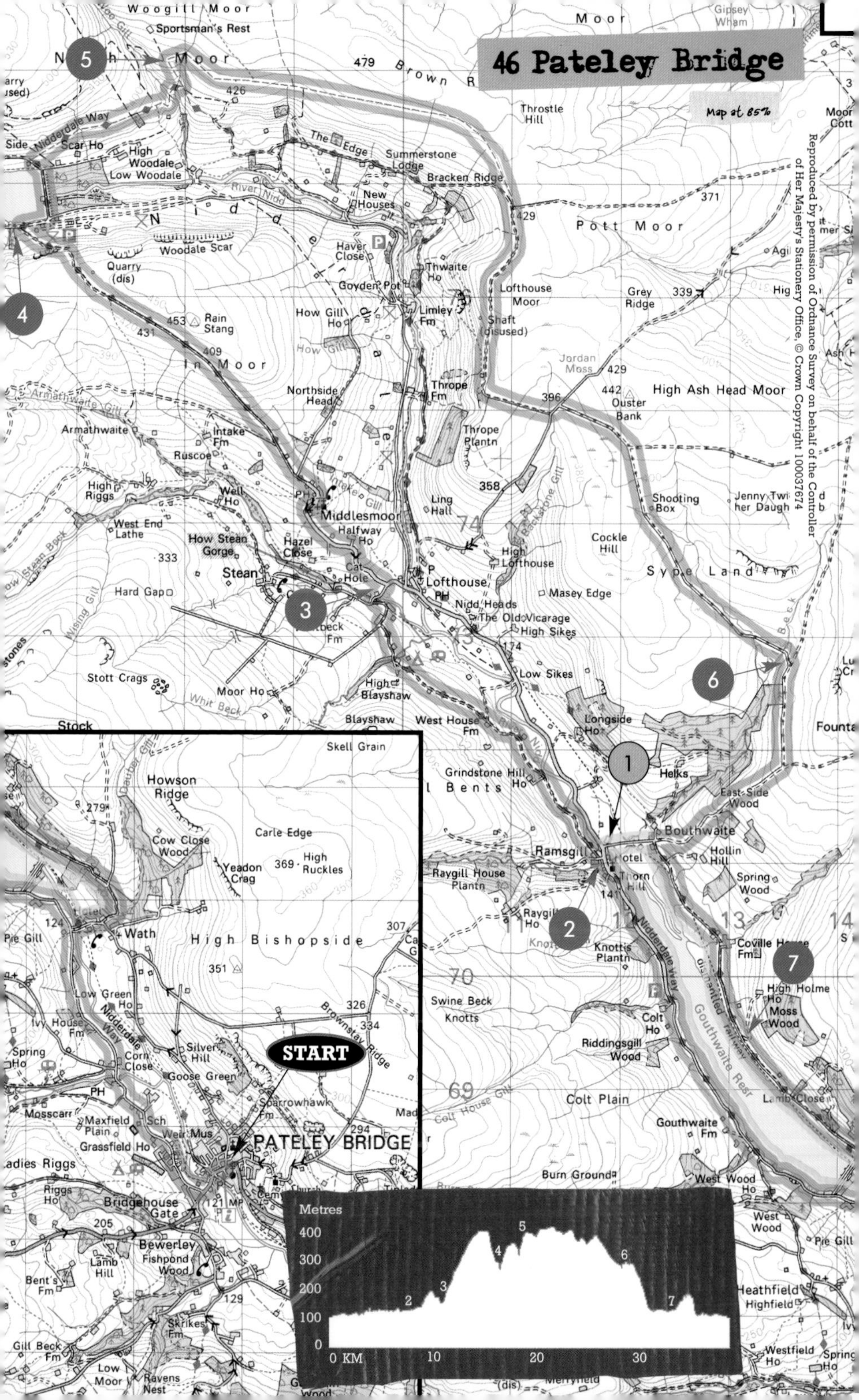
46 Pateley Bridge
Map at 85%
Reproduced by permission of Ordnance Survey on behalf of the Controller of Her Majesty's Stationery Office, © Crown Copyright 100037674
START
PATELEY BRIDGE
Woogill Moor
Sportsman's Rest
Brown Ridge
Throstle Hill
Nidderdale Way
Scar Ho
High Woodale
Low Woodale
River Nidd
The Edge
Summerstone Lodge
Bracken Ridge
New Houses
Pott Moor
Woodale Scar
Quarry (dis)
Haver Close
Thwaite Ho
Goyden Pot
Lofthouse Moor
Grey Ridge
How Gill Ho
Limley Fm
Shaft (disused)
Rain Stang
In Moor
Jordan Moss
Northside Head
Thrope Fm
High Ash Head Moor
Ouster Bank
Armathwaite
Intake Fm
Thrope Plantn
Ruscoe
High Riggs
Well Ho
Middlesmoor
Ling Hall
Shooting Box
Cockle Hill
West End Lathe
How Stean Gorge
Hazel Close
Halfway Ho
High Lofthouse
Stean
Hard Gap
Cat Hole
Lofthouse
Nidd Heads
Masey Edge
Syke Land
The Old Vicarage
High Sikes
Stott Crags
Moor Ho
High Blayshaw
Low Sikes
Blayshaw
West House Fm
Longside Ho
Skell Grain
Grindstone Hill Ho
Helks
East Side Wood
Howson Ridge
Bouthwaite
Carle Edge
Cow Close Wood
Ramsgill
Hotel
Hollin Hill
Yeadon Crag
High Ruckles
Raygill House Plantn
Thorn Hill
Spring Wood
Raygill Ho
Wath
High Bishopside
Coville House Fm
Knotts Plantn
Pie Gill
Swine Beck Knotts
High Holme Ho
Moss Wood
Low Green Ho
Ivy House Fm
Spring Ho
Silver Hill
Colt Ho
Gouthwaite Resr
Corn Close
Goose Green
Riddingsgill Wood
Mosscarr
Maxfield Plain
Sparrowhawk Fm
Colt House Gill
Colt Plain
Lamb Close
Grassfield Ho
Weir Mus
Gouthwaite Fm
Ladies Riggs
Burn Ground
West Wood Ho
Riggs Ho
Bridgehouse Gate
West Wood
Bewerley
Fishpond Wood
Lamb Hill
Bent's Fm
Heathfield
Highfield
Skrikes Fm
Gill Beck Fm
Low Moor
Ravens Nest
Westfield Ho
Metres
400
300
200
100
0
0 KM
10
20
30

Pateley Bridge

39KM (24.2M) & 1,030 METRES CLIMBING

START Turn L out of the car park on the B6265 west/towards Grassington, over the bridge then 1st R (SE 156/654) on Low Wath rd (SP Ramsgill). Follow this rd for 8km to Ramsgill & just after crossing a small bridge, turn L on a track, then bearing R on the (Stean) BW (118/710).

2 Follow this, keeping SA across the farmland, past track on L to Grindstone Hill House, UH to West House fm & keep SA/L (SP Nidderdale Way). To T-J (098 731) & go R, DH (SP Stean), through a fm onto tarmac, past a caravan park and take 1st rd on R, over stone bridge to T-J (098/734).

3 Go L (SP Middlesmoor) on this rd, steep UH, through the village and keep SA as tarmac track stops, keeping SA (ignoring a DT shortly on R & private rd on L). Long UH to top & views of Scar House reservoir & DH on loose stone track to a (tarmac) T-J at the reservoir edge (064/766).

4 Turn R then L over the dam, then bear L, UH on a cobble track, leaving the waters edge, then shortly going R on a (Nidderdale Way) BW (065/772). UH then DH through Woo Gill valley back UH to the top & bear L on rough track UH then bearing R through a gate on a better track.

5 Keep SA (improving along the way) for 5km, along the edge of the dale, to a rd & go L then shortly R on a track (114/750). Keep R at a fork along here, DH, on the grassy track along a wall, over bridge, short UH to a gate & T-J (136/727).

6 Go R & keep R, DH (SP unsuitable for motors) for fun descent to X-tracks (123/712) in Bouthwaite and turn L on the BW to Wath. Follow this track, tarmac stops after Coville House fm, keeping R at fork, alongside Gouthwaite reservoir (131/694).

7 Track climbs up away from the reservoir, to a T-J (148/681) just past a big house & go R DH, to a T-J with a rd (in Wath). Go R, past the hotel, to a T-J (144/677) & go L, rejoining the rd you started on, back to Pateley Bridge (3.5km's) (157/656).

Short Route

10KM (6.2M) & 250 METRES CLIMBING

1 From Ramsgill go east on the rd, over the bridge to Bouthwaite and turn R on the BW to Wath. Follow this track, tarmac stops after Coville House fm, keeping R at fork, alongside Gouthwaite reservoir (131/694).

2 The track climbs up away from the reservoir, to a T-J (148/681) just past a big house. Go R, DH to a T-J with a rd & go R, past hotel, to a T-J & go R and follow this rd all the way back alongside Gouthwaite reservoir back to Ramsgill (118/710).

NOTE: The impressive, surreal, weird & wonderful Bingham Rocks, just west of Pateley Bridge are worth checking out while you are in the area.

Getting there Start in the long stay car park in Pateley Bridge (157/656). Pateley Bridge is 16km north-west of Harrogate, leave the A61 at Ripley and follow the A6165 to Pateley Bridge. Railway at Harrogate.

Accommodation: The New Inn at Appletreewick (go west on the B6265) is a very mtb friendly B&B. Tel: 01756 720252. alternatively see www.harrogate.gov.uk/harrogate-266

Bike shops Psychlo Sport on 01423545413 & Boneshakers Performance cycles on 01423 709453, both in Harrogate.

Refreshments Pubs in Ramsgil, Middlemoor & of course lots of choice in Pateley Bridge itself.

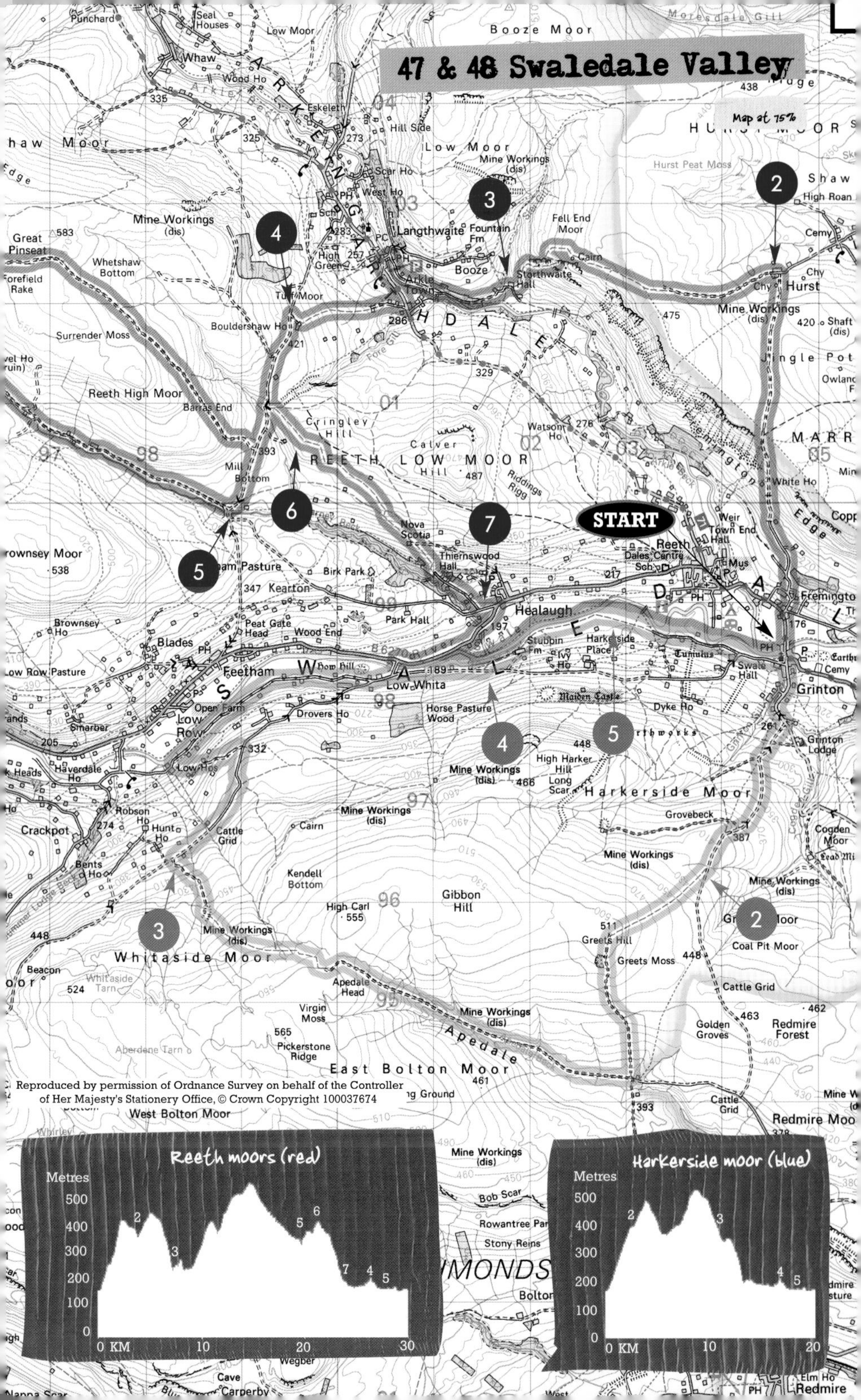
47 & 48 Swaledale Valley
Map at 75%
START
Reeth
Healaugh
Feetham
Low Row
Grinton
Fremington
Langthwaite
Arkle Town
Booze
Hurst
Crackpot
Kearton
Harkerside Moor
Whitaside Moor
Reeth Low Moor
Reeth High Moor
East Bolton Moor
Apedale
Reproduced by permission of Ordnance Survey on behalf of the Controller
of Her Majesty's Stationery Office, © Crown Copyright 100037674
Reeth moors (red)
Metres
0 KM
10
20
30
Harkerside moor (blue)
Metres
0 KM
10
20

Harkerside Moor

21 KM (13M) & 625 METRES CLIMBING

START From the Dales Bike Centre, go R/south on the B6270, over the bridge/river to Grinton & R keep SA (south) (SP Redmire) as the B rd bears L (046/984). UH for 1km & bear R on rd (past cattlegrid), UH for another 2km, ignoring BW's on R, until gradient eases off, bear R on a BW (038/963).

2 Faint grassy track. Head south west, UH, to a cairn then L to 2 cairns, through gate, SA, DH to X-tracks (030/942). Turn R & follow the DT through the valley, , keeping R at fork just after 1km, with Apedale Beck on LHS, then steep UH. To top & follow a track (R then L) DH, keeping L at BW fork, DH to a rd (982/964).

3 Go R on the rd for 1.4km go L through a gate (as DH steepens) by seat & FP to the R (GR 990 975). Keep R at a fork, to track at the bottom (982/973) & turn R (Grinton). Go between the trees, along valley bottom, to a rd & go L on this, keeping SA/R, climbing UH & L on BW after 1km (015/983), just after a FP, on a grassy track (Grinton).

4 DH to gate on L, DH through to a gate on the R & follow narrow track parallel to river (below on L). DH to L, gate by river & follow ST, to a gate (027/989). Join grassy track on R which bears R, away from the river, across a field to a gate on RHS of a fence.

5 Through gate to DT on R & go L on this, wall on L, until it turns sharp L towards a bridge, you keep SA on a grassy track.To a gate, UH, between walls & through gates, to a lane & go L into Grinton. Go L at X-rds, over the bridge, on B6270 & L back into the Dales Bike Centre (046/986).

NOTE: The excellent Dales Bike centre has accommodation, cafe, bike shop and offers guided rides, skills lessons & will be able to point you in the direction of much more riding in the area – see www.dalesbikecentre.co.uk

Reeth Moors

30KM (18.6M) & 1,030 METRES CLIMB

START Go L on the B6270 to Fremington & bear R 1st rd, then immediately L at fork, then shortly after it L, keep SA/R, UH out of village (046/991). Ignore RC on L, to gate by a house, follow obvious track, becom rough track, UH, keeping L at fork nr top, to a gate (N 044/007). Follow DT, DH to house & T-J past gates at bottom (045/022) and go L, through gates on DT, UH.

2 Keep SA/L, zig-zag to top & go L on the DT, through heather, to/through a gate (032/021), onto grassy sing track SA. To old quarry, follow the cairns, bearing R, DH rocky section, then wide grass DH, careful of ditch.. To c rocky track & bear L on it to far side of quarry then DH R, across bottom of quarry. Grass track, through gate o DH on a rocky track to Storthwaite hall (018/021).

3 Go R Turn right and follow the track SA, parallel to r to Langthwaite (005/024). Go L over the bridge to T-J & go L to Arkle Town, then R on BW on a gravel track just after a house (007/019). Through a gate on L of a hou UH, past last house (B&B), with wall on L, to Bouldersha house, go R to rd (995/019), then L on the rd.

4 After 1.4km (pass bends & ford) go R on DT (as rd sta to go DH) (991/005) & follow this, to top, bearing L, to c gate (960/022), SA to rd at Surrender Bridge (988/999).

5 Go L on rd, for 1km, over the ford from before, then UH to 2nd bend/LHB & go R through a gate (992/009), shortly bear R, off DT onto a ST, to RHS of Cringley Hill.

6 DH, keeping SA on grassy ST & follow this alongside c wall (on L), bearing R to X-tracks (005/999). Go over the DT, SA, on wide grassy trail to RHS of wall, bearing L, DH to wall on RHS. Follow this wall SA, around bends throug a gate & go R in the field, through a gate into trees, bearing L, SA at a junction, DH to a lane (014/989).

7 Go L to the B6270 & go R on this (Gunnerside) for 1.2km then turn L over a bridge (SP Askrigg) (006/984) & immediately over the bridge turn L on lane, UH to a (grassy) BW on the L (015/983). Follow the other routes directions from point no.4, back to the start (046/986).

Getting there West of Richmond, exit the A6108, on the B6270, heading west into the Swaledale Valley. Just after passing Grinton & goinging over the bridge, the Dales Bike centre is on your left (SE 046/986). For more detailed directions & maps, see www.dalesbikecentre.co.uk.

Accommodation: The Dales Bike centre in Fremington is specifically set up for cyclists, so makes an obvious place to head for. See www.dalesbikecentre.co.uk or call 01748 884 908 / for more info.

Refreshments Dales Bike centre has a great cafe. Pub in Grinton on south & in Langthwaite on north route.

Bike shops
The Dales Bike centre should be able to sort out your needs.

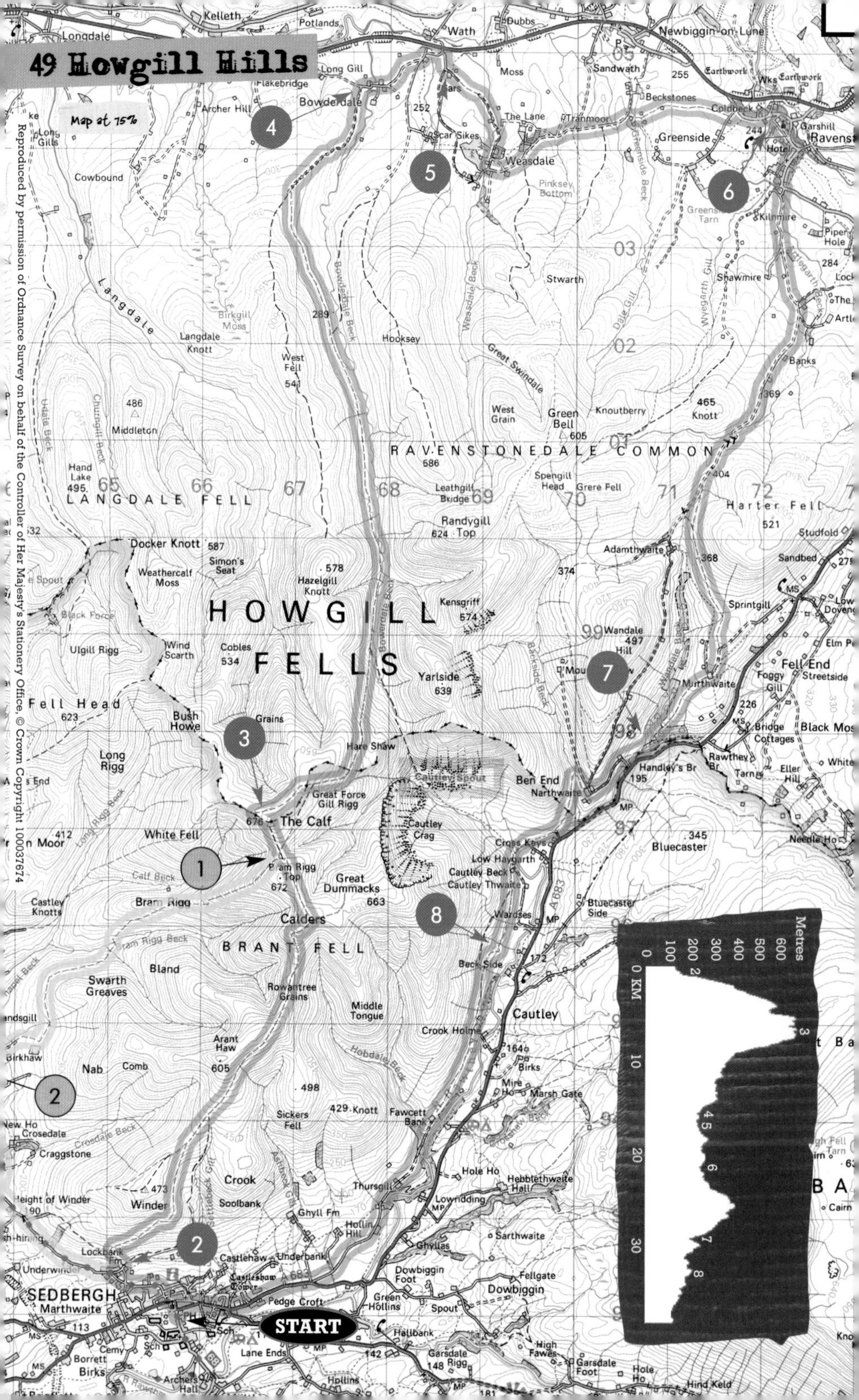
49 Howgill Hills
Map at 75%
Reproduced by permission of Ordnance Survey on behalf of the Controller of Her Majesty's Stationery Office, © Crown Copyright 100037674
HOWGILL FELLS
RAVENSTONEDALE COMMON
LANGDALE FELL
BRANT FELL
Kelleth
Longdale
Potlands
Wath
Dubbs
Newbiggin-on-Lune
Long Gill
Flakebridge
Bowderdale
Archer Hill
Moss
Sandwath
Earthwork
Beckstones
The Lane
Tranmoor
Coldbeck
Scar Sikes
Weasdale
Greenside
Garshill
Hotel
Cowbound
Pinksey Bottom
Greenside Tarn
Kilnmire
Piper Hole
Stwarth
Shawmire
Langdale
Birkgill Moss
Langdale Knott
West Fell
541
Hooksey
Great Swindale
Banks
Middleton
West Grain
Green Bell
605
Knoutberry
465
Knott
Hand Lake
495
586
Leathgill Bridge
Spengill Head
Grere Fell
Harter Fell
521
Randygill Top
624
Studfold
Docker Knott
587
Simon's Seat
Weathercalf Moss
578
Hazelgill Knott
Kensgriff
574
Adamthwaite
374
368
Sandbed
Sprintgill
Black Force
Ulgill Rigg
Wind Scarth
Cobles
534
Yarlside
639
Wandale Hill
497
Fell End
Foggy Gill
Streetside
Elm Pe
Fell Head
623
Bush Howe
Grains
Hare Shaw
Cautley Spout
Ben End
Narthwaite
Murthwaite
Bridge Cottages
Black Mos
Long Rigg
Great Force Gill Rigg
Handley's Br
195
Rawthey Br
Tarn
Eller Hill
676
The Calf
White Fell
Cautley Crag
Cross Keys
Low Haygarth
Cautley Beck
Cautley Thwaite
Bluecaster
345
Needle Ho
Calf Beck
Bram Rigg Top
672
Great Dummacks
663
Castley Knotts
Bram Rigg
Calders
Bluecaster Side
Wardses
Bram Rigg Beck
Bland
Beck Side
172
Swarth Greaves
Rowantree Grains
Middle Tongue
Cautley
Crook Holme
Arant Haw
605
Nab
Comb
Birkhaw
498
Hobdale Beck
Birks
Mire Ho
Marsh Gate
New Ho
Crosdale
Craggstone
Sickers Fell
429 Knott
Fawcett Bank
Crook
Soolbank
Thursgill
Hole Ho
Hebblethwaite Hall
Height of Winder
473
Winder
Ghyll Fm
Hollin Hill
Lowrdding
Sarthwaite
Lockbank Fm
Underwinder
Castlehaw
Underbank
Ghyllas
Castleshaw Tower
Dowbiggin Foot
Fellgate
Dowbiggin
SEDBERGH
Marthwaite
Pedge Croft
Green Hollins
Spout
START
Hallbank
113
Cemy
Borrett
Birks
Lane Ends
142
Garsdale Rigg
148
High Fawes
Garsdale Foot
Hole Ho
Hind Keld
Hollins
Archers Hall
Metres
0
100
200
300
400
500
600
0 KM
10
20
30
1
2
3
4
5
6
7
8

Howgill Hills

38KM (23.6M) & 1,210 METRES OF CLIMBING

START Go back to the A684 and go L on it bearing L then turn R on Howgill lane (SD 656/921), UH. Follow this, bears L, for 0.75km then turn R at Lockbank fm (650/924) where rd bears sharp L & bear R onto a steep UH, rocky trail.

2 Through couple of gates and bear L, then R as the track levels out (but not for long). This is the start to a very long, tough climb. Follow the DT UH keeping R at a junction, by a Col (658/937), admiring the fantastic views along the way, bearing L, then keeping SA to the trig point at 'The Calf' (667/970). See short)er) ride details here.

3 Drop DH, north-east from the trig point, making sure to bear R of the tarn, DH - not the track along the ridge to the L. Great BW along Bowerdale Back, with some great sections of singletrack, finally coming to a rd at Bowerdale (676/046).

4 Turn R on the rd here, to a T-J and go L here, DH, then shortly turn R before going under the bridge (683/050). Parallel to the rd then go R (Gars lane), UH, then L to pass a house and join a BW through a gate on the L.

5 Join alongside a stream, crossing it, to a rd just past some buildings (690/038) and go L on this, keeping SA at the fork, for 0.5km then go R through a gate, keep L, pass a barn & over a field to join a walled track. To a rd (716/043) and turn L on it, to a T-J & go R into Ravenstonedale.

6 Keep R in the village, aiming for Adamthwaite, UH, then just over the top of the hill, before Adamthwaite, turn L on a BW (713/005). DH, onto a wide stone track at bottom, turning R at the farm, for fun DH through the trees, across a field & through a stream (707/978).

7 UH, joining DT, to a farm and bear L on a BW, steep DH, through water and back UH. Joining along the RHS of the river, then go L over a footbridge (693/967), follow the BW track, UH then good DH on singletrack, through numerous gates.

8 Continue along through the valley with stream crossings, eventually joining a track at Fawcett Bank and becoming a rd, down to the A683 and go R on this to Sedbergh (657/920) and go L at the mini roundabout & L again into the car park.

Short(er) Ride

15.6KM (9.7M) & 815 METRES CLIMBING

1 From the trig point at 'The Calf' turn around to go back down the short climb, but bear off R just before you start the climb back up past Bram Rigg Top (668/967). This is a fast, grassy DH, passing Bram Rigg, which isn't too technical, but has a few rocks, jumps & drops to make it interesting.

2 Follow this main track back down the hillside, to a rd (636/945) and turn L on this and follow it (sustrans cycle path) back to Sedbergh (657/920).

NOTE: Can be done in reverse, but finish coming down west (not south) side of Winder Hill.

Getting there Really easy, just exit the M6 at junction 37 and follow the 'A' rd into the town. Go straight ahead at mini roundabout on Loftus Hill rd, as main rd goes left, just after the right hand bend, and car park is on the left GR 657/920.

Accommodation There are lots of places to choose from, such as B&B's, camspites, bunk barns, etc all listed on the towns very own website; www.sedbergh.org.uk or if you don't have internet access call 015396 20125.

Bike shop Evans bike shop in Kendal (other side of the M6) on 01539 740087 or Stonetrail Holidays hire bikes & offer skills courses & guided rides. See www.stonetrailholidays.com or call 015396 23444.

Refreshments Pub in Ravenstonedale halfway & lots of choice in Sedbergh, including cafes, fish & chips, etc.

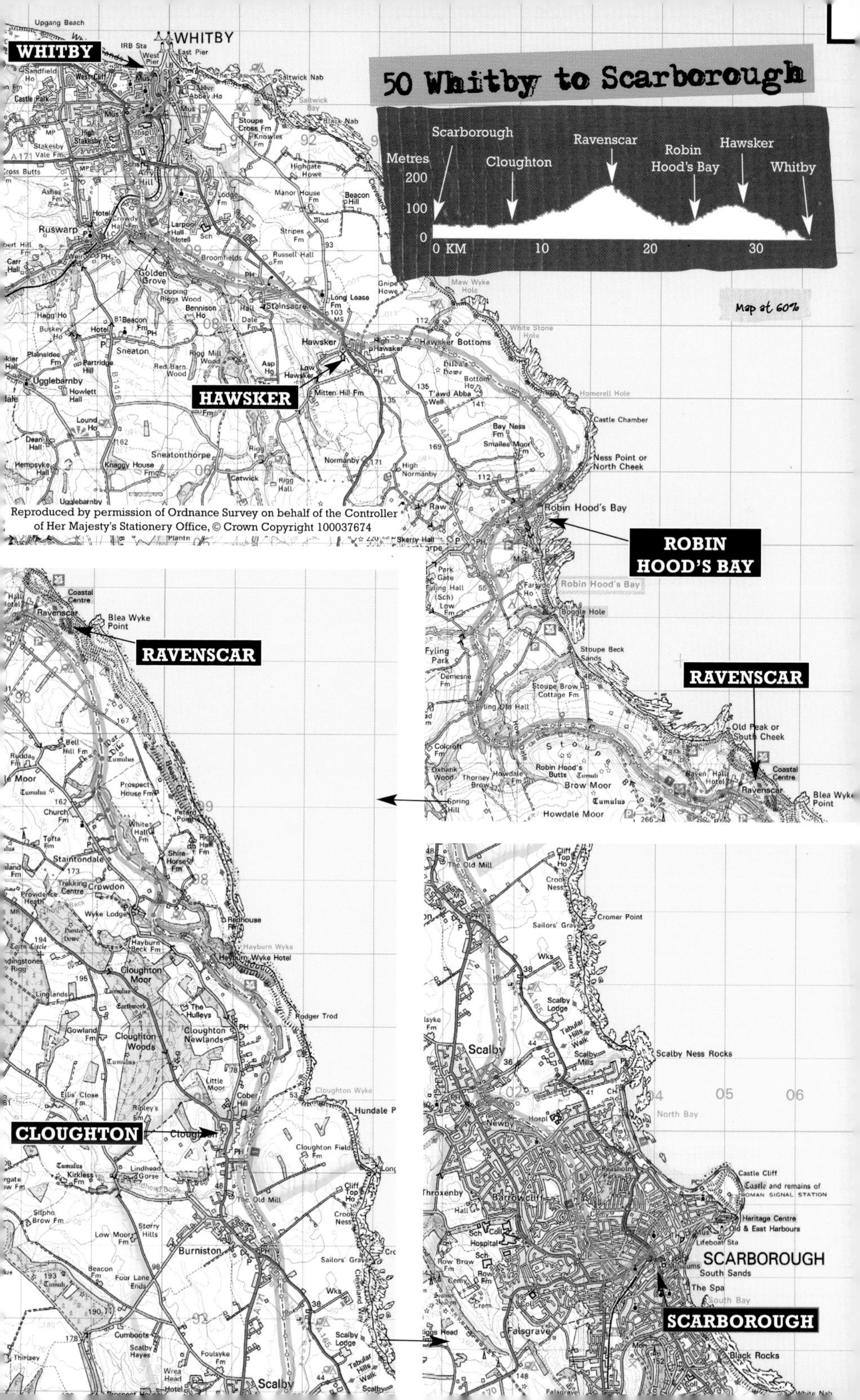

50 Whitby to Scarborough
Metres
200
100
0
Scarborough
Cloughton
Ravenscar
Robin Hood's Bay
Hawsker
Whitby
0 KM
10
20
30
Map at 60%
WHITBY
HAWSKER
ROBIN HOOD'S BAY
RAVENSCAR
RAVENSCAR
CLOUGHTON
SCARBOROUGH
Reproduced by permission of Ordnance Survey on behalf of the Controller of Her Majesty's Stationery Office, © Crown Copyright 100037674

Scarborough to Whitby

34.9KM (21.7M) & 610 METRES OF CLIMBI ONE-WAY

his is a lovely way to travel along this stretch of coastline, and it is very easy to follow and mostly pretty easy going on a good surface, but beware it has some hills that you don't always expect on old railway lines and a few rough tracks along the way.

NOTE: Please be aware that the route distances provided are all for 'one-way' only.

TOP TIP: See www.scarborough-online.co.uk or www.thisisscarborough.org for other activities to do in the area.

Scarborough to Cloughton

7.3KM (4.5M) & 60 METRES OF CLIMBING

he trail starts off Falsgrave rd (A171) in the centre of Scarborough, just southwest of the train station. Look for the Sustrans cyclepath signs no.1 around Commercial St (034/880). Simply follow this flat, easy going section of off-road cyclepath, to Cloughton (011/941), where you can stop for refreshments before turning back or continuing on.

Cloughton to Ravenscar

9KM (6.6M) & 235 METRES CLIMBING

Heading north along the Sustrans cyclepath no.1 his section of the trail climbs gradually for 9km to Ravenscar. There is a cafe here where you can have a break before turning around and enjoying he effects of gravity, back to Cloughton, or continue on to Robin's Hood Bay.

Ravenscar to Robin's Hood Bay

7.8KM (4.8M) & 130 METRES CLIMBING

This is a lovely section of the trail, made even be ter thanks to there being a gradual descent all th way to Robin's Hood Bay. Again it is simple to fo low and has a good surface and you can get refreshments in the village before heading back continuing on.

Robin's Hood Bay to Hawsker

4.6KM (2.9M) & 130 METRES CLIMBING

A gentle climb leads you north from Robin Hood Bay, before levelling out and brings you to Hawsker, where you need to cross the busy A17 There is a pub in Hawsker and one in Stainsacre which is easier to get to/find.

Hawsker to Whitby

6KM (3.7M) & 90 METRES CLIMBING

Follow the trail dropping down, over a bridge (ri & railway) passing some playing fields, into Whit Shortly after passing the A171 road, follow the Sustrans cycleway signs going right on South End Gardens rd, to a roundabout with the A174 rd. Go SA on Bagdale rd, to a roundabout (railway station on the R just before this) and bear L on N Quay rd, along the water front. Don't cross the bridge, keep L on St Ann's Staith rd, alongside t water, becoming Pier rd, to (you guessed it) the Pier, where you can take in the sights (& food).

NOTE: If you want to get the train back to Scarborough from Whitby, you need to go via Middlesborough and York. Reserve your bikes o the train 24hrs advance on 0845 7000125.

Getting there This will depend on what part(s) of the ride you want to do. Good start points are Scarborough, Cloughton, Ravenscar, Robin Hood's Bay and Whitby. Both Scarborough & Whitby have railway stations, but to go between them you need to go via Middlesborough & York.

Accommodation: There are lots of places available. Call Scarborough T.I. on 01723 373333 or Whitby T.I. on 01947 602674 for more info. Filey, just south of Scarborough is a lovely, popular holiday destination. Hooks House farm at Robin Hoods Bay is great, offering camping, caravan and cottage, see www.hookshousefarm.co.uk.

Bike shops The Bicycle Works (144 Victoria rd) in Scarborough nr the start on 01723 365 594 and Doctor Cranks Bike Shack in Whitby on 01947 606661.

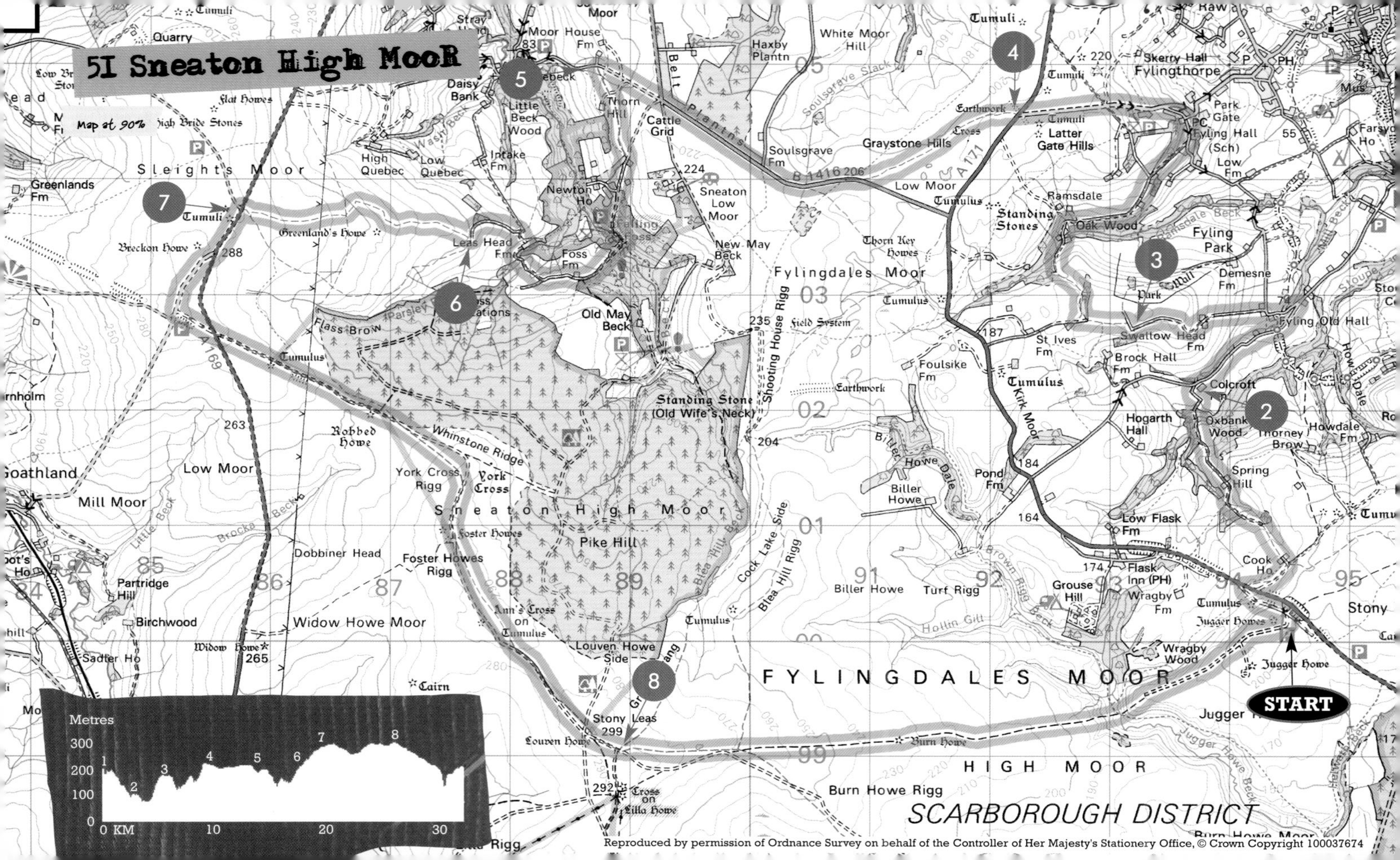
51 Sneaton High MooR
Map at 90%
START
Sneaton High Moor
Fylingdales Moor
FYLINGDALES MOOR
HIGH MOOR
SCARBOROUGH DISTRICT
Sleights Moor
Widow Howe Moor
Low Moor
Mill Moor
Goathland
Standing Stone (Old Wife's Neck)
Shooting House Rigg
Whinstone Ridge
York Cross
Pike Hill
Stony Leas
Jugger Howe
Fylingthorpe
Metres
300
200
100
0
0 KM
10
20
30

Sneaton High Moor

32.2KM (20M) & 730 METRES OF CLIMBING

ART Go L for 0.2km then R to cross the A171 to the track opposite (942/004) to Cook house. Cook house (944/006) turn L on a BW towards ring Hill, and follow this to the rd by Colecroft m (936/022).

Turn R on this rd, DH, to Flying Old Hall, taking t L (945/029) to head to/past Swallow Head m. Follow the BW (west) then shortly after the ck bears sharp R, turn L (931/027) along field ge (heading west).

At the trees, join a better track and turn R (north) the BW (927/027), to Ramsdale before St Ives m. Follow this BW, through Oak wood then UH Flying Hall, and keep bearing L, steep UH, past r park, now heading west, to the A171 rd 22/045).

Cross this rd to the BW on the other side and low this to the B1416 (909/039) and turn R on s towards Littlebeck. After 2.6km (0.6km) past X-rds), turn L on a BW to 'Falling Foss' 37/049), DH.

Join a rd and follow this (R), DH into the valley, d join a DT heading back UH, past Foss farm, to ork (882/031) and bear R. Just past Leas Head m keep R on the BW, then as the BW bears to L, turn R on a BW (876/034).

6 Follow the BW signposts across the fields, between 2 walls as the last gate, into the moors and go R on the BW then L on **(easy to miss BW)** BW path that fades, to a DT and the A169 rd (857/037) and turn L on this.

7 Take the minor rd on the R after a little way, to get off the A rd, then go L on a track at the far sic of the car park (852/028). Cross the A169 rd an follow this DT, and BW signs, for 5.3km (3.3m) to X-tracks (889/990).

8 Go SA on the middle BW (east), heading towards Robin Hood's Bay, and keep SA (L at fork on the track heading dead east, past Burn Howe (912/991). Good DH, cross Jugger Howe Beck, and bear L, UH, joining a DT, and keep SA, back to the car park by the A171 (944/002).

TOP TIP: see 'Dalby' in the trail centre rout for a choice of routes f Whitby to Scarborou cycle route for a family friendly ride.

Family activities

There are lots of nice beaches and coastal walks undertake. You should also visit the lovely village Robin Hood's Bay, famous for its role in smugglin

Whitby is a great town for all the family with lots activities and the usual seaside attractions. For more information see www.whitby-uk.com.

Getting there There is a car park by Flying-thorpe GR 931/045 (on north east edge of the route) which might be handier for some riders, but we start by Jugger How Moor on off the A171 (SE edge of the route) GR 944/002 as it means you finish with a good DH.

Accommodation: Quirky self catering railway carriages at Trailways, tel; 01947 820207 or see www.trailways.info. or the Flask Inn just up the rd from the start on tel: 01947 880305. For more options call Whitby T.I. 01947 602674

Refreshments Falling Foss tea garden at Midge Hall is in great location and distance on the ride (GR 888/038). There is also a pub (Flask Inn) just up the road from the finish, doing food..

Bike shops Doctor cranks bike Shack in Whitby, 01947 60661 or Trailways on 01947 820207 or see www.trailways.info for bike hire in Hawsker

52 High Cup Nick

Map at 60%

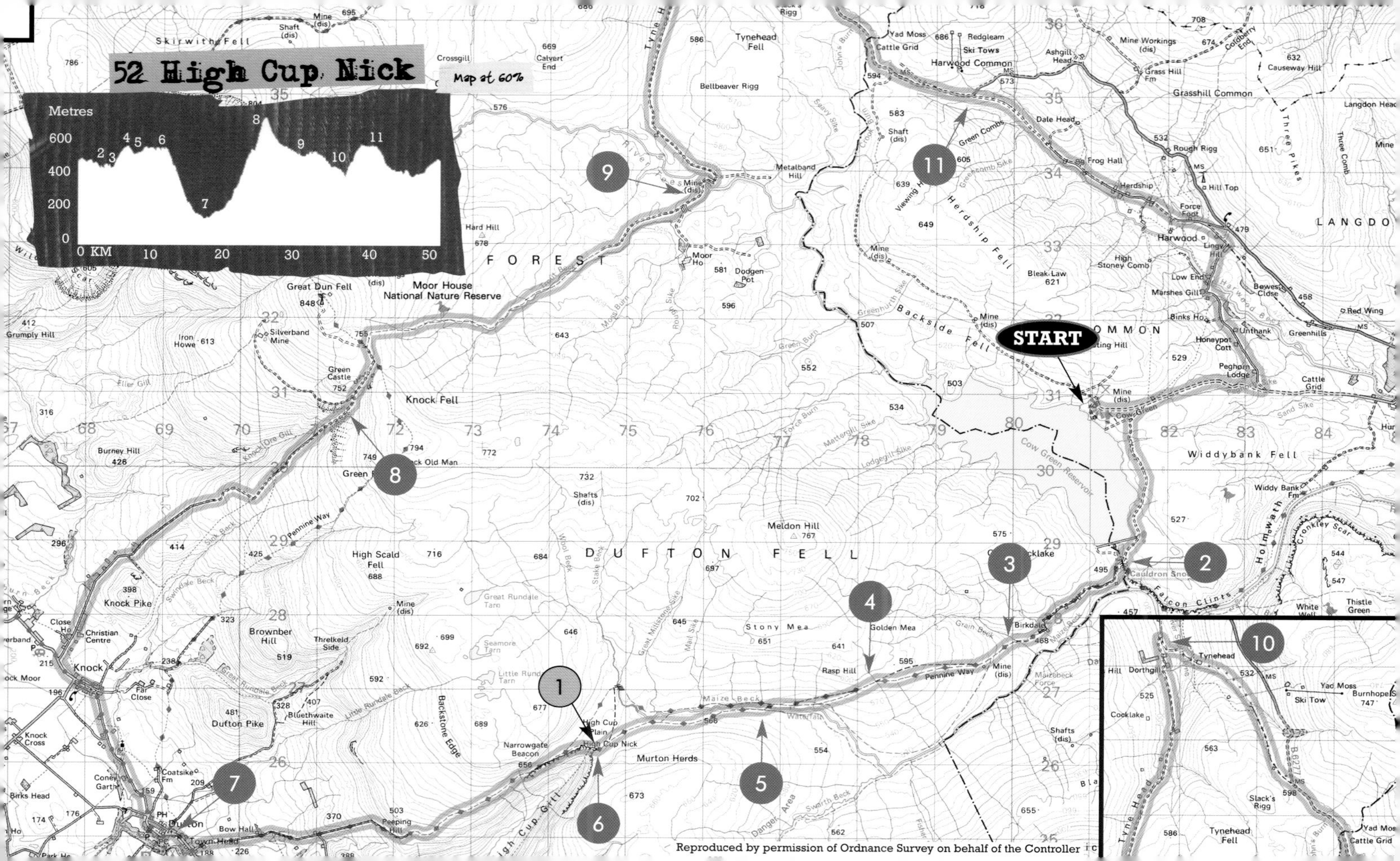

High Cup Nick

52 KM & (32.3M) 1,430 METRES CLIMBING

START From Cow Green car park head back along the rd & take next tarmac track on R. Please note this is a FP, so walk along here. Bear L (dirt track R), on rd through gate, past dam, to a bridge. Cross bridge & remount your bike, UH on track opposite.

2 Keep L at fork, following it bearing R, along Maize Beck valley, and bearing sharp L , DH to buildings. Ride past front of house, through gate & onto Grain Beck and leave track to cross bridge (801/276).

3 Keep R at fork, UH on on flag stone track, to RHS of an old mine and keep SA on stone track on the other side, UH. Follow this track, keep SA/R down steps at the end and bears L (Firing Range on L here).

4 Track becomes grassy and goes DH, crossing streams & down steep rocky ST to drop down to the flat flood plain, to follow alongside the river, eventually to a footbridge & cross the Maize Beck (766/268).

NOTE: The trail to the north of the Maize Beck does not make for good cycling.

5 Continue on south side of Maize Beck, bearing L UH away from the river on stoney track, becoming a grassy, following the cairns. Bears R, DH to the edge of High Cup Nick (745/261). See short ride.

6 Follow the BW to the RHS of the High Cup Gill (L at BW T-J) becoming a great descent (on Pennine Way), becoming a better track towards the bottom, and keep SA/R to a T-J with rd and go R into Dutton (688/251).

7 Follow the rd to Knock, keeping SA/R at the junction just after the village, then shortly R again on a rd (676/273) past the Christian Centre. UH, becoming a (tarmac) BW, Follow this track for a killer climb to a T-J on the edge of Green Castle (714/309).

8 Go SA/R up the valley, bearing L to view Great Dun Fell SA, leave the main track, bearing R on a BW (FP SA) (716/315). Follow this grassy rack, bearing R, DH to follow alongside Trout Beck, joining an old track.

9 Ignore bridge on R at the bottom, keeping SA/L, past old mine to another bridge and cross this then immediately bearing L and keep L on this track (to LHS of the hill/Bellbeaver Rigg. Follow this (Tyne Head) BW track up the valley, down to the head of a rd after a cattle grid (757/383).

10 Go R on this DT, DH, cross the river, pass Tynehead & UH on ROW (rough track) to the B6277. Go R on this rd for 2.7km then R on a DT on the other side (794/350). NOTE: There is no legal right of way on this track, so please do not use it if asked not to.

11 DH, joining a rd along the valley bottom & as it climbs UH to a fork just before the B6277 rd, bear R, following it to the R, DH, over bridge and follow the rd gently UH on the other side. At T-J (832/310) turn R, UH, back to the start reservoir (811/308).

Short(er) Ride

21.7KM (13.5M) & 480 METRES CLIMBING

1 Turn around and return the way you came, remembering to climb up the steep rocky ST 1km past the footbridge over Maize Beck. Follow the path as it bears L, UH, then bearing R by the firing range and keep L at fork to join the flagstone trail to the old mine.

__Getting there:__ Start from Cow Green Reservoir (NY 810/309), off the B6277, halfway between Barnard Castle & Alston. Alternatively start from Dutton (688/251), off the A66 from Appleby-in-Westmorland.

__Accommodation:__ YHA at Langdon Beck (nr start, on the B6277 rd) tel: 0845 371 9027 & another YHA in Dufton, on the other side of the route, tel 0845 371 9734. For more information on places to stay etc see www.northpennines.org.uk

__Bike shops__ Nothing close. Try Wood n Wheels at the Hamsterley Forest trail centre on 01388 488222.

__Refreshments__ Pub in Dufton, but nothing on the short(er) route.

ROUGH RIDE GUIDE

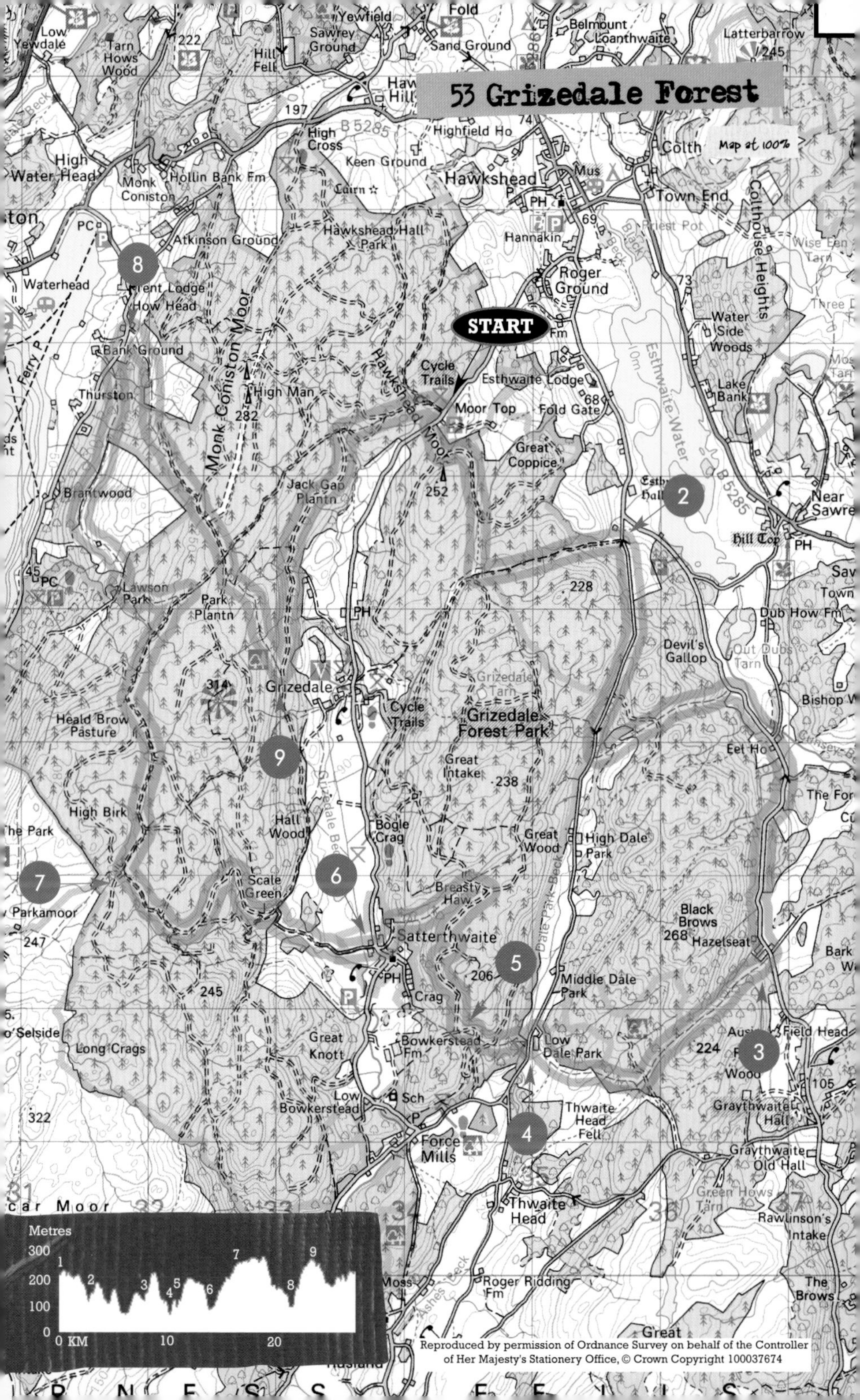

53 Grizedale Forest
Map at 100%
START
Hawkshead
Grizedale Forest Park
Grizedale
Satterthwaite
Monk Coniston Moor
Hawkshead Moor
Esthwaite Water
Roger Ground
Moor Top
Cycle Trails
Near Sawrey
Force Mills
Thwaite Head
Low Dale Park
Parkamoor
Brantwood
Metres
300
200
100
0
0 KM
10
20

Grizedale Forest

27.2KM (16.9M) & 1,220 METRES OF CLIMBING

START Turn R on the rd then shortly past a private driveway turn L on a forest fire track, 0.3km to a fork and bear L (east). Follow this track as it bear R (south) to a sharp LH bend where you keep SA (R) on a ST, UH (345/956). After 0.4km, at a forest track, turn L for fun technical DH to a rd at the bottom (356/955).

2 Turn R (south) on the rd, for 1.7km, steep UH, then DH, turning L on an (easy to miss) BW (shortly after a BW on the R) (354/938). Cross the field and into the wood, following the BW for fun DH to the rd (365/944) and turn R on this, for 2.3km, UH, then go R on a BW through Black Brows Close sawmills yard (368/924).

3 Follow the BW (R at fork), steeply UH, then becoming a DH, following the BW signs over a forest track, then shortly turning R through a deer gate at a X-tracks (358/914) on Low Dale Park BW. Superb technical ST trail, through some gates, DH to buildings at Low Dale Park, and go R then L, DH to the rd (349/917).

4 Go L on the rd then shortly R on a BW, over or through the stream, then UH, over a fire road, to a 2nd fire road (the BW goes SA but you don't). Turn L (south) on this fire road and R at the fork, to head back north, keeping SA on this main track for 0.5km to a fork (BW on L) and bear R (344/918).

5 Ignore a forest road to the R after 0.75km, and keep SA on the main track to a junction with deer fence SA, at Breasty Haw and bear L, then turn L after 0.1km on BW (SP to R), going south west, down to the rd at Satterthwaite and turn R then immediately L on a BW (337/924).

6 Follow this track UH, through a gate into the forest to a T-J with a forest track and go L, then R at the next fork, UH keeping SA/L, over a stream. Bear L at the next fork, keeping SA (ignore L turn) on the fire road to a main junction and bear L, to a X-tracks and turn R (north) (318/930).

7 Still going UH (north), bear L at the next fork and R at the following fork (SP Moor Top), to the top and 0.2km past Parkamoor BW on L, turn L on a BW (322/951). Superb DH through Lawson Park, to a rd and go R on this for 0.3km then turn R on a BW opposite a house (318/971).

8 SP to Satterthwaite/Grizedale, tough UH on a stoney track, keeping SA to a T-J with a forest track and turn R on this. See note below. UH past a junction with a BW, to a bigger junction and bear L, then shortly L again on a BW (326/952) for a steep, fun DH.

NOTE: You can turn L to join the North Face trail, following the markers all the way back to the start.

9 After the 1km DH, turn L on the forest track (330/944) and follow this, ignoring any turnings for 2km to a sharp RHB and turn L on a (easy to miss) ST BW (335/963). Keep SA/L at the forest track, then R at a fork, to Moor Top car park (343/965).

Shortcuts — VARIOUS

There are a number of suitable options e.g. use the BW through Great Wood by High Dale park to miss off the south east corner of the ride.

Family & other riding

There are some man-made trails at Grizedale trail centre (in centre of the route) with trails for various abilities. See route no.60 for more info.

16km (10m) North Face Trail
22.5km 14m) Silurian Way
17km (10.5m) Hawkshead Moor
11km 7m) Moor Top
9.5km (5.9) Grizedale Tarn Trail
3km (2m) Goosey Foot Tarn Trail

Getting there There are a few places you could start from (see the map), so the direction you approach the forest will determine where you park. Coming from Ambleside we used the B5286 to Hawkshead then right following the tourist signs. Moor Top car park is 2km (1.2m) up here on the right (SD 343/965) (2.3km/1.4m north of Grizedale visitor centre).

Accommodation: There is an increadible choice of places. Ask at The Hub in Ambleside (T.I) on 015394 32582. Grizedale camping (with wooden camping pods) on 01229 860208 www.grizedale-camping.co.uk is good and close to the trail. Also Low Wray campsite right on the shores of Windemere is lovely, tel 015394 328810.

Refreshments
Pub in Satterthwaite and Grizedaele visitor centre.

Bike shops Bike Treks in Ambleside on 015394 31245

54 Ambleside
Map at 90%
Reproduced by permission of Ordnance Survey on behalf of the Controller of Her Majesty's Stationery Office, © Crown Copyright 100037674
START
AMBLESIDE
Skelwith Bridge
Skelwith Fold
Elterwater
Chapel Stile
Clappersgate
Loughrigg Fell
Rydal
Rydal Water
Troutbeck
Troutbeck Bridge
Wansfell
The Hundreds
Holme Fell
Little Langdale
Black Fell
Metres
200
100
0
0 KM
10
20
5

Ambleside

24.3KM (15.1M) & 930 METRES CLIMBING

RT Go north on the A5095 (Borrans Rd), ring L on the one-way system then L at a junc- (on A593) over the bridge and immediately R on a rd, towards Rydal (371/039). After km turn L on a tarmac BW (370/045), UH, past w Head fm, keeping SA (southwest) on the rocky UH then DH to (BW) fork at Ivy Crag 3/040).

ear R on lovely ST DH, to a track and keep SA rd and go R then immediately L, and keep R he rd, to a X-rds with the A593 rd (344/035). SA on this, over Skelworth Bridge, UH for km then go L on a BW (335/029) as rd starts to cend.

ough UH, passing through a wall after 1km bearing L (buildings just ahead, UH following BW. Go through a gate into Iron Keld woods ore a track to the L at the gate), DH to a gate T-J (336/005). Turn R on this, DH to the A593 go SA on the (Smithy Brow) BW track, bearing eeping L on this, UH then DH.

Go SA through a gate on a BW when the tar- ends, UH to a gate, then DH to a gate at ge Close, to a T-J (318/019). Turn L, DH then a track opposite the last cottage, through a . Go R (north) at the fork just past Pierce How (313/020) to a X-tracks and go SA over a ge, to Little Langdale (315/033).

rn L on the rd then shortly R on rd, becoming past Dale End fm, DH, SA at gate, joining a ac track DH to a T-J with a rd (327/044). Turn the rd, over the water into Elterwater, keep between pub and PO, to a X-rds with the 43 (329/049) and go SA.

6 Past a car park, keep R and R at T-J, UH to a 2nd T-J by Loughrigg Fell and turn L then shortly R on a BW (340/056). Popular with walkers! Follow this BW along the southern shores of Rydal Water or alternative permissive route past the caves.

7 Keep R on the rd (Sustrans route no. 6) before Pelter Bridge and follow this back to the A593 rd and go L on the one-way system, then R back down (south) on the A593 to the car park (376/033).

Short Route

9.2KM (5.7M) & 370 METRES CLIMBING

Perfect for getting a quick (but challenging) spin in when time is tight - it should take between 1-1.5hrs

START Go south on the A593 for 3km, just past Brockhole centre, turn L on Kirk Lane, L (north) at T-J, past big building on the L (394/015). Steep UH, off rd, past a farm to the rd and turn R on this for 0.4km and go L on a BW (404/019) shortly after a BW that goes sharp R.

2 UH to a T-J and go L and keep L where SP Jenkin Crag, through a couple of gates, keeping R after the 2nd one, UH to High Skelghyll fm (390/028). Walk past the farm then remount for a fun technical DH through the woods, with rocks, roots and walkers.

3 The final part of the DH is on tarmac, bringing you out behind the mountain rescue centre, where you need to turn L to the A591 and go L on this back to the car park (on the R) (376/034).

TOP TIP: For further riding see our Grizedale route and 'Trail Centre' routes.

NOTE: There are plenty of water sports, walks and ferry trips to do with the family around here.

Getting there P&D car park between Waterhead & Ambleside, on the A591 (GR NY 038/377). Train stations in Windemere 6.3Km down the A591/Sustrans route no.6.

Accommodation: LOTS. see see www.amblesideonline.co.uk or call Ambleside T.I. on 015394 32582. Low Wray campsite right on the shores of Windemere is lovely, tel 015394 328810. Ambleside Backpackers on 015394 32340, YHA in Waterhead (at start) on 015394 32304, & Chapel Stile campsite (nr Elterwater) on 01539 437150.

Refreshments You will come across some tea rooms along the way as well as some pubs at Little Langdale, Elterwater & Rydal along the route and a sandwich shop in the car park at the start.

Bike shops Bike Treks in Ambleside on 015394 31245.

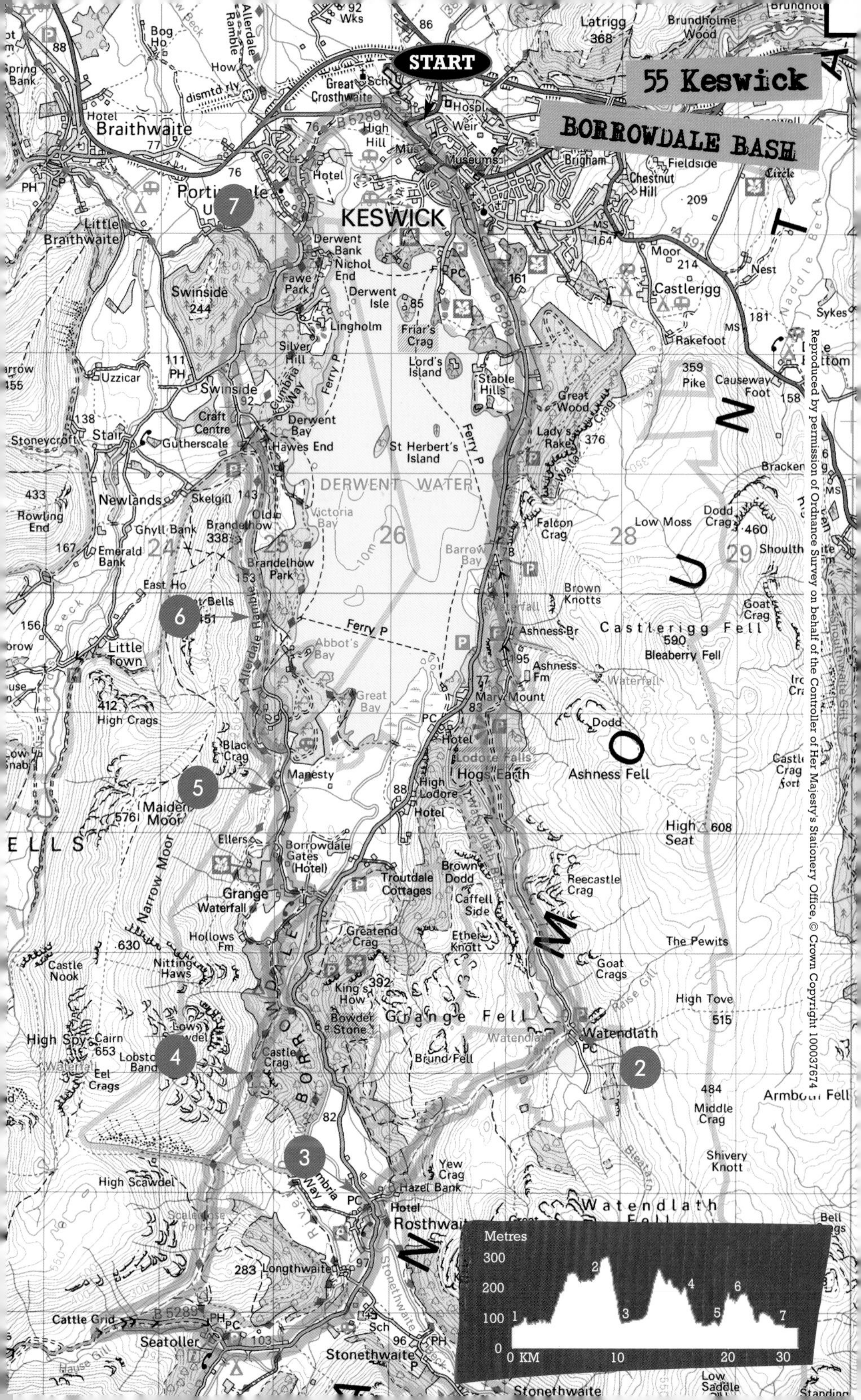

55 Keswick
BORROWDALE BASH
START
KESWICK
DERWENT WATER
Great Crosthwaite
Braithwaite
Portinscale
Little Braithwaite
Swinside
Derwent Bank
Nichol End
Fawe Park
Derwent Isle
Lingholm
Silver Hill
Friar's Crag
Lord's Island
Stable Hills
Uzzicar
Stair
Stoneycroft
Craft Centre
Gutherscale
Derwent Bay
Hawes End
St Herbert's Island
Newlands
Skelgill
Brandelhow
Brandelhow Park
Victoria Bay
Barrow Bay
Ferry P
Abbot's Bay
Great Bay
Little Town
High Crags
Black Crag
Manesty
Maiden Moor
Ellers
Borrowdale Gates (Hotel)
Grange
Narrow Moor
Hollows Fm
Nitting Haws
Castle Nook
High Spy
Eel Crags
Castle Crag
BORROWDALE
King's How
Bowder Stone
Grange Fell
Brund Fell
Troutdale Cottages
Greatend Crag
Brown Dodd
Caffell Side
Ether Knott
Lodore Falls
Hogs Earth
High Lodore
Mary Mount
Ashness Br
Ashness Fm
Ashness Fell
Dodd
Falcon Crag
Great Wood
Lady's Rake
Walla Crag
Castlerigg
Castlerigg Fell
Bleaberry Fell
Brown Knotts
Low Moss
Dodd Crag
High Seat
Reecastle Crag
The Pewits
Goat Crags
High Tove
Watendlath
Middle Crag
Armboth Fell
Shivery Knott
Watendlath Fell
Yew Crag
Hazel Bank
Rosthwaite
High Scawdel
Longthwaite
Cattle Grid
Seatoller
Stonethwaite
Cumbria Way
Alleradale Ramble
MOUNTAINS
Reproduced by permission of Ordnance Survey on behalf of the Controller of Her Majesty's Stationery Office, © Crown Copyright 100037674
Metres
300
200
100
0
0 KM
10
20
30

Keswick

26.5KM (16.5M) & 975 METRES OF CLIMBING

TART Follow signs for Borrowdale, joining the 5289, heading south, and after 3km (1.9m) turn L n a (dead-end) rd SP Watendlath (269/203). ollow this rd UH all the way to Watendlath 275/164) where the rd forks and bear R.

Cross the river and go through a gate, keeping , UH on Rosthwaite BW. Keep SA, steep UH, then ocky DH, staying on main track SA, which then ears L (Rosthwaite) and gradient eases at a gate. W to R is also fun. Follow the track DH, through a ate to a tarmac track and turn R on this, over a ridge to the B5289rd (258/149).

Turn L on this rd for 2.3km (1.4m) to Seatoller, en another 1km past here, VERY steeply UH, then o sharp R, on a BW (235/138) or R on permissive W just after (opposite YewTree). DH, looking for W forking off L after 1km and follow this technical ngle track BW SA (north), through gates, over ridges, etc, ignoring any turnings to some woods.

Rocky DH into a wood, on the main track to a J by the river Derwent (250/165) and turn L. Past campsite, then R at a T-J, to Grange (252/174). o L on the rd here, for 1.3km (0.8m) to just past e houses at Manesty, go L and walk along the otpath on the RHS, with boulder (250/184).

BW begins at the gate, climbing steeply UH, to fork (by a small cairn) and bear R along the edge the woods for some technical single track along at Bells BW. Keep SA on a grassy track and down a rd and parking area and keep L straight back nto the BW (248/197).

6 Follow this BW to the rd again and go L (SA) on it, keeping R at hairpin bend (247/211), and R at fork after 0.75km. Follow the SP's for Keswick, to the village of Portinscale, and turn R on the Sustrans no.71 cycle route (252/235).

7 Keep SA at the end of the rd, over cross the (foot) bridge and follow the Sustrans cycle track signposts, bearing R with the B5289 rd, for 1km back into Keswick and the end (262/237).

Further riding

Red & Blue grade waymarked man-made trails at Whinlatter forest trail centre, (GR NY209/245), ju west of Keswick. See www.forestry.gov.uk

Family activities

KESWICK LAUNCH

Take a ferry ride around Derwent water, or hire your own motor boat or rowing boat. Tel: 01768 72263 or see www.keswick-launch.co.uk

TROTTERS WORLD OF ANIMALS

Just north of Keswick, this place has a great range of usual & unusual animails, plus kids play area. Tel: 017687 76239 or see www.trottersworld.com

KESWICK MARKET

In the town centre, every Saturday, offering a goo wide range of products.

HONISTER SLATE MINE

Near Seatoller is the old slate mine (with zip wire ride). See www.honister-slate-mine.co.uk or call 017687 77230.

Getting there Head west off the M6 at junction 40, along the A66 to Keswick. There are a choice of pay & display car parks in Keswick, but be aware they get filled up quickly.

Accommodation: Lots of places in Keswick, see www.keswick.org. Hollows farm in Grange B&B and camping, tel: 017687 77298 or see www.hollowsfarm.co.uk and Keswick YHA on 0845 3719314 is good.

Bike shops Keswick Bikes are open 7 days week & do hire & repair; 017687 80586 or see www.keswickmountainbikes.co.uk

Refreshments Lots of places in Keswick, a pub in Rosthwaite, tea room in Grange and a choice of places in Portinscale.

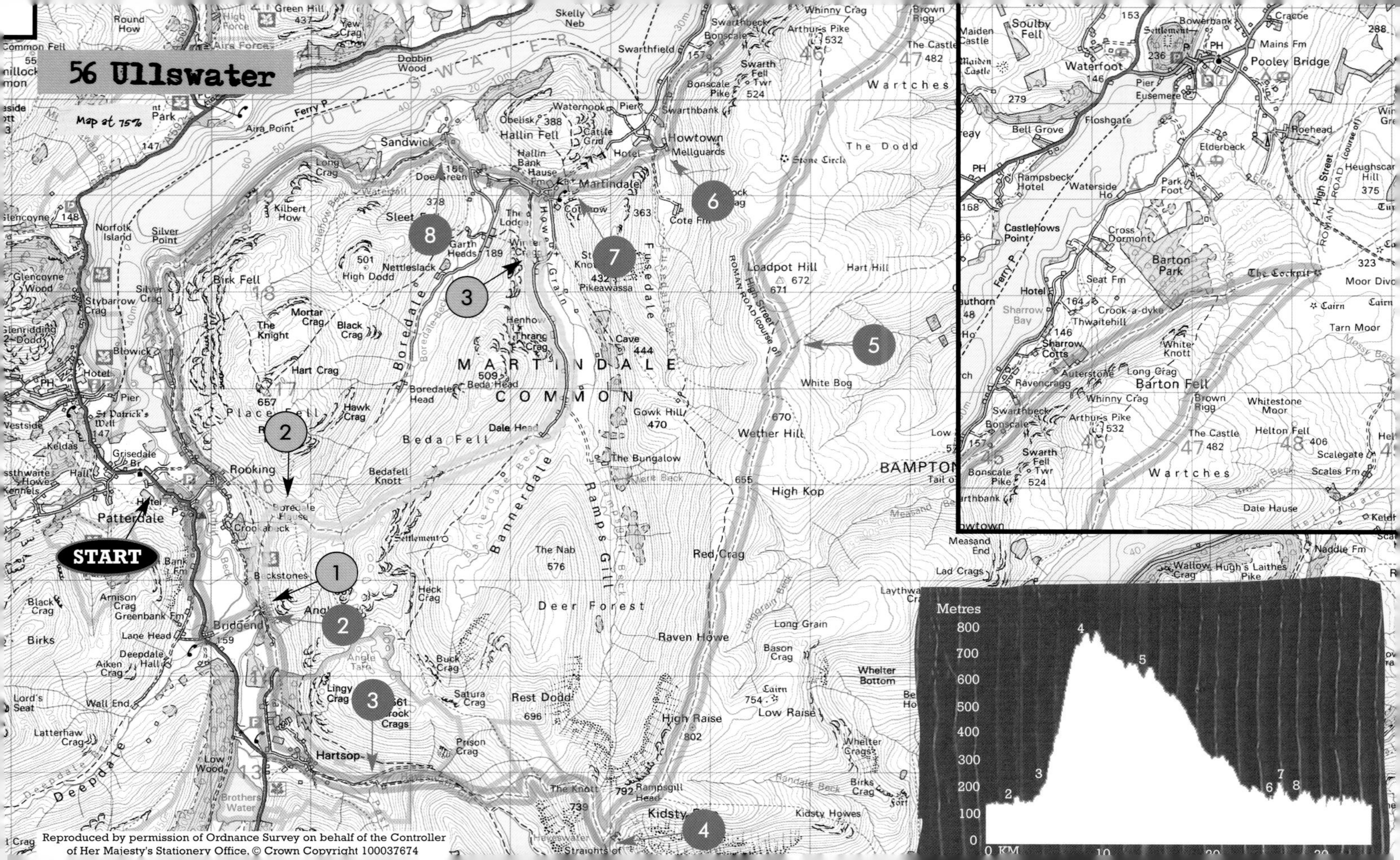
56 Ullswater
Map at 75%
START
Patterdale
Martindale Common
Place Fell
Hallin Fell
Howtown
Sandwick
Pooley Bridge
Loadpot Hill
High Street
ROMAN ROAD (course of)
High Raise
Hartsop
Bampton
Metres
800
700
600
500
400
300
200
100
0
0 KM
10
20

Ullswater - High Street

34.4 (21.4M) & 1,310 METRES OF CLIMBING

START Head south from Patterdale car park and go outh on the A592 for 1.6km (1m) to Bridgend and urn L on a BW by the last house (399/144). Follow his through the gates and across 2 fields, DH over the iver and bear L to a good track (404/147) and turn R or see the shortcut.

2 Keep SA on this BW for 1.6km (1m) to a rd 405/132) and turn L on this through Hartsopand a gate at the end of the car park (Hayswater). Just after going over a cattle grid bear R at the fork, DH over a bridge (416/128).

3 Shortly before Hayeswater follow the (easy to miss) BW over the river and up the (steep) hillside). Grassy zig zag UH (walk) to the ridge and bear R, following he track to the LHS of the Knott (gets boggy around here). Bears R down to a wall and T-J (439/123) with he 'High Street'.

NOTE: Turn R on the BW to get to High Street summit. You will have to walk the last part where you turn L after 0.8m, up to the trig point (440/110).

4 Turn L, UH to Rampsgill Head and at the summit urn L on the less obvious, feint grassy, trail, DH, then UH to High Raise (447/135). Keep SA on the main rack for (2.5m) (bearing R at the wall, over a stile, hrough a gate, keep fence on LHS, DH through gap n wall) to a fork (457/174) by cairn at bottom of Loadpot Hill (trig point on the top).

5 Bear L on the BW (on LHS of hill) and keep R at fork not L to Arthur's Pike) on the feint grassy track, for 2m) to a T-J (481/222) as the gradient levels out and urn L (The Cockpit is to R). Superb hillside track with views of Ullswater, keeping L at junction on the less obvious path to a gate by a house (445/195).

6 Walk along the RHS of the drive, then turn L hrough a gate on a BW (ride), cross the river, UH to X-racks and go SA on Martindale House BW. UH on teep grassy track, bearing L then turning R to a Chapel and the rd (435/191).

7 Turn L on the rd, shortly to a junction and go R (Sandwick), steep DH and shortly bear R on a track leaving the rd. **7A** DH and R when rejoining the rd, towards Sandwick, but turn L on the Patterdale BW by the car park just before the village (423/195).

8 Lovely technical single track along the waters edge but watch out for walkers - they like to taunt you on the tricky sections. After over 3km of this lovely trail bear R at the fork (397/183) and keep SA through Side farm to join a tarmac track. Bear R and down to the A592 (397/158) and turn R on this, back to the car park/start (395/159).

Shortcut

-16.7KM (10.4M) & 580 METRES CLIMBING

1 Shortly after going R, turn back sharp L, very steep UH to Boredale Hause on a wide track. Eases off and bears R, where you need to head east then L on the feint grass BW (ignore all other tracks). Bear L (north) at the far side, UH to the ridge top on a nice ST.

2 At the top go SA at a X-tracks, curving R then L, DH, staying on the main (fun single) track, which joins a road at the buildings / Dale Head (433/165). Follow this along the valley for until a grassy BW just before crossing the bridge by a farm (432/183).

3 Follow this to a rd and turn L (SA) on this, DH then shortly bear R on a track leaving the rd and join the main route at **7A**.

Variations to the ride

By using the Ullswater steam ferry you can create a variety of possible routes, as well as adding a unique and interesting element to the ride.

The ferry runs from Pooley Bridge, Howtown and Glenridding throughout the year now. Although it has to give priority to passengers it is usually fine getting bikes on. See www.ullswater-steamers.co.uk for info.

To miss out the hill top riding by getting the ferry from Glenridding to Howtown and just ride the fun technical trail along the edge of Ullswater.

Getting there Patterdale car park (395/159), north of Ambleside, on the A592 by Glenridding, at the southern end of Ullswater, or there is a car park in Pooley Bridge (470/245) which is easier to get to from the M6 (junction 40), along the A592, at the northern end of Ullswater. Train station in Penrith, 8km (5m) away – use the B5320 to Pooley Bridge.

Accommodation: Side farm campsite in Patterdale is excellent. Tel 017684 82337. Patterdale Hotel on 017684 82231, Patterdale YHA on 0845 371 9337, The Quiet Site with camping, cottage and huts in Glenridding on 07768 727016. Pooley birdge T.I. on 017684 86530.

Bike shops Harpers cycles 01768 864475, Arragons on 890344 and Halfords on 892960 all in Penrith, Keswick MTB centre on 01768 775202 and Lakeland Peddlar on 774492 both in Keswick and Bike Treks in Ambleside on 015394 31245.

Refreshments Patterdale only, or Pooley Bridge if starting there.

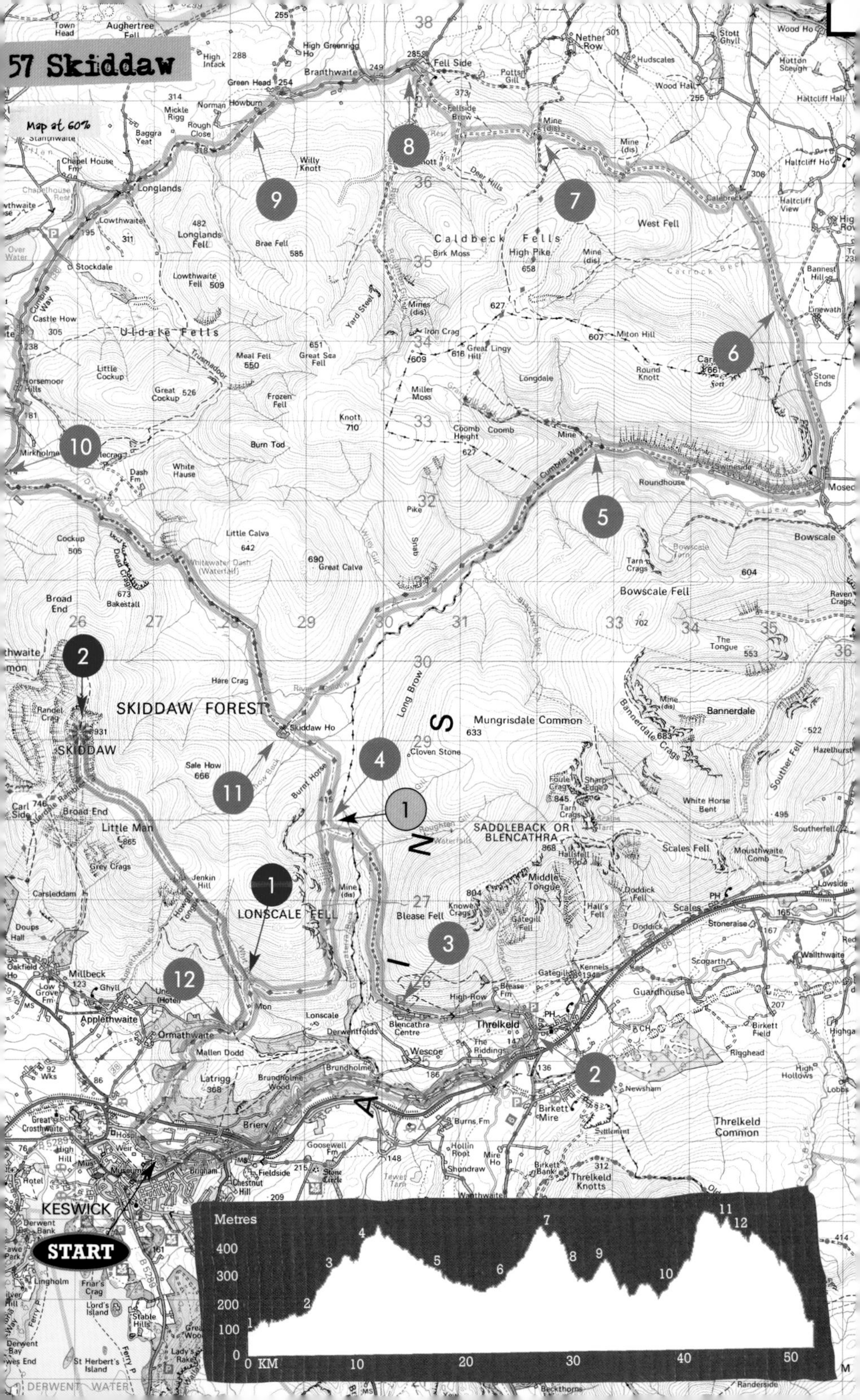

57 Skiddaw
Map at 60%
START
KESWICK
SKIDDAW
SKIDDAW FOREST
LONSCALE FELL
SADDLEBACK OR BLENCATHRA
Caldbeck Fells
Uldale Fells
Mungrisdale Common
Bowscale Fell
Threlkeld
Threlkeld Common
Skiddaw Ho
Little Man
Great Calva
Little Calva
Knott
High Pike
West Fell
Longlands Fell
Brae Fell
Great Cockup
Meal Fell
Bannerdale Crags
Souther Fell
Blease Fell
Latrigg
Applethwaite
Ormathwaite
Millbeck
Caldbeck
Mosedale
DERWENT WATER
Metres
400
300
200
100
0
0 KM
10
20
30
40
50

52.3KM (32.5M) & 1,550 METRES CLIMBING

TART From the old railway station car park (swimming ool), head East on the Keswick railway (foot)path, for KM (3m), over and under numerous bridges, to the main d (314/248) and keep L, following signs to Threkland.

In the village (319/253), turn L on Blease Road Blencathra), keeping SA, UH, past the Blencathra centre nd bear R at a fork on ST rd, to and through a car park nd onto a BW, (SP Skiddaw House).

Follow this trail northwards, along the valley, crossing 3 ords on the way, to the head of the valley. Follow the track a T-J (292/279) and turn R to Skiddaw house or see the hortcut.

Follow this trail to Skiddaw House, and turn R at the nd of the wall by the house, DH. Changing track surface, eeping SA, along the LHS of the river, the trail widens to become a better track, then a rd (328/327).

5 Follow the tarmac rd down the valley, to a T-J at Mosedale (357/322) and turn L and follow this rd north. After 2.25KM (1.4m) where the rd bears R, go SA on a track to cut the corner, rejoining the d again shortly.

6 After 0.6KM (1m) (at Calebreck) turn L on a Permissive BW track (NOT the grassy official BW), in the lay-by (just before a cattle grid) (345/358). Follow this past the 2nd disused mine up a short climb over a feint X-rds.

7 Shortly when the track disappears, turn R on a feint grassy track, DH, to a small stream, then UH, and back down on a grassy track to a T-J with a stone track and a wall alongside and turn R, DH, through a gate and farm-yard, to a rd (303/374) at Fell Side.

8 Turn L on this rd and follow it for 1.8KM (1.1m), then turn L over a small bridge, down the dead end rd. Keep SA/L on a dirt track, as the track bears R to a gate.

9 Follow this, and go through a gate just past a house, to a rd (266/358). Turn L and follow this rd for 4.3KM (2.7m) and turn L on a tarmac BW (SP Skiddaw House), just past Peter House farm (249/323).

10 After 1.37KM (0.85m) bear R on the BW to Skiddaw House and Threlkeld, steep technical UH. Go through a gate, and stay SA on this track, which levels out, then goes DH, then UH to Skiddaw House (287/291).

the track you came along earlier, but after 1.6KM (1m) don't turn L back towards Threlkeld, but keep SA (south) along the side of Lonscale Fell.

NOTE: This track does get quite technical and has a nasty drop near Whit Beck, so take great care.

12 Follow this thinning ST, DH then UH to a junction with the Skiddaw path (282/256). You could extend the ride by going up to the summit of Skiddaw - see 'Short hard route'. Keep L and follow the Keswick BW, turning R after the 2nd gate, through a gate into the car park.

13 Turn L through a gate at the other side of the car park, and bear R at the fork, steep DH, taking great care of walkers and drainage ditches. Through a gate to a rd and turn L, back to the car park (270/237).

Shortcut

-35.4KM (22M) & 985 METRES CLIMBING

1 Turn sharp L (south), on a higher track, around Lonscale Fell, to rejoin the route at no.12.

NOTE: This shortcut reduces the distance by a great deal, but there is still some technical riding.

Skiddaw Summit

9.7KM (6M) & 675 METRES CLIMBING

1 From the Ormathwaite car park (280/253) go through the gate at the far end and immediately turn L. Go through two more gates, and just after the 2nd one, fork L, on the Skiddaw path, and climb to the summit (260/290).

2 At the top, take in the view and some refreshments, and turn back around to go back down the way you came up, retracing your tyre tracks, all the way back the car park and your car (280/253).

Family route

For a nice easy family ride, follow the cycle track from Keswick to Threkland, 5.8km/3.6m (180 metres climbing). There is a pub in Threkeland for refreshments, then return back to Keswick, this time it is downhill. For more ideas see 'cycling' at www.lake-district.gov.uk.

Getting there start the ride from the old railway station / leisure centre 270/237 in Keswick, which is well signposted, or the car parks at Ormathwaite (280/253) for the Skiddaw summit ride.

Accommodation: Grassmoor B&B on 017687 74008 or see www.grassmoor-keswick.co.uk, Denton House Hostel on 017687 75351 or see www.vividevents.co.uk, Keswick YHA on 0870 7705894, Castlerigg Hall Caravan & Camping Park on 017687 74499 or see www.castlerigg.co.uk and Keswick T.I. on 017687 72645.

Refreshments Lots in Keswick, including The Lakeland Pedlar bike shop with its very good vegetarian cafe.

Bike shops Keswick Mountain Bike Centre on 01768 775202 and the Lakeland Peddlar on 01768 774492

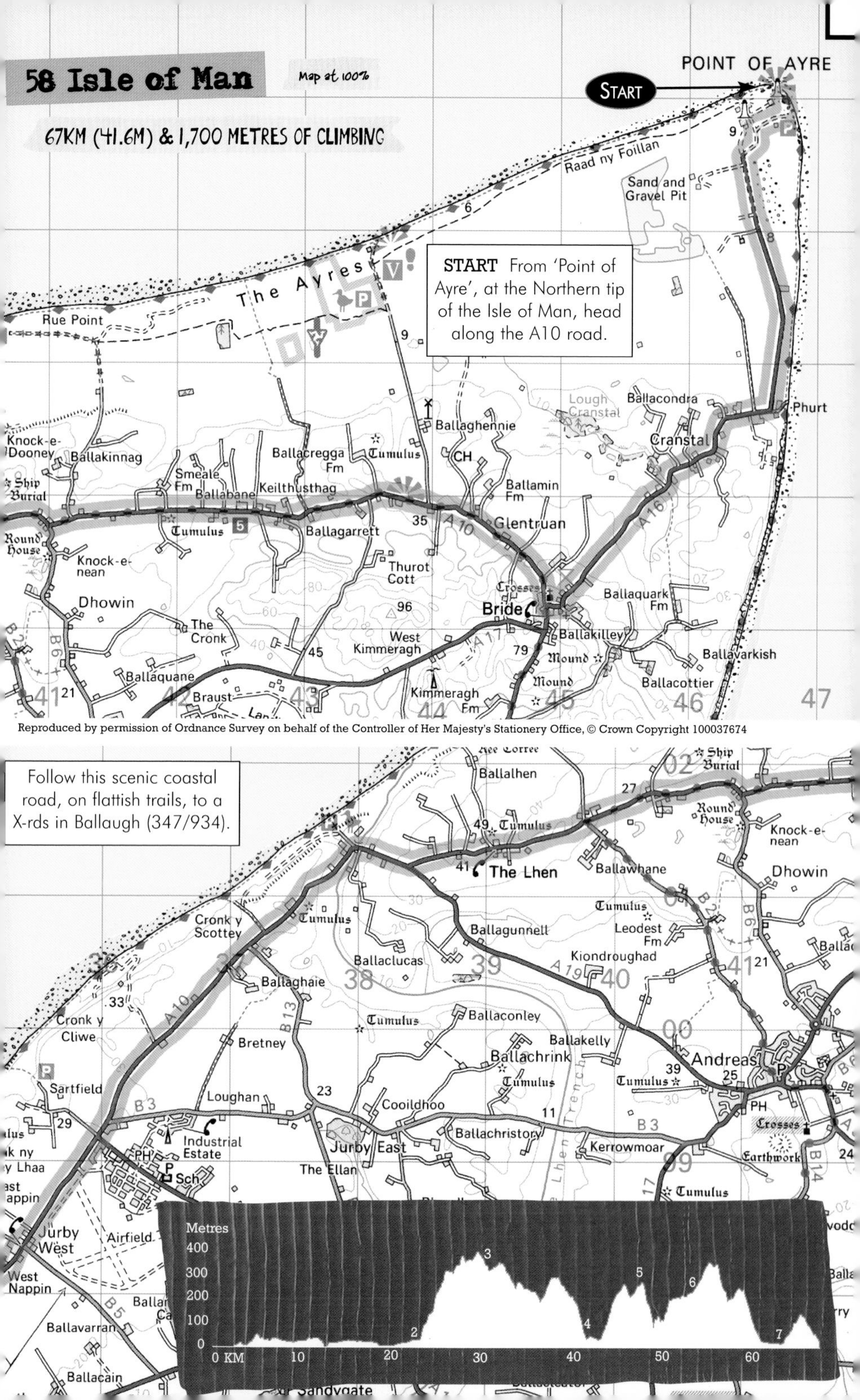
58 Isle of Man
Map at 100%
67KM (41.6M) & 1,700 METRES OF CLIMBING
START
POINT OF AYRE
START From 'Point of Ayre', at the Northern tip of the Isle of Man, head along the A10 road.
Reproduced by permission of Ordnance Survey on behalf of the Controller of Her Majesty's Stationery Office, © Crown Copyright 100037674
Follow this scenic coastal road, on flattish trails, to a X-rds in Ballaugh (347/934).
Metres
400
300
200
100
0
0 KM
10
20
30
40
50
60

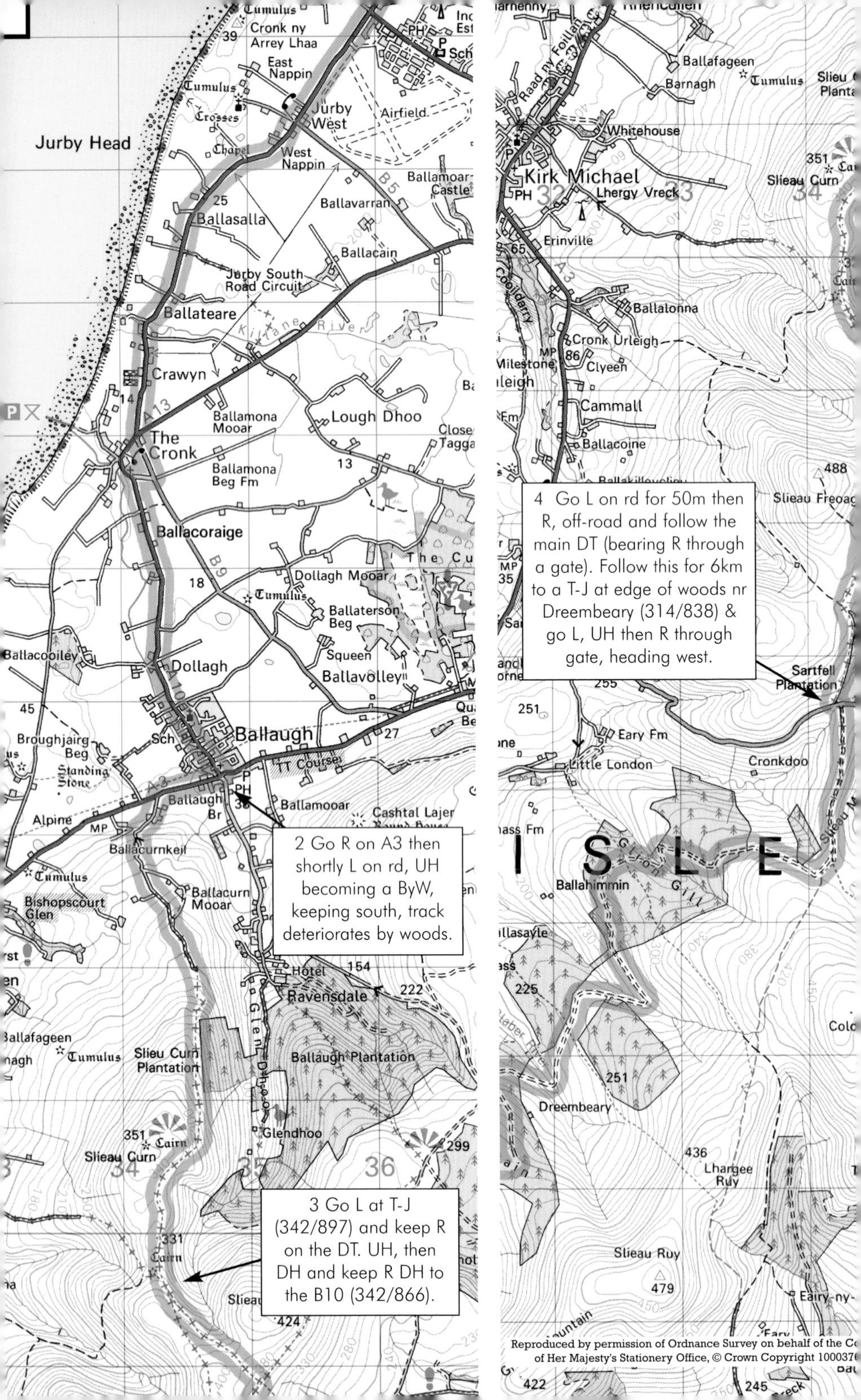

2 Go R on A3 then shortly L on rd, UH becoming a ByW, keeping south, track deteriorates by woods.
3 Go L at T-J (342/897) and keep R on the DT. UH, then DH and keep R DH to the B10 (342/866).
4 Go L on rd for 50m then R, off-road and follow the main DT (bearing R through a gate). Follow this for 6km to a T-J at edge of woods nr Dreembeary (314/838) & go L, UH then R through gate, heading west.
Jurby Head
Cronk ny Arrey Lhaa
East Nappin
Jurby West
Airfield
West Nappin
Ballamoar Castle
Ballavarran
Ballasalla
Ballacain
Jurby South Road Circuit
Ballateare
Crawyn
Ballamona Mooar
Lough Dhoo
The Cronk
Ballamona Beg Fm
Ballacoraige
Dollagh Mooar
Ballaterson Beg
Squeen
Ballavolley
Ballacooiley
Dollagh
Ballaugh
Broughjairg Beg
Standing Stone
TT Course
Ballamooar
Alpine
Ballacurnkeil
Cashtal Lajer
Ballacurn Mooar
Bishopscourt Glen
Hotel
Ravensdale
Ballaugh Plantation
Glen Dhoo
Glendhoo
Ballafageen
Slieu Curn Plantation
Slieau Curn
Kirk Michael
Whitehouse
Barnagh
Lhergy Vreck
Erinville
Ballalonna
Cronk Urleigh
Clyeen
Milestone
Cammall
Ballacoine
Slieau Freoaghane
Sartfell Plantation
Eary Fm
Little London
Cronkdoo
ISLE
Ballahimmin
Glion Gill
Dreembeary
Lhargee Ruy
Slieau Ruy
Reproduced by permission of Ordnance Survey on behalf of the Co
of Her Majesty's Stationery Office, © Crown Copyright 100037

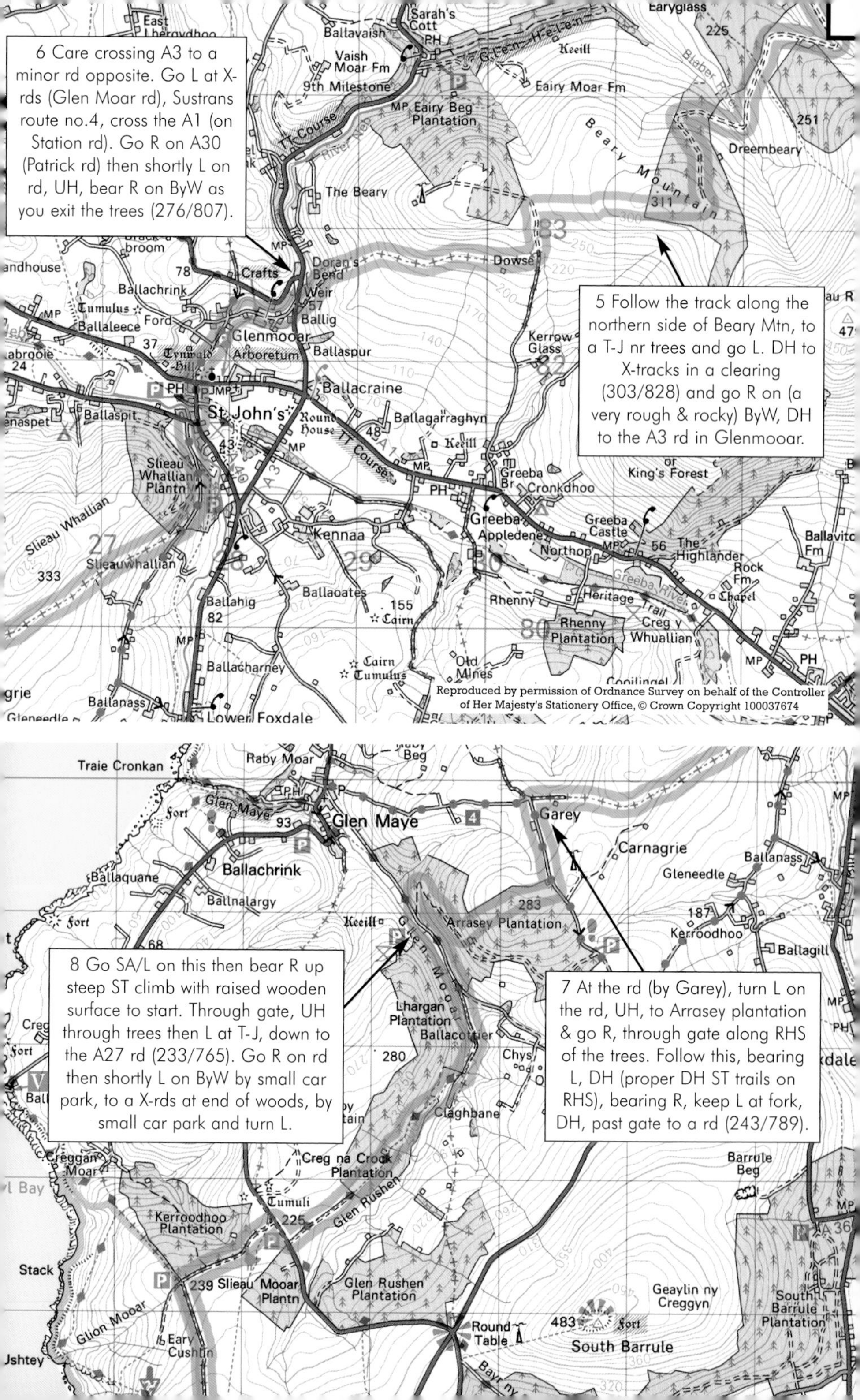
6 Care crossing A3 to a minor rd opposite. Go L at X-rds (Glen Moar rd), Sustrans route no.4, cross the A1 (on Station rd). Go R on A30 (Patrick rd) then shortly L on rd, UH, bear R on ByW as you exit the trees (276/807).
5 Follow the track along the northern side of Beary Mtn, to a T-J nr trees and go L. DH to X-tracks in a clearing (303/828) and go R on (a very rough & rocky) ByW, DH to the A3 rd in Glenmooar.
8 Go SA/L on this then bear R up steep ST climb with raised wooden surface to start. Through gate, UH through trees then L at T-J, down to the A27 rd (233/765). Go R on rd then shortly L on ByW by small car park, to a X-rds at end of woods, by small car park and turn L.
7 At the rd (by Garey), turn L on the rd, UH, to Arrasey plantation & go R, through gate along RHS of the trees. Follow this, bearing L, DH (proper DH ST trails on RHS), bearing R, keep L at fork, DH, past gate to a rd (243/789).
Reproduced by permission of Ordnance Survey on behalf of the Controller of Her Majesty's Stationery Office, © Crown Copyright 100037674

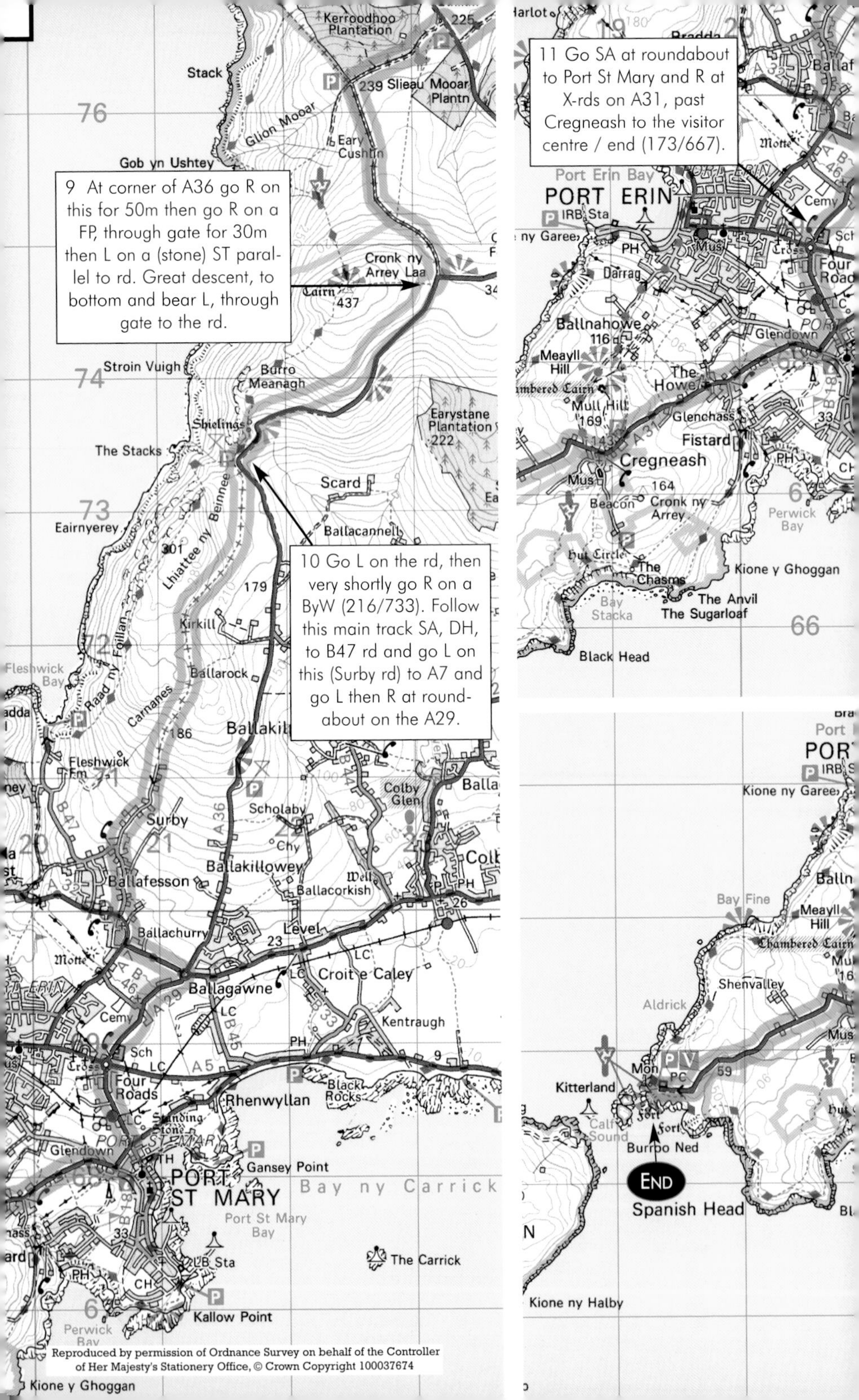
9 At corner of A36 go R on this for 50m then go R on a FP, through gate for 30m then L on a (stone) ST parallel to rd. Great descent, to bottom and bear L, through gate to the rd.
10 Go L on the rd, then very shortly go R on a ByW (216/733). Follow this main track SA, DH, to B47 rd and go L on this (Surby rd) to A7 and go L then R at roundabout on the A29.
11 Go SA at roundabout to Port St Mary and R at X-rds on A31, past Cregneash to the visitor centre / end (173/667).
END
Spanish Head
Kerroodhoo Plantation
Stack
Slieau Mooar Plantn
Glion Mooar
Eary Cushlin
Gob yn Ushtey
Cronk ny Arrey Laa
Cairn
437
Stroin Vuigh
Burro Meanagh
Shielings
Earystane Plantation
The Stacks
Scard
Eairnyerey
Lhiattee ny Beinnee
Ballacannell
Kirkill
Fleshwick Bay
Ballarock
Raad ny Foillan
Carnanes
Ballakilpheric
Fleshwick Fm
Scholaby
Colby Glen
Surby
Ballakilloweyy
Ballafesson
Ballacorkish
Ballachurry
Level
Croit e Caley
Ballagawne
Kentraugh
Four Roads
Rhenwyllan
Black Rocks
Standing Stone
Glendown
Gansey Point
PORT ST MARY
Bay ny Carrick
Port St Mary Bay
The Carrick
Kallow Point
Perwick Bay
Kione y Ghoggan
Port Erin Bay
PORT ERIN
Darrag
Ballnahowe
Meayll Hill
Chambered Cairn
Mull Hill
The Howe
Glenchass
Fistard
Cregneash
Beacon
Cronk ny Arrey
Hut Circle
The Chasms
The Anvil
The Sugarloaf
Bay Stacka
Black Head
Kione ny Garee
Bay Fine
Shenvalley
Aldrick
Kitterland
Calf Sound
Burroo Ned
Kione ny Halby

Other routes

SOUTHERN COMFORT

A 22.1km intermediate/hard route starting in Colby at Colby Glen pub car park (SC 233/ 701). Pass the smugglers route of the Whisky run then joins a section of the End 2 End route for great single track descent, back along the road to the start.

ST LUKES TO CREG-NY-BAA

A 27.km intermediate/Hard route starting from Grandstand, Douglas (382/774).

A GRAND DAY OUT

A 29.9km intermediate route that starts at the Bungalow Station (396/867).

DOUGLAS PEEL RAILWAY LINE

17.5km to Peel & 35km to Peel & back. An easy ride for all the family, starting from NSC Outdoor sports field car park, Douglas (366/761)

HELLS 8

A hard 24.6km ride starting at Glen Wyllin campsite, Kirk Michael (313/904). Figure of eight loop around the hills above Ballaugh & Kirk Michael, with lots of climbing & steep rocky descents.

LEG BURNER

A hard 20km ride starting at the Waterfall Pub, Glen Maye (235/798). A tough MTB route that is best done on a dry day.

ST JOHNS

An intermediate 20km ride starting from the Farmers Arms car park, St Johns (277/816).

THE CAMELS BACK

A 25.7km intermediate ride starting from Ballaugh village and touring the north of the Island with a couple of climbs and descents.

SOUTH BARRULE MTB TRAILS

Kipper route, 2km graded Blue (intermediate) with forest roads with some loose surfaces and a short section of single track.

VIKING TRAIL

5Km Red graded (difficult) route with some rough narrow trails, steep gradients, boardwalk & steps.

NOTE: For maps & detailed directions of all of the above routes, see www.gov.im/tourism/activities/events/mountainbiking.xml or www.gov.im/lib/docs/tourism/trails.pdf or www.gov.im/lib/docs/tourism/newbikesouthbarrule.pdf

TOP TIP: The Manx MTB club are a good port of call for guided rides. See www.manxmtb.org and contact them via the forum or by e-mail.

Downhilling

There is a downhill club on the Island with some good tracks all within just 30mins drive of one another. Visit www.iomdh.co.uk, ask on the forum or e-mail them to find out more information.

Getting there: In the Irish Sea, between Ireland & Cumbria. Ferries run from Heysham (nr Lancaster) & Liverpool. Bikes go for free, so its cheap(est) to go as a foot passenger. For timetables, prices, etc see www.steam-packet.com or tel 0871 222 1 333. It is possible to travel by train – Ramsey is closest to northern tip / start of the ride.

Accommodation: Sleepwell Hotel in Douglas on 01624 639 396, Glen Wyllin campsite in Kirk Michael (1/2 way along the west coast) on 01624 878231 is good. For a comprehensive listing see www.gov.im/tourism/travel/accommodation/isle-of-man-hotels.aspx.

Bike shops Eurocycles on 01624 624 909 and Bikestyle on 01624 673576 in Douglas.

Refreshments In villages and towns along the way and a cafe at the very end.

the isle of man

picture by Max

picture provided by the Isle of Man tourist board

pic provided by the IOM tourist board

picture by Max

picture provided by the Isle of Man tourist bo

picture by the Forestry commission

ENGLAND

TRAIL CENTRES

When you talk about man made trails you automatically think of Wales & Scotland, but England also has some great centres. While England doesn't have mountains of Wales or Scotland, the Forestry Commission has helped develop some superb twisty singletrack forest trails. For more information see www.forestry.gov.uk/england-cycling, www.enjoyengland.com & www.visitbritain.co.uk

picture by Mathew Clark 'Rider Gary Ewing'

Hamsterley

picture from Forestry commission

picture from Forestry commission

picture from Forestry commission

picture from Forestry commission

picture from Forestry commission

picture from Forestry commission

picture from Forestry commission

NO.59 HALDON FOREST

A good range of routes for all ablities, from easy family cycle tracks to extremely challenging Northshore trails. Although the Red trail isn't particularly long there are some nice natural trails just off the Blue route, which itself has some nice fast single track in it.

picture by Forestry Commission

Family Route 5 KM

Follow the purple markers, for an easy going, gentle ride on wide, well surfaced trails, with a couple of steep(ish) hills, but not very long.

Adventure Trail 3.7 KM

Using well surfaced (fairly wide) single track trails which are pretty flat, but flow well so that more experienced riders can ride at speed. Makes a good addition to either the green or red route.

Freer Route 9.6 KM

A technically challenging ride, with some steep gradients, easy northshore and big berms. It is pretty short, but the blue Adventure trail makes a fun addittion when ridden at speed. Also see our tip about exploring the natural trails in the forest.

Freer Freeride Area

Just off the Red route (about half way around), is an area set aside for some Northshore constructions, which offer some very technical challenges, such as skinnies, wall ride, step-ups, jumps & drops and a corkscrew - for very experienced riders only.

TOP TIP

The trails are a bit on the short side, but there are some good natural (singletrack) trails around the forest to explore – look for the tell-tale tyre tracks off the blue 'Adventure' route.

Getting there: Follow A38/signs for/past (horse) race course, to Haldon Gateway (car park) is just past the cross roads. Railway in Exeter 10km away.
Grid Ref: SX 885/847 / Sat Nav: EX6 7XR

Opening times & cost: Pay & display parking

Facilities: Toilets, Green Box food at the hub (nr Rangers office) at weekends & bank holidays.

Bike shop: Partridge Cycles in Kennford on the A38, tel: 01392 833303

Map: www.forestry.gov.uk and search for 'Haldon forest trail map'

Tourist info: Exeter TI on 01392 665700

Website: www.haldonforestpark.org.uk and www.haldonfreeride.org

NO.60

THETFORD FOREST

This large forest in slap bang in the middle of a flat area which is largely devoid of 'good' mountain biking. It may not have much in the way of hills, but it makes up for it with lots & lots of superb undulating single track, which provide an oasis of smooth, flowing trails.

NOTE: The technical challenge of the riding comes from how fast you ride the singletrack, making it perfect for all abilities.

High Lodge Loop 10.5 KM

This is a nice gentle ride along wide forest roads, which is perfect for families & beginners.

Brandon Park loop

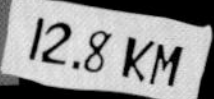

Starting from Brandon Country park, although it can be linked to the High lodge forest centre. There are a few narrow tracks and loose surfaces, but no real hills and makes a good introduction to mountain biking, especially for confident children.

Red route 17.8 KM

A fast but also tight & twisty single track trail that undulates through the forest, which is suprisingly tiring. Nothing too challenging, but the faster you ride it the more technical it becomes. Make sure you do both loops of this figure of eight course.

Black Route 17 KM

This is not actually a very technically challenging ride (and may be re-graded), but if it is ridden very fast, the tight twisty singletrack becomes harder to stay on and you might start missing corners.
The trail urges you to ride it fast, so be prepared to get tired and have great fun doing so.

FAMILY ACTIVITIES

Go Ape: A high ropes assault course of ropes swings and zip slides in the tree tops. Tel; 0845 643 9215 or see www.goape.co.uk

Grimes Grave: A Neolithic flint mine which you can descend into (some 9 metres down), tel; 01842 810656

Picnic sites: There are plenty of picnic tables located around the main High Lodge and BBQ hire is available from the Forestry Commission, tel; 01842 815434.

Walking: There are a number of waymarked walks, including wildlife or sculpture trails. Maps are availavle at the High Lodge Forest Centre.

Orienteering: There is a large permanent orienteering course at High Lodge Forest Centre with different routes/distances. Get a map (small fee) from High Lodge Forest Centre.

Getting there: From Thetford, take B1107 towards Brandon and turn left to High Lodge Forest centre. Brandon railway station is just down the road.

Grid Ref: TL 811/851 Sat Nav: IP27 0AF

Opening times & cost: (expensive) Pay & display and gates to High Lodge are locked at night.

facilities: bike shop with bike hire, toilets, cafe & lots of activities for the whole family.

bike shop: www.bike-art.com / 018428 100090

map: www.forestry.gov.uk and search for 'Thetford bike map

More info: High Lodge centre on 01842 815434

website: www.forestry.gov.uk/thetfordforestpark

NO.61 LEE QUARRY

An impressive setting providing some great, technical rocky trails and skills & trials areas.

The rocky trails blend in well to the surroundings and being permeable rock, having steep slopes and good drainage means it makes a great all year round venue. It is also used for a number of MTB events & their are plans for developments, so keep an eye on their website.

Picture by Ian Donohoe

Red Route 5KM

Being in a quarry the route is rocky but has some nice flowing single track in it, especially towards the end, that most riders will have fun on. The route may not be very long but there are some Red & Black options along the way, so you can do some laps of the whole trail with some changes each time. Also, keep an eye for extensions of the route, going out onto the moors.

Black Route 2KM

This is a slower much more technical and rockier affair than the red route which will require very good balance & riding skills, so might be best ridden with flat pedals & body armour.

Skills Area

A place to practice your bike handling skills on the rocky drop offs, skinny logs etc. There are also 3 purpose built trials areas and lots of natural stuff, suitable for beginners through to experts.

TOP TIP: Body armour e.g. shin & knee pads are a good idea for this rocky terrain. There are also some big drops, so take care.

Getting there: Go into Rawtenstall, at the end of the M66 (north of Manchester) then A681 (Bacup) looking for Futures Park on right after Stacksteads, and Quarry is on the right.

Grid Ref: SD 860/206 Sat Nav: OL13 OBB

Opening times & cost: Free (see parking below)

facilities: Parking at King Fiher centre at weekends and after 6pm weekdays Town for facilities.

Bike shop: Ride-on 01706 831101 / www.rideon.co.uk in Rawtenstall (1 mile away) is very good.

map: www.adrenaline-gateway.co.uk/LeeQuarry.aspx

tourist info: Rawtenstall T.I. 01706 244678

website: www.adrenaline-gateway.co.uk

Dalby Forest

NO.62

A great venue with a wide variety of trails for all abilities, including short family trails, a long XC single track, a technical black XC and a jump/northshore area. The entry fee is somewhat expensive, but the riding and facilities (good bike shop & cafe) make it worth it. There are also some other activities e.g. family walks, paintballing and Go Ape (high ropes course)..

picture from Forestry commission

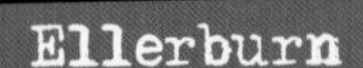 

Ellerburn 4 KM

An easy and gentle fire road route ride for families, starting from the visitor centre and heading into the forest, along the valley bottom.

Adderstone 10 KM

Using a mix of fireroads and grassy tracks, with a few short climbs & descents to provide a slightly more challenging family ride. Can also be combined with the Blue route (see below).

Blue Route 14 KM

Starting at Low Dalby car park, on mixed terrain, this route tackles a good distance and some steep hills, but without technically challenging trails.

Red Route 37 KM

A long and mostly single track route with berms, drops and some technical trail features (with 'escape' options), such as rock gardens and northshore constructions. Start at Dalby Courtyard or Dixon's Hollow. Experienced riders only.

Black route 10 KM

A very technical and steep trail with some fast fun downhills, nothshore, big (5ft) drops, for experienced riders only.

Dixon s Hollow

Bike Park providing a 4X course with table tops, berms, rhythm bumps and corkscrew bridge, and some skinnies and north shore trails.

OTHER STUFF

Go Ape on 0845 643 9215 or see www.goape.co.uk & Paintballing on 07765 243 672 or see www.abilityoutdoors.co.uk.
Vale of Pickering caravan & campsite in Allerston is highly recommended, especially for families. See www.valeofpickering.co.uk or call 01723 859280.

Getting there: Inland from Scarborough, follow the brown signs to Thornton-Le-Dale & join the toll road/forest drive heading north (to trail centre)..
Grid Ref: SE 857/873 / Sat Nav: YO18 7LT

Opening times & cost: see www.forestry.gov.uk

facilities: Toilets, cafe and bike shop with bike hire (see below).

bike shop: Purple Mountain Bike centre (& cafe) on 01751 460011

map: www.singletraction.org.uk

Tourist info: Dalby visitor centre 01751 460295

website: www.singletraction.org.uk

No.63 HAMSTERLEY FOREST

A good range of routes for all ablities, from easy family tracks to technical XC & extreme downhill & jumps. There are also some Trailquest cards available from the visitor centre.

picture by Mathew Clark

Windy Bank 5KM

A nice easy ride for families, looping around the Bedburn Beck.

Spurls Wood Valley 14.5KM

The single track start soon gives way to wide, well surfaced trails, for a long and pleasant ride.

Neighbour Moor Tour 16KM

This extends the blue route, with steeper, longer climbs and descents, but not much of a technical challenge, making it a fast ride. The red grade is awarded for the physical effort required, not the technical challenge. **NOTE**: There are plans to make this route 25km long.

Bedborn Bash 11KM

A tough technical trail on rooty singletrack trails, for experienced riders and although not long, is hard going with short steep techincal climbs and descents. It can also be extended by joining with the Red route by Grove House.

Descend Bike Park

Downhill's: Fast and flowing with berms, drop-offs and a huge table-top jump at the top, then steep, rocky and technical towards the bottom.

4X: Huge table tops, triples, big berms & more.

Duel course: race head-to-head, over table tops, around berms & jumps, etc. Fast, furious fun.

NOTE: Register at the Descend cabin (at mid-point of the course) before riding the DH or 4X trails.

NOTE: There is a good Skills Loop with various grades of technical features which is very useful for testing and developing your skills.

Getting there: Follow brown tourist signs for Hamsterley forest from the A68 to the (pay & display) car park, or for the DH & 4X go through Hamsterley village, for 5km to Grove car park (NZ 066/288). Grid Ref: NZ 092/312 / Sat Nav: DL13 3NL

Opening times & cost: Pay & display parking

facilities: Toilets, cafe, shop, bike wash, bike shop with ire & servicing. and an uplift for the downhill.

bike shop: Wood n Wheels (on site) 01388 488222

map: www.forestry.gov.uk and search for 'Hamsterley Forest cycle map'

Visitor centre: 01388 488312

website: www.hamsterley-trailblazers.co.uk

NO.64 Grizedale

OK so the Lakes may have lots of natural riding, but this is a great place for safe, all weather riding, with something suitable for all abilities, especially newer riders. However the fact that it isn't too technical means that experienced riders can ride it fast to really test their high speed cornering skills. Great fun!

picture by Forestry Commission

Goosey Foot Tarn 3 KM

A moderate ride from Moor Top car park, follow the red signs along wide and relatively flat forest trails - good family ride.

Grizedale Tarn 9.5 KM

A moderate ride from Bogle car park, following the black signs, offering a longer ride than Goosey Foot, to challenge the fitter riders.

Moor Top Trail 11 KM

Starting from the Grizedale visitor centre or Moor Top car park, and as the name suggests, it goes to the top of the moor. A good introduction on the next step up from the family 'Green' graded trails.

Hawkshead Moor Trail 17 KM

Starting from the visitor centre Moor Top or High Cross car parks, this trail explores the western side of the forest.

Slurian Way 22.5 KM

Starting from the visitor centre Moor Top or Force Mills car parks, this is a fairly demanding ride for a Blue grade, as it is fairly long and involves some reasonable gradients. Makes a good stepping stone for those wishing to progress to red routes.

North Face Trail 15.6 KM

This trail has some nice single track, rocks, and quite a lot of (easy) northshore sections, such as boardwalks, wooden berms and log rides. The riding isn't actually too tehnical though and intermediate riders will find it a good place to advance their skills, while experienced riders will want to ride it fast to get the most from it.

Getting there: In Cumbria, south of Ambleside, between Coniston Water and Lake Windemere, off the B5285. Follow the signposts.

Grid Ref: SD 335/943 / Sat Nav: LA22 0QJ

Opening times & cost: see www.forestry.gov.uk

Facilities: Toilets, cafe, bike wash and a bike shop with bike hire (see below).

Bike shop: Grizedale MTB at the start 01229 860335 or Bike Treks in Ambleside on 015394 31245

Map: From the shop (cost £1)

Tourist info: Visitor centre 01229 860010

Website: www.forestry.gov.uk

NO.65

KIELDER FOREST

Lots of trails to choose from & castle wood skills loop to test your skills on first. Experienced riders should ride the (red) Deadwater & (black) 'up & over' trails.

Borderline Trail 11.3 KM

Easy going trail that largely follows the former Border Counties railway line, it takes you to the Scottish Border at Deadwater Station and back.

Lakeside Way 24 KM

Passing around the lakeside, this route has gentle gradients, making it suitable for families.

Castle Hill

Starting from the Kielder castle, along undulating tracks and a few small obstacles such as roots & rocks, make it suitable for intermediate riders.

Village Connection

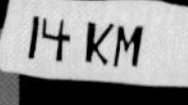

An easy trail linking Kielder and Falstone with great views, tea rooms and pubs to visit on route.

New Blue

A new route for 2009 providing intermediate riders with opportunity to experience more of remote trails in the vicinity.

Cross Border 48 KM

Ride anti-clockwise, from the Kielder Calvert Trail, and follow the Bloody Bush toll road to Dykecrofts centre, then back along the Kershope Burn.

Kielder to Calvert 21 KM

From Kielder village to the Calvert Trust and back, and can be linked with the Lakeside Way, Cross Border trail and Deadwater Trails.

Humble loop 12 KM

Starting at the Calvert Trust and passes through the forest, providing wonderful views.

Deadwater 14.7 KM

With good, fast single track and technical features such as boardwalks, berms, rocks & drop-offs, this is a great route for more experienced riders.

(new) Red Run 18.7 KM

A new addition for experienced riders, featuring a 1.2km section of North shore style boardwalk.

Up & Over 2.3 KM

A technical option to the end of the Deadwater route, by start of 'All Along the Watch Tower' with berms & jumps (don't roll the gap jump at end).

MTB Trails Park

A good range of jumps and northshore trails to hone (or learn) some extreme skills.

Getting there: on the scottish borders, off the A68, well signposted. There are two main centres; Leaplish waterside park & the Kielder castle forest park at the northern end of the lake (head for this).

Grid Ref: NY 632/936 / Sat Nav: NE48 1HX

Opening times & cost: Pay & display

Facilities: bike wash, hire, shops, toilets, choice of food & drink, accommodation & other activities.

Bike shop: www.thebikeplace.co.uk / 0845 6341895

Map: www.visitkielder.com/site/things-to-do/mountain-biking

Visitor centre: 0845 6341895

Website: www.kieldertrailreavers.org.uk & www.purplemountain.co.uk for the bike centre.

Breaks with bikes

www.scottishmountainbikeguides.com

IN

SCOTLAND

Scotland

Scotland is home to remote rugged adventures. Epic, inspiring scenery & riding at its most creative. In contrast the man-made trail centres offer amazing (world class in fact) riding in a more controlled environment, with the 7 Stanes in southern Scotland and more in the north such as Fort William and Glospie.

If Wales encourages mountain biking, Scotland almost forces you into the sport; with the Right to Roam law, cyclists are allowed to ride virtually anywhere they like; if there is a path, you can ride it. This makes the scope for epic rides even more enormous. What really is exciting is when you start to think of the potential for the adventures to be had, especially when you add a bivy bag, bothies & friends. Experiences we could all benefit from & aspire to do one day...

Useful sites: www.scottishmountainbike.com, www.midgforecast.co.uk, www.visitscotland.com, www.midgforecast.co.uk, www.forestry.gov.uk/mtbscotland, www.syha.org.uk, www.hostel-scotland.co.uk, & www.7stanes.gov.uk & www.mountainbothies.org.uk.

picture by A Horning

www.scottishmountainbikeguides.com

Ben Alder - cairngorms

Seals on Isle of Skye

picture by Max

Isle of Skye

picture by Max

Meannach bothy

picture by www.scottishmountainbikeguides.com

www.scottishmountainbikeguides.com

pic by A Horning / Ben Alder

picture by Steve Makin

picture by Mid Argyll Tri-cycle Club

Fire Tower Trail

www.scottishmountainbikeguides.com

picture by Steve Makin

www.scottishmountainbikeguides.com

picture by D Rainsford

picture by Steve Makin

SCOTLAND

Trail centres

picture by Steve Makin

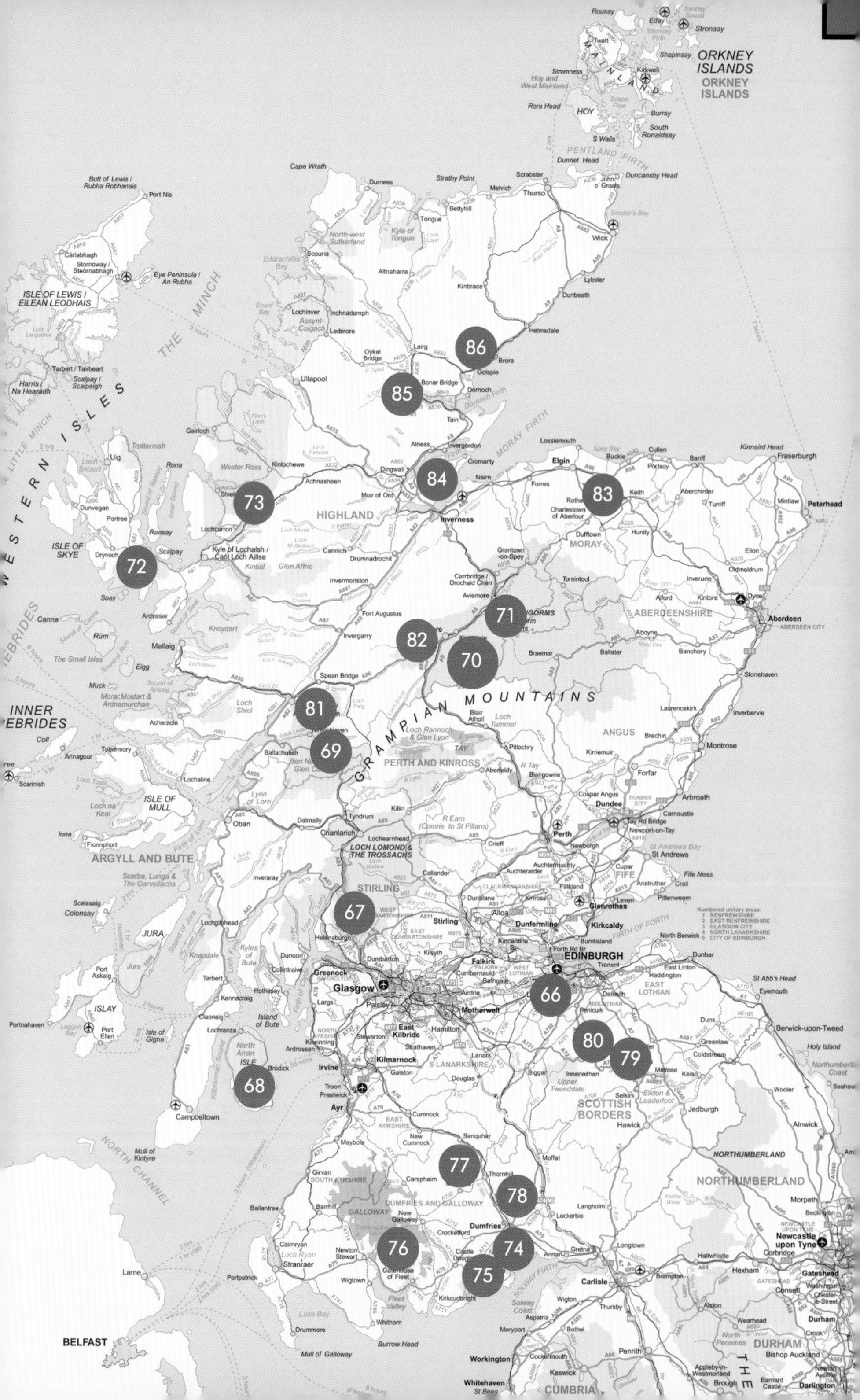

ORKNEY ISLANDS
Rousay
Eday
Stronsay
Shapinsay
Twatt
MAINLAND
Stromness
Kirkwall
Hoy and West Mainland
Rora Head
HOY
Burray
South Ronaldsay
S Walls
PENTLAND FIRTH
Dunnet Head
Scrabster
John o' Groats
Duncansby Head
Cape Wrath
Durness
Strathy Point
Melvich
Thurso
Butt of Lewis / Rubha Robhanais
Port Nis
Tongue
Bettyhill
North-west Sutherland
Kyle of Tongue
Wick
Càrlabhagh
Stornoway / Steòrnabhagh
Eye Peninsula / An Rubha
Scourie
Eddrachillis Bay
Altnaharra
Kinbrace
Lybster
Dunbeath
ISLE OF LEWIS / EILEAN LEODHAIS
THE MINCH
Lochinver
Inchnadamph
Assynt-Coigach
Ledmore
Helmsdale
Tarbert / Tairbeart
Scalpay / Scalpaigh
Harris / Na Hearadh
Oykel Bridge
Lairg
Brora
Golspie
Ullapool
Bonar Bridge
Dornoch
Dornoch Firth
WESTERN ISLES
LITTLE MINCH
Gairloch
Tain
MORAY FIRTH
Lossiemouth
Uig
Trotternish
Alness
Invergordon
Cromarty
Buckie
Cullen
Kinnaird Head
Fraserburgh
Rona
Wester Ross
Kinlochewe
Dingwall
Nairn
Elgin
Portsoy
Banff
Achnasheen
Forres
Keith
Aberchirder
Dunvegan
Muir of Ord
Charlestown of Aberlour
Turriff
Mintlaw
Peterhead
Portree
HIGHLAND
Inverness
Raasay
Lochcarron
Dufftown
Huntly
ISLE OF SKYE
Drynoch
Scalpay
Kyle of Lochalsh / Caol Loch Aillse
Kintail
Glen Affric
Cannich
Drumnadrochit
Grantown-on-Spey
MORAY
Ellon
Oldmeldrum
Carrbridge / Drochaid Charr
Tomintoul
Inverurie
Invermoriston
Soay
Aviemore
Alford
Kintore
Dyce
Canna
Ardvasar
Fort Augustus
CAIRNGORMS
ABERDEENSHIRE
Aberdeen
ABERDEEN CITY
Knoydart
Rùm
Mallaig
Invergarry
Aboyne
Banchory
The Small Isles
Eigg
Braemar
Ballater
Spean Bridge
Stonehaven
Muck
Morar, Moidart & Ardnamurchan
GRAMPIAN MOUNTAINS
Loch Shiel
INNER HEBRIDES
Acharacle
Blair Atholl
Loch Tummel
Laurencekirk
Inverbervie
Coll
Loch Rannoch & Glen Lyon
ANGUS
Brechin
Tobermory
Arinagour
Ballachulish
Montrose
PERTH AND KINROSS
Pitlochry
Kirriemuir
Scarinish
Lochaline
Aberfeldy
Blairgowrie
Forfar
ISLE OF MULL
Lynn of Lorn
Coupar Angus
Arbroath
Loch na Keal
Dundee
DUNDEE CITY
Killin
Carnoustie
Oban
Tyndrum
Tay Rd Bridge
Newport-on-Tay
Iona
Fionnphort
Dalmally
Crianlarich
Lochearnhead
Perth
R Earn (Comrie to St Fillans)
Crieff
Newburgh
St Andrews Bay
St Andrews
ARGYLL AND BUTE
LOCH LOMOND & THE TROSSACHS
Auchtermuchty
Cupar
Fife Ness
FIFE
Scarba, Lunga & The Garvellachs
Inveraray
Callander
Auchterarder
Crail
STIRLING
Anstruther
Falkland
Pittenweem
Dunblane
Kinross
Leven
Glenrothes
Scalasaig
Colonsay
Stirling
Alloa
Dunfermline
Kirkcaldy
WEST DUNBARTONSHIRE
Numbered unitary areas:
1 RENFREWSHIRE
2 EAST RENFREWSHIRE
3 GLASGOW CITY
4 NORTH LANARKSHIRE
5 CITY OF EDINBURGH
Lochgilphead
FIRTH OF FORTH
JURA
Helensburgh
EAST DUNBARTONSHIRE
Kincardine
Burntisland
North Berwick
Dunbar
Knapdale
Kyles of Bute
Dunoon
Kilsyth
Falkirk
Forth Rd Br
EDINBURGH
Jura
Dumbarton
Port Askaig
Colintraive
Greenock
Tranent
East Linton
Tarbert
Glasgow
Cumbernauld
Bathgate
WEST LOTHIAN
Haddington
St Abb's Head
Kennacraig
Rothesay
Paisley
Airdrie
EAST LOTHIAN
Eyemouth
ISLAY
Largs
Motherwell
Penicuik
Dalkeith
Portnahaven
Claonaig
Island of Bute
Port Ellen
Isle of Gigha
Lochranza
East Kilbride
Hamilton
Duns
Berwick-upon-Tweed
Holy Island
North Ayrshire
Stewarton
Strathaven
Greenlaw
North Arran
ISLE
Ardrossan
Kilwinning
Kilmarnock
Lanark
Coldstream
Irvine
Brodick
Galston
S LANARKSHIRE
Biggar
Innerleithen
Melrose
Kelso
Northumberland Coast
Troon
Prestwick
Douglas
Upper Tweeddale
Selkirk
Eildon & Leadervoot
Wooler
Ayr
Campbeltown
Cumnock
SCOTTISH BORDERS
Jedburgh
Hawick
EAST AYRSHIRE
Alnwick
NORTH CHANNEL
New Cumnock
Sanquhar
Mull of Kintyre
Moffat
NORTHUMBERLAND
Girvan
SOUTH AYRSHIRE
Carsphain
Thornhill
Ballantrae
DUMFRIES AND GALLOWAY
Langholm
Morpeth
Barrhill
GALLOWAY
Lockerbie
Bedlington
New Galloway
Dumfries
Crocketford
Cairnryan
Loch Ryan
Newton Stewart
Castle Douglas
Annan
Gretna
Longtown
Newcastle upon Tyne
Haltwhistle
Corbridge
Larne
Stranraer
Portpatrick
Gatehouse of Fleet
Wigtown
SOLWAY FIRTH
Carlisle
Brampton
Hexham
Gateshead
Consett
Washington
Chester-le-Street
Kirkcudbright
Fleet Valley
Solway Coast
Wigton
Aspatria
Thursby
Alston
Luce Bay
Whithorn
Drummore
Maryport
Bothel
Wearhead
Durham
Crook
North Pennines
DURHAM
BELFAST
Burrow Head
Mull of Galloway
Penrith
Bishop Auckland
Workington
Cockermouth
Appleby-in-Westmorland
Newton Aycliffe
Keswick
Whitehaven
St Bees
CUMBRIA
Brough
Barnard Castle
Darlington
66
67
68
69
70
71
72
73
74
75
76
77
78
79
80
81
82
83
84
85
86

ROUTE	GRADE	DISTANCE	+/–
66 Pentland Hills	Medium	25.2Km	+6Km
67 Loch Lomond	Easy – Hard	29.6Km	various
68 Isle of Arran	Medium – Very hard	10 / 10 / 18 & 35 Km	
69 Kinlochleven	Hard – Very Hard	27.5Km	–9.5Km
70 Gaick Pass	Very hard	80Km	–22Km
71 Aviemore	Easy – Medium	28.3Km	+2.9 or –11.6Km
72 Isle of Skye	Hard – Very Hard	50Km	
73 Torridon	Very Hard	45.5Km	

Trail centres	Green	Blue	Red	Black	Orange
74 Mabie	1	1	1	1	1
75 Dalbeattie	1	1	1	0	0
76 Kirroughtree	1	2	1	1	0
77 Drumlanrig	4	2	1	1	0
78 Ae	1	1	1	0	2
79 Glentress	1	1	1	1	1
80 Innerleithen	0	0	1	0	4
81 Fort William	0	2	3	0	2
82 Laggan	1	0	1	1	1
83 Moray Monster Trails	1	2	2	2	2
84 Learnie Red Rock	1	2	0	0	1
85 Kyle of Sutherland	0	2	1	1	0
86 Golspie	0	1	1	1	0

ROUTE DESCRIPTION

Great riding close to Edinburgh city, offering an escape & great views of the city.

Lovely loch side ride, with a couple of ferry crossings & not far from Glasgow.

4 routes; something for all abilities & a superb adventure just to get there.

A tough ride up & down the Devil's staircase & down the very technical Ciaran path

A big hard ride venturing deep into the Cairngorms, for a very memorable experience

Easy'ish, but remote & wild introductionary to the Cairngorms, to Loch Einich & back

A classic, epic ride into the wilderness on technical & remote trails – awesome.

hard wilderness ride with superb singletrack & stunning scenary – a 'must do' ride

ood mix of trails & a very challenging northshore trail. YHA & hotel with a bar on site

Great singletrack trails on grippy hardrock trails – home to 'The Slab'

A favourite centre for many riders – home to the grippy 'McMoab' granite rock.

reat setting & trails for everyone, with tight, rooty singletrack for the experts

Offering a jumpy, bermy style of trail – quite different to the other centres.

A VERY popular destination with great facilities & great trails for everyone.

Best known for its superb downhill tracks, but also home to a technical XC route

ome to the World Cup Downhill & a red (XC) grade downhill, plus superb XC routes

Great facilities & great trails for all abilities, including a good bike park for all

Good range of short trails to join up. Not much singletrack but some technical bits

Best for Blue & Black grade riders, but see our route suggestion for a 'Red' route

Made up of the Balblair & Carbisdale centres – well suited to intermediate riders

Out of the way & quiet, with technical rocky trails & lots of superb singletrack

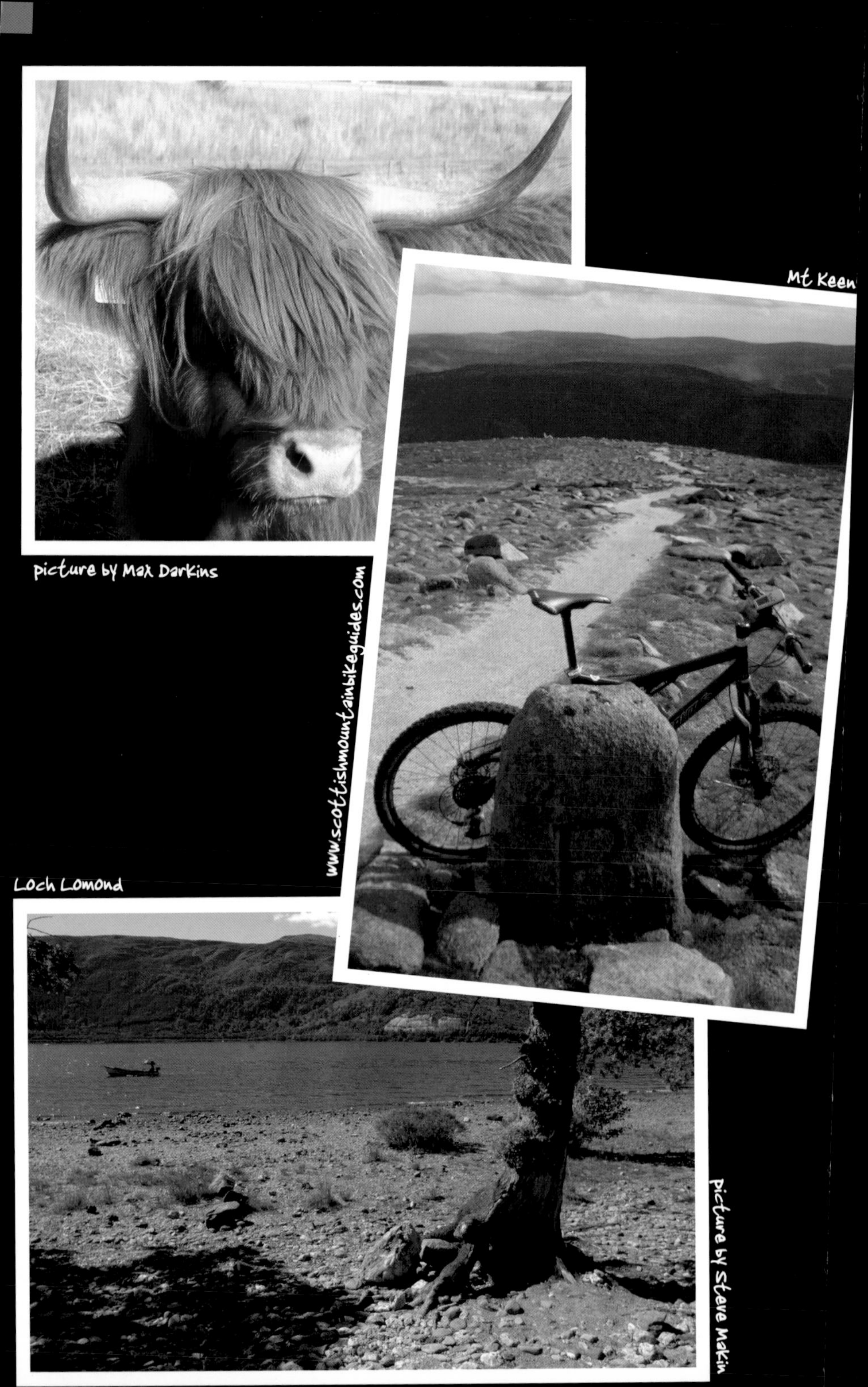
picture by Max Darkins
Mt Keen
www.scottishmountainbikeguides.com
Loch Lomond
picture by Steve Makin

66 Pentland Hills

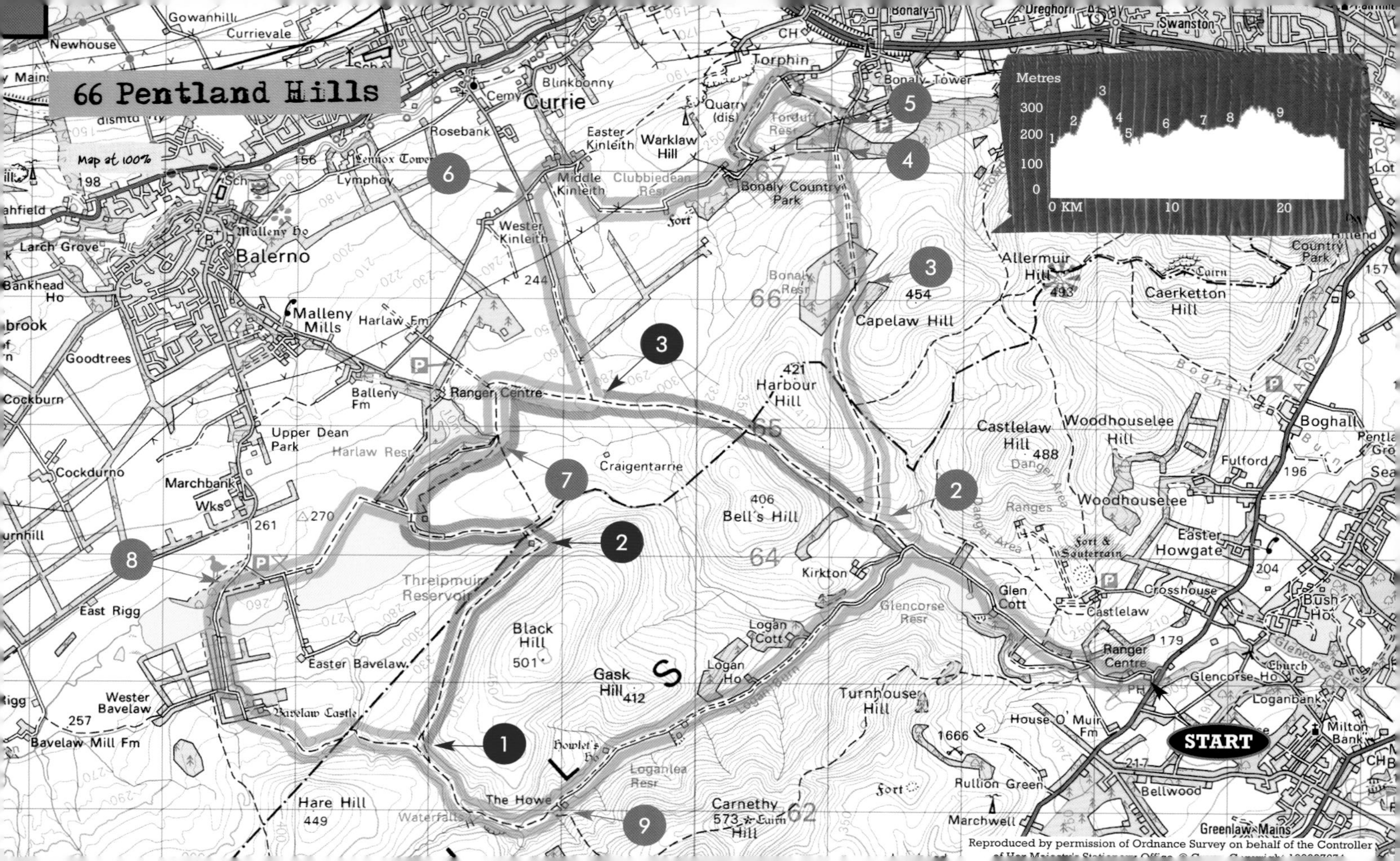

Pentland Hills

25.2KM (15.7M) & 710 METRES OF CLIMBING

START Ride up the (Great Glen road) track to Glencourse reservoir, joining alongside this, then keep SA (over a little bridge) at the far end, then shortly after this go through the gate on the R, signposted to Bonaly, UH on a DT.

2 Keep R at the fork, UH onto the moors, through another gate and along a ST to Bonaly reservoir. After riding to the RHS side of the woods for a short while, go L (north) through a gate onto a DT (211/661), DH.

3 To/through another gate for a fast track (but watch out for other users), coming to and going through a gate into the woods (210/672) and turn L. Nice technical trail of roots, rocks and steps, to edge of woods and turn R.

4 Follow the path down, out of the wood to a path up Torduff Hill (SA), but go R in the dip before on a grassy track. Through bushes, SA, to the main track (210/673) and go L, UH then shortly L on a ST trail that crosses you, round Torduff Hill (210/674).

5 DH to a gate at Torduff reservoir and go through this over the dam and L, alongside it then follow the tarmac track up to Clubbiedean reservoir. Follow this to a T-J in Middle Kinleith and go L, to a X-rds (187/667) and turn L on the DT here.

6 There is a nice ST in the woods on the L, UH, through gate, to a T-J at the top and turn R (or L for an 8km shortcut - see extension for directions), DH towards Harlaw reservoir. Bear L at the fork in a field shortly past a gate, alongside trees and wall, and use stone stile over the wall, before the gate.

7 Go L on other side and around then over the wier/reservoir and L along Threipmuir reservoir. Shortly past a (private) track/bridge on L, keep SA on a ST into a wood, as the main track bears R, to a rd on the other side (164/637) and go L on this.

8 Over (Redford) bridge, steep UH to T-J at the top and go L then R, past Bavelaw castle and through a gate onto the moor (166/626). Wide grass track to L, over the top, becoming a lovely ST, to gate at base of the hills (179/624).

9 Continue through the valley on a great trail to Loganlea reservoir or see the extension. Take the track on the LHS of the reservoir, then turn R at the end of Glencorse reservoir (216/640), back to the start (234/631).

Extension

+6KM (3.7M) & 230 METRES CLIMBING

NOTE: Only do this is very dry conditions. Stronger riders could ride down the (fun) trail to Loganlea res. (where they leave the weaker riders to carry along the track back to the start), then double back to the start of ext.

1 Turn L on a narrow stoney track through the heather for a tough UH to a wall and a view of Threipmuir reservoir. Follow the trail alongside the wall and follow it L, to the end of the reservoir and a pump house (187/641).

2 Go over a stile and reservoir then go L SP 'Thriepmuir car park' alongside the reservoir, through some trees then down to a DT and go L then shortly R back along the way you came from earlier, alongside the reservoir, R (east) at the junction (184/653), and continue SA past the L turning you came up from before (192/652).

3 Climb steadily along this (new) trail, passing inbetween Harbour and Bell's Hills, and keep SA a the gate. Fast, fun descent to Glencorse reservoir, and keep SA back to the start.

TOP TIP: There are some nice trails in the woods around Harlaw reservoir to explore.

NOTE: Some areas of this area have problems with erosion, so please refrain from cycling on any trails in the wet which would get damaged i.e. Black Hill/the extension route. Also Caerketton Hill and the track that runs from the start of the ride to West Kip along the ridgetops are not on the route, but are best avoided if you are exploring further.

Getting there: From the centre of Edinburgh follow the sustrans cyclepath no.75 (for 8km) to Currie, where there is also a train station. If driving, there is a car park at the Harlaw House visitor/Rangers centre (181/654) nr Balerno, off the A70, or we start at the Rangers centre off the A702, nr Penicuik, behind the Flotterstone Inn (234/631).

Accommodation: There is lots of choice in & around Edinburgh, see www.edinburghguide.com for information.

Bike shops Plenty in Edinburgh; Edinburgh Bicycle in the centre on 0131 2283565, Bike Chain on 0131 5572801 or Motavation in Penicuik (for basics spares) on 01968 673127.

Refreshments The very good Flotterstone Inn at the start.

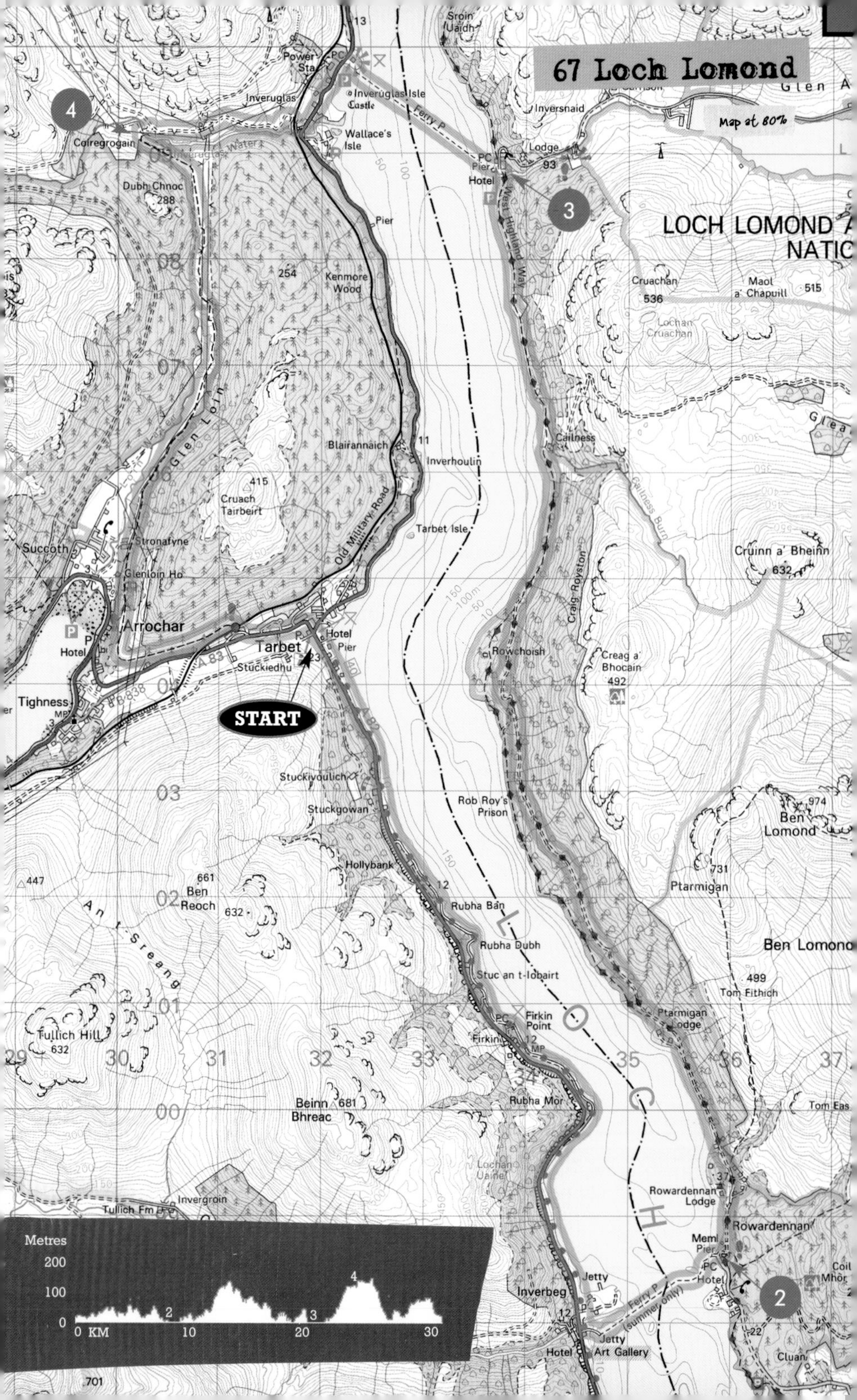

67 Loch Lomond
Map at 80%
START
LOCH LOMOND
Arrochar
Tarbet
Succoth
Tighness
Inveruglas
Inversnaid
Glen Loin
Old Military Road
West Highland Way
Ben Lomond
Ptarmigan
Rowardennan
Inverbeg
Ben Reoch
Beinn Bhreac
Tullich Hill
Rob Roy's Prison
Craig Royston
Cruach Tairbeirt
Metres
200
100
0
0 KM
10
20
30

Loch Lomond

29.6KM (18.4M) & 1,165 METRES OF CLIMBING

START From Tarbet, head south on the West Loch Lomond cycle path, alongside the A82 rd and follow it all the way (nearly 8km), all the way to Inverbeg (NS 346/979). Bear L, down to the jetty, to catch the ferry over Loch Lomond, to Rowardennan (358/986).

2 One the east side of the Loch, head L (north) on the West Highland Way trail, passing Rowardennan Lodge YHA, becoming off-road. Keep R at the next 2 forks (the 1st L goes to Ptarmigan lodge & the 2nd goes along the shoreline, past Rob Roy's Prison and isn't suitable for bicycles). The paths rejoin just past Rowchoish bothy, along the shoreline & over footbridges, to Inversnaid (337/088).

3 Catch the ferry back over Loch Lomond to Inveruglas (322/098) & cross the A82 then turn L (south) for 0.75km then turn R on an access road to Loch Sloy (317/092). Go under the railway line, UH, ignoring the access road to R/north, for 1km to Ardvorlich and keep straight ahead, then left over a bridge (302/092).

4 UH on the single track (power cables overhead), then down the other side, joining a double track and keeping left at the fork. UH & bear hard L, past Tarbet train station, back to Tarbet (319/044). This is a beautiful ride around Loch Lomond with 2 ferry crossings, allowing you to have a break and take in the scenery - as long as they are running, so please check beforehand.

FERRY DETAILS

The ferrys usually run 3 times a day between April to September. For the Inverbeg to Rowardennan ferry, call the Loch Lomond Ferry service on 01360 870273 & for the Inversnaid to Inveruglas ferry, call Inversnaid Hotel on 01877 386223.

Loch Lomond cycle path

As the main route involves some technical trails, steep climbs & good time keeping (to catch the ferries), people looking for an easier & more relaxing ride may like to just ride the flatter, well surfaced West Loch Lomond cycle path, on a 'there & back route'. The trail runs for 24km's from Balloch (at the southernmost point of Loch Lomond) to Tarbet.

Other riding

If you are based in or near Glasgow, Mugdock Country Park (to the north-east has a superb amount of singletrack in this (small) area. They are not marked on maps, but the place is well worth exploring, although it can get busy at weekends.

OTHER ACTIVITIES

Lots of other activities to do in the area, such as boat tours or hire, water sports, golf, fishing, walks etc. For more info see www.visit-lochlomond.com or www.seeglasgow.com or www.visitscotland.com

Getting there Start from the village of Tarbet, on the west side of Loch Lomond. Follow the A82 from Glasgow, past Alexandria, alongside the Loch to Tarbet where there is parking available down by the pier (319/044). Train station in Tarbet.

Accommodation Rowardennan YHA on 01360 870259 / www.syha.org.uk, Inverbeg Inn hotel on 01436860678 / www.inverbeginn.co.uk, Colquhoun arms hotel in Luss on 01436 860282 / www.lochlomondarms.co.uk, Inversnaid Hotel on 01877 386223 or lot more at www.loch-lomond.net.

Refreshments Hotels at Tarbet, Inverbeg, Rowardennan & Inversnaid (useful when waiting for the ferry), and a visitors centre (with snacks) in Inveruglas.

Bike shop Lots of choice in Glasgow.

68 Isle of Arran
Map at 80%
START
Brodick
Brodick Bay
Lamlash
Lamlash Bay
Whiting Bay
Kingscross
Cordon
Clauchlands
Clauchland Hills
Strathwhillan
North Corriegills
South Corriegills
Corriegills Point
Glen Cloy
Glen Ormidale
Meall Buidhe
Cnoc Dubh
Ferry (P) (summer only)
Gortonallister
Lag an Daer
The Knowe Fm
Auchencairn
Knockenkelly
North Kiscadale
South Kiscadale
Largymore
Giants Graves
Glenashdale Falls
Cycle Route
Merkland
Merkland Wood
Brodick Castle and Country Park
Wine Port
Old Quay
Cladach
Home Fm
Strabane
1
BLACK ROUTE
Metres
0 KM
10
20
30
Lamlash
Whiting Bay
Lamlash

Isle of Arran

VARIOUS

Arran is known as 'a mini Scotland' because it has pretty much everything that features in Scotland - mountains, deep glens, rivers and stunning beaches.

NOTE: These routes use natural trails, but hey do have some (limited) signing, so you should take a map with you. These trails are shared with walkers and horse riders, so please ride carefully.

Castle blue route

10KM (6.2M) & 250 METRES CLIMBING

This mainly off-road circular route is a long established route around Brodick Castle. It is aimed at families, but be aware there is a fair bit of climbing involved. Starting in Cladach it heads north on the A841, then off road, climbing in Merkland wood, then heads west o loop around the back of Brodick Castle.

Blue route

10KM (6.2M) & 260 METRES CLIMBING

START Go south-west out of Brodick, along Glen Coy, before turning east to the A841 rd. Here you join the return leg of the Red route and opposite way to start of the black route) heading north, downhill, back into Brodick.

Red route

18KM (11.2M) & 600 METRES CLIMBING

START This figure of 8 loop starts with a short uphill on the tarmac, before climbing off-road into the Clauchland Hills forest, and joining the natural tight, twisty single track. Cross a road for a fast descent down to Lamlash village (pubs & shops here), then climbing Cnoc na Dial Hill and going back down the other side sharing the same trail as the Blue route (and going the opposite way to the Black route so watch out for riders).

Black route

35KM (21.8M) & 1,190 METRES CLIMBING

START This route probably isn't much more technical than the Red route, but it gets its 'Black' grade from the length. Heading south, it climbs the final descent of the Red & Blue routes, and on past Lamlash for a loop past Glenashdale Falls, and into Whiting Bay. It then heads back north, past Lamlash to the Stone Circle X-tracks, to descend back to Brodick via Glen Cloy (the opposite way to the start of the Blue route), back to Brodick.

TOP TIP: There are so many tracks you could make any length ride you require.

For more info see www.arranbikeclub.com who have a very active role in the trails, and offer a MTB Leader Training courses.

Getting there: Head for Androssan on the west coast of Scotland and follow the Isle of Arran ferry signposts from the A78. You could leave your car on the mainland as the trails all start in Brodick. About 1hr crossing to Brodick. See www.calmac.co.uk for ferry info.

Accommodation: Lots of choce. See the accommodation listed on www.visitarran.com or call the Brodick T.I. on 01770 303774, who will be happy to help.

Refreshments: Arran Adventure centre 01770 302244 Brodick Boat & cycle Hire 01770 302868

Bike shop: Shops etc in Brodick town and the other towns you pass.

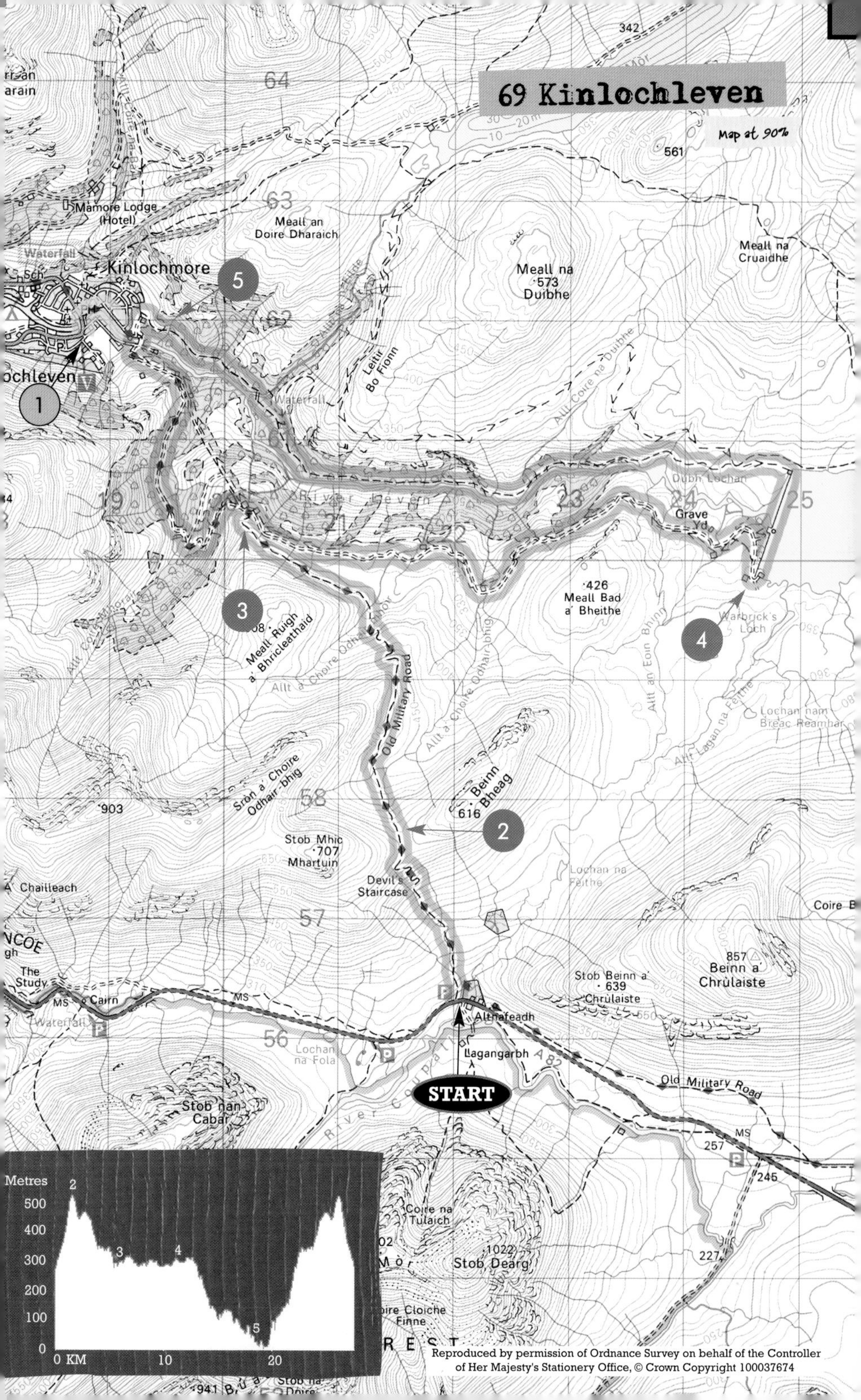
69 Kinlochleven
Map at 90%
Mamore Lodge (Hotel)
Waterfall
Kinlochmore
Kinlochleven
Meall an Doire Dharaich
Meall na 573 Duibhe
Meall na Cruaidhe
Leitir Bo Fionn
Allt Coire na Duibhe
River Leven
Dubh Lochan
Grave Yd
426 Meall Bad a' Bheithe
Warbrick's Loch
Meall Ruigh a' Bhricleathaid
Allt a' Choire Odhair-mhoir
Old Military Road
Allt a' Choire Odhair-bhig
Allt an Eoin Bhinn
Lochan nam Breac Reamhar
Allt Lagan na Feithe
Sron a' Choire Odhair-bhig
Beinn Bheag 616
903
Stob Mhic 707 Mhartuin
Devil's Staircase
Lochan na Feithe
Coire B
The Study
Cairn
MS
Stob Beinn a' 639 Chrùlaiste
857 Beinn a' Chrùlaiste
Altnafeadh
Lagangarbh
A 82
Lochan na Fola
Old Military Road
START
River Coupall
Stob nan Cabar
257
245
227
Coire na Tulaich
1022 Stob Dearg
Coire Cloiche Finne
342
561
1
2
3
4
5
Metres
500
400
300
200
100
0
0 KM
10
20
Reproduced by permission of Ordnance Survey on behalf of the Controller of Her Majesty's Stationery Office, © Crown Copyright 100037674

Kinlochleven

27.5KM (17M) & 1,300 METRES OF CLIMBING

START From the car park at the foot of the Devil's staircase (220/563), head north on part of the West Highland Way trail, for a BIG climb (well a mix of climbing and walking). Enjoy the views at the top and get your strength back for the descent.

NOTE: Watch out for walkers on the way down.

2 The descent is all rideable, but big stones, water bars, with a few short sharp climbs along the way, down to a 4x4 track (202/603).

3 Turn R (east) along this track, all the way to the dam along the undulating track (or along the water conduit, which is smooth and level all the way to the dam).

4 'Past' the dam to the other side (you should cross at the base which is very tricky, but there is a good path along the top). Over the other side go parallel to concrete water pipe and L to descend the excellent and VERY technical Ciaran path, on the northern side of the river Leven to the edge of Kinlochmore (192/620).

5 Turn L and cross the water to join the West Highland way, and follow the DT southwards (R at fork) , staying on the WHW, leaving the 4x4 track, back over the hill, to descend the Devil's staircase, back to the car park (220/563).

NOTE: This is a very strenuous & technical ride which includes the VERY challenging Ciaran path & Devil's staircase trails. A superb ride, but not suitable for everyone.

Shortcut

-9.5KM (5.9M) & 615 METRES CLIMBING

1 Start from Kinlochleven and follow the WHW south, but stay on the 4x4 track, where the WHW bears R, UH. Follow this 4x4 track to the dam, and follow the main route (from no.3), back to Kinlochmore, then over the water to Kinlochleven.

NOTE: This misses out the Devil's Staircase, but takes in the VERY technical Ciaran path.

Other Activities

WALKS

There are a few recommended walks in/from Kinlochleven, many which have some historical, scientific or visual interest, from; explore the remains of an old POW camp, panoramic views of Loch Leven, spot red squirrels, or visit Grey Mare's waterfall. For a leaflet/more info call 01855 831779.

FISHING

There is good fishing to be had in Loch Leven (sea water) and the river Leven (freshwater). Equipment hire is available at Caolasnacon campsite on tel; 01855 831279 or www.kinlochlevencaravans.com.

Getting there: South of Fort William, start from the car park on the A82 at Altnafeadh (220/563) or in Kinlochleven for the shorter route, which is on the B863, by Loch Leven.

Accommodation: Mamore Lodge hotel nr Kinlochmore on tel: 01855 831213 or see www.mamorelodgehotel.co.uk. Blackwater Hostel, campsite and lodge in Kinlochleven, tel; 01855 831253 or see www.blackwaterhostel.co.uk. Caolasnacon caravan & campsite with static vans, just down the road from Kinlochleven on 01855 831 279 or www.kinlochleven caravans.com or for more life & choice head to Fort William (T.I. centre on 0845 2255121).

Bike shops Off Beat bikes in Fort William on 01397 704 008 or see www.offbeatbikes.co.uk

Refreshments In Kinlochleven & Kinlochmore only.

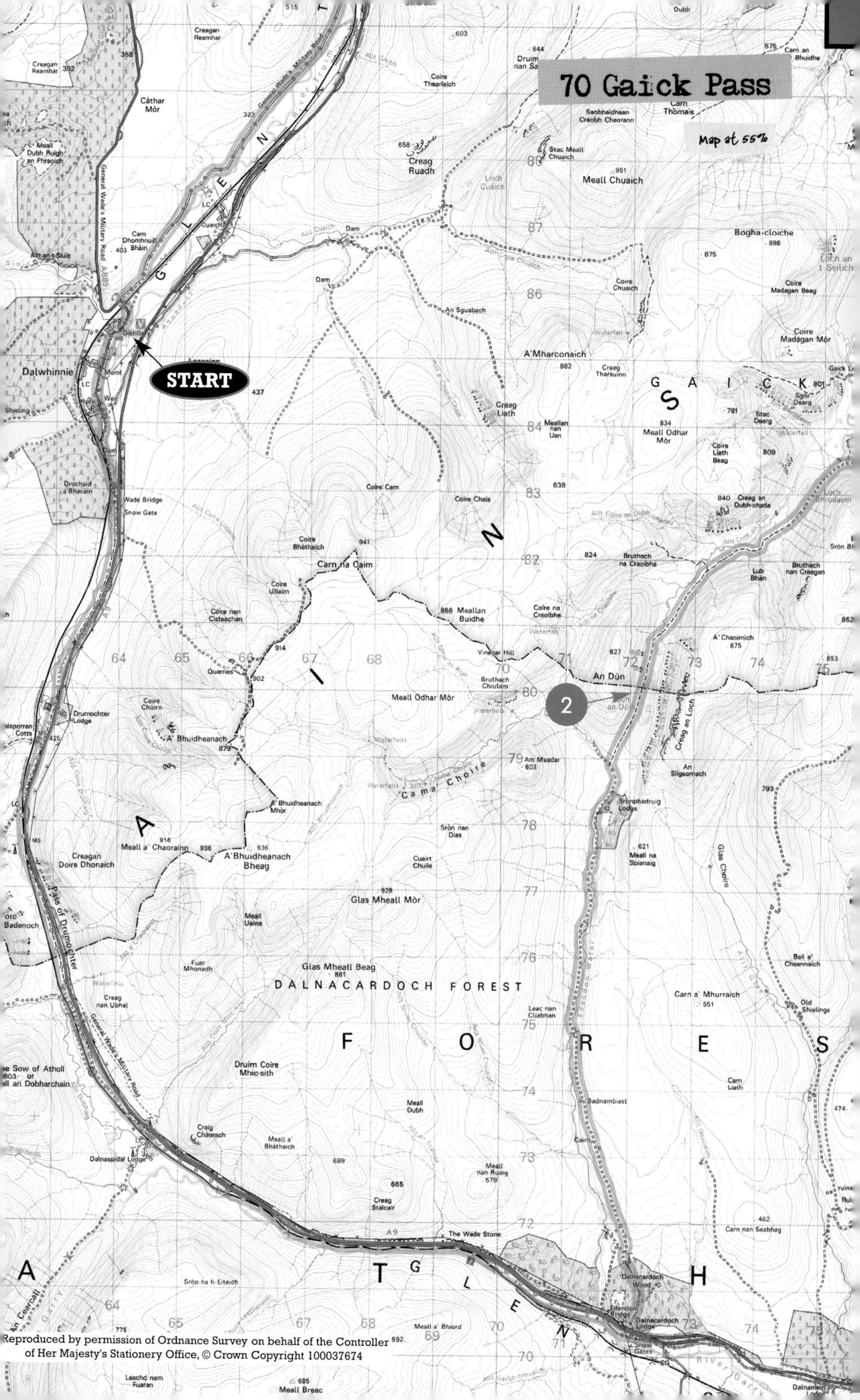

70 Gaick Pass
Map at 55%
START
Dalwhinnie
Distillery
Cuaich
Loch Cuaich
Meall Chuaich
Creag Ruadh
Càthar Mòr
Carn Dhomhnuill Bhàin
General Wade's Military Road
Allt Cuaich
Dam
An Sguabach
A'Mharconaich
Creag Tharsuinn
Creag Liath
Meallan nan Uan
Meall Odhar Mòr
Bogha-cloiche
Coire Chuaich
Coire Madagan Beag
Coire Madagan Mòr
Sgòr Dearg
Stac Dearg
Coire Liath Beag
Creag an Dubh-chadha
Loch an Dùin
Bruthach na Craoibhe
Coire Cam
Coire Chais
Coire Bhàthaich
Carn na Caim
Coire Uilleim
Coire nan Cisteachan
Meallan Buidhe
Vinegar Hill
Bruthach Chulaim
An Dùn
A' Chaoirnich
Lub Bhàn
Bruthach nan Creagan
Meall Odhar Mòr
Am Meadar
Cama' Choire
Creag an Loch
An Sligeamach
Sronphadruig Lodge
Meall na Spianaig
Glas Choire
Quarries
A' Bhuidheanach
A' Bhuidheanach Mhòr
A'Bhuidheanach Bheag
Meall a' Chaorainn
Creagan Doire Dhonaich
Drumochter Lodge
Pass of Drumochter
Sròn nan Dias
Cuairt Chuile
Glas Mheall Mòr
Meall Uaine
Glas Mheall Beag
DALNACARDOCH FOREST
Fuar Mhonadh
Creag nan Ubhal
Leac nan Cliabhan
Carn a' Mhurraich
Bail a' Cheannaich
Old Shielings
F O R E S T
ATHOLL
Druim Coire Mhic-sith
Meall Dubh
Badnambiast
Carn Liath
Craig Chaorach
Meall a' Bhàthaich
Dalnaspidal Lodge
Meall nan Ruaig
Creag Stalcair
The Wade Stone
Carn nan Seabhag
Dalnacardoch Wood
Edendon Bridge
Dalnacardoch Lodge
GLEN GARRY
Sròn na h-Eiteich
Meall a' Bhiord
Meall Breac
River Garry
Reproduced by permission of Ordnance Survey on behalf of the Controller of Her Majesty's Stationery Office, © Crown Copyright 100037674

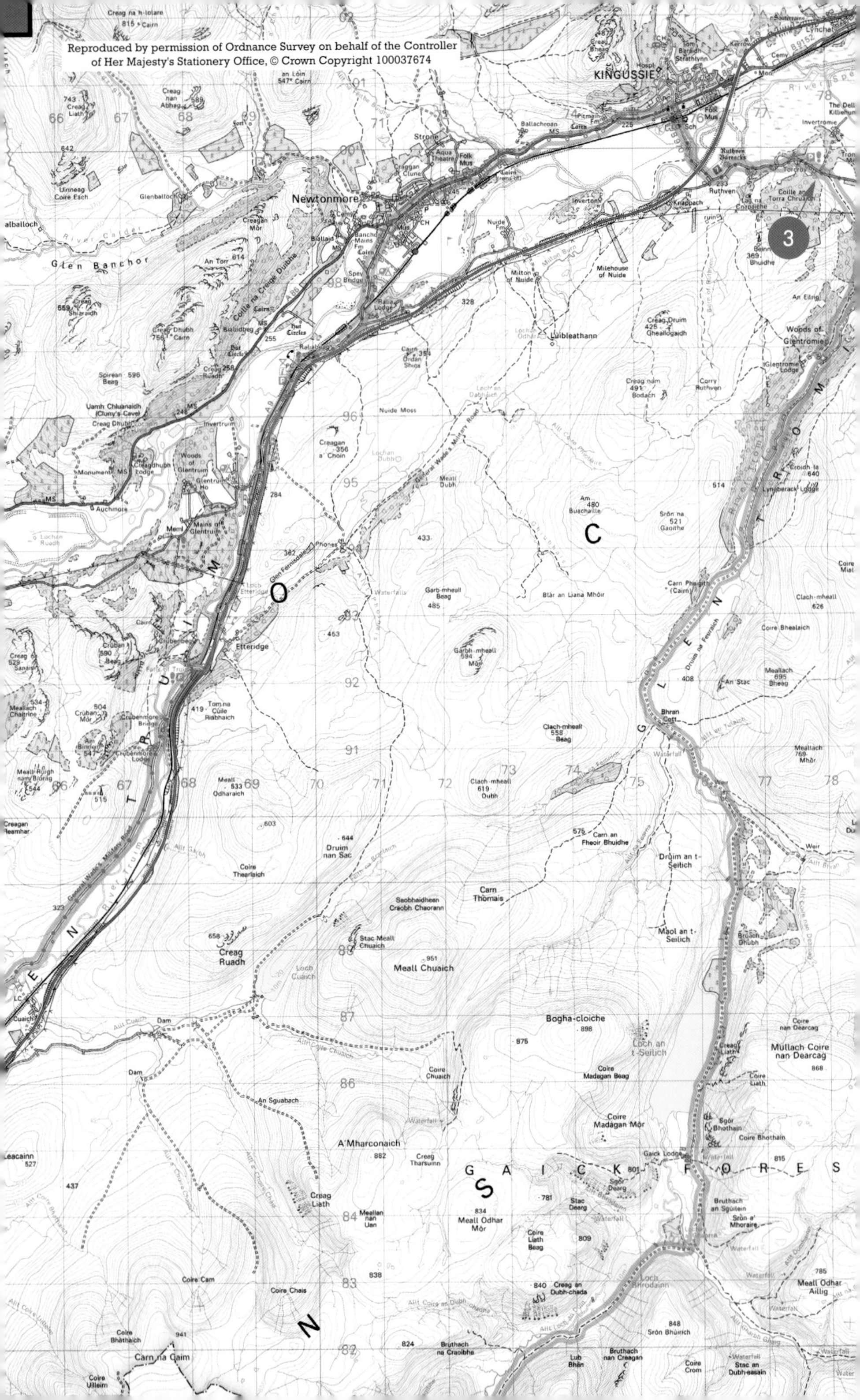
KINGUSSIE
Newtonmore
Glen Banchor
River Calder
Strone
Ruthven
Knappach
Inverton
Nuide Fm
Milton of Nuide
Milehouse of Nuide
Luibleathann
Creag Druim 425 Gheallogaidh
Creag nam 491 Bodach
Corry Ruthven
Woods of Glentromie
Glentromie Lodge
Lynaberack Lodge
Nuide Moss
Creagan 356 a' Choin
Meall Dubh
Am 480 Buachaille
Sròn na 521 Gaoithe
Blàr an Liana Mhòir
Carn Phaigith (Cairn)
Garbh-mheall Beag 485
Garbh-mheall 594 Mòr
Glen Fernisdale
Etteridge
Loch Etteridge
Phones
Crubenmore Lodge
Tom na Cùile Riabhaich
Clach-mheall 558 Beag
Clach-mheall 619 Dubh
Bhran Cott
Carn an Fheoir Bhuidhe
Druim an t-Seilich
Maol an t-Seilich
Druim nan Sac
Coire Thearlaich
Carn Thomais
Saobhaidhean Craobh Chaorann
Stac Meall Chuaich
Creag Ruadh
Loch Cuaich
Meall Chuaich
Bogha-cloiche 898
Loch an t-Seilich
Mullach Coire nan Dearcag
Coire Chuaich
An Sguabach
A'Mharconaich
Creag Tharsuinn
Coire Madagan Beag
Coire Madagan Mòr
Gaick Lodge
G A I C K F O R E S T
Creag Liath
Meall Odhar Mòr
Stac Dearg
Coire Liath Beag
Sgòr Bhothain
Coire Bhothain
Bruthach an Sgùilein
Sròn a' Mhoraire
Loch Bhrodainn
Meall Odhar Aillig
Sròn Bhùirich
Coire Chais
Coire Cam
Carn na Caim
Coire Bhàthaich
Coire Uilleim
Bruthach na Craoibhe
Bruthach nan Creagan
Lùb Bhàn
Coire Crom
Stac an Dubh-easain
General Wade's Military Road
Dam
Cuaich
Auchmore
Invertruim
Woods of Glentruim
Glentruim Ho
Mains of Glentruim
Uamh Chluanaidh (Cluny's Cave)
Coille na Creige Duibhe
Creag Dhubh 756
Spirean Beag 596
Creag Shiaraidh 559
An Torr 614
Glenballoch
Unneag Coire Esch
Ralia Lodge
Spey Bridge
Coille an Torra Chrudzich
Beinn 369 Bhuidhe
An Eilrig
Croidh la 640
Clach-mheall 626
Coire Bhealaich
Meallach 695 Bheag
An Stac
Meallach 769 Mhòr
Coire nan Dearcag
Coire Liath
G L E N T R O M I E
C O M N
G L E N T R U I M

Gaick Pass

80KM (50M) & 1,345 METRES OF CLIMBING

NOTE: This is an very challenging ride that requires some planning beforehand, to be safe and to get maximum enjoyment from the ride. You can then appreciate the wonderful views and trails you encounter as you pass through this magnificent part of the Cairngorms.

The best place to start is in Dalwhinnie, so you can attempt the hilly, technical, off-road trails of the Gaick Pass early on, and finish with the easy cycle track (or the train) from Kingussie, for the last 22km. This also means you have some refreshment stops at the end, when they are most needed. The navigation is pretty straight forward, with one half using the fast, well surfaced, Sustrans cycle track, and the other half on the off-road, mountainous, and technical at times, easy to follow Gaick Pass.

START Go south on the Sustrans cycle track no.7, alongside the A9 rd, for 21km to Dalnacardoch (722/703). Cross the A9, and head north along a double track, keeping left at a fork, past a radar mast, then keep right at a fork, above, then alongside and crossing Edendon Water a few times, and bearing right to pass alongside Loch an Duin, between the peaks of An Dun and A' Chaoirnich.

2 Stay on this track along the valley, and shortly past Loch Bhrodain bear left at a junction (758/835), heading due north, to the right hand side of Loch an t-Seilich, and keep straight ahead/left towards the woods, descend to Glen Tromie, staying on the valley floor. At a bridge near the Woods of Glentromie (779/968) turn left over this, then first right, through the woods.

3 Follow this trail to the B970 road and turn left on this, into Kingussie (756/006) and turn left on the Sustrans cycle track no.7 (or get the train). Follow the cycle path no.7 signposts, all the way, through Newtonmore, along the B9150, alongside the A9, then onto General Wade's Military Road, back into Dalwhinnie (638/850).

Shortcut

-22KM (13.7M) & 300 METRES CLIMBING

1 Catch the train from Kingussie to Dalwhinnie. See www.nationalrail.co.uk or call 08457 484950 for times, etc.

Family activities

The Sustrans cyclepath no.7 is family friendly, but mostly runs close to the A9, so is not very idyllic. However, the section between Etteridge and Dalwhinnie peels away from the main road, and offers a pleasant ride down the valley on the quiet General Wade's Military road. There is a car park at Etteridge, by the Falls of Truim, where you can then head south along the road, to Dalwhinnie.

Distillery at Dalwhinnie, tel; 01540 672219 or see www.discovering-distilleries.com/dalwhinnie.

The Falls of Truim is a great location to watch the salmon leaping. There is also a footpath downstream for those who wish to go for a walk.

Learn how the early highland people lived, built homes, etc. Located in Newtonmore, on 01540 673551 or see www.highlandfolk.com.

Getting there: Dalwhinnie car park, off the A9, on the south west edge of the cairngorms (GR 638/850). There is also a train station here.

Refreshments: in Dalwhinnie at the end/start, and Kingussie and Newtonmore near the end.

Bike shops: Bothy Bikes in Inverdruie, 01479 810111.

Accommodation: Self catering in Newtonmore on 01355 260498 and Invernahavon camping & caravan site in Newtonmore www.newtonmore.com /invernahavon, on 1540 6735 & also see the website www.kingussieaccommodation.co.uk.

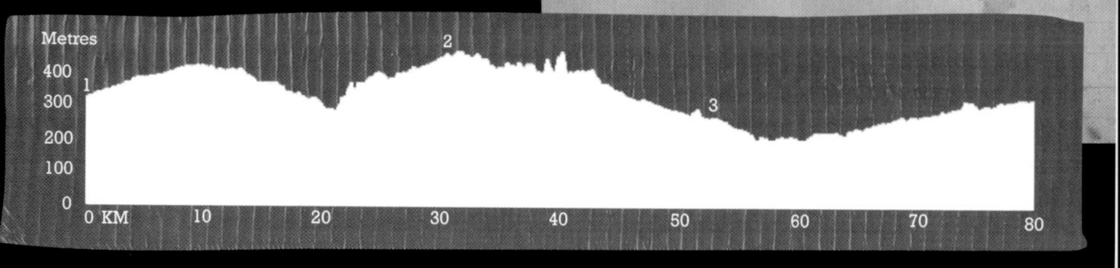

picture by Ae Bike Shop www.ae7.co.uk

pic by www.scottishmountainbikeguides.com

corrour

Glen Tanar

pic by www.scottishmountainbikeguides.com

pic by Ae Bike Shop www.ae7.co.uk

picture by Ae Bike Shop www.ae7.co.uk

7I Aviemore
Map at 90%
START
Aviemore
The Aviemore Centre
Fish Farm
Farm
Dell
Ski Centre
Inverdruie
Corrour Ho
Kinakyle
River Druie
Mus
Coylumbridge
Hotel
Mountain Rescue Post
Clay Pigeon Shooting
Aultnancaber
Guislich Farm
Achnahatnich Farm
Druimintoul Lodge
Moormore
Creag a' Ghreusaiche
Slugan
Blackpark
Lower Tullochgrue
Upper Tullochgrue
Croft
Hut Circles
Cairn
Whitewell
Achnagoichan
Cairngorm Club Footbridge
ROTHIEMURCHUS
Doune
Mon
The Polchar
Ord Bàn
PC
Castle (rems of)
Loch an Eilein
Inshriach
Loch Gamhna
River Luineag
Coire Buidhe
Cadha Mòr
Carn Eilrig
Cairn
Allt Druidh
Allt a' Phris-ghiubhais
Carn a' Phris-ghiubhais
Allt Ruigh na Sròine
Clach Mhic Cailein or the Argyll Stone
Loch Mhic Ghille-chaoil
Coire Bogha-cloiche
Coire nan Clach
Loch Einich
Gleann Einich
Rothiemurchus Lodge
Metres
KM
1
2
3
4
5
Reproduced by permission of Ordnance Survey on behalf of the Controller of Her Majesty's Stationery Office, © Crown Copyright 100037674

Aviemore

28.3KM (17.6M) & 645 METRES CLIMBING

TART From the car park, head east along the 970 for 1.6km (1m), to Coylumbridge then turn ght by/to the side of the caravan & campsite NH914/106), heading south. SP Braemar, along ne Lairig Ghru trail, but keep right (leave the Lairig rail), following SP for Glen Einich, passing through ates along the way, to a X-tracks (916/079).

Keep straight ahead or see the shortcut. Shortly go past a gate, and carry on through the forest, to a fork by a ford. Keep L, following alongside the iver Am Beanaildh, with some interesting water crossings along the way (the ford with Beanaidh Bheag (925/029) may just be best to walk hrough). Some more climbing brings great views of the loch, and a nice descent to the shores.

3 After having a rest (dip!) and look around, turn around and head back the way you came, which as you will know is mostly downhill now (and probably wind assisted).

4 Back at the X-tracks (916/079) turn left to Loch an Eilein, and bear to the right hand side of this or see the extension.

Just past the end of the loch, by car park, turn ght off the road (897/086), then after 1km (0.6m) bear left on a single track trail, through the woods 903/095) back to Inverdruie (901/109).

Extension

+2.9KM (1.8M) & 75 METRES CLIMBING

1 Bear to the left hand side of Loch an Eilein following a nice single track trail through the trees, keeping R, around the edge of the loch to the car park at the northern end & rejoin the route at no.5. **NOTE**: There is more ST to find/ride around here.

Shortcut

-11.6KM (7.2M) & METRES CLIMBING

1 Turn right at the X-rds to Loch an Eilein, and bear to the right hand side of this, and join the route at no.5.

Family Activities

The ride is quite remote, but the terrain is gentle and stream crossings will entertain the children (an get your feet wet), however, the extension may not be suitable with its forest singletrack. The Rothiemurchus Estate has lots of outdoor activities on offer for all ages, and there is also a visitor cen tre, cafe and shops to keep the family entertained.

Some of the activities on offer include safaris by foot or 4x4's, pony trekking, water sports & boat trips at Loch Insh down the road by Kincraig, and the fenicular railway to the top of cairn Gorm mountain (6th highest in Britain) isn't very far. See www.visitaviemore.com/family for more details.

Getting there Inverdruie is on the B970, just south of Aviemore, which is on the northern edge of the cairngorms, and is reached via the A9 or A95. car park in Inverdruie, opposite the visitor centre (901/109). By train: Aviemore, just over 1 mile away. The sleeper train also stops here.

Accommodation Lots available, see www.visitaviemore.com for something to suit your needs. The Rothiemurchas caravan & campsite on the route at coylumbridge, on 01479 812800 comes recommended.

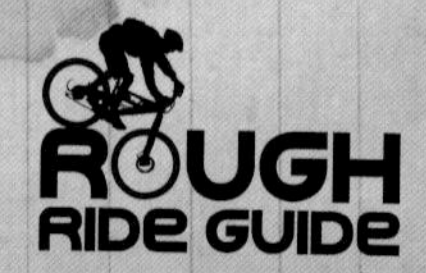

Refreshments There is nothing on the ride apart from at the start/end (café), and some light refreshments at the Loch an Eilein visitor centre near the end.

Bike shop Bothy Bikes in Inverdruie, 01479 810111 is very good & offers bike hire & more route ideas (ask about Lairig Ghru).

72 Isle of Skye
Map at 65%
START
Sligachan Hotel
Sconser
Pier
Sconser Lodge Hotel
Glamaig
Sgurr Mhairi
An Coileach
Leathad Dubh
Meall Buidhe
Maol na Gainmhich
Meall a' Mhaoil
Luib na Moil
Maol Bàn
Druim nan Cleochd
Leathad Chrithinn
Rubha Reireag
Rubh' an Àird Dhuirche
Ard Dorch/ An Aird Dorcha
Am Meall
Loch Ainort
Luib
Aricharnach
Sròn Ard a' Mhullaich
Loch nam Madadh Uisge
Glen Sligachan
River Sligachan
Loch Dubh
Nead na h-Iolaire
Coire na Sgairde
Bealach na Sgairde
Coire nan Laogh
Beinn Dearg Mhòr
Bealach Mosgaraidh
Am Fuar-choire
Druim na Ruaige
Beinn Dearg Mheadhonach
Coire na Ciche
Ciche na Beinne Deirge
Màm a' Phobuill
Bruach nam Bò
Eas a' Bhradain
Waterfalls
Glas Bheinn Mhòr
Marsco
Fiactan Dearg
Coire nan Laogh
Coire nam Bruadaran
Coire Choinnich
Coire na Seilg
Druim Eadar Dà Choire
Belig
Garbh-bheinn
Am Fraoch-choire
Ruadh Stac
Bloody Stone
Meall Dearg
Strath na Creitheach
Loch an Athain
Sgurr nan Each
Coire Dubh
Choire a' Caise
Loch na Sguabaidh
Clach Oscar
Blà Bheinn
An Stac
Loch na Creitheach
Slat Bheinn
Sgurr na Stri
The Bad Step
Camasunary
Camas Fhionnairigh
Am Màm
Rubha Bàn
Rubha na h-Airigh Bàine
Beinn Leacach
Shielings
Stone Circle (rems of)
Strathaird Ho
Kirkibost
Kilmarie
Graveyard
Ringill
Dùn Ringill
Nead an Fhir-eòin
Tobar Ceann
An Càrnach
Druim an Fhuarain
Rubha Cruaidhlinn
Slipway
Faoilean
Torrin
STRATHAIRD
SKYE
Strath Mòr
Metres
0 100 200
0 KM 2 3 4 5 6
0 10 20 30 40 50
Reproduced by permission of Ordnance Survey on behalf of the Controller of Her Majesty's Stationery Office, © Crown Copyright 10003674

Sligachan (Isle of Skye)

50KM (31M) & 1,070 METRES OF CLIMBING

START From Sligachan hotel, cross the bridge (closed to motor vehicles) and go south on the track, south bound, along Glen Sligachan. Keep straight ahead for 6km to a fork by Lochan Dubha (NG 501/240).

Bear left on the main path, passing 2 lochs, and staying to the right, on the lower path alongside the Loch, to Camusunary, by the sea (516/186).

TOP TIP: There is a bothy over the far R (west) side of the bay, which makes a good shelter / lunch stop.

Turn L (east) along a farm track, uphill on a stony track with switchbacks, then downhill to Kilmarie and the B8083 rd (545/172).

Turn L (north) on this road to the top of Loch Sapin, over a bridge and turn left, off road, heading north (565/224).

NOTE: The track disappears at times, but keep heading north, following the water.

After 3km, at the start of the 2nd Loch look for another path beginning on the other side. Cross the stream to join the track on the other side, north, to Luib (563/277).

Go L to & on the A87 rd (or R to Pipers Moon tea room), then shortly right on a minor rd around the coastline, later rejoining the A87, back to Sligachan Hotel (485/298).

pic by max darkins

This is a classic Scottish ride, with magnificant landscapes and a tough technical & physical challenge. The jagged mountain peaks, glistening sea, deep glens will leave you with wonderful memories of the ride, but the steep, technical, rocky terrain and remoteness of this ride may not be for everyone (ok, it's for very experienced riders only) but you could get a taste of it by riding as much of the first leg as you like (caw) before turning back to Sligachan.

TOP TIP: September is one of the best times to do this ride. The weather has a good (ok, better) chance of being nice, and there should be less midges around.

Getting there: 5hr drive from Glasgow – take A82 to Fort William, then either carry on to Invergarry and take the A87, or between March – October, the A830 to Mallaig to get a ferry (www.calmac.co.uk) to Armadale Bay & take the A851 to rejoin the A87. Start the ride at Sligachan Hotel, over the bridge, by the A863 rd (NG 486/298). Train station in Kyle (15 miles from Luib).

Accommodation: Sligachan Hotel has it all; rooms, self-catering cottages, camping and a bunkhouse. See www.sligachan.co.uk or 01478 650204. Visit www.skye.co.uk

Bike shops: Fairwinds Bicycle Hire in Broadford on 01471 822270 and Island Cycles in Portree on 01478 613121

Refreshments: Sligachan hotel (at the start/end) does food, as does Pipers Moon tea room in Luib, on 01471 822594.

73 Torridon
Map at 60%
START
Metres
400
300
200
100
0
0 KM
10
20
30
40

Torridon

45.5KM (28.3) & 1,275 METRES OF CLIMBING

START Head east on the A896 road, to just beyond Loch Clair, then turn right on some single track alongside this Loch, then Loch Coulin, and at the end of this bear right, to junction (019/546).

2 Go left, then at a junction along here (023/531), along Easan Dorcha. Follow this uphill, past Drochaid Coire Lair, at the foot of Beinn Liath Mhor, and keep left (south) at the junctions (990/502).

3 Superb steep, single track descent alongside River Lair, to the A890 at Achnashellach (002/481). Turn right on this road for 5.6km to Coulags and turn right (north) on a double track (958/451).

4 Follow this track, uphill, alongside Fionnabhainn, past Loch Coire Fionnaraich then keep left, for a short climb to Loch an Eion, then a wonderful single track descent to Annat, and the end of the ride (893/544).

Torridon at rush hour

picture by scottishmountainbikeguides.com

NOTE: A wonderful, remote, challenging ride, with superb wilderness singletrack. Definately one to go on your 'to do' list.

other activities

Torridon Activities offer climbing, kayaking & clay pigeon shooting. Tel; 01445 791242 or see www.thetorridon.com/activities.

There are of course the beaches to explore and other usual beach activities such as crabbing, as well as boat trips in Torridon. On boat trips you may be lucky enough to see seals, dolphins and possibly whales.

Getting there From Fort William head north on the A82, then left (west) on the A87 at Invergarry, then just past Loch Duich, before Kyle of Lochalsh, turn right on the A890, then A896, past Lochcarron, and on to Annat/Torridon (905/557). There is a train station at Achnashellach, on the route.

Accommodation: See the website www.visittorridon.co.uk for a list of wonderful places to stay. The Loch Torridon hotel looks fantastic www.lochtorridonhotel.com, or there are more modest places such as the YHA on 01445 791284 or in Achnashellach at www.gerryshostel-achnashellach.co.uk / 01520 766 232.

Bike shops Nothing nearby. Head for Fort William where there are a couple of good bike shops;. Off Beat Bikes on 01397 704008 and Nevis Cycles on 705555.

Refreshments Ben Damph Inn in Annat (nr Torridon).

Pic by Andy McCandlish / Forestry Commission

SCOTLAND

TRAIL CENTRES

The Forestry Commission is helping to put mountain biking on the world stage. With the growing network of fun & challenging trails being built, Scotland ranks as one of the top places on the planet to go biking. For world-class trails, stunning scenery and a warm welcome, look no further. See www.forestry.gov.uk/mtbscotland for more information.

TOP TIP: You can catch a (sleeper) train to Scotland and book lifts to

picture by Andy McCandlish / Forestry

picture by Forestry Commission

picture by Forestry commission

picture by Andy Mccandlish / Fc

picture by Mid Argyll Tri-CYCLE club

picture by Forestry commission

MABIE

picture by Forestry Commission

Mabie offers a great range of natural feeling trails, for all abilities

Although Mabie sits in-between Dalbeattie & Ae, it offers something quite different, with a more naturally feeling trail, flowing single track through beech trees, with roots rather than rocks to provide the challenges.

A good selection of trails for all abilities, great northshore, a bike shop, Youth Hostel & hotel (with bar) on site.

Big Views Loop

Mostly forest road, with some gentle climbs & great views along the way. Provides a very pleasant way for a family to explore the area together.

Woodhead Loop

Only slightly longer than the Big Views loop, but with more climbing (but nothing too taxing), using mostly fireroad, with some single track.

Phoenix Trail 17 KM

This trail mixes the natural with the man-made for a very rewarding ride, although some sections suffer in the wet. If it is dry, there is an optional leg after the boardwalk, to 'The Ridge' on the left, to a good viewpoint. There are also some optional Black graded sections along the way if you feel the need/desire to spice things up at all.

Kona Dark Side 3.8 KM

A very technical raised northshore featuring step-ups, gap jumps, 10cm skinnies, drop-offs and a gap-jump at the end. For experienced riders only, happy with heights & jumps. We recommend you walk through the trail before riding it.

Skills Park

Various graded trails & Mini-X (mini 4X) suitable for all abilities (as the jumps are rollable). There are also jumps & northshore for experienced riders.

Getting there: From Dumfries go south on the A710 towards Dalbeattie and the trail centre is about 4 miles along here on the right.

Grid Ref: NX 950/707 Sat Nav: DG2 8HB

Opening times & cost: Pay & display

Facilities: cafe, bike shop, with hire, toilets, bar & accommodation (hotel & YHA).

Bike Shop: Cycle centre / The Shed Cafe on 01387 270275 (on site) or in town on 01387 259483

Map: www.forestry.gov.uk/forestry/ACHS-5RNFL6

Tourist info: Dumfries T.I. on 01387 245555

Website: www.7stanes.gov.uk

NO.75 DALBEATTIE

A memorable trail centre that is at the top of many peoples 'to ride' list, thanks to the large natural slabs of bedrock that are adapted into the trail. The easier trails are mostly fireroad, but the Hardrock trail provides some very unique and challenging obstacles, such as 'The Slab' and 'The Terrible Twins'.

TOP TIP: Test / grade your abilities in the (excellent) skills area at the start & try a Taster loop before embarking on a whole ride.

picture by Forestry Commission

NOTE: 'The Slab' on the Hardrock trail in Dalbeattie is probably one of the most famous features of any trail in the county. It offers a very steep, long descent on an incredibly grippy and impressive hunk of rock.

Ironhash 11.5KM

An easy route, starting in the skills loop on wide single track, before going deeper into the forest, mostly using fireroads. After going around the marshland of the 'Dry Lock' keep a look out for any riders descending 'The Slab', before you start heading back, along trails that mostly run downhill.

Moyle Hill 14KM

This shares some of the easier sections of the red Hardrock route, including the easy (low & wide) boardwalk over the boggy ground at the start. It's great for getting some distance covered and views in, without any technically challenging obstacles along the way. There is a final (optional) section around 'Volunteer Ridge' at the end.

Hardrock 27KM

Graded red, but with a number of optional Black graded sections (with chicken runs) along the way. Look out for the likes of 'The Qualifier' a long slab of rock to test you before the infamous 'Slab' a 45 degree, 14 metre high hunk of rock. Other trails include 'The Terrible Twins' which are smaller but steeper versions of the Slab. The rock here is very grippy and you can impress folk with riding stuff that looks a lot harder than it is (honest).

Getting there: south west from Dumfries on A711, past Dalbeattie (after 13 miles) and join A710 for 1 mile to Dalbeattie Forest & the car park is off the road, on the right. Grid Ref: NX 836/590 Sat Nav: DG5 4QU.

Opening times & cost: pay & display

facilities: Bike wash but not much else, although Dalbeattie village is just 1 mile down the road. Urr Lodge Hostel is good – see www.urrlodge.co.uk

Bike shop: G & G cycle centre, in Dumfries on tel: 01387 259483 / www.cycle-centre.com

map: www.7stanes.gov.uk

tourist info: Dumfries T.I. on 01387 253862

website: www.7stanes.gov.uk

NO.76

KIRROUGHTREE

The trails here have a very remote & wilderness feel to them as well as some wonderful unique terrain which is incorporated into the trails. A prime example of this is the infamous rock slab known as 'McMoab' (on the black route).

There is a good selection of trails to suit all abilities & a skills area to test your skills. The red & black routes offer some brilliant & original technical challenges, lots of excellent flowing single track & grippy granite rock features that make it the favourite 7 stanes trail centre for lots of riders.

Bargaly Wood — 6 KM

Using forest & farm tracks, quiet country roads and woodland trails, this pleasant route is a perfect introduction for new riders and families alike.

Larg Hill — 10 OR 14 KM

Over half the route is single track, with small drops and challenges along the way, which is perfect for new riders & those wanting to try sections of the red route. The 4km 'Doon Hill' extension adds some more single track and a good viewpoint.

Taster Loop — 2 KM

Perfect short loop to test your ability to make the

Twister — 17 KM

This is a hard Red route, with technical rocky features (many of which don't have easier chicken run options) and some optional Black runs. It is however, also one of the best trails around. If all is going well, you can continue on the **Black Craigs** route, otherwise stay on this route to 'Jabberwocky'.

Black Route

An extension to the red 'Twister' route after the 'Rivendell' section, where you join the black grade 'Stairway to Heaven' singletrack. This leads on to trails such as 'The Judgement' and 'McMoab' a huge granite slab of rock which Kirroughtree is famous for. Keep a look out for the skull & cross bones to warn of the leap 'Hissing Sid'.

picture by Andy McCandlish / Forestry Commission

Getting there: Go west on the A75 from Dumfries towards Newton Stewart and 4 miles before the town go right on a minor road then 1st left on a lane and follow this to the trail centre car park.

Grid Ref: NX 452/644 Sat Nav: DG8 7BE

Opening times & cost: Pay & display

Facilities: Bike shop, bike hire, maintenance, bike wash, toilets, cafe & childrens play area.

Bike shop: The Break Pad (on site), 01671 401303

Map: www.forestry.gov.uk search 'Kirroughtree map'

Tourist info: Newton Stewart T.I. 01671 402431

Website: www.7stanes.gov.uk

NO.77 DRUMLANRIG

These trails are on the private estate of Drumlanrig Castle and a small (but very worthwhile) fee is charged for riding here. The routes have been designed by Rik Alsop (who owns the bike shop here). The trails are natural, tight, twisty single track with natural obstacles such as roots (and lots of them).

A superb destination for riders to progress & develop from the very beginning, through to the very experienced. The trails are well maintained and there is a bicycle museum here too.

Policy Trail 3 KM

Quiet country roads around Drumlanrig Castle suitable for total beginners.

Burnsands 13 KM

Passing through the hamlet of Burnsands, using quiet country roads, offering more of a physical challenge, due to the distance covered.

Rocking Stone 5 KM

Off-road, through the woods, passing some lochs along the way, the forest tracks and quiet country roads make a good introduction to off-road.

Low Gardens 8 KM

Starting on tarmac, but heading off-road with more varied terrain and steeper gradients than Rocking Stone, for a bigger challenge. Can be combined with the Rocking Stone route to make a bigger challenge, on par with a Blue graded route.

Copy Cat 9 KM

Running parallel to and on some of the red graded trails, this route allows you to sample and even just join the (red) Old School trail if you feel confident.

Secret Forest

If you want a physical but non-technical challenge this is the ride for you. Expect some steep gradients and great views, along these dirt trails.

Old School

A great natural feeling trail packed with action all along the way. Expect challenges back to back as you weave through the trees on the lovely flowing, twisty single track, with bombholes, jumps, drop offs, berms and especially LOTS of roots. Physically and technically challenging. Great fun.

NOTE: See below for the (8km) black grade extension option to this route.

Hells Cauldron

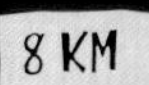

8km Black grade extension to the (red) Old School route, to make a total route of 23.5km. Expect bigger hills, even tighter corners and even more roots on this highly technical, tiring, fun trail.

Getting there: From Dumfries head north on A76 for 17 miles, through Thornhill and follow Drumlanrig castle signposts (left) on minor roads.
Grid Ref: NX 852/993 Sat Nav: DG3 4AQ.
Opening times & cost: Around £4
Facilities: Bike shop, hire & repair, museum, cafe, toilets, showers, and a castle..
bike shop: Rik's Bike Shed (on site), tel: 01848 330 080 (does hire, repairs, etc).
map: Available from Rik's bike shop
tourist info: www.visitsouthernscotland.co.uk
website: www.drumlanrig.com

NO.78

AE

A great destination for riders of all abilities. The green trail (& blue extension) are a great introduction, while the Ae Line & downhills runs will appeal to experienced riders.

A great selection of trails which loves the use of berms & jumps along the way – great fun for everyone.

Ae Valley 9KM

This low level trail has little climbing and uses wide single track type tracks that wind through the trees to make/keep it exciting, while still being perfect and suitable for families. It passes a lovely view-point overlooking the Water of Ae, which makes a good spot to spot for a picnic.

Larchview 13.5 KM

A 4.5km extension to the green Ae valley ride, for families wanting to push themselves a bit more. The extra distance is along forest roads, easy boardwalk and single track sections.

Ae Line 24 KM

The Ae line has taken some inspiration from the downhill trails, offering a fast, rocky route with lots of jumps, drops and berms, allowing you to get some airtime or just roll over. The best is saved to the end, with 'The Omega Man' with it's choice of a Red or Black line; the Red line (on right) has lots of jumps, drops and berms, while the Black line running parallel does the same but is supersized. There is also an optional (black graded) long, skinny log ride or a wider, easier timber trail.

NOTE: Be aware that the last section of this trail is quite busy as lots of people 'session' it (practice it again & again).

Ae Downhill 1.6 KM

A well established world class downhill course, with features such as the 22ft 'Coffin Jump' and 20ft 'Field Drop' to contend with on the way down.

The Shredder 1 KM

This is a fast flowing, steep, freeride style trail with some great features and a stunning road gap jump! Built as a progression towards the main downhill, but as always, walk it first to check it out.

picture courtesy of Ae Bike Shop

Getting there: From Dumfries, follow the A701 (north) towards Moffat for 8 miles then go left on a minor rd to Forest of Ae. Just past the village of Ae is the trail centre, on the right. Grid Ref: NX 982/901 Sat Nav: DG1 1QB

Opening times & cost: pay & display

facilities: bike shop/hire, cafe, toilets, showers, uplift for the downhill, see www.upliftscotland.com

bike shop: Ae bike shop/hire, cafe toilets, showers, & bike wash open 7 days a week. Tel: 01387 860541

map: www.7stanes.gov.uk

tourist info: Dumfries T.I. on 01387 253862

website: www.ae7.co.uk or www.7stanes.gov.uk

NO.79 GLENTRESS

A superb trail centre that offers great riding for all abilities and really encourages & enables riders to progress & develop their skills. The facilities are also top notch, including the superb Hub cafe (run by bikers) that has good food & also offers bike hire, night rides & skills training. A very popular trail centre so it gets very busy at weekends.

Green Route

Starting from the Buzzard's Nest car park, this beginners route uses family friendly single track for over half of its length and signs to guide you through the challenges along the way.

Blue Route 8 OR 14 KM

8km from Buzzard's Nest car park or 14km from the Osprey car park. Over half of the route is on single track and provides a few technical challenges, making it a great introduction route. The longer route saves the best to last, with the lovely 'Falla Brae' single track trail - graded red.

Red Route

A very popular and fun ride, designed with speed in mind and home to 'Spooky Wood'. This is a superb 1.6km single track descent with twelve 180-degree bermed corners, eighteen jumps and seventeen tabletops (chicken runs available), as well as some other superb, fun & technical trails.

Black Route 30 KM

A superb trail with around 75% singletrack with great black sections such as 'Soor Plooms' the rocky descent of 'Goat Track' and fast bermed corners of 'Britney Spears'. If your legs tire before the end you can opt to miss out 'Deliverance' & 'Redemption Climb'. The skinny northshore 'Ewok Village' is optional, then it joins the Red route but with optional Black sections along the way back.

Freeride Park

'The Unnamed' trail is packed with 23 jumps (mostly tabletops) and berms, while the 'Cycopath' uses northshore obstacles, with skinnies, ladder drops (that require jumping off) and 2 wall rides. Both trails end with a couple of tabletop jumps and the 'Funbox' (8ft high, 6ft wide, 15ft long) to jump (or use the ramps) on & off.

The 'Essentials' trail is designed for riders new to freeride, enabling you to have a go on easier versions, with bigger & harder options alongside them, to progress onto when you are ready.

picture by Forestry commission

Getting there: South from Edinburgh on A703, signposted to Peebles, then left (east) on the A72 for 2 miles. Grid Ref: NT 284/397 Sat Nav: EH45 8NB. Train: Caledonian Sleeper to Edinburgh & book lift with www.go-where.co.uk or www.bikebus.net in advance.

Opening times & cost: Pay & display.

Facilities: Bike shop & cafe with hire, repairs, skills lessons, group rides & cake. Showers & toilets.

Bike shop: The Hub cafe (on site), tel: 01721 721736 or see www.thehubintheforest.co.uk

Map: www.forestry.gov.uk search 'glentress trail map'

Tourist info: Edinburgh T.I. on 0845 2255 121

Website: www.7stanes.gov.uk

NO.80

INNERLEITHEN

Best known for its brilliant choice & quality downhill runs with uplift service this. However due to the lack of facilities and beginners (green & blue graded) routes, it is often over looked by XC riders, but there is a superb, highly technical red/black graded route. It also means that this site is much quieter than the popular Glentress one just down the road.

NOTE: A place for experienced riders, but not just downhillers.

Downhill Tracks

TOP TIP: Book ahead for uplifts (see notepad) or prepare to push up the paths for 45-60 mins.

MAKE OR BREAK 3.8KM

A wide, fast flowing track packed with huge berms, lots of jumps, and drops, most of which can be rolled over. Some bigger optional jumps at 'Diks Dinnerparty', then 3 rocky steps (3rd being nearly 4ft), 10 big rollers for a rollercoaster ride, a rock chute, with a few more jumps, drops, a massive bomb hole, and a few more jumps to finish.

GOLD RUN 1.5KM

A natural feeling trail, with fast flowing, rooty, off-camber sections which joins the Cresta Run to end.

CRESTA RUN 1.5KM

Similar to the Gold Run, this natural, technical, tight, rooty, track, with sweeping turns and berms.

MATADOR 2KM

Set away from the other downhill tracks, offering big drops (up to 8ft, which you can get serious air) rocks, tabletops, a gap jump and berms to finish.

Traquair XC 19 KM

This trail is close to being graded Black, even without all the Black options along the way. It has lung busting climbs, bermed single track and hard technical riding, finishing with the superb 'Cadon Bank' trail; 2km of fast flowing rollercoaster downhill singletrack, with jumps, bomb holes, drop-offs & big berms, it will leave you battered but happy.

NOTE: There is a shortcut to the left just before the 'Minch Moor Climb' to the 'Endura Trail'.

picture by Forestry commission

Getting there: South from Edinburgh on the A703 to Peebles, then left (east) on A72 past Glentress, to Innerleithen. Go right (SP Traquair) to T-junction and the car park is on the left. Grid Ref: NT 336/357 Sat Nav: EH44 6PD. Also, see Glentress.

Opening times & cost: Pay & Display + uplift

facilities: Nothing at the trail head, but Innerleithen is just down the road and has lots.

bike shop: Alpine Bikes in Innerleithen on 01896 830880 or www.alpinebikes.com

map: www.forestry.gov.uk/forestry/achs-5rnfvj

tourist info: Peebles T.I. on 0870 6080404

website: www.7stanes.gov.uk, www.upliftscotland.com & www.redbullprojectdownhill.co.uk

NO.81 FORT WILLIAM

This wonderful location has been / is home to the (very tough) round for the World Cup Downhill, 4 cross & XC events, plus there is a gondola uplift available for the downhill runs.

All the trails here are world class and generally offer some serious technical challenges, apart from the blue grade trails and some (unmarked) natural trails. The red routes also get changed each year to keep things fresh.

Small World

This is a short taster route for new riders, going around the start of the World Championship trail and back along the old World Cup circuit.

Broomstick Blue

This new blue route uses cycleways, forest tracks & lots of great flowing singletrack, which isn't too technical. This makes it ideal for beginners who want an interesting & exciting ride.

IO Under the Ben 16.5 KM

This trail, as used in www.nofussevents.co.uk, uses some familiar trails to the World Champs course. Generally a fast and not too technical route until you come to the very tricky steep, rocky descent called 'Nessie' - be warned, this beast is real!

World Champs 9.5 KM

Designed for the 2007 World Championships XC race, this tough, technical trail is aka the 'Witch's Trail'. It basically consists of a big long climb followed by a superb descent back down along some wonderful trails. If you want even more of a challenge, there are some optional black graded sections of trail along the route.

NOTE: The professional men do 5 laps of this and the women do 4. Can you?!

Nevis Red 5.5 KM

Graded the same as a red XC route, but you take a Gondola up Aonach Mor, so the ride is mostly downhill & has a lovely long boardwalk section. It iisn't too technical though, as it is designed for experienced (XC) riders, not hardcore downhillers. You will need to be correctly clothed, biked & sign a participation statement to ride it though.

World Cup Downhill 2.8 KM

After a tranquil 15 min journey in the Gondola, up Aonach Mor, you face a superb, technical descent dropping 555 metres. Expect massive drop-offs, jumps rock gardens, mud & roots as you descend one of the longest & toughest downhill routes in the world. Only recommended for expert riders with the proper bike, equipment & skills.

4X Race track

Situated at the bottom of the main DH track, the 4X track is designed to allow 4 riders to race down the track together, tackling a course of berms, jumps, step ups & other features.

Getting there: Just a few miles up the A82 from Fort William, at the Nevis ranges / Aonach Mor ski centre car park. There is a railway station in Fort William. Grid Ref: NN 171/774 Sat Nav: PH33 6SW

Opening times & cost: Fee for the Gondola ride - open all year & for bikers mid-May to mid-September.

Facilities: cafe at the bottom, restaurant & bar at the top of Anoach Mor, bike wash,

Bike shop: Off Beat Bikes: 01397 704008 & Nevis Cycles: 01397 705555, in Fort William & on site in the summer.

Map: www.forestry.gov.uk & search 'witch's trail map'

Tourist info: Fort William T.I. 01397 701801

Website: www.ridefortwilliam.co.uk or www.nevisrange.co.uk

NO.82 LAGGAN WOLFTRAX

Well known for its (double) black graded route as it is probably one of, if not the most technically difficult XC trails in Scotland. However, less experienced riders also have some nice trails to choose & the Bike Park is suitable for a whole range of abilities and has an uplift.

TOP TIP: The 'Gateway' feature at the start of the trails is a good place to test your skills and determine which trail would suit you best.

Green Route

4.8 KM

This easy, family trail goes through some lovely woodland, making a nice introduction to mtb'ing. It starts with an easy wide track to Gorstean car park (alternative start point), which you can return along now, or climb a bit further to ride a gentle single track descent that is smooth and easy to ride, but with some twists & turns to make it interesting.

Red Route

17 KM

'Upper Red Route' uses the black grade single track climb and then a 3km descent which is fast and not too technical unless you take the optional drop-offs and rock gardens along the way.

'Lower red route' provides a more technical and fun rocky route with drop-offs, the Black graded 'Air's Rock' (huge granite slab of rock), the 'Bhadain Boulder Field' and the 'Wolf Run' (a bermy boardwalk descent) to the Bike Park, where you can finish the ride some with jumps & berms.

Black Route

9.4 KM

After the 3km fireroad climb, the trail becomes VERY technical and has no chicken runs. Starting with the double black graded 'Back, Crack, Sack Attack' and other such evil sounding trails such as 'Surgeon's Slab', 'Heart of Darkness', 'Two Ton Drop', and of course the 'Devil's Chessboard' a 40 metre slab of rock staircase with 24 levels.

Fun Park

3.5 KM

Originally this was graded Blue, but it is now graded Orange as all Forestry Commission bike parks are, so it isn't actually too technical, so everyone can enjoy it. Experienced riders can ride the jumps fast, while less confident riders can roll over them, and become more daring as they develop. There is also a shuttle bus service back to the top, but it's not too hard a climb if its not running.

picture by www.basecampmtb.com

Getting there: From Fort William follow the A86, or from Inverness follow the A9 to Kingussie then join the A86 and it is just a few miles along here.

Grid Ref: NN 594/923 Sat Nav: PH20 1BU

Opening times & cost: Free

facilities: A great cafe, toilets, showers, bike wash & bike shop with hire, repair & uplift service.

bike shop: Basecamp (on site), 01528 544786 or see www.basecampmtb.com

map: www.forestry.gov.uk/wolftrax

tourist info: see website below

website: www.basecampmtb.com

NO.83

MORAY MONSTER TRAILS

A good variety of trails, starting from 3 different car parks: Whiteash Hill Wood, Ordiequish, and Ben Aigan. Slightly out of the way and not as technical as some centres, but good fun all the same, especially for intermediate riders.

WHITEASH HILL WOOD

Fochabers Ring 8 KM

A varied and technical ride with section named after the Lord of the Rings. First its the smooth single track of 'The Shire' the tough 'Lord of the Granny Rings' climb, then the option of riding Fochabers Freeride (see below). After 'Rohan' & Fangorn' comes the technical rocky single track of 'Middle Earth', and on through 'Gondor' & 'Rivendell' to the (natural) muddy rooty 'Helms Deep' then back on 'Aragorn Alley' single track.

Fochabers Freeride

Found on Fochabers Ring ride, is a very challenging trail for experienced riders only - walk before you ride. It starts with some technical northshore, then introduces some big drops, jumps and berms, then rejoins the Fochabers Ring route.

BEN AIGAN

Ben Aigan Hammer 8 KM

Going around the summit of Ben Aigan, this trail isn't very technical, although it is fun and has a lovely 6.7km of uninterrupted single track. Also, at the end you get to choose between riding either;

Pink Fluffy Bunny

The most technical trail, with tabletop jumps to start, before getting steeper & tighter in the woods, through rock gardens back out the woods for some berms and jumps.

or

Mast Blast 1 KM

A fast, fun, bermed trail, with rollable jumps and nothing too technical, enabling you to ride fast.

ORDIEQUISH

Skills area - great for newer riders to test their skill.

Soup Dragon 4 KM

A fun route for all riders, as the difficulty lies within the speed with which you ride it. There is also an optional extension called 'The Dragon's Tail'.

The Haggis 6 KM

A fun intermediate route, which can also be used to link with the Ben Aigan Hammer trail, by taking 'The Haggis Connection' and following the signs for 7km (4.3m), heading south.

Gordzilla 5 KM

A good intermediate route with a big climb to start, then a descent on varied terrain. It can be added to extend 'The Haggis' or 'Soup Dragon' rides.

Gully Monster 2 KM

A 3km ride up 'Godzilla' brings you to the start of this very tight & technical trail. With steep slopes, drops, blind bends and narrow off camber trails you will need good balance and concentration to avoid falling down the steep sides. Great fun!

Getting there: Just south of Spey Bay, there are 3 starting points; 2 near Fochabers, one in Whiteash Hill wood (GR NJ 358/585), off the A96/A98, the other at Ordiequish Hill car park (GR NJ 340/562) just south of Fochabers, and 3rd off the A95 near Mulben (GR NY 333/492). Sat Nav: Fochabers.

Facilities: All 3 start points have parking, Fochabers has toilets. cafes & shops in Fochabers, Elgin & Craigellachie.

Bike Shop: Rafford Cycles in Forres, 01309 672811

map: www.forestry.gov.uk/forestry/infd-6mrfe5

tourist info: www.visitscotland.com

website: www.moraymountainbikeclub.co.uk

NO.84 LEARNIE RED ROCK

The centre is made up of a collection of graded trails, so riders basically 'pick n mix' their own route. There are some superb Blue & Black graded trails, a fun park & dirt jump area but nothing in-between i.e. red grade. However, if you follow our suggested route you will get something similar to a red run, with optional Black extensions (some of which are VERY technical).

The layout: A Dirt jump area at the start and on this / western side of the public road are the Green and Blue trails. On the other / eastern side of the road are the technical rocky Black trails and another Blue trail.

(our) Pick n Mix route

VARIOUS

Leave car park on the fireroad then go R to climb **Callachy Hill** (1.5km) singletrack, to the Bike / Fun Park (but save that for later) & go down the superb, fast flowing **Callachy Downhill** (1.3km) to the start of **Muirhead climb** (1.1km) for a single track climb & cross the public road to Fir Hill.

Follow the **Fir Hill** (0.5km) for a fast and descend to **Firth View** (2.2km) and admire the views before continuing through Boulder Boulevard and climb back up to Firth Hill. Here you can choose to ride the (Double) **Black** graded Learnie Hill (3.4km) trail, but beware it it has some seriously challenging sections along it. Trails to look out for include 'Seismometer', 'Tracy's Trees' (with chicken run), 'Dextrality', and finishing with 'Gyroscope' and the 10ft stone drop of 'Mephisto'. Scary stuff.

NOTE: If it has been rebuilt, there is another **Black** graded trail, **Fir Hill**, but if you have problems with 'Amen Corner' at the start, bail out before you reach the likes of the 'Meek Machete' (a twisty, wooden berm section of trail).

Cross back over the public road and turn left along the fireroad to and down the **Fun Park** (1.1km) near the start of the Callachy Downhill, for some big berms & jumps, then follow the **Home** (0.5km) single track back to the start.

Pick n Mix your own route

picture by Andy McCandlish / Forestry Commission

Getting there: From Inverness go north on the A9 to Tore then right on A832 (SP Cromarty) then 3 miles past Rosemarkie village turn right to the trails.

Grid Ref: NH 736/614 Sat Nav: Rosemarkie (village)

Opening times & cost: 24/7/365 & Free

Facilities: Parking, but nothing else. Head back to Rosemarkie village for refreshments.

Bike Shop: Square Wheels in Strathpeffer on 01997 421000 or Highland Bicycle Co in Inverness on 01463 234789.

Map: www.forestry.gov.uk/forestry/INFD-6NZE9W

Tourist info: Kingussie T.I. 01540 661297

Website: www.forestry.gov.uk

NO.85

KYLE OF SUTHERLAND

The trails are located at 2 trail centres, which are in close proximity to each other; Balblair & Carbisdale.

CARBISDALE

Both of the trails are pretty short, but they can be combined with the Balblair trails for a bigger day out. One their own they make a good introduction for intermediate riders to test their skills on while also offering some wonderful views of the area. Novices may find the trails a bit too technical though.

Blue Trail 3 KM

Mostly singletrack, with some technical descents such as 'Goldie Rocks' & 'Hissing Sid' but the more technical obstacles are optional/avoidable, so it can be ridden by less experienced riders. If you are happy riding this trail you could try the red route, which isn't too much harder.

Red Trail

This is an extension to the blue route, after 'Hissing Sid' to provide some more technical riding on sections such as 'Little Red Riding Wood' & 'What Big Teeth'. As you'd expect from a red route, it is slightly harder than the blue route, but not a massive jump, as some other red graded trails would be. You'll face an extra couple of climbs & descents on tighter twistier singletrack to provide some experience of 'the next step'.

TOP TIP: Experienced riders could ride all 4 of the trails to provide a good days riding.

NOTE: You can cycle between the two centres along the Sustrans cycle path.

BALBLAIR

Balblair offers some great technical riding (even the blue route is technical for its grading). The trails, designed by Rik Alsop, have a great natural feel to them and are pretty quiet & offer some great views.

Blue Trail 3 KM

A short but sweet trail offering some nice sections, such as 'Whoopy do' and the smooth fast 'Ceilidh Trail'. For a blue grade it is quite hilly & rough with some tight corners, so be careful, but it isn't very long so makes a good transition to red grade trails.

Black Route 7.5/11.5 KM

A very natural feeling & technical trail, with some timber constructions as well. With trail names such 'Rock Hard', 'Candy Mountain', 'Loopy Loo', 'Slab & Tickle' & 'Slab Happy' you may have guessed that rocks feature heavily, so you may want to take some body armour with you.

Getting there: North of Inverness & west of Golspie, exit the A9 on the A836 nr Tain (or A949 nr Dornoch from Golspie) & Balblair is 1.5 miles past Bonar Bridge on the left GR NH 604/930 / Sat Nav: Bonar Bridge. For Carbisdale, either cycle (see map info) or turn off the A836 just before Bonar Bridge, to Culrain & follow signs to Carbisdale Castle YHA Grid Ref: NH 574/953 / Sat Nav: IV24 3DP.

Facilities: Nothing at Balblair, but there is a cafe & YHA with accommodation & bike hire, tel 0870 0041109

Bike shop: Square Wheels, Strathpeffer 01997 421000

Map: www.forestry.gov.uk/forestry/INFD-74EJDM

Website: www.forestry.gov.uk

NO.86

COLSPIE WILDCAT

It may be a bit out of the way, but this trail centre offers some truely superb (& quiet) routes, in a beautiful setting. The (very technical) black route has some of the most challenging climbing of any of the trail centres & rewards those who conquer it with a truely fantastic 7km singletrack descent - one of the longest in the country.

NOTE: The red & blue trails are good, but if you aren't going to attempt both and / or the Black route it might be a bit farto travel to.

picture by Andy McCandlish / Forestry Ciommission

The Black route offers some of the most technical riding available, as well as the longest singletrack descent (7km). Awesome.

Blue Trail

This trail offers some nice, but not too technical singletrack & forest roads, with superb views of the sea. Great fun for intermediate riders.

NOTE: You can start from the town an follow the red route until you see the blue markers, or see 'Getting there' for directions to the start.

Red Trail

You start at sea level, so face a big climb to start off with, using some good singletrack that zig-zags up the hill and some rocky challenges to keep your mind off the exertion - kind of. The route is fast, flowing & relatively smooth, with some great berms, jumps & drops along the way. The jumps are rollable, but also enable some good air when taken at speed - which is easy to build up.

Black Trail

This is an extension to the Red trail (from the top of 'Cat's Climb' onto the single track climb of 'Fox Farm') and it provides some of the most technical riding in the country, as well as the longest single track descent in Scotland (7km). Once you have completed the very technical climb, there are some jumps at the top before the superb, very technical, steep, tight, rocky descent.

NOTE: If you are struggling, there are shortcuts & chicken runs available to help you out.

Getting there: Go north on the A9 from Inverness, for 50 miles! Park in town centre GR NC 832/999 Sat Nav: Golspie or for the blue route, keep straight ahead, through the town and turn left on minor road, under the railway bridge SP 'Backies' up to car park on your right (838/014) nr the waterfall.

facilities: car park, cafe etc in town.

Bike Shop: Square Wheels in Strathpeffer; 01997 421000 & Highland Cycles in Inverness; 01463 234 935

map: www.highlandwildcat.com

tourist info: www.visitscotland.com

website: www.highlandwildcat.com

Breaks with bikes

IN WALES

picture by Andy Lloyd

Wales

The home to mountain biking? certainly home to the first purpose built mtb trail centre (coed-y-Brenin) to which everyone who considers themselves a serious mtb'er should maybe make a pilgrimage to at some point in their life.

Quintessential Wales for me has to be winding fire roads through damp pine forests with the sound of mountain streams rushing past. It reminds me of holidays as a child and adventures as an adolescent. Wales also has such variety that includes the majesty of snowdonia to the beauty of coastal Pembrokeshire. It's not all extremely challenging riding; there are plenty of places to ride with the family and get introduced to the sport if you're just starting out.

Wales is also completely geared up to mountain biking which is so refreshing - the tourist board can't do enough to encourage people to come & visit. so if you have never ridden in Wales before start planning your trip now!

Useful sites: www.mbwales.com, www.mtb-wales.com www.visitwales.com, www.cycling.visitwales.com & www.forestry.gov.uk/mtbwales.

picture by Richard Williams on Snowdon

pic by Max Darkins

picture by Jeremy Atkinson

picture by Paul Knott

WALES

Trail centres

picture by Chris Malone

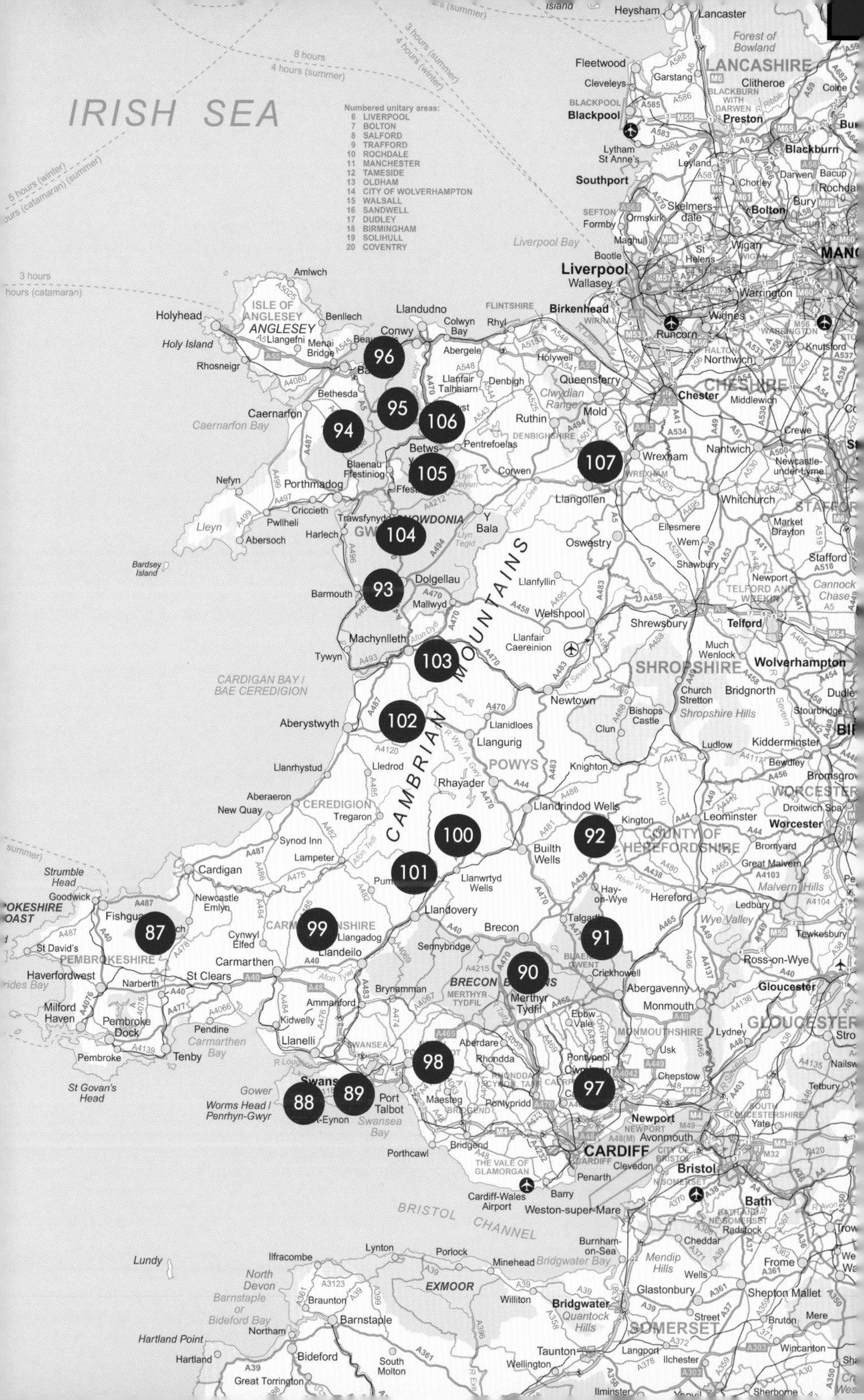

IRISH SEA
Numbered unitary areas:
6 LIVERPOOL
7 BOLTON
8 SALFORD
9 TRAFFORD
10 ROCHDALE
11 MANCHESTER
12 TAMESIDE
13 OLDHAM
14 CITY OF WOLVERHAMPTON
15 WALSALL
16 SANDWELL
17 DUDLEY
18 BIRMINGHAM
19 SOLIHULL
20 COVENTRY
8 hours
4 hours (summer)
3 hours (summer)
4 hours (winter)
5 hours (winter)
3 hours
hours (catamaran)
Heysham
Lancaster
Forest of Bowland
LANCASHIRE
Fleetwood
Garstang
Clitheroe
Cleveleys
Blackpool
Preston
Blackburn
Lytham St Anne's
Leyland
Southport
Chorley
Darwen
Bacup
Rochdale
Skelmersdale
Ormskirk
Formby
Bolton
Bury
Maghull
Wigan
St Helens
Liverpool Bay
Bootle
Liverpool
Wallasey
Warrington
Birkenhead
Widnes
Runcorn
Knutsford
Northwich
CHESHIRE
Chester
Middlewich
Crewe
Nantwich
Newcastle-under-Lyme
Whitchurch
Market Drayton
Stafford
Newport
TELFORD AND WREKIN
Cannock Chase
Telford
Shrewsbury
Much Wenlock
Wolverhampton
SHROPSHIRE
Bridgnorth
Church Stretton
Shropshire Hills
Stourbridge
Kidderminster
Ludlow
Bewdley
Bromsgrove
WORCESTERSHIRE
Droitwich Spa
Worcester
Leominster
Kington
COUNTY OF HEREFORDSHIRE
Bromyard
Great Malvern
Malvern Hills
Hereford
Ledbury
Wye Valley
Tewkesbury
Ross-on-Wye
Gloucester
GLOUCESTERSHIRE
Lydney
Chepstow
Tetbury
Yate
Avonmouth
Bristol
Clevedon
Bath
Radstock
Cheddar
Mendip Hills
Wells
Frome
Glastonbury
Shepton Mallet
Street
Bruton
Mere
Bridgwater
Quantock Hills
SOMERSET
Langport
Ilchester
Wincanton
Taunton
Wellington
Ilminster
Sherborne
Yeovil
Burnham-on-Sea
Weston-super-Mare
Bridgwater Bay
Minehead
Williton
EXMOOR
Porlock
Lynton
Ilfracombe
North Devon
Braunton
Barnstaple
Barnstaple or Bideford Bay
Northam
Bideford
South Molton
Great Torrington
Hartland Point
Hartland
Lundy
BRISTOL CHANNEL
Cardiff-Wales Airport
Barry
Penarth
CARDIFF
THE VALE OF GLAMORGAN
Bridgend
Porthcawl
Maesteg
Pontypridd
Newport
Caerphilly
Cwmbran
Pontypool
Usk
MONMOUTHSHIRE
Monmouth
Abergavenny
Crickhowell
BLAENAU GWENT
Ebbw Vale
Merthyr Tydfil
MERTHYR TYDFIL
Aberdare
Rhondda
RHONDDA CYNON TAFF
BRECON BEACONS
Brecon
Sennybridge
Talgarth
Hay-on-Wye
River Wye
Builth Wells
Llandrindod Wells
Knighton
Rhayader
POWYS
Llangurig
Llanidloes
Newtown
Bishops Castle
Clun
Welshpool
Llanfair Caereinion
Llanfyllin
Oswestry
Ellesmere
Wem
Shawbury
Llangollen
Wrexham
WREXHAM
Corwen
Mold
Ruthin
DENBIGHSHIRE
Clwydian Range
Queensferry
Holywell
FLINTSHIRE
Denbigh
Rhyl
Abergele
Colwyn Bay
Llandudno
Conwy
Llanfair Talhaiarn
Pentrefoelas
Betws-y-Coed
Y Bala
Llyn Tegid
River Dee
SNOWDONIA
Blaenau Ffestiniog
Ffestiniog
Trawsfynydd
Harlech
Dolgellau
Mallwyd
Barmouth
Machynlleth
Afon Dyfi
Tywyn
CAMBRIAN MOUNTAINS
CARDIGAN BAY / BAE CEREDIGION
Aberystwyth
Llanrhystud
Lledrod
Aberaeron
New Quay
CEREDIGION
Tregaron
Synod Inn
Lampeter
Afon Teifi
Llanwrtyd Wells
Llandovery
Cardigan
Newcastle Emlyn
Strumble Head
Goodwick
Fishguard
PEMBROKESHIRE
St David's
Haverfordwest
Narberth
Milford Haven
Pembroke Dock
Pembroke
St Govan's Head
Tenby
Pendine
Carmarthen Bay
St Clears
Carmarthen
Cynwyl Elfed
Llangadog
Llandeilo
Afon Tywi
Brynamman
Ammanford
Kidwelly
Llanelli
SWANSEA
Gower
Worms Head / Penrhyn-Gwyr
Port Talbot
Swansea Bay
Caernarfon
Caernarfon Bay
Bethesda
Bangor
Menai Bridge
Llangefni
Benllech
Amlwch
ISLE OF ANGLESEY
ANGLESEY
Holyhead
Holy Island
Rhosneigr
Nefyn
Porthmadog
Criccieth
Pwllheli
Lleyn
Abersoch
Bardsey Island
87
88
89
90
91
92
93
94
95
96
97
98
99
100
101
102
103
104
105
106
107

ROUTE	GRADE	DISTANCE	+/–
87 Preseli Hills	Easy–Medium	24Km	
88 Gower	Family – Medium	32.2Km	Various
89 Mumbles	Family	Various	
90 Talybont-on-Usk	Family – Hard	31.2Km & 22.5Km	+3.3Km
91 Black Mountains	Hard – Vary hard	36.5Km	+0.3Km
92 Kington	Easy – Medium	31Km	Various
93 Barmouth	Family – Medium	34.5Km	Various
94 Snowdon	Very hard	18.3Km	–3.7 or +2.8Km
95 Capel Curig	Medium – Hard	26.8Km	
96 Colwyn Bay	Family	Various	

Trail centres	Green	Blue	Red	Black	Orange
97 Cwm Carn	0	0	1	0	2
98 Afan Argoed	1	0	3	1	0
99 Brechfa Forest	1	1	1	1	0
100 Coed Trawllwm	0	1	1	1	0
101 Cwm Rhaeadr	0	0	1	0	0
102 Nant Yr Arain	0	0	2	1	0
103 Machynlleth	0	1	2	1	0
104 Coed Y Brenin	1	0	3	2	0
105 Penmachno	0	0	2	0	0
106 Gwydr Forest	0	0	1	0	0
107 Coed Llandegla	1	1	1	1	0

ROUTE DESCRIPTION

A beautiful area, largely devoid of mtb trails, but for this route. A saviour.

Picturesque seaside route, with great riding (& surfing), with a family option

A lovely family ride along the seafront, with an added extension heading inland.

classic Welsh ride, known as 'The Gap'. Head into the mountains or keep it easy & low

A big day out in the Welsh mountains. Big challenge with big rewards & big views

Good mix of tracks & forgotten lanes. A good introduction to the area.

A lovely ride along the estuary to the seaside – great ride for all the family

Proper mtb'ing. A tough hike to the top & a very technical descent. A must do.

Superb natural singletrack route, often overlooked for surrounding trail centres

Lovely family ride along the seafront, with attractions along the way

Only 1 red XC route but its nearly all singletrack. Good freeride & downhill trails

Over 100km of trails, 2 trail centres, bar & camping. Great for experienced riders

Fun BMX style trails with jumps & berms to pump the bike along, for all abilities

Great facilities & nice singletrack trails, but quite short. Good base for more trails

Another great flowing, jumpy, bermy (but short) trail designed by Rowan Sorrell.

Great mix of natural & man made trails to provide some wonderful, remote rides

Good natural trails from town & the technical singletrack Cli-Machx trail close by

The birthplace of the trail centre & still leading by example. A must go place.

No facilities & still not officially open, but nice riding with lots more trails close by

Only 1 red route & no facilities, but nice flowing trail with lots more riding close by

Smooth, fast flowing trails with jumps & berms for everyone. Great cafe & bike shop

picture by Andy Lloyd @ cwm carn

picture by Andy Lloyd @ Afan

picture by Andy Lloyd @ cwm carn

87 Preseli Hills
Map at 100%
Reproduced by permission of Ordnance Survey on behalf of the Controller of Her Majesty's Stationery Office, © Crown Copyright 100037674
PEMBROKESHIRE COAST NATIONAL PARK /
PARC CENEDLAETHOL ARFORDIR PENFRO
START
MYNYDD PRESELI
Foel Drygarn
Carn Breseb
Carn Goedog
Bwlch Ungwr
Carnmenyn
Carn Gyfrwy
Carn Bica
Bedd Arthur
Carn Arthur
Carn Siân
Mynydd-bach
Foel Feddau
Carnau Lladron
Foel Cwmcerwyn
Pantmaenog Forest
Pant-maenog
Rosebush
Burial Chamber
Eithbed
Bwlch-y-pant
Mynydd Crwn
Glynaeron
Cnwc Rhudd
Carn Afr
Glynsaithmaen
Cattle Grid
Standing Stones
Cwm-garw
Craig Talfynydd
Cors Tewgyll
Pantithel
Mynachlog-ddu
Cemy
Rhos Fach
Llain
Gors Fawr
Stone Circle
Mohair Centre
Henbarc
Dolaumaen
Waun Lwyd
Caermeini
Glan-rhyd
Crug-yr-hwch
Llainban
Blaen-gors
Waunclеddau
Tafarn-y-bwlch
Rhos-y-Bryn
Waun Brwynant
Mirianog Ganot
Carnalw
Coedcefnlas
Fronlas
Brynberian
Banc Du
Penanty
Mynydd-du Commin
Mynydd Bâch
Pisgah
Travel
Wern
Tirbach
Llandre
Blaendyffryn
Allt-y-gôg
Pen-yr-allt
Eithinduon
Portis-pant
Afon Wern
Afon Tewgyll
Metres
400
300
200
100
1
2
3

Preseli Hills

24KM (14.9M) & 490 METRES OF CLIMBING

START Head south-west along the road, along the Sustrans cycle route no.47, and follow this for 12km (7.5m), to the B4313 (SN 074/286), nr Burial chamber, and go R on the rd, leaving the Sustrans route.

2 Shortly only this rd go R on a rd just past bridleway track, passing a pub and quarry (074/290). Keep SA, as rd ends, becoming a bridleway, steep climb up through Pantmaenog Forest, for 3.6km (2.2m), to a bridleway X-tracks at the top (085/321).

3 Turn right (east) on the bridleway along the ridge top. Starts off with a short climb, which is then followed by a good downhill. Keep following the BW signposts (east), which involves a couple of short climbs along the way, but mostly descending back to the car park (165/332).

NOTE: Pembrokeshire and the Preseli Hills are a beautiful, but it is quite limited for mountain biking. However you are not far from (and may be driving close to) Brechfa Forest which has some lovely man made trails suitable for all abilities. For more information see **'Brechfa'** in the trail centres section.

Family activities

BOAT TRIPS

Voyage of Discovery, inc. whale & dolphin watching & fishing trips. Nr St David's on 0800 854367 www.ramseyisland.co.uk.

ADVENTURE SPORTS

TYF Adventure offer coasteering, kayaking, rock climbing & surfing days. In St David's Tenby on 01437 721611 or www.tyf.com.

NOTE: For families around (or willing to tr el to) the south Pembrokeshire coast (nr Tenby) should check out the following;

Silent World Aquarium nr Tenby on 01834 844498 or www.silentworld.org.uk

Dinosaur Park: Great place for the kids, wi LOTS of activities on offer. Tel 01834 8452 or see www.dinosaurpark.co.uk.

Folly Farm Adventure Park: A fun fair, zoo, indoor & outdoor play areas and (usual & unusual) farm animals. Great day out tel 01834 812731 or see www.folly-farm.co.u

Oakwood Theme Park: Great fun family dc out, see www.oakwoodthemepark.co.uk.

Pembroke Castle: Fun day out for the fami 01646 684585 www.pembroke-castle.co.u

Getting there The Presili Hills are in Pembrokeshire coast National Park, south-east of Fishguard. The ride starts from a car park just west of crymych (SN 165/332), on the A478 which runs from cardigan, on the north coast, to Tenby on the south coast.

Accommodation: Fforest bring a whole new (luxurious) side to 'camping'. see the website www.coldatnight.co.uk or call 01239 623633. The Salutation Inn in crymych has various sized rooms, see www.salutationcountryhotelc.o.uk or tel; 01239 820564. TYF for groups of 8–16 on 01437 721678 or www.tyf.com.

Bike shops New Image Bicycles in cardigan, on 01239 621275

Refreshments Pub in crymych near the start/end, and a pub in Rosebush, just before the big climb half way around.

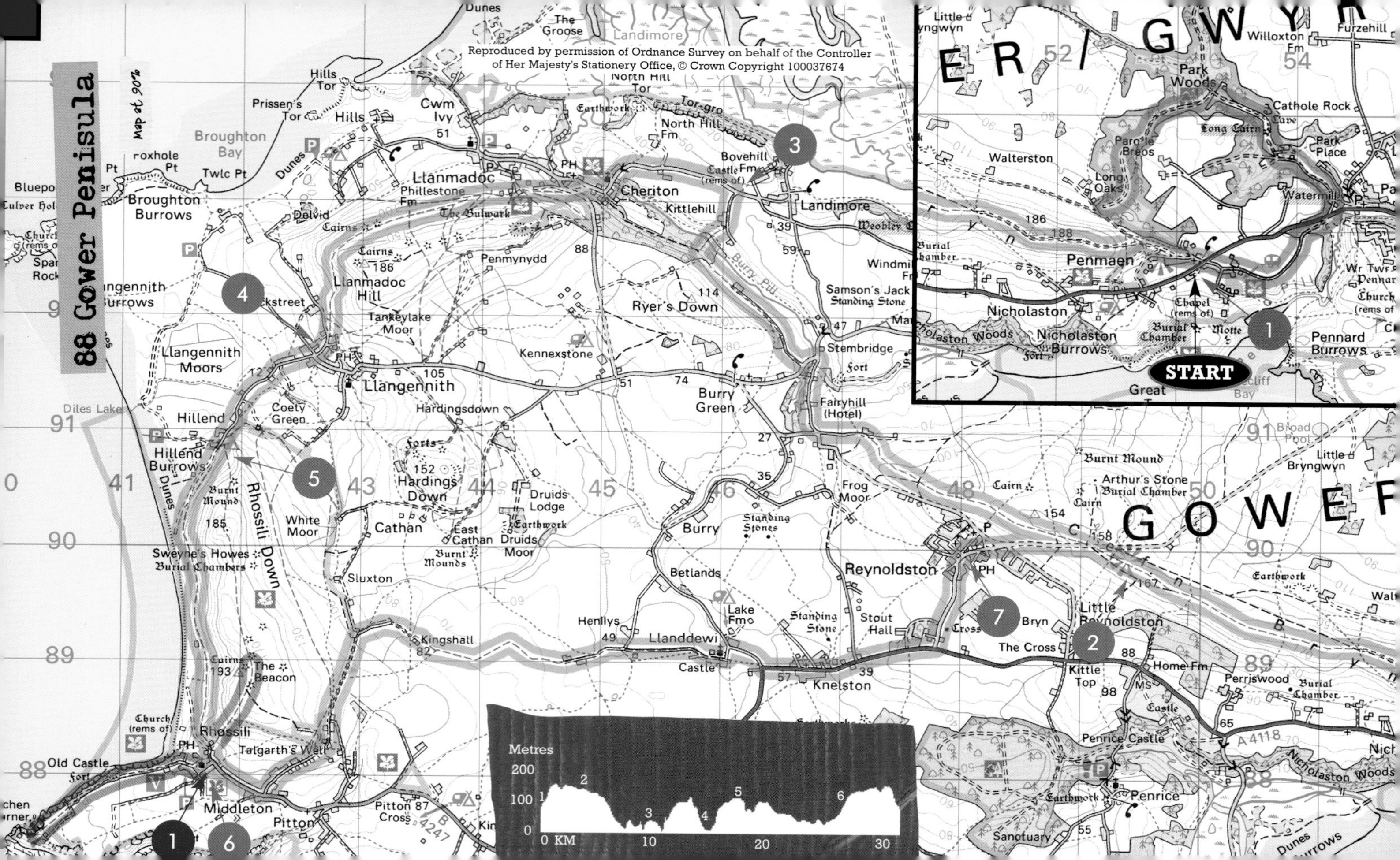
88 Gower Penisula
Map at 90%
Reproduced by permission of Ordnance Survey on behalf of the Controller of Her Majesty's Stationery Office, © Crown Copyright 100037674
START
Rhossili
Middleton
Pitton
Rhossili Down
Hillend
Llangennith
Llanmadoc
Cheriton
Landimore
Burry Green
Reynoldston
Llanddewi
Knelston
Penrice
Nicholaston
Penmaen
Metres
KM

Gower Peninsula

32.2KM (20M) & 780 METRES OF CLIMBING

START Turn left out of the Penmaen car park 529/888) then shortly right onto a rough track, to he top then turn left and then left again at the fork, o climb the Cefn Bryn. Follow this bridleway running along the top (known as Talbots Way), west, to he viewpoint (493/899).

2 Cross the road and keep straight ahead on the bridleway opposite, downhill, and past Fairyhill hotel and join a bridleway near Stembridge, along Burry Pill, to a road by the castle remains 460/931).

3 Go left, through Cheriton then climb past the Britannia Inn and turn left, to the top and turn right past Stormy Castle to the Bulwark. Follow the bridleway along the northern side of Llanmadoc Hill, past the 2 northern most Cairns, then heading south to Llangennith (426/916).

4 Go straight ahead at a X-roads in Llangennith, o Hillend Burrows. To the caravan site and take BW to L and go R (not UH) and go along ST alongside a wall, to a rd in Rhossili (417/881).

TOP TIP: Keep R, past church on a BW to the viewpoint at Kitchen Corner, or go UH to The Beacon on Rhossili Down, for great views.

5 Turn left on the B4247, then shortly left on a dead end road/Talgarth's well, keeping straight ahead on the main track, then bearing right (east) past Kingshall and Llanddewi, joining the A4118, past Knelston, then left to Reynoldston.

6 Bear right to a X-roads and go straight ahead, uphill, then right on the bridleway, past the viewpoint again (493/899). Retrace your earlier tyre tracks back into Penmaen.

Family ride

VARIOUS

1 Go back to the A4118 and cross over this join North Hills Lane. Keep SA/L on this, past caravan park, becoming a BW track, which re the A road (542/891). Cross over this onto a minor rd/drive and keep L at the junction past house on the L (543/892).

2 Follow this good track through the woods, t parking place and bear R (538/896). Ignore th turn immediately after, keeping SA through the open grounds, for 0.85km (0.5m) to a X-tracks turn L (533/901).

3 Follow the wide forest track for 1.6km (1m) end and retrace your steps, or see below.

NOTE: The short section where the track disappears nr Long Oaks may be unsuitable for som riders i.e. those towing trailers. If so, make you way to the track just beyond the end of the fore track and turn L on it, back to the start (529/88

TOP TIP: If you can't afford the time t the whole ride, you can have a great time exploring the trails on Rhossili Down (espec going north, DH past Burnt Mound is good f Harding Down and Llanmadoc Hill on the we coast. These will provide you with some sti climbs and excellent descents (and excelle views) for as long as you care to ride.

NOTE: Non-cyclists can lie on the beach or surfing. For hire & lessons; 01792 360 370 or www.surfgsd.com (they also do indoor lesso

Getting there Follow the M4 to Swansea, and exit at junction 42 and follow the A483, then A4118 to Penmaen. Park up by the view point (529/888).

Accommodation: Lots of choice; see www.the-gower.com or call Rhossili T.I. on 01792 390707. The Three Cliffs Bay holiday park in Penmaen is very nice. See www.threecliffsbay.com or tel: 01792 371218. Hillend campsite in Llangennith on 01792 386204.

Refreshments There are pubs in Llanmadoc, Llangennith, Rhossili, and Reynoldston. There are also some shops at Parkmill just down the A4188 road, near the start of the ride.

Bike shops Lots of choice in Swansea, including Cycle World on 01792 702555 and Wheelies on 01792 472612.

89 Swansea to Mumbles
Map at 90%
Gowerton
Swansea
Marina
Black Pill
Mumbles

Swansea to Mumbles

VARIOUS

'his is a lovely coastside cycle route, along the ovely sweeping beaches, on what was the old Mumbles railway line (the first passanger train in he world) from Swansea to Mumbles Head.

'he (red) off-road cycle trail from Black Pill, up the ovely dense wooded Clyne valley to Gowerton if you want a change of scenary.

NOTE: It is uphill from Black Pill to Gowerton.

TOP TIP: You can catch the train between Swansea & Gowerton, however it only takes 2 bikes at a time, so book ahead make sure you book ahead, tel; 0870 9000 773.

Family activities

CLYNE GARDENS

Situated by Black Pill, this is a very pretty garden, open all year and free. Tel: 01792 401737.

LEISURE CENTRE

With water slides, rides, pools and a climbing wall. On the A4067 rd, tel; 01792 484730.

PLANTASIA

A tropical hothouse in the centre of Swansea, with over 5,000 unusual exotic plantsfree-flying butterflies, a cologny of endangered Tarmarind monkeys, a collection of reptiles, fish, insects and a Burmese python. Tel; 01792 474555.

SURFING

Ask at PJ's Surf shop on 01792 386669 / www.pjsurfshop.co.uk, or www.gowersurfing.com / 01792 360 370 for hire & lessons.

Swansea to Coast/Marin

2.8KM / 1.

Park in the car park (663/948) in Swansea, j the rounabout on the A4217, by the river, an head south out of the car park. Goes south between the road and the river, under the A4 then cross the river at the A4067. Continue s (some sections of quiet roads), through the m to the coast (659/923) and turn right (west).

Swansea Marina to Black Pi

4.6KM / 2.9M

This is a VERY easy to follow and family friendl section of the route, following the coastline, pa lel to the A4067. When you come to a fork in trail, bear L on the narrower track over the bric to continue to Mumbles, along the coast, or ke to cross the A4067 and join the Clyne valley tr

Black Pill to Mumbles

4.3KM / 2.7

This is an easy, family friendly section of the rou that simply follows the coastline to the peir at Mumbles Head (630/874).

Black Pill to Gowerton

7.4KM / 4.6

Use the Clyne valley country park, car park, oppsite Blackpill Lido, on Oystermouth road (toilets here too). Follow the cycle path from the car park/bicycle traffic lights, and head north into the Clyne valley, gently climbing (140 metres in all). There is the Railway Inn pub along the way, and lots of choice in Gowerton (592/962). Either retrace your steps back to Blackpill.

NOTE: The wooded hillsides of the Clyne Valley provides some good (dirt track) trails, suitable for mountainbiking.

Getting there see the different sections for more details. Train station in Swansea.

Accommodation: Lots of places. Best to call Swansea T.I. on 01792 468321 or Mumbles on 01792 361302. Also, the Clyne Farm centre offers a range of places (and activities), tel: 01792 403 333 or see www.clynefarm.com for more info.

Bike shops Action Bikes in St David's Sq Swansea, over the A4067 from the Marina on 01792 464 640 (also do bike hire). Tredz is good, but further north, in Swansea, see www.tredz.co.uk.

Refreshments: Lots in Swansea & Mumbles, Junction cafe at Black Pill. Dunvant & Gowerton also have a choice.

90 Talybont-on-Usk

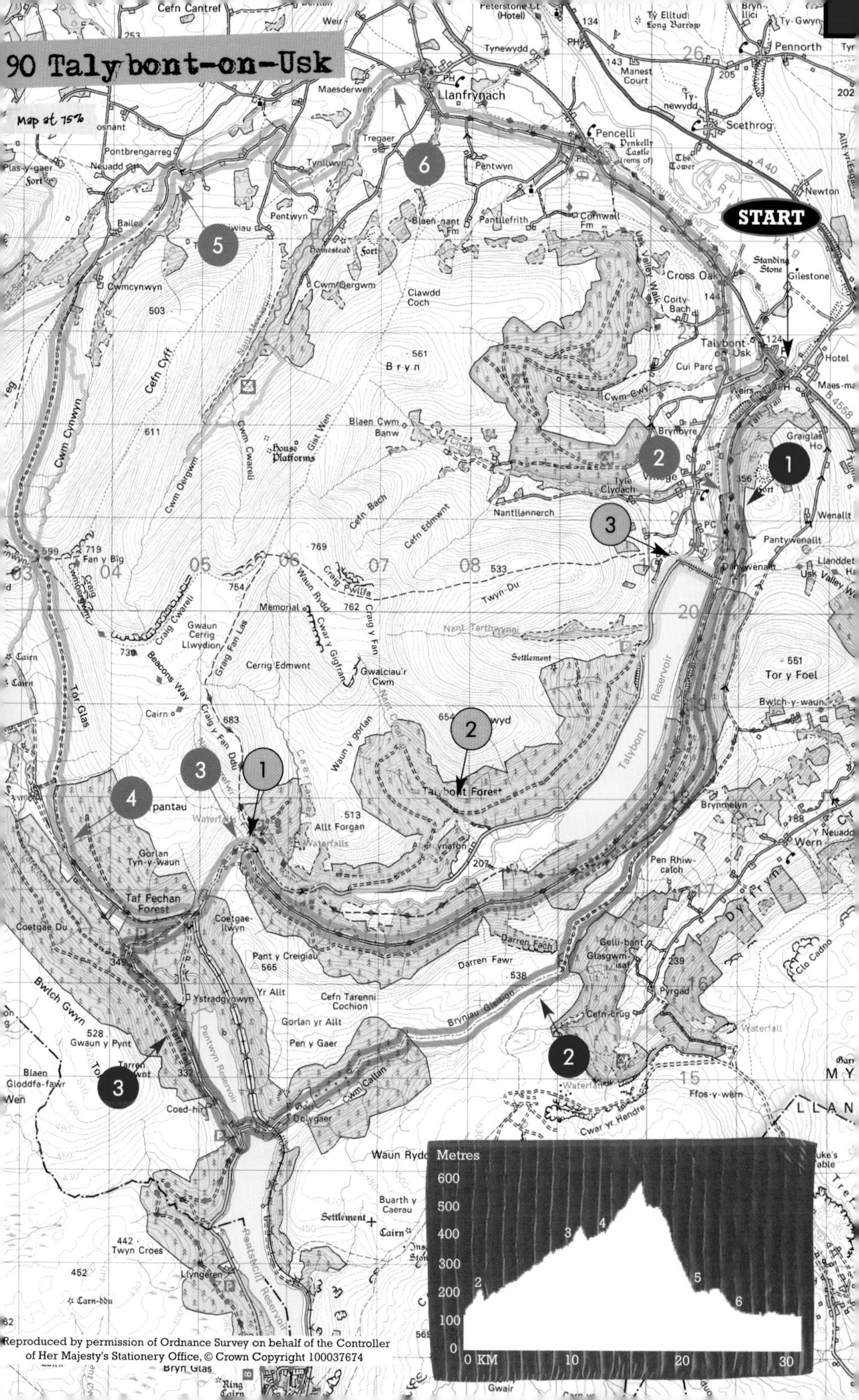

Talybont-on-Usk

31.2KM (19.4M) & 770 METRES OF CLIMBING

START From the White Hart pub (SO 115/225) join the 'Taff Trail' over the steep concrete ramp, over the water, bearing R at the fork, over the old railway line, UH on the Brinmore Tramroad heading southwest and keep SA at a gate.

2 At a X-track turn R on the Taff Trail or see the extension. DH, keeping SA, following the Taff Trail along the old railway line, for a long UH, eventually to and through a gate, to a rd (055/174) and turn L or see the shortcut.

3 Go UH then DH for 0.9km and bear R on a BW (048/167) and keep R at the fork (not L on the cycle track). **3A** Keep L at fork along here, to end of a rd and keep R, then R again at a fork on a track (No Vehicles Except 1-31 March, 1-15 Sept).

4 After dropping down and up a deep ravine (ignore L turn at top), keep SA for a BIG UH climb to 'The Gap' and keep SA for a superb long rocky descent. At the tarmac, 1 gate on L & 3 on R, go through the middle (wooden) R one, for more rocky DH to a T-J by a bridge (046/247).

5 Turn R on the rd for 1.5km to a T-J and turn R, keeping L at a fork after 0.5km, for 0.3km then turn L on a BW (upgraded from FP) (059/245). Go down the LHS of field to a stream and rejoin/follow the BW signposts, with the river on your RHS.

6 At the rd (071/257) turn R and R again in Llanfrynach, then R again, following the Taff Cycle Trail to Pencelli, and continue along the B4558, back to Talybont-on-Usk (115/225).

Shorter ride

22.5KM (14M) & 730 METRES CLIMBING

1 Turn R on the road, steeply DH, and look for a forest rd on the L after crossing the river (066/170). Through a gate, steep UH, keeping SA then bearing L, still climbing UH. Levels out then descends, into the valley, then back UH.

2 After a level section with views of the reservoir, bear R at a forest track junction, DH, through a gate, then another gate to the rd (099/196). Turn L on this, to the reservoir dam wall, and go R to this.

3 Cross the dam and take the 2nd L, UH, back up Brimore Tramroad, to a junction and go L, following your earlier tracks, back to the start (115/225).

Extension

+3.3KM (2.1M) & 140 METRES CLIMBING

1 Go SA/L on the (Pen Rhiw-Calch) BW, UH along the Bry Ore Tramroad, up steep section to a track and turn R (101/176 SP Dolygaer. 1.5km to a gate at Pen Bwlch Glascwm, through narrow gorge, steep UH to a fork at the top and bear R.

2 Follow this rough track across the moors, then through a gate, DH through a a wood, keeping SA to a rd at the bottom, past an outdoor centre. Keep SA on the tarmac, over the dam, then R on the rd (SP Talybont-on-Usk) (054/142).

3 Keep SA/L at the for in the rd, then over a bridge and immediately turn R on the cycle path, UH for 0.75km then turn L on the DT (048/167), and rejoin the main route at **3A**.

TOP TIP: If you've come all this way but the weather is bad, ride the extension and return to Talybont on the main route (Taff Trail) for a 26km & 730 metres climbing) 'medium' grade route.

Getting there The ride starts from Talybont-on-Usk, which is just off the A40, between Brecon and Abergavenny. You will need to find street side parking (GR115/225 is a good spot) or if you are staying/eating/drinking at one of the pubs, ask the landlord. There is no railway near by, but there is a bus service (allowing bicycles on) from Cardiff and surrounding areas.

Accommodation: B&B & Bunkhouse at the White Hart 01874 676227, Travellers rest 01874 676233, Bunkhouse at Upper Cantref on 01874 665223, Brecon YHA on 0870 7705718.

Refreshments Nothing on the route, but the Travellers rest in Talybont is good.

Bike shops Brecon Cycles in Brecon on 01874 622651

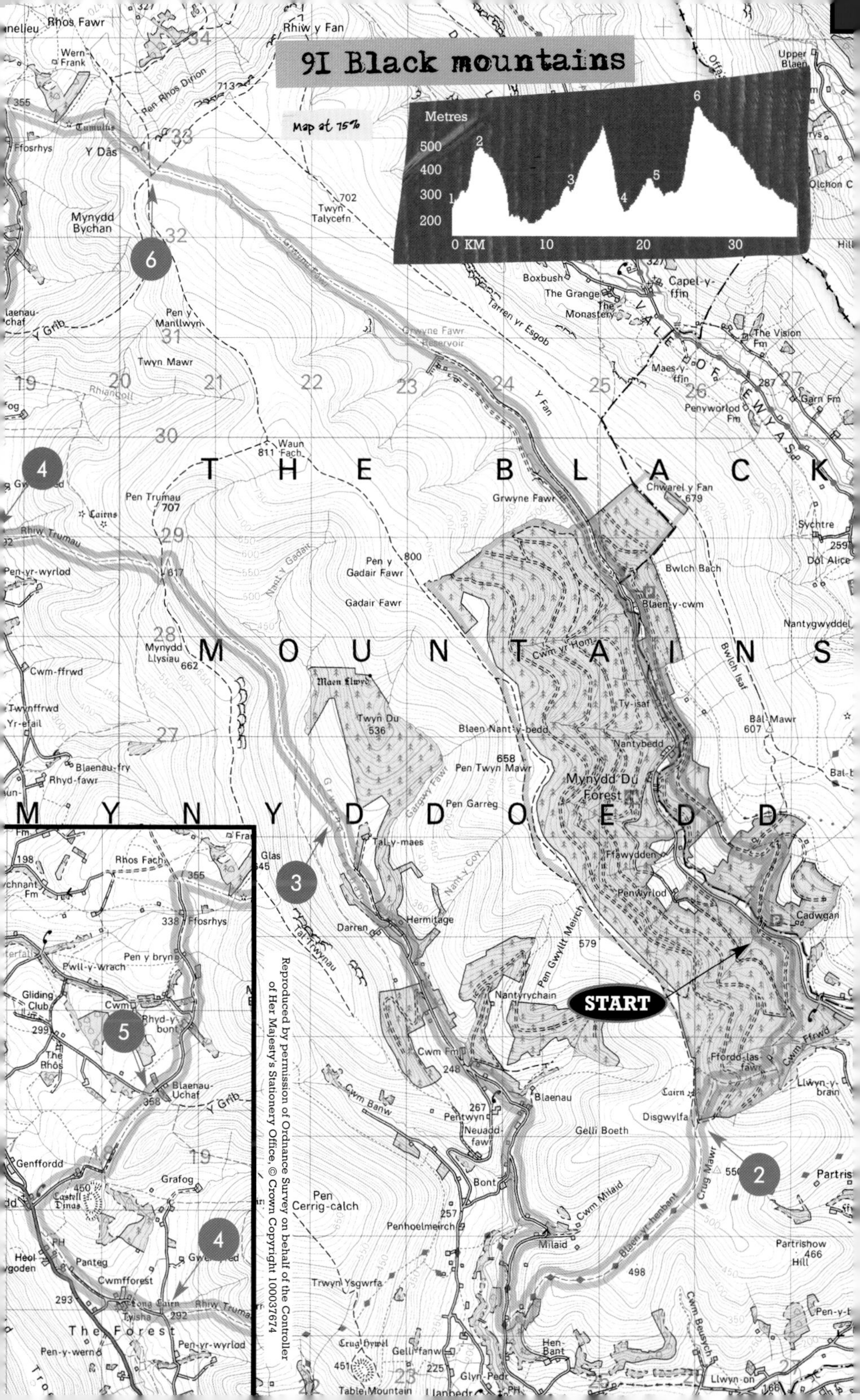

91 Black mountains
Map at 75%
Metres
500
400
300
200
0 KM
10
20
30
1
2
3
4
5
6
THE BLACK MOUNTAINS
MYNYDD DU
START
Rhos Fawr
Rhiw y Fan
Wern-Frank
Pen Rhos Dirion
713
Tumulus
Ffosrhys
Y Dâs
Mynydd Bychan
Twyn Talycefn
702
Upper Blaen
Olchon C
Boxbush
The Grange
The Monastery
Capel-y-ffin
VALE OF EWYAS
Tarren yr Esgob
Grwyne Fawr Reservoir
The Vision Fm
Maes-y-ffin
Penyworlod Fm
Garn Fm
287
Pen y Manllwyn
Y Grib
Twyn Mawr
Rhiangoll
Y Fan
Waun Fach
811
Pen Trumau
707
Cairns
Rhiw Trumau
Pen-yr-wyrlod
617
Grwyne Fawr
Chwarel y Fan
679
Sychtre
Dôl Alice
259
Bwlch Bach
Pen y Gadair Fawr
800
Gadair Fawr
Nant y Gadair
Blaen-y-cwm
Nantygwyddel
Mynydd Llysiau
662
Cwm-ffrwd
Cwm yr Hom
Bwlch Isaf
Maen Llwyd
Twyn Du
536
Ty-isaf
Twynffrwd
Yr-efail
Blaen Nant-y-bedd
Bâl Mawr
607
Nantybedd
658
Pen Twyn Mawr
Blaenau-fry
Rhyd-fawr
Mynydd Du Forest
Pen Garreg
Grwyne Fawr
Tal-y-maes
Ffawydden
Rhos Fach
Glas
645
Penwyrlod
Cadwgan
355
Ffosrhys
338
Darren
Hermitage
Tal Trwynau
Nant y Coy
Pen Gwyllt Meirch
579
Pen y bryn
Pwll-y-wrach
Gliding Club
Cwm
Rhyd-y-bont
299
The Rhos
Nantyrychain
Cwm Fm
248
Ffordd-las-fawr
Cwm Ffrwd
Llwyn-y-brain
Blaenau-Uchaf
358
Y Grib
Cwm Banw
Blaenau
267
Pentwyn
Neuadd-fawr
Cairn
Disgwylfa
Gelli Boeth
Genffordd
Grafog
Castell Dinas
450
Bont
Pen Cerrig-calch
Crug Mawr
550
Partrishow Hill
466
Cwm Milaid
Blaen-yr-henbant
257
Penhoelmeirch
Milaid
498
Heol Caradoc
Panteg
Cwmfforest
Gwernyfed
Trwyn Ysgwrfa
Long Cairn
293
292
Tyisha
Rhiw Trumau
The Forest
Pen-y-wern
Pen-yr-wyrlod
Cwm Beusych
Crug Hywel
451
Gelli-fanw
225
Table Mountain
Glyn-Pedr
Llanbedr
Hen-Bant
Llwyn-on
Pen-y-
Reproduced by permission of Ordnance Survey on behalf of the Controller of Her Majesty's Stationery Office, © Crown Copyright 100037674

Black Mountains

36.5KM (22.7M) & 1,550 METRES CLIMBING

START Go back to and over the rd (south), and follow the FP, bearing L, UH, to a X-tracks 269/243) and turn L on the BW. Keep R at both he BW forks at Ffordds-las-fawr, involving some valking, then leave the forest onto the ridgetop single track past the tombstones (260/231).

2 UH to a junction and head south west, DH to 2 gates and go through the R one, DH, zig-zag o a rd (240/211). Go R on the rd, up the valley, keep to the R, to the end of the rd, up gravel track, along field edge, DH to a bridge 221/262).

3 Cross bridge, long UH, to a junction by the cairn at the top after the zig-zags, and head north-west, DH, bearing L at the fork after 0.1km. Steep, rocky DH (Rhiw Trumau) through a gate, to the rd (186/289).

4 Turn R then immediately L, DH to a sharp LH bend and bear R on the track, parallel to the main rd. Turn R at the junction (172/300), up a rocky track, through a gate, alongside a fence o a minor rd (185/311).

5 Follow this rd for 2.5km (1.5m) to a common and turn R on the DT (187/333) for the VERY steep walk up Y Das, keeping on the BW to th top and junction of tracks (203/326).

6 Keep SA (fence on L), for a long DH, splash through a stream, down past the reservoir and gate, joining a DT to a rd (251/286). Go L on this (effectively SA), for 4.5km (2.8m) back to the car park (267/251) or see the extension.

Extension

+0.3KM (0.2M) & 50 METRES CLIMBING

1 Shortly past the car park (and building), turn L on a BW (253/283), parallel with the rd, then climbing up the side of the valley. Follow this BW along the forest track, eventually dropping down to the car park at the end (267/251).

NOTE: There is a bit of a 'debate' about whic direction to ride this route – you can ride it reverse to provide a very technical descent o Y Das, but you will lose two good long descents

TOP TIP: If starting from an alternative start point you may like to miss out the push up Ffordd-las-fawr (especially if it isn't at the start anymore) so follow the forest tracks through Mynydd Du forest, but be aware it is pretty easy to follow the wrong track.

Getting there North of Abgervenny on the A465, exit this at Llanvihangel Crucorney, left (west) to Stanton, then go left here towards Llanbedr, but turn right (north) at the 5-way junction, up the Grwyner Fawr valley, to Mynydd Du Forest. The car park is on the right after entering the forest (SO 267/252). By train: Abergavenny 8km away.

Accommodation Crickhowell makes a nice base and has a few good places to stay, inc. Bear hotel on 01873 810408, White Hart Inn on 810474, Britannia Inn with bunkhouse on 810553 or Perth-y-Pia farm bunkhouse just 2 miles north on 810164. The Bridge cafe in Brecon is bike friendly 01874 622024 or www.bridgecafe.co.uk and the Castle Inn bunkhouse in Pengenffordd, on the A479 (and route) is good, tel: 01873 711353.

Bike shop Brecon Cycles, in Brecon, on 01874 622651 or Halfords in Abergevenny on 01873 853128.

Refreshments Talgarth has a pub, and so does Llanbedr about half way around, just off the route.

92 Kington
Map at 90%
Reproduced by permission of Ordnance Survey on behalf of the Controller of Her Majesty's Stationery Office, © Crown Copyright 100037674
START
Metres
400
300
200
100
0
0 KM
10
20

Kington

31KM (19.3M) & 950 METRES CLIMBING

START From Kington clocktower (SO 291/567) head west, UH, past the church & take the 2nd L tarmac rd UH to gate, onto the moor, staying on the ridge, UH for 1km to X-tracks where gradient eases, go SA on narrow track past small Monkey Puzzle trees on L. 0.3km past small dew pond on L, to X-tracks & BW fingerpost (254/564).

2 Turn L (south) on feint track, aiming between the 2 cairns, after 0.5km it descends and follow a feint track down the centre of a shallow depression, through clumps of gorse to a fingerpost 0.1km before a field gate, (258/554).

3 Turn R (west) on a narrow landrover trail, leaving gorse after 0.3km & head slighty UH, heading for a large (Ash) tree at the fence corner. Follow the trail down to the R, into & out of a steep little cwm. To the top of the short steep UH, take the R fork on field corner, edging UH into the moor & away from the field boundary. Follow the track as it traverses the sloping moor, to a BW fingerpost at the rutted track junction on the top of the ridge (241/555).

4 Follow the rutted rocky track DH (west) through a gate, off the moor, through another gate & DH to a tarmac lane. Bear R into Gladestry village, with the Royal Oak pub on L (232/551).

5 After 0.1km turn R then L past a church, then R at a fork & keep R to the end of the tarmac rd. At the farm follow the stone lane past a house, down to/through a ford, & a gate and follow this lane up to the new farm buildings & gates (216/573).

6 Leaving the fm on your L, bear L after 0.15km & follow the rd up through a gate, becoming stone track. Follow this level track with valley below & R, to a gate nr Blaen-y-cwm (head of the valley). Go through the gate, on shale track to the top of the hill, by a pond & track to sheep pens (198/580).

7 With pond to your L, follow the top of the field east for 0.3km to a small gate & go SA. Track improves, pass through a gate by a line of trees, to a derelict farmhouse. Keep on the track DH past some large Limes to a gate into a wood directly SA (208/593

8 Go through the wood gate & follow the grassy round to R, out of the wood & follow the line of th track down to the road gate. Bear L, to X-rds with old track dropping away on R (220/596).

9 Go R, DH on the old sunken rocky track, to a s white stone chapel at X-rds & turn sharp R, UH pas Wolfpits fm.Turn L directly after the fm, down to a gated grass lane through the bog holes to/through wooded ford. UH on rocky lane, to tarmac at Llan cottage. Follow the tarmac rd SA for 0.7km to a T- go R then bear L, 0.2km to a farmhouse (216/573

10 With the fm on R do down the rd past Trewern for 1km, to a widening in the rd & go R through a gate, to a dirt lane (225/571).

11 Go down the lane to/through a ford & UH on tough bedrock lane out of the dingle, to rd and ke SA, down to Gladestry village. At the T-J turn L, ba to the pub (232/551).

12 Leaving the pub on your R, take the 1st R, then L on tarmac rd, UH, through two gates, into the mo Follow the rutted track until it levels & ruts peter out BW fingerpost (241/555).

13 Looking up at the main body of the moor rising front of you, take the L track UH & keep on this, ov false summit, you will see a small dew pond after approx 0.8 km. Leave this on your L & keeping to th track, follow it to the top of the ridge & fingerpost a the footpath/bridleway X-tracks (254/564).

14 Keep SA (east) along the ridge, past the dewpo on your R after 0.2km & keep on the highpoint of t ridge. Starts to become a fast DH, following the wa markers, past a gate (town SA) & take 1st rough tra on R after 0.2km. Through a gate at the smallholdi & follow the gravel track down to cattlegrid & tarmc lane. Bear L & follow the rd to a T-J opposite a chu & turn R, back down into Kington (291/567).

TOP TIP: For more routes in the area see www.roughrides.co.uk

Getting there Kington is due west of Worcester, (65km) along the A44 from junction 7 of the M5. Park in the town.

Accommodation see see www.roughrides.co.uk for a list of accommodation as well as lots of other useful info, such as places to eat & drink (inc. real ale pubs).

Bike shop Slim Willys cycles in Leominster on 01568 614052 & the Petfood shop in Kington has some basic spares.

Refreshments Plenty in Kington & a pub in Gladestry.

93 Dolgellau to Barmouth

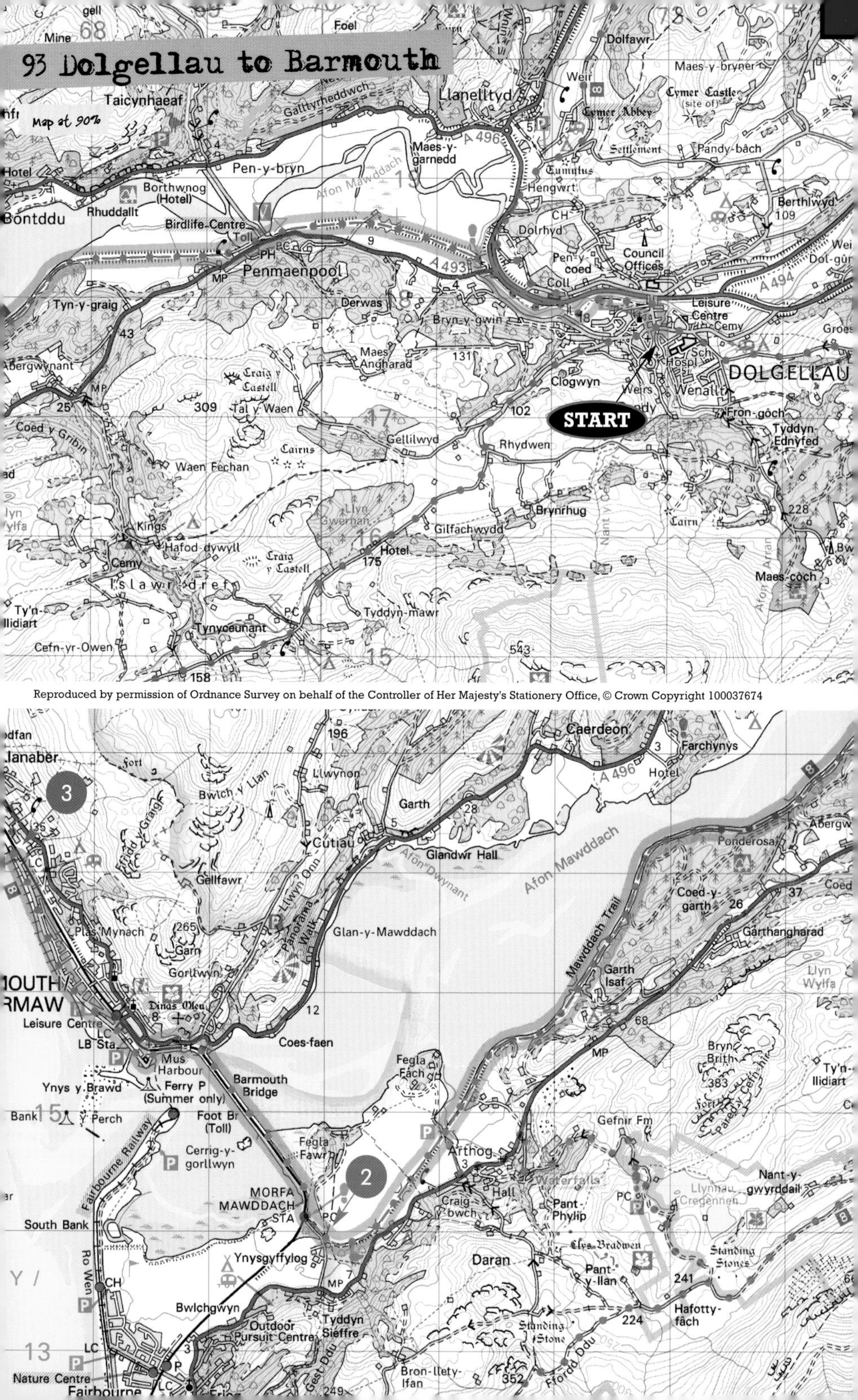

Dolgellau to Barmouth

34.5KM (21.4M) WITH GENTLE GRADIENTS

THE RIDE: This is a beautiful ride on the Mawddach Trail, along the Mawddach estuary, and over the beautiful Barmouth (toll) bridge, to the town of Barmouth on the coast. Once here, take a break (eat an ice cream), take in the views, then head back along the same trail, back to Dolgellau.

The tracks are well surfaced, with a gentle gradient and no technical features along the way, so makes an ideal ride for people of all abilities, especially families.

NOTE: Because this is a there and back route, you could easily reduce the length by turning back early.

START Head west on the Sustrans cyclepath No.8 (which actually takes you all the way to Barmouth), past Penmaenpool, along the inlet, and on to Marfa Mawddach train station (628/141).

2 Continue over the Barmouth Bridge,and bear left, into Barmouth and continue on the cycle track no.8, along the seafront (602/171).

3 Turn back around and retrace your wheel tracks, all the way back to Dolgellau (728/177).

NOTE: The excellent MTB trail centre of Coed-Y-Brenin is just up the road.

Family activities

BARMOUTH MARKET

Every Thursday throughout the year and most Sundays & Bank Holiday Mondays in the holidays.

THE BEACH

Excellent sandy beach, now awarded the prestigious blue flag

CRICCIETH CASTLE & VISITOR CENTRE

Perched on a rocky outcrop overloooking the sea, Established by LLewelyn the Great around 1230. Tel: 01766 522227

THE HARBOUR

Still used by a few commercial fishing boats, though now mostly pleasure craft. Popular with kids for crab lining. Some nice cafes overlooking the quay, also the Last Inn.

LIFEBOAT MUSEUM & SHOP

Now part of the new Lifeboat station. View the lifeboats and associated exhibits.

HARLECH CASTLE

One of Wales' most formidable and dominant castles. Panoramic views of sea and Snowdonia. On site exhibition. Tel: 01766 780552

LLANFAIR SLATE CAVERNS

Descend into the tunnels and caverns hacked out by candlelight over a century ago. A496 Llanfair, towards Harlech. Tel: 01766 780247.

Getting there Dolgellau is west of Telford, at the end of the M54. Head west on the A458, past Shrewsbury & Welshpool, then join the A470, north-west to Dolgellau. From the north, head south from Colwyn Bay on the A470, or south-west on the A494 from Mold, off the A55, near Chester.

Accommodation Graig Wen B&B, camping and holiday cottages, see www.graigwen.co.uk or tel; 01341 250482 nr Barmouth Bridge. Shell Island campsite (up the A496 rd), see www.shellisland.co.uk or call 01341 241453. The grand Penycoed Hall guest house, www.snowdoniaguesthouse.co.uk or call 01341 423403. Plas Isla for self catering groups (up to 24) tel; 01341 421949 or see www.plasisa.co.uk. Dolgellau T.I. on 01341 422888.

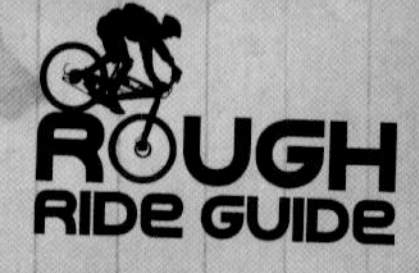

Bike shops Greenstiles in Dolgallau on 01341 423332 and Dragon Bikes & Kites (hire bikes out) on 01341 423008 & Redbikehire on 01654 700411.

Refreshments Plenty in Dolgellau & Barmouth, and a pub in Penmaenpool just outside Dolgellau.

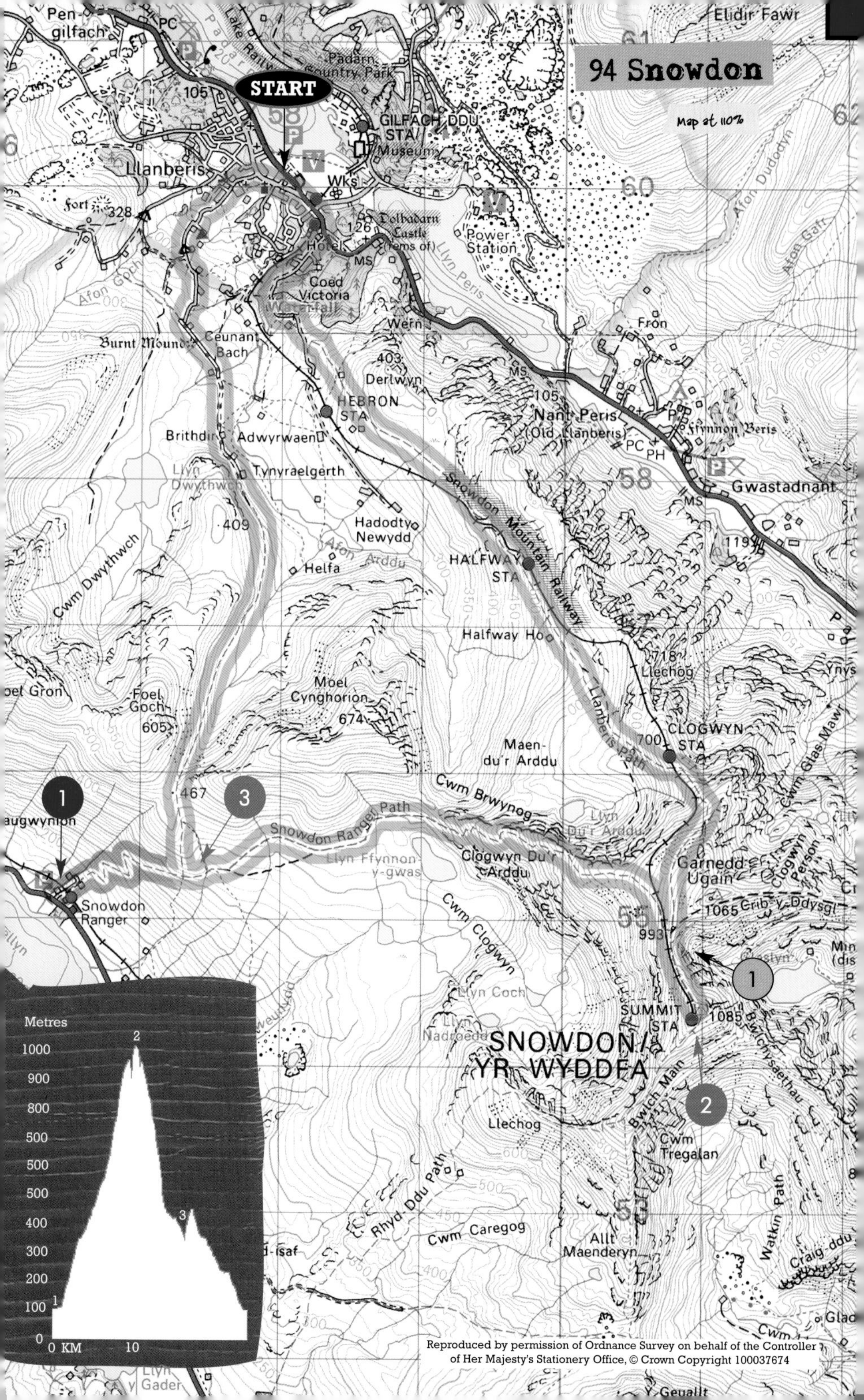
94 Snowdon
Map at 110%
START
Llanberis
Pen-gilfach
Padarn Country Park
GILFACH DDU STA/ Museum
Dolbadarn Castle (rems of)
Power Station
Llyn Peris
Hotel
Coed Victoria
Waterfall
Ceunant Bach
Burnt Mound
HEBRON STA
Derlwyn
Nant Peris (Old Llanberis)
Ffynnon Peris
Gwastadnant
Brithdir
Adwyrwaen
Tynyraelgerth
Llyn Dwythwch
Hadodty Newydd
Helfa
HALFWAY STA
Snowdon Mountain Railway
Halfway Ho
Cwm Dwythwch
Moel Cynghorion
Foel Goch
Llechog
CLOGWYN STA
Maen-du'r Arddu
Llanberis Path
Cwm Brwynog
Llyn Du'r Arddu
Snowdon Ranger Path
Llyn Ffynnon-y-gwas
Clogwyn Du'r Arddu
Garnedd Ugain
Crib y Ddysgl
Snowdon Ranger
Cwm Clogwyn
Llyn Coch
Llyn Nadroedd
SUMMIT STA
SNOWDON/ YR WYDDFA
Bwlch Main
Cwm Tregalan
Rhyd Ddu Path
Cwm Caregog
Allt Maenderyn
Watkin Path
Craig-ddu
Elidir Fawr
Afon Dudodyn
Afon Gafr
Fron
Metres
0 KM
10
Reproduced by permission of Ordnance Survey on behalf of the Controller of Her Majesty's Stationery Office, © Crown Copyright 100037674

Snowdon

18.3KM (12M) & 1,220 METRES OF CLIMBING

START Head through Llanberis, past the railway station and turn right on Victoria Terrace, over a cattle grid, and steeply uphill. Shortly after the cafe, bear left through a gate (signposted 'Snowdon') and the start of the off-road section. Some technical climbing brings you to the halfway house, which can provide a sheltered stop. Keep on up, under a bridge, and on to a Finger Stone marker for the last push to the summit (609/543).

2 Turn around and descend back to the X-tracks/finger post (607/549) and turn L (west) on the Rangers Path (or retrace your steps for the easier descent, down the Llanberis path). Cross the railway and look out for the obvious track further ahead. The trail gets more technical as you go.

3 After the trail levels out, then starts to descend again, keep a good look out for the small (and easy to miss) BW signpost on the right (going north) (573/553), up a grassy bank. There is a better track at the top, which you follow (north), downhill, all the way back, (watching out for the drainage channels), past the YHA, back into Llanberis.

TOP TIP: Take a pump & some spare inner tubes.

(slightly) Easier option

-3.7KM (2.3M) & 120 METRES CLIMBING

1 Head back down the way you came up i.e. the Llanberis path, for a slightly easier & less technical descent (and you'll know what you are in for).

Extension

+2.8KM (1.7M) & 210 METRES CLIMBING

1 Start from the car park at the base of the R path (SH 563/551), by the YHA on the A4085 climb the obvious (Rangers path) zig-zagging join the main route & use the same track to fir

IMPORTANT NOTES

There is a voluntary restriction on cycling the b ways on Snowdon between 10am to 5pm from May to 30th September. Please respect this or could risk a complete ban for all cyclists altoge

It takes roughly 2.5 hrs up to the top, and 1.5h down the rangers path, or just 0.5hrs back dov the Llanberis path.

Getting there This ride starts from the car park by the lake in Llanberis, at the foot of Snowdon. It's pretty easy to find (it's the big lump on the horizon) as once you get to Caernarfon, which in on the A487, just follow the A4086 to Llanberis. The nearest main line railway is at Caernarfon, about 7 miles away.

Accommodation: Pete's Eats in Llanberis on 01286 870117 or www.petes-eats.co.uk should satisfy all your needs (including food).

Refreshments Cafe at the bottom of the Llanberis path, and a cafe at the summit of Snowdon, but check before to see if it is open. There is lots of choice in Llanberis, where Pete's Eats is highly recommended.

ROUGH RIDE GUIDE

Bike shops Beics Beddgelert on 01766 890434 and Beics Betws in Betws-Y-coed on 01690 710766

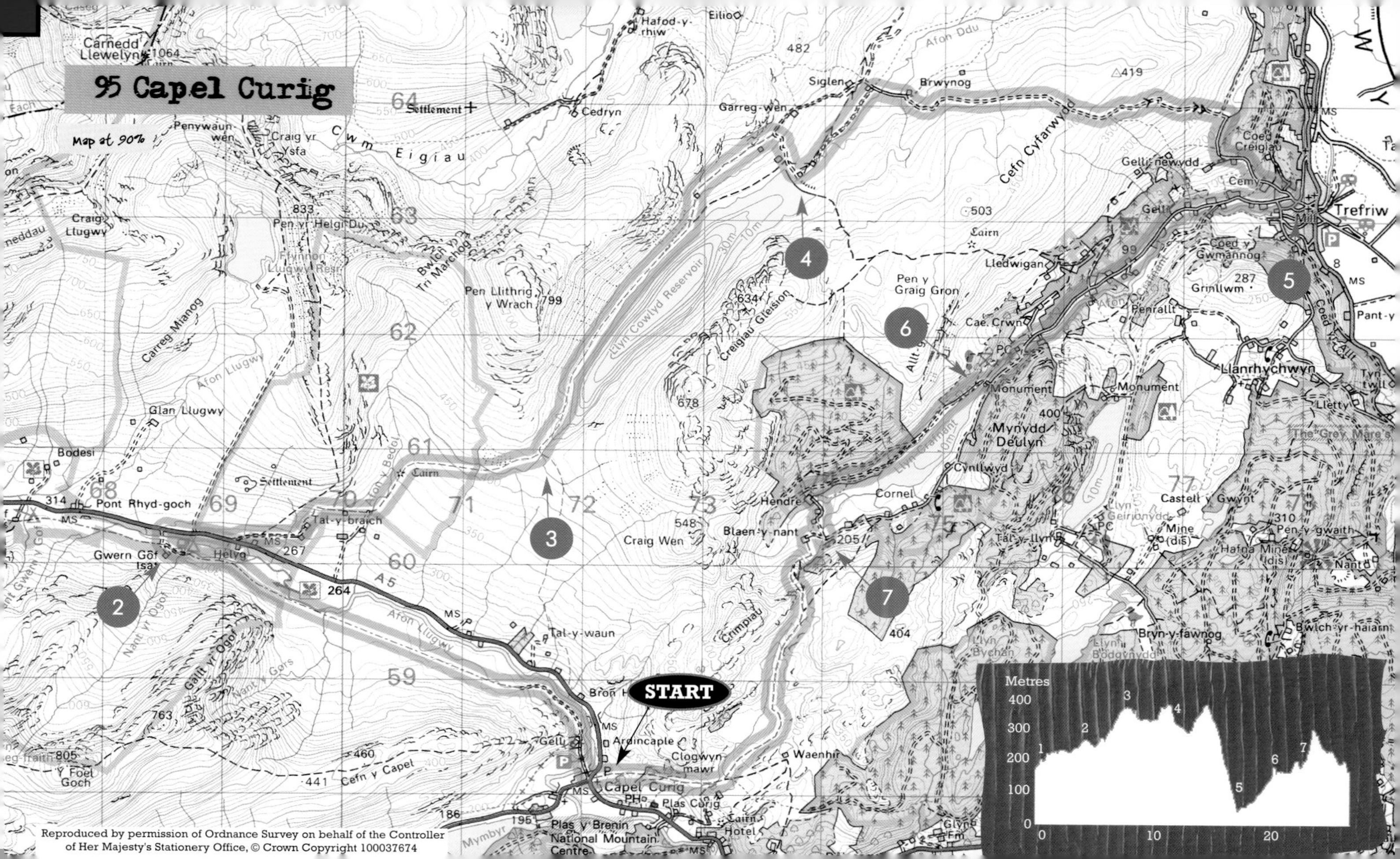

95 Capel Curig
Map at 90%
START
Carnedd Llewelyn 1064
Penywaun-wen
Craig yr Ysfa
Cwm Eigiau
Settlement
Cedryn
Hafod-y-rhiw
Eilio
482
Siglen
Garreg-wen
Brwynog
Afon Ddu
419
Cefn Cyfarwydd
Gelli-newydd
Coed Creiglau
Trefriw
Craig Llugwy
833
Pen yr Helgi Du
Ffynnon Llugwy Resr
Bwlch y Tri Marchog
Pen Llithrig y Wrach 799
Llyn Cowlyd Reservoir
Creigiau Gleision
634
503
Cairn
Lledwigan
Coed y Gwmannog
287
Grinllwm
Pen y Graig Gron
Cae Crwn
Allt-g
Penrallt
Llanrhychwyn
Pant-y
Carreg Mianog
Afon Llugwy
Glan Llugwy
Bodesi
Settlement
Afon y Bedol
Cairn
678
Monument
Mynydd Deulyn
400
Monument
Llyn Geirionydd
Lletty
The Grey Mare's
Cynllwyd
Cornel
Hendre
548
Craig Wen
Blaen-y-nant
205
Castell y Gwynt
310
Pen-y-gwaith
Mine (dis)
Hafna Mine (dis)
Nant
Tal-y-llyn
314
Pont Rhyd-goch
Tal-y-braich
Gwern Gôf Isaf
Helyg
267
264
A5
Nant yr Ogof
Gallt yr Ogof
Nant y Gors
763
Tal-y-waun
Bron Heulog
Ardincaple
Clogwyn-mawr
Crimpiau
404
Waenhir
Llyn Bychan
Llyn Bodgynydd
Bryn-y-fawnog
Bwlch-yr-haiarn
805
Y Foel Goch
441
Cefn y Capel
460
Gelli
Capel Curig
Plas Curig
Cairn
Hotel
186
195
Plas y Brenin
National Mountain Centre
Mymbyr
Glyn
Fm
Metres
400
300
200
100
0
0
10
20
1
2
3
4
5
6
7

Capel Curig

26.8KM (16.7M) & 930 METRES OF CLIMBING

ART In Capel Curig, carry on along (north) the ad that lead you to the car park, and follow this e old Ogwen road) BW track, alongside the river d A5 on the far side. After 4.4km (2.7m) you ass through Gwern Gof Isaf campsite, and come a X-rds (684/601) where you go R to the A5 rd.

Turn R on this rd for 0.6km then bear L on a ack (possibly still signposted as a FP but it is a W), (691/602). Follow the signs past the house at e end where the path has been diverted and con- ue UH along the worn trail, to Llyn Cowlyd reser- ir at the top (716/609).

Keep L, down to the waters side and follow this vely trail along the LHS of the reservoir. The BW ars L, UH, away from the waterside, past some umbled down buildings, to a DT (735/637). ep R to drop down a zig-zag DT to the dam, here you keep SA/L to go over the dam wall.

When you are half way across the dam wall, n L (737/634) on a good track, following along e RHS of the Afon Ddu. Follow this to a rd (743/ 1) and turn R on this, UH, then steep, fast bendy H (watch out for gates & cars on the way down).

Ignore a rd on the L as you approach a wood, lowing the rd as it bears hard R for more steep H riding on the road, to a junction (778/632). n R here, steep UH on the rd for 3.2km to Llyn afnant (753/616).

6 Turn R at the start of the lake, through a gate, then L along the RHS of the lake, keeping L at any junctions along the way, to keep close to the wate edge. After 0.5km (0.3m) past the end of the lake turn L on a track (738/606), to a T-J (& small park ing area) (739/602) and turn R.

7 Follow the BW around the back of a house anc up a big tough climb (eventually) to the top. Take in the views (get your breath back) and keep R, over a footbridge and stream, and follow this fun technical ST (BW) down into Capel Curig, for a great finish to a great ride. Go SA/R at the rd island back to the car park (720/583).

Family activities

The Old Ogwen road between Capel Curig & Gwern Gof Isaf is a good traffic free route, which although a bit rough and muddy in places, shoulc make a nice, easy going family cycle ride.

Capel Curig is a great base for some lovely walks whether they are mountain walks, such as on Moe Siabod and the Glyder range, or low level strolls along the lakes and rivers. There is also good white water rafting on the Afon Llugwy - ask at the local outdoor shops.

Capel Curig is also home to the National Mountain Activity Centre (Plas y Brenin) which has climbing walls, dry-ski slope, and a whole range mountain and water activity courses. For more information see www.pyb.co.uk.

For more MTB'ing, the Gwydyr (nr Betws-Y-Coed) and Penmachno trail centres are very close by. Fo more info on these see the Welsh road trip in this book or our 'Man-Made trails' supplement pack.

Getting there: Park behind the shops in Capel Curig (720/580), which is just along the A5 from Betws-Y-Coed (so head for here), where the A470 and A5 roads cross one another, and follow the A5 west. Parking also available at Gwern Gof Isaf by the campsite. There is a train station in Llanrwst, just a couple of miles off the route.

Accommodation: YHA in Capel Curig on 0845 371 9110, a campsite & bunkhouses at Gwern Gof Isaf. see www.gwerngofisaf.co.uk or tel: 01690 720276. For more choices see www.betws-y-coed.co.uk or www.snowdonia-active.com. T.I. office on 01690 710426

Bike shops Beics Betws in Betws-Y-coed on tel: 01690 710766 who do bike hire, parts, repairs, etc.

Refreshments There are shops, pub, etc in Capel Curig.

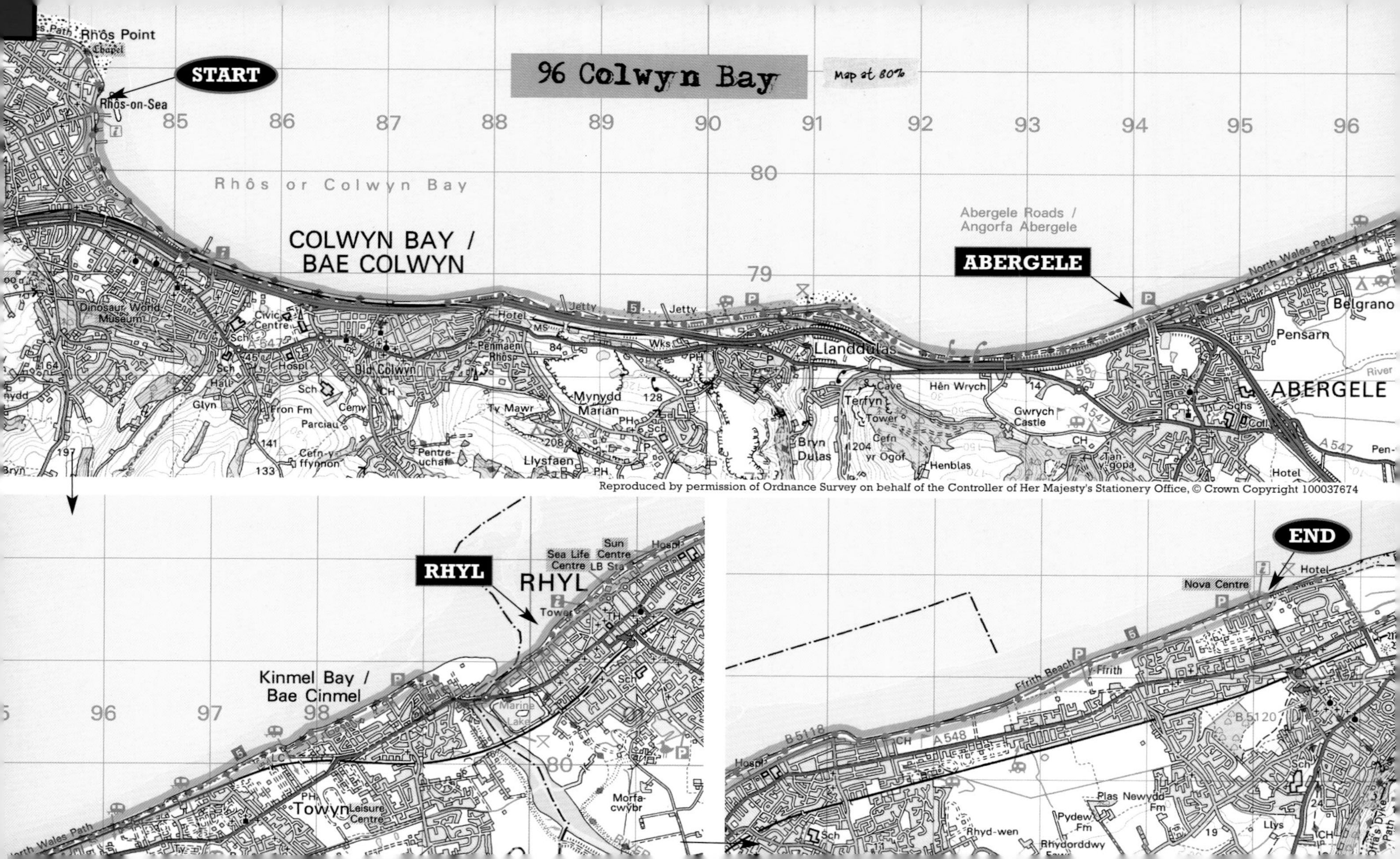
96 Colwyn Bay
Map at 80%
START
Rhôs Point
Rhôs-on-Sea
Rhôs or Colwyn Bay
COLWYN BAY /
BAE COLWYN
Abergele Roads /
Angorfa Abergele
ABERGELE
Llanddulas
ABERGELE
Pensarn
Belgrano
North Wales Path
RHYL
RHYL
Sea Life Centre
Sun Centre
Kinmel Bay /
Bae Cinmel
Towyn
END
Nova Centre
Ffrith Beach
Offa's Dyke Path

Colwyn Bay

VARIOUS DISTANCES

his is a lovely coastal ride that can be started or stopped at any number of places, to provide a ride of variable length, depending on your needs.

he whole ride, from Rhos-on-Sea to Prestatyn, one-way, is 24.5km (15.2m). You can either cycle back or catch the train, or shorten the ride by catching a train back from either Abergele, 11.5km along the route, or Rhyl, a further 7km on from Abergele (19km from start). Colwyn Bay train station is on the route, just 2km from Rhos Point.

t is very easy to follow, simply keep the close to the coastline on one side, and follow the Sustrans no.5 cyclepath signposts.

NOTE: The wind is usually blowing west to east, so if catching the train back for the return leg we suggest you start from Colwyn to make use of the wind. If you plan to cycle in both directions, we suggest riding into the wind to start, and have it aid you on your return journey.

lmost all of this route is free of traffic along flat, tarmac or stone tracks, with the sand & sea to one side and the wooded hills on the other, making it a great family ride.

Care should be taken when crossing the Blue bridge as you enter Rhyl, or use the footpath.

Family activities

RHYL

Rhyl provides a good ice cream break point, with an outside events area, as well as a Sea Life centre (includes sharks & walkthrough underwater tunnel), tel 01745 344660 or www.seaquarium.co.uk/rhyl. Rhyl Sun Centre is a water park with rides, slides and pools for all the family. Tel; 01745 344433 or see www.rhylsuncentre.co.uk.

COLWYN BAY

Welsh Mountain Zoo is a great day out for all the family, tel: 01492 532 938 or see the website: www.welshmountainzoo.org. Ther are also lots of other seaside attractions and places to eat and drink, as you'd expect in a seaside town.

picture by max

Getting there: On the north coast of Wales, off/parallel to the A55 road. There is some parking along the promenade at Rhos-on-Sea and in Prestatyn. Train stations in colwyn bay (2km from Rhos-on-Sea) and in Prestatyn.

Accommodation: There are lots of places offering accommodation, so best to call Rhos-on-Sea T.I. on 01492 548778, Colwyn Bay T.I. 01492 530478 on and Prestayn T.I. on 01745 889092 or see www.iknow-wales.co.uk.

Bike Shops: West end cycles in Colwyn Bay (do bike hire) on 01492 530269 or see www.westendcycles.com.

Refreshments: Lots of places all along the route.

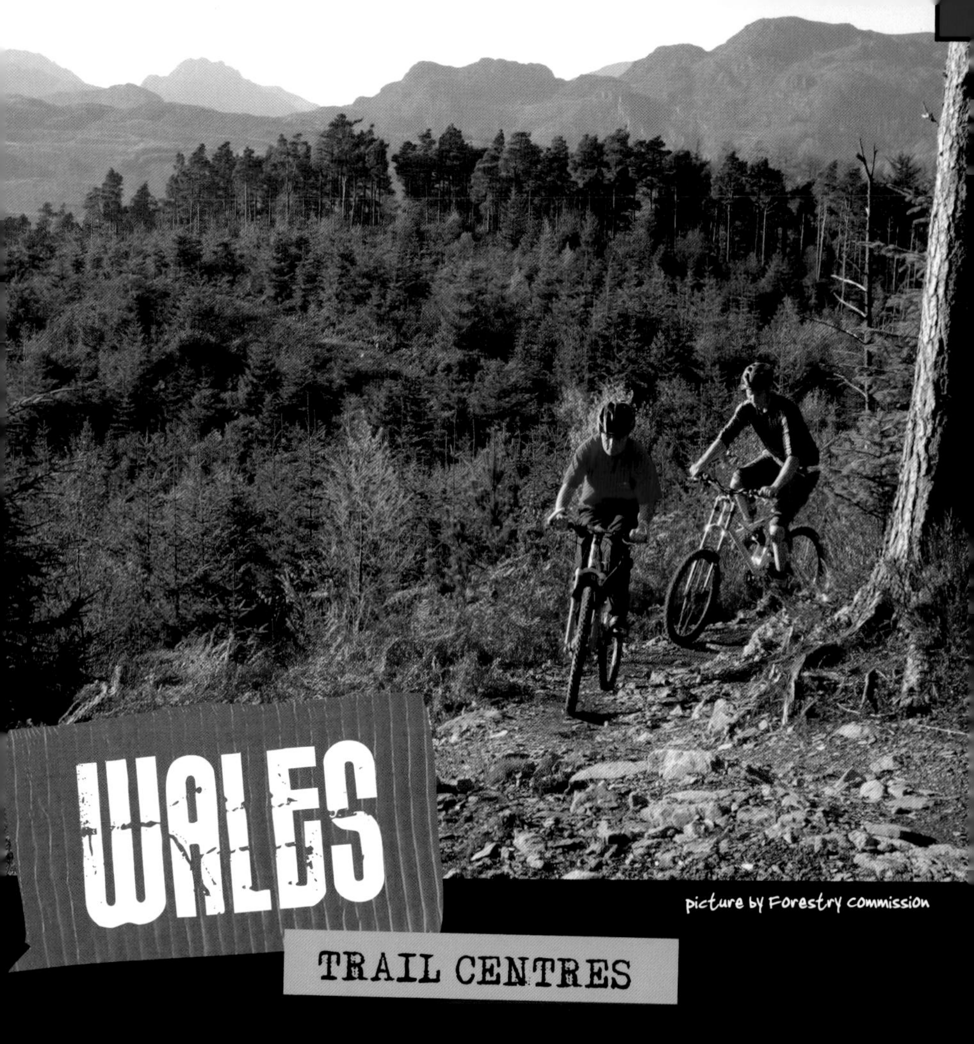

picture by Forestry Commission

WALES

TRAIL CENTRES

The Forestry Commission started developing mtb trails in Coed Y Brenin & now has a whole number of superb trail centres throughout the country. With terrain so suitable for mtb'ing its no wonder it has been voted as one of the top places in the world to ride. For more information see www.forestry.gov.uk/mtbwales & also www.mbwales.com

picture by Forestry commiss

picture by Forestry commission

pic by Forestry commission

coed-Y-Brenin

picture by Forestry commission

NO.97 CWMCARN

Well known for its superb downhills (with uplift service), but there is also a very nice red XC trail which is almost all singletrack, with a technical 'Freeride' option. Being very accessible and great in all weather conditions, make this a very popular destination for experienced riders.

TOP TIP: Book your uplift tickets (for the downhill) on-line well in advance as it is very popular. See www.cwmdown.co.uk for details.

Twrch 14 KM

Almost all singletrack, the start involves a big climb alongside the stream, on a challenging singletrack, to the top, where there is an optional freeride section (see below). Continue along the Twrch trail for a natural feeling trail, breaking out of the darkness of the woods, to exposed steep sided valleys with big drops (which is why some call this place little Switzerland). The trails drain very well, so you'll have good traction and confidence to blast down the final descents berms & jumps.

Freeride 1 KM

An optional extra on the red route, this is for advanced riders only. Expect ladder drops, a cork screw, tabletop jumps and a wall.

Y Mynydd Downhill 1.9 & 1.7 KM

There are 2 downhill runs; a 1.9km red & a 1.7km black. Both have roots, drops, switchbacks, big berms & jumps, but there is often a choice of lines and most of the jumps are rollable. There is also a bridge & a tunnel, plus a huge quarry jump before the bottom section which is totally flat out fast fun.

The red should be ok for competent XC riders, while the black run has more challenging & steeper sections for experienced / downhill riders.

NOTE: Pre-book uplifts at www.cwmdown.co.uk.

picture by Andrew Lloyd

A superb downhill venue, with lots of berms, switchbacks, jumps, a tunnel, rock steps, bridge & a flat out section at the bottom.

Getting there: Exit the M4 at junction 28 and go north on A467, following signs for Cwmcarn Forest drive keeping straight ahead. At 5th roundabout go right then right at another roundabout and its 2nd right from here. GR ST230/936 / Sat Nav: NP11 7FA

Opening times & cost: Free except the uplift.

Facilities: Bike wash, cafe, camping, toilet and an all year round uplift – see www.cwmdown.co.uk

Bike Shop: PS Cycles in Abercarn on 01495 246555 / www.pscycles.co.uk.

Map: www.mbwales.com

Tourist info: Newport TI 01633 842962

Website: www.mbwales.com

NO.98

AFAN ARGOED

An easily accessible and very popular trail centre with over 100km's of superb, technical, all weather trails. With great facilities & accommodation it makes a top weekend destination.

The trails are between 2 sites: Afan Forest & Glyncorrwg aka 'The Drop Off'. The Penyhdd & Wall trails start at Afan car park and White's Level & Skyline start at Glyncorrwg. Both sites are best suited to experienced riders, although there is the easy 'Rheilffordd' trail along an old disused railway, which also links the 2 centres.

NOTE: The 'W2' trail combines the 'Wall' & 'White's Level' trails, to make a 44km, Black grade trail.

There are also some other less technical trails in the area, such as the 39km (one-way) celtic high level scenic trail from Neath to Pontprydd and a 11km family route. For more information see www.cycling.visitwales.com & www.mbwales.com.

Penyhdd 17 KM

This was the first of the trails in Afan, but additional work has meant it has kept right up-to-date, with lots of tight, twisty, single track and sections such as the Hidden Valley, Side Winder and Dead Sheep Gulley. It's a great introductory route to the area as the riding isn't too technical, but still offers some challenging sections. Be aware that you will be exposed to bad weather on the higher trails.

The Wall 23 KM

Don't be fooled by the gentle flat spin along the cycle track to start, this route soon starts climbing, but is interspersed with some single track descents. Then comes a long section of singletrack from Nant y Bar farm, leading to some great views, then a rock infested roller coaster section named 'The Graveyard', before the fast and furious final section which gives the trail its name 'the Wall' , bringing you back to the start.

Whites Level 15 KM

A long (2.5km and 200m) single track climb greets you at the start, and impressive views of a wind farm great you at the top. Here you can opt to take a black DH run (go back up the fire-road to re-join the route again after). The trail is nearly all downhill (in a gravity way) from here, using flowing single track, small rock jumps, natural berms and a flowing boardwalk section, finishing with a fast, fun single track descent, back to the café.

Skyline 48 KM

Venturing higher & deeper into the wilderness, this trail is recommended for experienced riders only. However, there are a couple of optional shortcuts named; 'July' & 'August'. The 'August' option misses out a lot of fire road without losing very much single track, so is quite a good (and a popular option). All 3 options still finish with the superb 6km 'Jetlag' descent which has lots of rock jumps along the way, leaving you smiling no matter which option you decided on.

Getting there: Exit M4 at junction 40 nr Port Talbot and go north on A4107. Afan centre is on right GR SS821/951 / Sat Nav: SA13 3HG & Glyncorrg 3 miles further on at GR SS 872/984 / Sat Nav SA13 3EA. Train at Port Talbot, 7 miles on Afan Valley cycle route

Opening times & cost: Pay & Display

Facilities: Both have cafes, showers, campsite, bike hire & bike wash, but everything at Glyncorrwg is newer & more impressive, plus has a bike shop & bar.

Bike Shop: Skyline cycles at Glyncorrwg, 01639 850011 & the Glyncorrwg MTB centre on 01639 851900.

Map: www.forestry.gov.uk & search 'afan cycle map'

Tourist info: www.afanforestpark.co.uk

Website: www.mbwales.com

NO.99

BRECHFA FOREST

The trails here are quite different from the other centres, feeling something like a big BMX park. They are fast & swoopy, with big berms and jumps – all of them are great fun. The green & blue trails are a superb introduction to mtb'ing & even experienced riders will enjoy them, especially when ridden fast.

There are LOTS of great (unmarked) natural trails in this 'enchanted' forest to explore.

Derwen trail

A superb introduction to MTB'ing, staying low, along the valley sides on fun, flat, wide trails, with gentle climbs & descents. It is even great fun for experienced riders when ridden fast as it flows wonderfully. Great place to bring (& hook) new riders.

Derwen extension 5 KM

An extension to the Green route (half way along) this adds another climb & descent along some more challenging trails. Expect tighter corners & bigger hills, and even some table top jumps near the end. Perfect for those who enjoyed the Green route and want to advance.

Gorlech trail 22 KM

A very scenic route with a natural, flowing feel to it, using some hard, fast, all weather surfaces, with berms, switchbacks, step-ups, and (optional) jumps, which get more challenging the faster you ride. The grand finale is a superb 1km long section of huge switchbacks & berms, with very steep hairpins & tabletop jumps for those inclined. This last section is the most technical of the ride (more like a black grade) and gets used lots by downhillers.

Raven Trail 18 KM

Much like the red trails, this route is largely based around big berms & jumps, with some lovely additional, natural singletrack trails. It isn't actually too technical for a black graded route and it gets better & better the faster and more you ride it.

picture by Richard Sanders

Getting there: Follow M4 to the end, then the A48 & B4310 past Brechfa. Parking for green, blue & black trails is 3km on left (before Nany-y-ffin) & Red trail is 5km further, in Aber Gorlech on left. GR SN 545/315 / Sat Nav: Brechfa & GR SN 585/340 / Sat Nav: Abergorlech.

Opening times & cost: Free

Facilities: None on site, but there is a pub in Abergorlech. See website below for more info.

Bike Shop: Beiciau Hobbs Bikes in Carmarthen on tel: 01267 236785 / www.hobbscycles.com

Map: www.forestry.gov.uk/mtbwales – see Brechfa

Tourist info: Carmarthen TI on 01267 231557

Website: www.bikebrechfa.co.uk – which is also the best place to stay over.

NO.100 COED TRALLWM

Run on a private farm, the routes use natural trails, with forest roads to climb & singletracks for the descents. It is well suited to intermediate riders due to the relative shortness of the routes.

Great cafe that is all to happy to feed muddy bikers with home made cakes, hot drinks & lunches. It is also open in the winter months (between 12–4pm and has a nice wood burning stove to warm you up). You can also arrange a shower & hot home cooked for after a nightride – call 01591 610546 for more info.

It also makes a great base because of its good facilities & accommodation, is in driving distance of Afan, Brechfa & the natural trails in the Brecon Beacons (see our Talybont-on-Usk ride).

Blue 4 KM

All routes share the same winding trail up through the woods, to the top and onto a singletrack descent. Take care at 'Fox's Den' a dark narrow section & at a tricky stream crossing and be sure to use the single track down to the cafe just before joining the black route.

Red 5 KM

Continue climbing, leaving the Blue route, to the top of Bryn Mawr, onto a fast single track with switchbacks, then down through the trees. Cross your previous ascent, then through 'five springs' and down to the county road back to the cafe.

Black 6 KM

Continue climbing on a forest road after the Blue route, onto singletrack and great views from the summit. Nice technical descent through the woods and a twisty, turny section past a giant Oak tree and down to the Visitor Centre car park.

NO.101 CWM RHAEADR

Cwm Rhaeadr is only a short way from Coed Trallwm & as both centres only have short routes it makes sense to ride them together.

Cwm Rhaeadr was designed by Rowan Sorrell (who also designed Brechfa) so you can expect the same fast, fun, bermy, jumpy type of ride. There are no facilities here though.

From Coed Trallwm go past Llanwrtyd Wells on A483 then go right on minor roads Cynghordy, to Cilycwm, then right (north) towards Llyn Brianne Reservoir & folow signs for Cwm Rhaiadr. Grid Ref: SN 765/422 / Sat Nav: SA20 0TL.

Cwm Rhaeadr Red

Starts with a big forest road climb, with great views, then a bit of singletrack to the top which is a bit more challenging. The reward is a fantastic, fun BMX style type trail back downhill with jumps, drops & berms, which is excellent for riders to practice 'pumping' their way down.

coed trallwm

Getting there: In the middle of Wales, 3 miles off the A483 (15 minutes west of Builth Wells). Follow the brown signs off the A483 in Beulah or Llanwrtyd Wells. Grid Ref: SN 882/543 / Sat Nav: LD5 4TS

Opening times & cost: £2 (at time of print) to park, ride, map & for bike wash.

Facilities: Bike hire (call in advance), bike wash, cafe, shop and showers. There are also holiday cottages available., see www.forestcottages.co.uk

Bike Shop: Basic spares at the visitor centre

map: www.coedtrallwm.co.uk

tourist info: Visitor centre on 01591 610546

website: www.coedtrallwm.co.uk

NO.102 NANT-YR-ARIAN

sat up high on the mountains, with great views, this is the only centre to start at the top of a pass. The riding could be described as 'wilderness' and containing a good mixture of different terrains. There are some great stretches of singletrack as well as some wide rocky natural trails, but isn't really suitable for beginners.

NOTE: Please be aware that these are shared trails, so take care of horses & other trail users out on the trails.

picture by Dave Reed, Rider: Al

location: Pendam trail

Pendam Trail 9 KM

Don't be fooled by the relative shortness of this route, as it combines sections of the 'Summit' and 'Syfydrin' trails, so although not as technical overall, it still offers a good challenging ride, providing a good taster of what you can expect on the other two routes on offer.

Summit Trail 16 KM

This is a demanding route with some technical single track descents, long climbs & exposed sections. There is a superb series of switchback turns named 'The Italian Job' & 'Mark of Zorro' and a climb aptly named 'Leg Burner' before the sexy 'Emmanuelle' single track leads you back to the start. This route has the most singletrack and its a fast flowing ride - great fun.

Syfydrin Trail 35 KM

This route combines the technical, flowing single track of the 'Summit trail' with the backcountry mountain tracks for a wonderful wilderness route with stunning views and rugged, exposed remote countryside, so go well equipped & prepared.

Getting there: 13km inland (east), along the A44 from Aberystwyth (where there is a railway station). Park in the forestry commission car park. Grid Ref: SN 718/813 / Sat Nav: SY23 3AD

opening times & cost: Pay & Display

facilities: cafe, bike wash, shop & toilets. The nearest town is Aberystwyth or for local accommodation, the bike friendly George hotel in Ponterwyd, 01970 890230

Bike Shop: Summit cycles in Aberystwyth on tel: 01970 626061 or www.summitcycles.co.uk

map: www.forestry.gov.uk/mtbwales

tourist info: Visitor centre on 01970 890694

website: www.mbwales.com

NO.103

THE MACH TRAILS

There are 4 trails; the 3 Mach trails which offer the natural but less technical riding, to the south of the village & the cli-Mach-X trail which provides the technical singletrack riding.

MTB'ing is very much a part of the village of Machynlleth, with everyone working together towards creating a real mountain biking vibe to the town.

Mach I 16 KM

A mix of quiet roads, forest trails & farm tracks, this route makes a great introduction for inexperienced riders. Heading south west out of Machynlleth, to the village of Derwenlas, then along the Llyfnant Valley, returning via Bryn Coch Bach (where Mach 1, 2 and 3 routes all meet), finishing with a super fast descent back down to Machynlleth.

Mach 2 24 KM

Aka Middle-Mach, the route heads south east along the river Dulas, across open farmland on the Glyndwr's Way, then drops down to Talbontdrain. A steep climb up to the forest is followed by a flowing descent to Bryn Coch Bach, to the meeting point of the Mach1, 2 and 3 trails, where you do the final descent (shared with Mach 1). Not very technical riding, but makes a good challenge for intermediate riders - not your normal challenging red grade.

Mach 3 30 KM

Starting with the same trail as the Mach 2, the route soon peels off, heading south through the forest and onto the moors, for some remote wilderness riding. The return leg takes in some fast and furious (non-technical) descents From the furthest point, the adventurous can take a spectacular cross country ride all the way to Nant yr Arian.The highlight of the return leg is 'the Chute', very steep and very rocky, and then to top it off it gets very dark.

Cli-Machx 15 KM

The start leads you along wide singletrack trails, climbing until you enter the forest, where the rocks, roots and tight bermed singletrack takes over. From the track 'Where's my ball' the trail really kicks in - be aware that the 'Tony the Tiger' section along here is graded black, then its 'Woody's Leap' and the huge jump of 'Eye of the needles' which has a narrow landing between two trees. The descent is (was!?) the longest uninterrupted singletrack descent in Wales, and ends with with a sequence of eight huge berms that following quickly after each other – go high.

NOTE: There is a track at the start of this technical downhill if you feel it would be too much for you, or alternatively this track can be used to get you back to the top to do it again (& again & again).

TOP TIP: You'll need a route leaflet (& map) from The Holy Trail for the Mach 1, 2 & 3 trails. They'll also be able to point you in the direction of some good freeriding in Dyfi forest.

Getting there: Mach 1, 2 & 3 all start from town & cli-Mach-X is 6km north on the A487 road or follow Sustrans cycle route no.8 by bike. Trail is 1 mile past the centre for Alternative Technology. Railway station in Machynlleth. Grid Ref: SH 759/063 / Sat Nav: Machynlleth for the cli-Machx trail.

Facilities: Nothing at start of cli-Machx trail, but plenty in the town of Machynlleth.

Bike Shop: The Holey Trail, in Machynlleth on tel: 01654 700411 or www.theholeytrail.co.uk

map: www.dyfimountainbiking.org.uk

tourist info: T.I. on 01654 702401

website: www.mbwales.com

NO.104 COED Y BRENIN

A superb choice of technical XC trails for the more experienced riders, but still enough to entertain beginners & some short Red routes for them to progress on to. The facilities are also very good, so it does get very busy here.

The birth place of man made trails & still a top destination, especially for technical XC riders.

Yr Afon 7 KM

Based on forest roads and contouring the hillsides this family trail avoids the single track, but takes in some magnificent views, including waterfalls, the river Mawddach and the old gold mines.

Temtiwr 9 KM

This route provides a taster of the Dragon's Back and MBR trails, and although it isn't long, it squeezes in 5 sections of singletrack; from very technical rocky sections, to fast flowing tracks through the trees. Great fun for a quick blast, but don't underestimate the technical riding skills required - this is not a ride for novices.

MBR 18.5 KM

A nice mix of open, flowing trails and long sweeping descents with tight, technical, rocky single track such as the 'Badger', 'Pink Heifer' and the most challenging of all 'The Beginning of the End' all squeezed into a relatively short ride. Great fun.

Tawr 20 KM

Formally known as 'Red Bull' this is a technically challenging ride with rocky descents, fire road climbs and plenty of singletrack. It includes the superb 'Pins & Needles', 'Snap, Crackle & Pop', 'Rocky Horror Show' and 'Mantrap'.

Cyflym Coch 11 KM

A mix of the other trails, starting on the Yr Afon Trail, the Cyflym coch bears off left up a short technical climb onto Pinderosa. It then uses the best of the fast & flowing trails from MBR & Dragon's Back.

Dragons Back 31 KM

Formally known as 'Karrimor' this long, challenging trail contains a wide variety of terrain; from forest roads to technical single track, huge climbs and long sweeping descents. Highlights include sections of trails, such as the rooty, rocky 'Big Doug' and the fast, flowing corners of 'Herman'.

Beast of Brenin 38 KM

This route is made up of a combination of the MBR and Dragon's Back trails, to provide a very challenging ride. Lots of superb single track trails, but only recommended for fit, technical riders. There is a (very welcome) cafe half way around the route.

Getting there: Go south from Colwyn Bay on the A470 and the is on the right, 8km's before Dolgellau (inland from Barmouth), signposted 'Maesgwm visitor centre'. From the Midlands follow the A458 from Shrewsbury. GR SH 720/270 / Sat Nav LL40 2HY.

Opening times & cost: Pay & Display.

Facilities: Parking, toilets, showers, cafe, bike wash, a shop and a bike shop.

Bike shop: Greenstiles bike shop in Dolgallau 01341 423332 & Dragon Bikes & Kites on 01341 423008.

Map: www.forestry.gov.uk search 'coed y brenin cycle m

Tourist info: Dolgellau T.I. on 01341 422888

Website: www.mbwales.com

NO.105 PENMACHNO

Nice natural, flowing trails with wonderful views and nearly all singletrack. All very understated; no trail center, no big claims, no wild names or key features, just good honest singletrack trails, which aren't too technical, but great fun, especially when ridden fast.

TOP TIP: The Marin Trail over in Gwydyr isn't far away and offers another great flowing red graded route.

picture by the Forestry commission

Loop 1 — 20 KM

With no big berms, rock gardens, jumps, etc along the way, it may sound like this trail is lacking something. However, when you ride it, it all just makes sense, flows and blends together to provide a lovely ride, which is finished off with some cracking descents.

Loop 2 — 10 KM

This is an additional section to Loop 1, to include more single track, without much more climbing, but does take you out into the more exposed parts of the hills. Again, this trail isn't too technically challenging, but the singletrack is nice & flows well and involves minimal amounts of fireroad.

NOTE: Beics Betws in Betws-y-coed offer bike hire & are open 7 days a week in the summer. If they are closed, give them a call to make arrangements - they can even deliver the bikes to you.

Getting there: From Betws-y-coed go east on the A5, over bridge, then right on the B4406 and follow this through Penmachno village for 1km to a (small) car park on the right.

Grid Ref: SH 786/498 / Sat Nav: Penmachno

opening times & cost: Free

facilities: None on site, but the pub in Penmachno village is nice & friendly.

Bike Shop: Beics Betws in Betws-y-coed on tel: 01690 710766 www.bikewales.co.uk

map: None

tourist info: www.walesdirectory.co.uk

website: www.mbwales.com

NO.106 GWYDYR FOREST

There is only the one trail but the great natural feeling to the ride makes it a popular place with lots of riders. It is often described as a very 'real mountain bike experience' as the trail has a very organic, free flowing feel to it. The route hugs the snowdonia hillsides, providing some wonderful views and a trail that urges you to go faster and make use of the wonderful big berms. Not for novices / beginners.

TOP TIP: For more way marked (red) XC trails see Penmachno which is just down the road There is also lots of natural riding close by – see our wonderful capel curig route.

Marin Trail 25 KM

A great fast, flowing ride with some jumps & berms, but without being too technical, so may appeal to some riders making the transition from Blue to Red.

Route Description: Starts of quickly with a roller coaster single track named 'Parc & Ride' before climbing up & up on a mix of fire road and single track to the highest point of the ride. You are soon rewarded for your efforts with 'Pigs might fly' a technical rocky descent. The trail then rises and descends along some technical trails to the 'Dragon's Tail', a razorbacked ridgeline of off camber slate single track, then some handy northshore construction to keep you above the swamp. The steep off camber descent of 'Stumpdance' leads you to the last big climb for the grand finale, a superb flight of bermed switchbacks, chicanes & jumps leading back to the start.

NOTE: There are no facilities on site, but Betws-y-coed is just down the road & has lots to offer – including a very good bike shop.

picture by Forestry commission

Getting there: Take the A470 towards Llanrwst (before Betws Y coed) and the trail is (west) in the village of Trefriw on the B5106 rd. Follow the green forestry parking signs with a bike. Railway station in Llanrwst. Grid Ref: SH 790/610 / Sat Nav: LL26 0PN

opening times & cost: Free

facilities: Nothing on site, but Betws-y-coed is just down the road & has lots to offer.

Bike Shop: Beics Betws in Betws-y-coed on tel: 01690 710766 www.bikewales.co.uk

map: www.biking-wales.co.uk/maps/gwydyr.pdf

tourist info: Betws-y-coed TI on 01690 710426

website: www.mbwales.com

NO.107 COED LLANDEGLA

coed Llandegla Forest covers 650 hectares & is owned by UPM Tilhill. It offers a range of trails to suit all abilities and although not too technical, it offers some great all weather riding and the black route has some great berms & jumps to keep experienced riders happy.

NOTE: There is a good bike shop & a great cafe on site – both are very friendly & helpful.

Family Route

A great family trail, avoiding big climbs & technical terrain, along safe but fun hard pack trails with some loose & uneven (sometimes muddy) sections at times to make it interesting. The route passes through the forest to a reservoir, with views of the Clwydian Range, then back, finishing with a sweeping descent to finish, where tea & cake awaits.

Beginner Route

12 KM

A long gradual climb (shared with the red & black routes) takes you through the forest to the top then splits, to gradually descend on fun, but non-technical trails. There are a few short little climbs along the way, but its mostly downhill and has the likes of small humps & berms to keep it interesting.

Intermediate Route

Using the same start i.e. the long climb as the Blue & Black routes, you split from them at the top to ride some unsurfaced singletrack with a few steep sections, through the more remote areas of the forest. There are some nice flowing sections with huge bermed switchbacks, whoops, water crossings, tabletops & boardwalk. A good step up from the blue route in terms of fitness & skills required, but not too technical still.

Black Runs

Departs from the Intermediate/red route, to provide a series of black runs, providing 6km of excellent fun trails that provide steeper & more technical trails with features such as steps, gaps & drop-offs. Great fast, BMX style ride with fun berms and flowing singletrack, recommended for experienced bikers only, but don't let that put you off if you are a competent rider as you can control the ride.

picture by Chris Malone

Getting there: 7 miles west of Wrexham along the A525 (signposted Ruthin) & the forest is (on the left) signposted from the road. Train station in Wrexham. Grid Ref: SJ227/520 / Sat Nav: LL11 3AA

opening times & cost: P&D. check centre & car park times at www.coedllandegla.com/about/opening.htm

facilities: Bike hire, shop, bike wash and great a cafe at the start/end.

Bike Shop: One Planet bike shop, on site, tel; 01978 751656 is very good.

map: www.coedllandegla.com/trails

tourist info: coed Llandegla on 01978 751656

website: www.coedllandegla.com

picture by the Forestry Commission

Brechfa

pic by the Forestry Commission

pic by the Forestry Commission

pic by the Forestry Commission

Suggested road trips & WEEKEND BREAKS

picture by Tim Boarder

ROAD TRIPS

Road Trips involve getting in your car or van and travelling to new destinations to ride. It's a great way to escape normal life and bring some adventure and variety to your cycling, with memories that will stay with you forever. They also allow great flexibility, not just in where you ride, but also where you eat & sleep – be it in the van, camping, B&B or living it up in hotels.

The following suggested road trips are ideas for multiday trips visiting some highly ecommended places. They will no doubt require some manipulation in some way to suit your needs, fitness, ability & time schedule, but hopefully they'll provide some inspiration and a starting point from which to plan your perfect break.....

Checklist

*service bike a few days before & order any parts / spares.

* Plot route on Sat Nav or RAC / AA route planner websites.

shoes (check cleats)

helmet

gloves

buff

cycle shorts

rucksack & hydration pack

cycle tops (base, mid, outer)

waterproof / windproof coat

cycling socks

chamois (bum) cream

sun cream!

(sun) glasses

midge repellant (Deet or Avons 'Skin so soft')

1st aid kit & space blanket

Multi tool

SRAM link

chain lube & GT85

little pot / tube of grease

bike cleaner & brushes

basic tools (if you have space)

inner tubes & repair kit

spare tyre(s)

shock & tyre pumps

zip ties & gaffa tape

camera, mobile + chargers

GPS or compass

spare brake pads

Guidebook / maps

mech hanger!

Top Tip: Wear compression tights for after rides & especially for travelling.

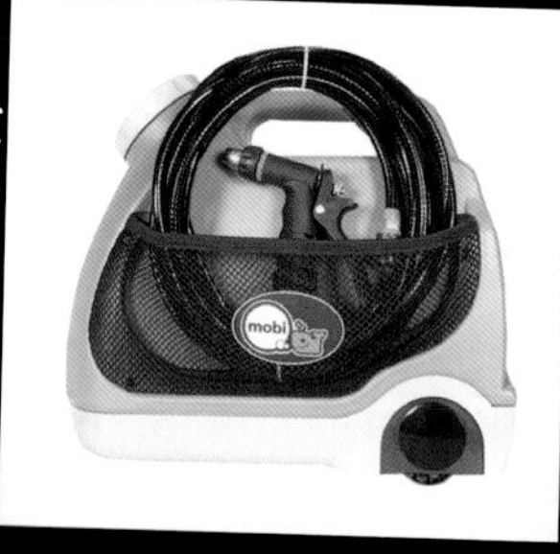

by www.mobiwasher.co.uk

A portable (bike) pressure washer that runs off the car battery is ideal when on the move.

pic & bag by www.ultrasporteu.com

A bike bag keeps your bike (& car) protected from scratches & tangles, keeps the bike out of view, is an easy way to haul all your (muddy) luggage around & maybe get you on trains & buse

pic by Jon Ross aka Shaggy
pic by Paul Knott
pic by Steve Makin

South Wales

ROAD TRIP

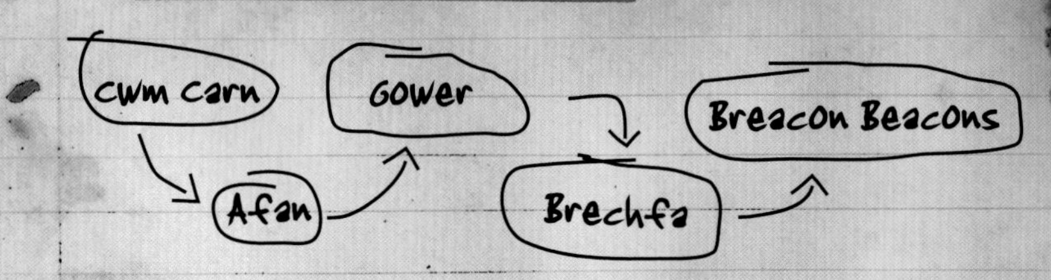

Day 1 – Cwm Carn. Ride the Twrch trail (& the downhill if feeling up for it) then drive to Afan (& quick ride around Penyhdd if time). Camp at the Drop Off or stay at Bryn Bettws log cabins 01639 642040.

Days 2 & 3 – Afan. Big breakfast at cafe, then ride 'W2' (White's Level & 'Wall' trails combined). The next day ride 'Skyline' & if you haven't / want / can ride Penyhdd, before heading on to The Gower (3/4hr drive).

NOTE: Afan on its own, makes a great weekend destination

Day 4 – Gower (route in book). Nice natural ride with sea views (1+hr drive).

Day 5 – Brechfa. Ride the Black trail in the morning, then Red in the afternoon. Head for Brecon (1 1/2hr drive) & stay at the Canal Bunkhouse on 01874 625361 or see www.mtbbreconbeacons.co.uk

Day 6 – Ride the Talybont-on-Usk (aka 'The Gap') route in the book.

Day 7 – Ride the 'Black Mountain' route in the book, then head home.

Accommodation in Builth Wells; www.midwalesonline.co.uk/bwcycles. For more information on accommodation in Wales see www.visitwales.com & for more information about cycling in Wales see www..cycling.visitwales.com

North Wales

ROAD TRIP

Coed Llandegla → Gwydyr → Penmachno → Capel Curig → Snowdon → Coed-Y-Brenin → Machynlleth

Day 1 – Coed Llandegla. Red run, refuel at the cafe & back out to do the black run. Eat at cafe & head to Betws-Y-Coed (see bottom).

Day 2 – Gwydyr. Ride the Marin trail, back to Beyws-Y-Coed for lunch, then on to Penmachno & back to Betws-Y-Coed for the night again.

Day 3 – Capel Curig route (in the book), then head to Llanberis for the night at Pete's Eats www.petes-eats.co.uk.

Day 4 – Snowdon. Early breakfast at Pete's (see route for time restrictions). After, head to Coed-Y-Brenin to ride Temtiwr (taster) trail. Stay at the Log cabins at www.logcabinswales.co.uk.

Days 5 – Coed-Y-Brenin. 'The Beast' (combination of MBR & Dragon's Back).

Days 6 – Ride Tawr trail & your favourite one again, then on to Machnylleth.

NOTE: Coed-Y-Brenin is the place to head to for weekend only breaks.

Day 7 – Machnylleth. Ride the Cli-Mach-X route & 'session' the last section or ride a Mach trail if you have time, before heading home.

For accommodation in Betws-Y-Coed see www.betws-y-coed.co.uk & for Machnylleth see www.dyfimountainbiking.org.uk. For more information, see www.visitwales.com, www.mbwales.com & www.mtb-wales.com.

South Scotland

ROAD TRIP

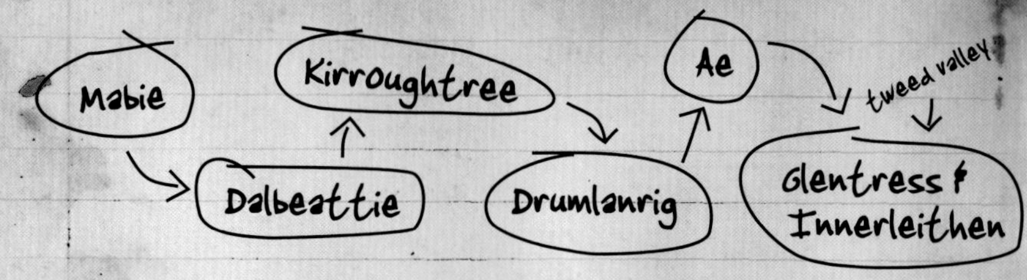

Day 1 – Mabie. Skills area, look/ride Kona Dark side, then ride the red route.

Day 2 – Dalbeattie (1/2hr drive). Ride the Hardrock trail.

Day 3 – Kirroughtree (1hr drive). Ride Black craigs then drive (2hrs) to Thornhill, close to & ready for Drumlanrig, for the next day.

Day 4 – Drumlanrig. Ride the red (& black extensions), then drive (3/4hrs) to Ae forest (use back roads past closeburn).

Day 5 – Ride red Ae Line route & watch/ride downhill. Drive 2hrs to Peebles.

Day 6 – Glentress. Ride Blue trail, lunch at Hub cafe, then ride the Black.

Day 7 – Glentress. Ride Red route, have lunch at the hub cafe, then go to Innerleithen to ride the red Traquair trail & watch the downhillers.

NOTE: Glentress gets very busy at weekends (as it makes a superb weekend break) especially as sleeper trains to Edinburgh are available.

Accommodation: www.marthrown.com for Mabie, www.breakpad.co.uk for Kirroughtree, Hillcrest Barn in Thornhill; 01848331557. For Innerleithen; www.thebikelodge.co.uk, www.tweedvalleybikehouse.com & www.visittweedvalley.co.uk. More @ www.7stanes.com & www.visitscotland.com

North Scotland

ROAD TRIP

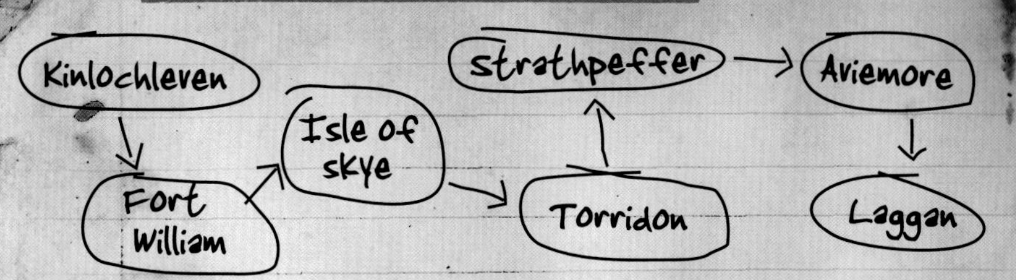

Day 1 – Kinlochleven route (from book) for a great, technical, natural ride.

Day 2 – Fort William – red XC loop, then after lunch get the gondola up the mountain & do the Nevis red run.

Day 3 – Isle of Skye route (from book). Afterwards drive to Achnashellach to stay at www.gerryshostel-achnashellach.co.uk / 01520 766 232.

Day 4 – Torridon route (from book), for a classic (epic) natural ride.

Day 5 – Strathpeffer – call in at Square Wheels bike shop to get a map & advice (www.squarewheels.biz / 01997 421000 / Sat Nav: IV14 9DW) – or ride the trails at Learnie Red Rock, on Black Isle (nearby).

Day 6 Aviemore – ride loch Einich or Gaick Pass (both in the book).

Day 7 Laggan – Ride red trails & after lunch do Black or Fun Park.

For accommodation see the specific routes in the book and / or check out the following websites: www.visitscotland.com, http://cycling.visitscotland.com, www.visithighlands.com & www.scottishmountainbike.com

Keep your passion for riding alive by doing new things & having new adventures. Here are a few ideas....

TOP 10 THINGS TO DO ... before its too late

1. Go on a road trip - ride the trails & live the lifestyle
2. Ride from coast to coast - for an unforgettable journey
3. Do a weekend of downhilling or freeriding - with uplifts.
4. Ride different bikes - cyclocross, road, downhill, bmx anything...
5. Bivy / bothy ride - ride, camp out under the stars, have a campfire, wake up at dawn, cook breakfast & ride some more.
6. Take part in a bike event - challenge yourself
7. Introduce someone new to riding - kids if you have them.
8. Go nightriding - get some lights & friends to discover a new world
9. Ride down a 'proper' mountain e.g. Snowdon
10. Early morning ride - leave in the dark & see the sun rise

rough ride guide presents...

our unique ring binder design not only enables you to carry just the route page you need, but also allows you to add new routes & sections to the book. create your very own unique guidebook, custom made to your requirements in an economical & flexible way – here are some sections available....

available from **www.roughrideguide.co.uk**

INTRODUCTION TO MOUNTAIN BIKING

Discover how to set your bike up to suit you (including for women), learn about the equipment & clothing, night riding and tackling aches & pains. Also, learn the secrets to off-road riding skills with our step-by-step instructions; from pedalling to jumping.

HEALTH, FITNESS & TRAINING

A great guide to get the most from your body & cycling. Learn when, how, where & what to train, what & when to eat & drink, as well as how to avoid, cope & deal with injuries & illness. Great for anyone wanting to improve their performance & essential for anyone thinking of undertaking a big ride, event or race.

MAN MADE TRAILS

Over 70 destinations, hundreds of trails & thousands of km's of superb trails at trail centres & other mtb hot spots across the UK.

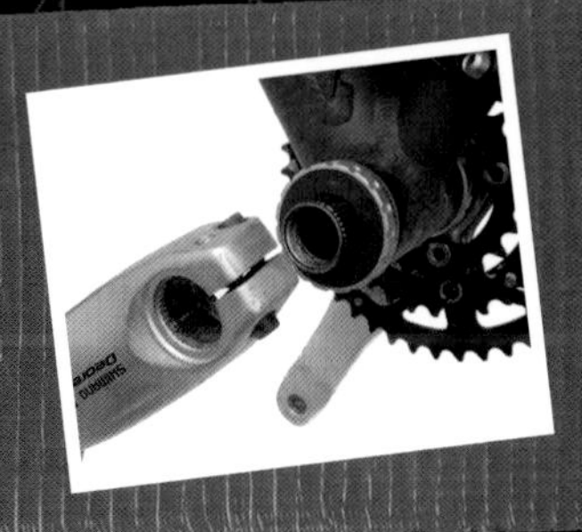

MAINTENANCE & REPAIR MANUAL

Over 100 pages of step-by-step instructions with full colour pictures covering just about every job; from cleaning to changing the bottom bracket. Designed to give you a sound understanding of your bike & to save you time & money.

LONG DISTANCE RIDES

A superb collection of long distance rides around the UK; ride from coast to coast across Scotland or England, cycle from London to Brighton off road, ride classics such as the South Downs Way or tackle 3 day (bivvy!) rides in Dartmoor, Lakes, Cairngorms etc.

& others

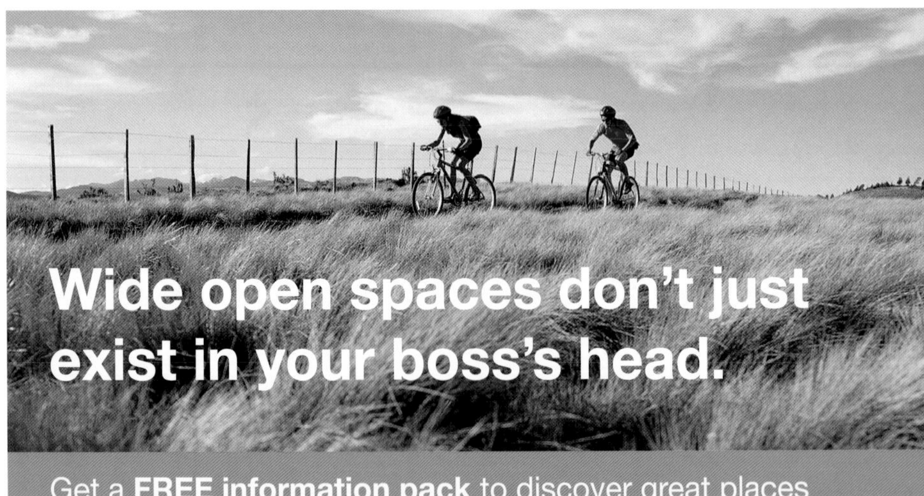

Wide open spaces don't just
exist in your boss's head.

sustrans
JOIN THE MOVEMENT

brought to you by

picture by Dave Lowe

rough ride guide